FRANCE

THE VENDÉE

WITH NANTES & PORNIC,
PLUS LA ROCHELLE & THE ÎLE DE RÉ

T0274131

ANGELA BIRD & MURRAY STEWART
UPDATED BY ED COOPER

www.bradtguides.com

Bradt Guides Ltd, UK
The Globe Pequot Press Inc, USA

Bradt GUIDES
TRAVEL TAKEN SERIOUSLY

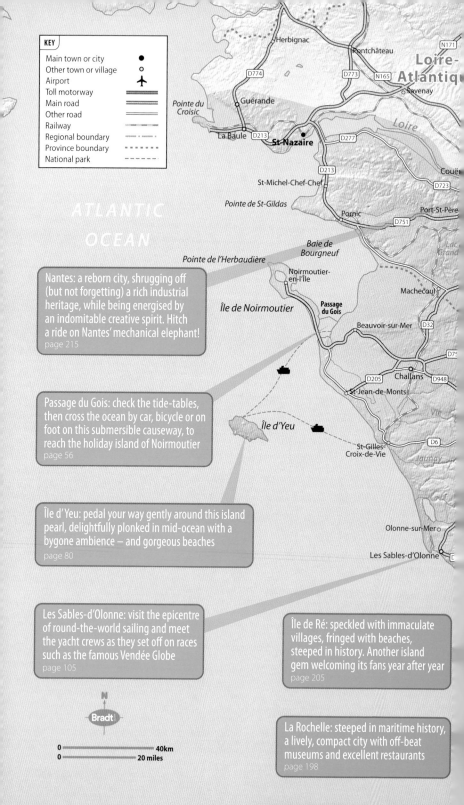

KEY

Main town or city	●
Other town or village	○
Airport	✈
Toll motorway	
Main road	
Other road	
Railway	
Regional boundary	
Province boundary	
National park	

ATLANTIC OCEAN

Herbignac
Pontchâteau
Loire-Atlantiq
N171
D774
D773
N165
Savenay
Pointe du Croisic
Guérande
D277
Loire
La Baule
D213
St-Nazaire
D213
Couë
St-Michel-Chef-Chef
D723
Pointe de St-Gildas
Pornic
Port-St-Père
D751
Baie de Bourgneuf
Lac Grand
Pointe de l'Herbaudière
Noirmoutier-en-l'Île
Machecoul
Île de Noirmoutier
Passage du Gois
Beauvoir-sur-Mer
D32
D7
D205
Challans
D948
St-Jean-de-Monts
Vie
Île d'Yeu
D6
St-Gilles Croix-de-Vie
Jaunay
Olonne-sur-Mer
Les Sables-d'Olonne

Nantes: a reborn city, shrugging off (but not forgetting) a rich industrial heritage, while being energised by an indomitable creative spirit. Hitch a ride on Nantes' mechanical elephant! page 215

Passage du Gois: check the tide-tables, then cross the ocean by car, bicycle or on foot on this submersible causeway, to reach the holiday island of Noirmoutier page 56

Île d'Yeu: pedal your way gently around this island pearl, delightfully plonked in mid-ocean with a bygone ambience – and gorgeous beaches page 80

Les Sables-d'Olonne: visit the epicentre of round-the-world sailing and meet the yacht crews as they set off on races such as the famous Vendée Globe page 105

Île de Ré: speckled with immaculate villages, fringed with beaches, steeped in history. Another island gem welcoming its fans year after year page 205

La Rochelle: steeped in maritime history, a lively, compact city with off-beat museums and excellent restaurants page 198

N

Bradt

0		40km
0		20 miles

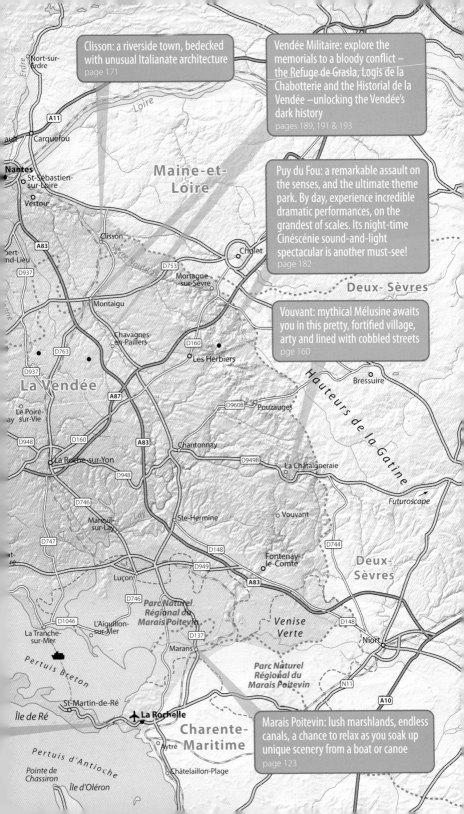

Clisson: a riverside town, bedecked with unusual Italianate architecture
page 171

Vendée Militaire: explore the memorials to a bloody conflict – the Refuge de Grasla, Logis de la Chabotterie and the Historial de la Vendée – unlocking the Vendée's dark history
pages 189, 191 & 193

Puy du Fou: a remarkable assault on the senses, and the ultimate theme park. By day, experience incredible dramatic performances, on the grandest of scales. Its night-time Cinéscénie sound-and-light spectacular is another must-see!
page 182

Vouvant: mythical Mélusine awaits you in this pretty, fortified village, arty and lined with cobbled streets
pge 160

Marais Poitevin: lush marshlands, endless canals, a chance to relax as you soak up unique scenery from a boat or canoe
page 123

THE VENDÉE
DON'T MISS...

LA ROCHELLE
Lively La Rochelle's harbour is a favourite with sailors and landlubbers alike PAGE 198
(ShR/D)

LA VENISE VERTE
Tranquillity awaits discovery inland on the Marais waterways PAGE 139
(UHP/S)

ÎLE D'YEU
Among the delights of the Île d'Yeu are some tiny, secluded beaches PAGE 80
(AL/VE)

LE PUY DU FOU
The description 'theme park' does not do justice to Le Puy du Fou, a truly spectacular assault on the senses PAGE 182
(SA/VE)

PASSAGE DU GOIS
The Passage du Gois links the mainland to Noirmoutier island… but only at low tide! PAGE 56
(RAP/S)

THE VENDÉE
IN COLOUR

above
(JG/VE)
Sea views and clifftop walks are among the main
attractions in Jard-sur-Mer PAGE 117

below left
(T/D)
In Les Sables-d'Olonne, meet the stars of the world's most
exciting yacht race – the Vendée-Globe PAGE 112

below right
(GP/D)
Climb the Grand Phare to experience spectacular views across the Île d'Yeu PAGE 86

In St-Martin-de-Ré, quaint, whitewashed houses sit alongside the impressive Vauban fortifications PAGE 209
above left (M/S)

Enjoy fresh oysters and other seafood delights on the Vendée coast PAGE 34
above right (SB/VE)

Feel the wind in your hair and sun on your face as you whizz along the beaches of St-Jean-de-Monts in a sand yacht PAGE 71
right (D/D)

Barbados? No, it's the turqouise water and white sands of Île de Noirmoutier PAGE 57
below (IV/D)

Angela Bird studied and worked in France, and has owned a home in the Vendée for almost 50 years. In 1995, she wrote her first guidebook to the area, which ran to four editions before transferring to the Bradt stable. Back home, she has worked for *The Illustrated London News* and *Country Living* magazines, and was for four years Vendée correspondent for the French publication *Côté Ouest*.

Murray Stewart spent two months living and travelling around the Vendée and its borders, researching and writing the first edition of Bradt's guidebook to the area. When his legs were significantly younger, he enjoyed cycling holidays on the flat coastal terrain along the Vendean Atlantic coast. Murray wrote the first edition of Bradt's *Basque Country and Navarre: France and Spain*, which won the British Guild of Travel Writers' Best Travel Guidebook of 2016. He has twice updated Bradt's guide to North Cyprus, twice updated their guide to Cape Verde, and has also updated their popular Azores guide. He has written several blogs on these destinations and contributed prize-winning articles online on other countries.

Ed Cooper is an experienced traveller, adventurer and writer. His work has included *The Inuit Way: A Journey Across Greenland and the Canadian Arctic Archipelago* and contributions to the first edition of *Greenland*, both published by Bradt, along with several articles for the *Telegraph* and other UK magazines. Ed loves anything to do with the water and being in nature. He has travelled and worked across the globe including countries in the Arctic, Antarctic, South America, Eastern Europe, Africa and the Middle East. He is also a keen walker and regularly goes on long trails with his wife Tara and their daughter Indie. He is a frequent traveller to France, with his longest sojourn spent working in the south for six months in Antibes, Juans Les Pins and Nice, where he developed a lasting and positive impression of the country. Ed has spent a significant amount of time in the Vendée and has a passion for its infinite coastlines and landscapes.

Second edition published September 2024
First published 2018
Bradt Travel Guides Ltd
31a High Street, Chesham, Buckinghamshire, HP5 1BW, England
www.bradtguides.com
Print edition published in the USA by The Globe Pequot Press Inc,
PO Box 480, Guilford, Connecticut 06437-0480

Text copyright © Bradt Travel Guides Ltd, 2024
Maps copyright © Bradt Travel Guides Ltd, 2024; includes map data
© OpenStreetMap contributors
Photographs copyright © Individual photographers, 2024 (see below)
Project Manager: Elspeth Beidas
Cover research: Pepi Bluck, Perfect Picture

ISBN: 9781804692219

British Library Cataloguing in Publication Data
A catalogue record for this book is available from the British Library

Photographs AWL Images: Hemis (H/AWL); Dreamstime.com: Andrew Allport
(AA/D), Coatchristophe (C/D), David Havel (DH/D), Davidmartyn (D/D), Gueret
Pascale (GP/D), Inglebert Valery (IV/D), Olrat (O/D), Ondřej Prosický (OP/D),
Rudmer Zwerver (RZ/D), Sharad Raval (ShR/D), Slowmotiongli (S/D), Stephane
Rochon (StR/D), Sylvain Robin (SyR/D), Thomaspajot (T/D); Shutterstock.com:
Altitude Drone (AD/S), benoitgade (B/S), Christine LaCroix (CL/S), JeanLucIchard
(JL/S), MC MEDIASTUDIO (MCM/S), mehdi33300 (M/S), MisterStock
(MS/S), Olivier Malard (OM/S), Pierre-Olivier (PO/S), RobArt Photo (RAP/S),
slowmotiongli (S/S), Unai Huizi Photography (UHP/S); Vendée Expansion:
Alexandre Lamoureux (AL/VE), Julien Gazeau (JG/VE), simonbourcier.com
(SB/VE), Stéphane Audra (SA/VE), Valéry Joncheray (VJ/VE)

Front cover Noirmoutier-en-l'Île (H/AWL)
Back cover Île d'Yeu (*top*; B/S); mechanical elephant, Les Machines de l'Île, Nantes
(*bottom left*; MCM/S); La Venise Verte (*bottom right*; UHP/S)
Title page, clockwise from top left Windmill, Île-d'Olonne (SB/VE); Catamaran, Île de
Noirmoutier (VJ/VE); seafood platter (SB/VE); Marais Breton (AL/VE)
Part openers Page 51: Brem-sur-Mer (PO/S); page 197: Tour St-Nicolas, La
Rochelle (JL/S)

Maps David McCutcheon FBCart.S. FRGS; colour relief base by Nick Rowland FRGS

Typeset by Ian Spick, Bradt Travel Guides and Geethik Technologies, India
Production managed by Imprint Press; printed in India
Digital conversion by www.dataworks.co.in

Acknowledgements

As ever, writing or updating a book is a team effort. First, a big thank you to Angela Bird whose deep knowledge and love for the Vendée oozed from the original book and whose unstinting assistance in creating the Bradt first edition made my task much easier. Also thanks to Juliette Dagois, a native of the area who shared her tips on the region. Thanks to the various tourist offices and in particular to those in La Rochelle and Nantes for showing me the best of their engaging cities. Simone Ostoj kindly introduced me to elegant La Baule and its neighbouring towns. A thank you to Brittany Ferries, who generously provided me with a complimentary ferry crossing to France (and back), and also to the Compagnie Vendéen, who took me as their guest to the beautiful Île d'Yeu (and back). Hats off to the Puy du Fou for their hospitality, too. As always, gratitude must be expressed to everyone at Bradt, especially to Rachel Fielding for the commission and to Claire Strange for her excellent editorial assistance. And finally, to Sara Lister for her support throughout and in particular for lending me her satnav. Quite literally, I would be lost without her.

ED COOPER   In addition to the above, I would like to thank the following for their assistance with this second edition: Murray Stewart for his previous work, which built on Angela's; the team at Vendée Expansion who accommodated my family and I while we were there – in particular the generous time and support provided by Eléonore Fourre and Charly Boutevin; Claire Strange and Elspeth Beidas at Bradt; and my wife Tara, for her constant support.

Contents

HOW TO USE THIS GUIDE

LISTINGS Places to stay and eat are listed first by descending price code then alphabetically within each price code.

MAPS
Keys and symbols Maps include alphabetical keys covering the locations of those places to stay, eat or drink that are featured in the book. Note that regional maps may not show hotels and restaurants in the area: establishments may be located in towns shown on the map.

Grids and grid references Several maps use gridlines to allow easy location of sites. Map grid references are listed in square brackets after the name of the place or site of interest in the text, with page number followed by grid number, eg: [106 D2].

WEB ADDRESSES A web address includes '/en' when this offers a quick route to a version in English. Some websites might display the English version automatically or via an English-language button on the home page.

TOURIST INFORMATION OFFICE OPENING TIMES While these were correct at the time of researching this edition, be aware that these opening times can vary from season to season and from year to year.

LIST OF MAPS

Introduction

'The Vendée; oh yes, we used to camp there years ago with the children – wonderful beaches.' That was the refrain in the 1970s, but accommodation, entertainment and gastronomy here have moved resolutely upmarket since then. Motorways speed you towards the coast, modern museums are fitted with state-of-the-art displays, and dedicated cycleways and footpaths criss-cross the area – so it's time to go back to this large French *département*, and discover its many other attractions. Some, like the world-famous Puy du Fou theme park, are blockbusters; some, such as the causeway to Noirmoutier island, have been formed by nature; some, like prehistoric stones and Romanesque churches, bear witness to humans' beliefs and building skills through the centuries.

Lying between the major cities of Nantes and La Rochelle, the Vendée is tucked cosily into the top of the Bay of Biscay, just south of Brittany. Admittedly, unless you are heading specifically to it, you are unlikely to pass through. But that would be a pity.

The Vendée's turbulent post-Revolutionary wars have been airbrushed out of French history for a couple of centuries, causing the département to be seen as an ultra-Catholic and rabidly royalist stronghold. Added to this undeserved air of suspicion, the bourgeois French from everywhere else can be snooty about the region's surge of mass tourism as paid holidays became the norm in the 1930s. Ironically, nowadays some of the poshest Parisians have sought out their own boltholes here: either a traditional stone *logis*, or manor house, on the edge of an inland village; an elegantly updated dwelling in the chic streets of Noirmoutier island; or a sun-bleached pad on the even less accessible – and therefore even more upmarket – island of Yeu.

There are stately homes, unusual museums and charming gardens to visit, plus quirky rural events and busy market days; flea markets, craft fairs and – of course – local food, such as the region's ham and *mogettes* (white haricot beans), barbecued quail, grilled sardines, or eels cooked over cowpat fires. Village festivals make for a fun Sunday outing, usually headlined by a different, often food-related local tradition – from oyster-fishing to the baking of *brioche*.

Houses connected with local celebrities such as politician Georges Clemenceau, painter Charles Milcendeau and military hero Marshal Jean de Lattre de Tassigny, give fascinating insights into provincial French life.

Extra treats on the coast include watersports of all kinds, and some 200km of coastal cycleway. Inland, you can take to treetop trails in the forests, pedal mountain bikes up and down the hills, paddle canoes through the marshes, ride on a steam train, go birdwatching, sip wine at a vineyard, or visit some breathtaking summer son et lumière shows.

Oh, and the beaches are still brilliant, of course.

Part One

GENERAL INFORMATION

Location Mid-western France, bordering on the Atlantic Ocean to the west, the departments of Charente-Maritime to the south, Loire-Atlantique to the northwest, Maine-et-Loire to the northeast and Deux-Sèvres to the east

Size 6,720km^2

Climate Oceanic climate, with hot, sunny summers and mild winters

Status Département number 85, within the Pays de la Loire region

Population (Vendée) 685,442 (INSEE, 2019)

Life expectancy (France) 80 years (male), 85 years (female)

Main towns La Roche-sur-Yon (departmental capital), Challans, Les Herbiers, Olonne-sur-Mer, Les Sables-d'Olonne, Fontenay-le-Comte. Outside the Vendée, but covered in this book: Nantes, St-Nazaire (both Loire-Atlantique), La Rochelle (Charente-Maritime).

Economy Services (especially tourism), light industry/manufacturing, food processing, agriculture

GDP per capita (France) US$40,890

Official language French

Religion Roman Catholicism, with some adherents to Protestantism

Currency Euro (€)

Exchange rate £1 = €1.18, US$1 = €0.92 (June 2024)

Airports (both outside the Vendée) Nantes (Aéroport Nantes Atlantique), La Rochelle (Aéroport La Rochelle-Île de Ré)

International telephone code +33 (France)

Time GMT+1 (GMT+2 in summer months)

Electrical voltage 220V (50Hz)

Weights and measures Metric

Flag Half-red, half-white background, with two red interlocking hearts, a crown and a small cross

Public holidays 1 January, Easter Monday (March/April, date varies), 1 May, 8 May, Ascension (39 days after Easter Sunday), Whit Monday (50 days after Easter), 14 July, 15 August, 1 November, 11 November, 25 December

1

Background Information

GEOGRAPHY

Occupying one corner of France's distinctive hexagonal shape, the Vendée stretches out over 6,720km² of territory, ranking it as the 22nd largest in area among the 95 French *départements*. Over half of its 250km of Atlantic coastline is fringed with fine white sands, much of it backed by dunes and the rich forest which helps to hold the fragile structure together. At certain points along the seashore, rocks are dominant. The Vendée is further characterised by a largely flat terrain: its highest point, far from the sea, fails to exceed even 300m. Gentle slopes continue into the ocean, the tides going out a long way and returning quickly. Equally striking are the marshlands which can be found both inland and along much of the coast, the saltpans which are prevalent in the north of the territory, the delightful islands, and the five principal rivers which cross the mainland. The shortest of these four, the 70km-long Vendée, is responsible for the name of the area. It is a département with no significant cities, its administrative seat being located in La Roche-sur-Yon, which can claim only around 53,000 inhabitants; the larger conurbations of Nantes and La Rochelle – both covered in this book – respectively lie to the north and south of the Vendée's borders.

MARAIS (MARSHLANDS) Perhaps the most distinctive geographical features of the region are the *marais*, or marshlands, which can be found across the region from north to south and east to west. Visitors arriving from the northwest will first of all encounter the Marais Breton, the salty marshes which adjoin the northern Atlantic coast between the Vendée and the neighbouring département of Loire-Atlantique to the north. These marshes then stretch all the way south down the coast to St-Hilaire-de-Riez and eastwards across to Challans. Discovering this largely treeless region by boat or canoe is recommended. Look out here for the traditional *bourrines*, the low, thatched houses of which only a few now remain. At the southern end of the Vendée is the Marais Poitevin, extending right across the territory and encroaching into next-door Deux-Sèvres and Charente-Maritime départements. Part of this area of nearly 200,000ha comprises the open landscape of the Marais Desseché ('dry marsh'). Starting in the 11th century, astonishingly this area was drained over a period of many centuries, first by Benedictine monks, then later with the help of the Dutch who introduced to the area their expertise in separating low-lying lands from the sea. Sea walls keep the ocean at bay, while the principle of the canals is for them to irrigate the land in summer and drain it in winter. East of the dry marshes is the Marais Mouillé ('wet marsh'), a network of tree-lined canals known as the Venise Verte, or 'Green Venice', whose lushness and tranquillity provide such a lure for the many visitors who come to potter about in watercraft of various types.

BOCAGE Defying any suitable, single-word English translation, the *bocage* covers much of the rest of the landmass – the *Haut-Bocage* being the hilly, wooded region down the eastern fringe of the département, and the *Bas-Bocage* the gently undulating land that surrounds La Roche-sur-Yon and continues towards the coast. This area is dotted with small farmhouses and cottages, their doorways often outlined in white and topped by a painted cross to keep witches and ill-fortune at bay. Here, geography merges with history: Neolithic humans built dolmens and raised the enormous standing stones known as menhirs; more than 4,000 years later – after the French Revolution – 18th-century guerrillas hid in the dense forests to escape the flames and the bayonets of Republican troops.

THE PLAINE Blending into the Marais Poitevin and the *bocage* is the *plaine*, a series of rolling prairies that stretch between Ste-Hermine and Fontenay-le-Comte and provide crops of sunflowers, maize and wheat. The red-roofed houses here exude prosperity. Tall and substantial, they are built of fine, white stone, unlike the more primitive, ground-hugging cottages of the windswept marshes.

ISLANDS Two main islands belong to the Vendée. **Noirmoutier** extends over nearly 5,000ha and stretches itself out over 20km. Accessible from the mainland by a bridge and at low tide by the Passage du Gois, this popular holiday island shares geographical characteristics with the nearest mainland. Saltpans spread across its northwest, and its fine sandy beaches mirror those across the water. In contrast, the **Île d'Yeu** is literally more insular, being 18km off the coast and an hour away by boat. Half the size of Noirmoutier, its northern coast is the calmer, sprinkled with beaches and forest, and home to the main town, pretty Port-Joinville. Wild and rocky, the graveyard of many ships over the decades, the southern coast hosts fewer beaches.

The third island covered by this book, but outside the Vendée, is the Île de Ré, a delightful holiday haven for the inhabitants of nearby La Rochelle and beyond.

RIVERS In addition to the Vendée itself, the major rivers impacting the area are the Sèvre Nantaise and the Sèvre Niortaise, as well as the Vie, the Lay and several smaller ones – more than a dozen in total.

LAKES Lakes are also a feature of the Vendée, with nearly 20 of them inside the departmental boundaries. **Apremont** is the largest, but **Mervent** and **Jaunay** are among others which provide welcome inland opportunities for summer visitors and residents. In high season, they are popular for their 'beaches' and nautical activities. Again outside the Vendée, but inside the subject matter of this book, is the **Lac de Grand-Lieu**, a huge expanse of water south of Nantes and a popular haven for birds.

FORESTS In parts, the territory here is heavily wooded. The forests of Olonne, Mervent, Longeville and the Pays de Monts are the most significant, and together they cover nearly 10,000ha. Pine – especially the maritime pine – oak, ash and poplar are among the common species to be found. As well as shoring up the fragile dune ecosystem along the Atlantic, trees also provide home to wild boar and deer – and shade to campers both inland and by the sea.

CLIMATE

The Vendée and its surroundings are gloriously sunny, particularly on the coast, which experiences over 2,000 hours of sunshine annually. Temperatures in high

LES SABLES-D'OLONNE
Average maximum temperatures in °C

Jan	Feb	Mar	Apr	May	Jun	Jul	Aug	Sep	Oct	Nov	Dec
9	10	12	15	18	21	24	23	21	18	13	9

Average minimum temperatures in °C

Jan	Feb	Mar	Apr	May	Jun	Jul	Aug	Sep	Oct	Nov	Dec
3	4	5	7	10	13	15	14	13	10	6	4

Average sea temperatures in °C

Jan	Feb	Mar	Apr	May	Jun	Jul	Aug	Sep	Oct	Nov	Dec
10	10	10	12	14	17	20	20	19	17	14	12

summer can be hot, winters are generally mild and somewhat humid but colder in the areas away from the ocean. There's little in the way of snow and even the interior claims only a modest number of frosty days. November to January are the rainiest months, and the coast generally experiences less precipitation than the interior of the département. Wind is often a feature here, a welcome provider of cooling breezes in summer. Occasional storms can brew in autumn or winter, with the islands being particularly susceptible. Only very rarely can these be serious (page 128).

NATURAL HISTORY *Mike Unwin*

MAMMALS Many of France's 100-plus species of mammal live in the Vendée. The great majority are small rodents, bats and insectivores – nocturnal creatures that you are unlikely to see, let alone identify – but a few are more easily recognised. **Brown hares** are common in the fields, dashing about during their spring courtship rituals. **Red squirrels** thrive in the forests where, unlike in the UK, they do not have to compete with the American grey squirrel.

At dusk, both **red deer** and **roe deer** venture out into fields and forest edges, the former much larger, with impressive antlers in the stags. **Wild boar** are common but shy, their telltale tracks and diggings more easily seen than the animals themselves. Among several carnivores also largely active after dark are the familiar **red fox** and **badger** and, less well known to UK visitors, two species of marten: the **pine marten**, confined to forests, and the **beech marten**, which has a white rather than yellow bib and makes itself unpopular by chewing through cables under car bonnets. Headlights might also reveal a **common genet** crossing the road. This lithe, spotted cat-like hunter was introduced to Spain from Africa by the Romans and has since colonised much of France.

Several aquatic mammals inhabit the region's waterways. The **otter** is widespread but seldom seen, usually offering just a glimpse of sleek body and long tail as it swims across a lake or canal. Equally shy, and largely nocturnal, the **European beaver** is enjoying a comeback across France, courtesy of targeted reintroductions, and has spread into the Vendée from the Loire. The **coypu**, another aquatic rodent, is often mistaken for a beaver but is only half the size and has a rat-like rather than paddle-shaped tail. Introduced from South America, it now thrives across France. Much smaller than either coypu or beaver is the diminutive **water vole**, often seen swimming across quiet waterways or nibbling plants at the edge.

1

There are also a few curiosities among the region's livestock. Perhaps the most distinctive and endearing is the *baudet du Poitou*, a large, shaggy-coated donkey said to be the oldest race in France. This once-threatened breed is now increasing thanks to a conservation plan. Some protected areas also harbour **highland cattle**, which help in ecological management through their rough grazing.

BIRDS Birds are probably the Vendée's greatest wildlife draw and at certain seasons this region offers some of the richest birdwatching in France. The coast is especially productive, with its extensive wetlands providing vital pit stops for spring and autumn migrants travelling to and from Africa, as well as wintering quarters for others. These travellers include huge flocks of wildfowl, such as **pintail**, **greylag geese** and **brent geese**, plus waders, such as **black-tailed godwit**, **curlew**, **knot** and **dunlin** that swirl in hundreds of thousands between their high-tide roosts and the food-rich mudflats. Top spots for such spectacles include the bays of Bourgneuf and L'Aiguillon, the latter one of the most important protected areas in France.

In spring, after the big flocks have departed, the marshes and salt meadows host breeding wading birds such as **avocet**, **little egret**, **black-winged stilt** and **spoonbill**. In recent years, the **sacred ibis** – an invasive species from Africa – has also secured a foothold in the Marais Breton region. **Ospreys** pass through on migration and the exquisite little **bluethroat** breeds in the coastal scrub in sites such as the Réserve Naturelle de Lilleau des Niges, on the Île de Ré. Further inland, freshwater marshes host such reed-bed skulkers as **bittern** and **purple heron**, while **kingfishers** zip along waterways and **great reed warblers** fill the air with their relentless, mechanical song. **White storks** breed in the marshland around Châteauneuf and Velluire, building their big stick nests on tall platforms. **Yellow-legged gull**, **Mediterranean gull** and **Sandwich tern** breed on the coastal lagoons, while more sea-going seabirds, including **skuas**, **shearwaters** and **auks**, pass offshore – especially outside the breeding season.

Inland, each habitat offers new birds. Woodland is home to woodpeckers – some unfamiliar to UK birdwatchers, including **middle-spotted woodpecker**, **grey-headed woodpecker** and, in larger forests, the impressive **black woodpecker**. As well as numerous **common buzzards**, the raptor ranks are swelled in summer by **honey buzzard**, **black kite** and a few rare **short-toed eagles** – specialist snake-catchers that hover over open ground like oversized kestrels. In the broader countryside, spring brings the songs of **nightingales** and **turtle doves**, while **red-backed shrike** and **hoopoe** forage around farm and orchard, and **golden orioles** make their fluting call from poplar stands. **Black redstarts** flit around village rooftops, red tails quivering, while **barn owls** hunt around farms and fields at night.

The more open fields and plains may not look the most appealing habitat, but they are also home to many special birds. These include the three species of harrier – **marsh harrier**, **Montagu's harrier** and **hen harrier** – all of which can be seen quartering open country for prey, wings upheld in a characteristic shallow 'V'. **Corn bunting** and **crested lark** sing from fences, while **stone-curlew** and **little bustard** stalk the bare ground and long grass.

Birdwatchers will find numerous observatories around the region. These include Les Landes-Genusson, St-Denis-du-Payré, Le Poiré-sur-Velluire, Réserve biologique de Nalliers Mouzeuil-/St-Martin and Île-d'Olonne. Other excellent sites for watching birds and other wildlife include the Marais Breton, the Marais d'Olonne, the Marais Poitevin, the Baie de L'Aiguillon, the Mervent-Vouvant Forest and the rivers Sèvre Nantaise, Lay, Vie, Vendée and Payré. Details of ornithological outings with the Vendée branch of the Ligue pour la Protection des Oiseaux (LPO) are listed on the organisation's website: w vendee.lpo.fr.

REPTILES AND AMPHIBIANS France's milder winters leave the country much better endowed with reptiles and amphibians than the UK, and the Vendée region offers a fair selection. Snakes, as everywhere, are shy and seldom seen. One of the more impressive is the fast-moving **western whip snake**, a greenish-yellow species, finely banded in black, which may reach 1.5m in length and often suns itself in dry clearings. In the marshes and ditches, **grass snakes** hunt for frogs, as does their close relative the **viperine snake**, which has black adder-like markings. The common adder is not found here – instead replaced by its close relative the **asp viper**, the region's only venomous snake, which basks on sunny hillsides and retreats quickly from disturbance.

Lizards are more easily seen. The most common is the **wall lizard**, a small species that is found where its name suggests. The larger and brighter **green lizard** often dashes away beneath a hedge, the male revealing a blue throat. The **ocellated lizard**, found in the south of the region, has a long tail and 'eye' spots along its green flanks, and may exceed 60cm. In quiet marshy pools, look out for France's rarest reptile, the **European pond terrapin**, basking on logs. This habitat is also the haunt of several frog species, including the **marsh frog** and **edible frog**, which strike up an impressive chorus during the spring breeding season. Other amphibians include the diminutive **European tree frog**, which clings to overhanging vegetation with sucker-pad toes, and the **fire salamander**, found around mossy logs and damp leaf litter, whose vivid black and yellow colours warn of its toxic skin secretions.

INSECTS Butterflies are the most conspicuous representatives of the region's rich insect fauna. In summer, field margins attract a good selection, including the spectacular **common swallowtail** – extremely rare in the UK – and its paler cream relative the **scarce swallowtail**. Numerous **fritillary** species glide and flutter over wild flower meadows, **map butterflies** haunt woodland rides and **great-banded graylings** join **painted ladies** to sup nectar from garden buddleia bushes – which also, invariably, host the buzzing attentions of **hummingbird hawkmoths**. Other striking insects include numerous dragonflies that patrol the waterways, such as the large **emperor dragonfly**, and the **cicadas** that fill the summer woods with their relentless call. Less popular are the **hornets**, a large relative of the wasp, which are less aggressive than their reputation suggests but do pack a nasty sting, and the **mosquitoes**, which may be a problem in some weather conditions. Plug-in insect repellents are effective in deterring the latter, as is *citronelle* oil from chemists, rubbed on the skin.

FLORA In spring, the fields and wetlands of the Vendée region are alive with wild flowers. Botanists will be particularly interested in the rich variety of orchids, including **lizard orchid**, **bee orchid** and **tongue orchid**. Top spots include the Île d'Yeu, where **white asphodel**, **rock rose** and **sand dune wallflower** (helianthemum) are among more than 760 species of wild flower. Inland, clearings among the beech and oak forests offer a different selection, with **pink asphodel** and **yellow broom** especially conspicuous.

HISTORY

You can have a great time in the Vendée wining, dining, sunbathing and absorbing the rich present-day culture while remaining blissfully unaware of its past.

Nevertheless, to dig a bit deeper and to get closer to the identity of the département it is essential to understand more about the Vendée Wars, a period unknown to many and perhaps conveniently forgotten even by many French citizens.

FRENCH AND VENDEAN HISTORY Dating from 2500BC and before, the menhirs and dolmens scattered all around the region are evidence enough that the Vendée was inhabited from prehistoric times; the areas around Avrillé and Le Bernard are particularly rich in this respect. From the end of the 10th century AD, after the collapse of Frankish king Charlemagne's empire across western Europe, feudal castles began to be built at places such as St-Mesmin, Ardelay, Noirmoutier, Tiffauges and Talmont. (Today's visitors still frequent these historic places, or at least what has been left of them by the passage of time and the pursuit of conflicts.) A new religious phenomenon took hold in the 11th century across much of France – including the Vendée – in which people made pilgrimages from northern countries towards the shrine of St James the Elder at Santiago de Compostela, in northwest Spain. During the following 200 years, abbeys, churches, convents, almshouses and hospitals sprang up along the most popular routes to shelter the thousands of people who made the long journey, though in the Vendée these Romanesque buildings would receive heavy damage during the waging of later wars.

FAMOUS AND INFAMOUS VENDEANS

Memorable names connected with the Vendée include:

Gilles de Rais (1404–40) Companion-in-arms of Joan of Arc, famous Satanist, prolific child killer and notorious in legend as the murderous 'Bluebeard'.

Pierre Garcie-Ferrande (c1430–c1520) Intrepid navigator from St-Gilles-sur-Vie, praised by King François I for his charting of Europe's coastline.

François Rabelais (c1494–1553) Renaissance writer, monk and father of good living, who spent time at Fontenay-le-Comte and Maillezais.

François Viète (1540–1603) Inventor of modern algebra, born at Fontenay-le-Comte.

Cardinal Richelieu (1585–1642) Prime minister to Louis XIII and Bishop of Luçon from 1606 to 1622.

Nau l'Olonnais (c1630–71) Bloodthirsty pirate from Olonne-sur-Mer who was chopped up and eaten by cannibals (perhaps serves him right for being a bloodthirsty pirate).

Paul Baudry (1824–86) A painter and native of La Roche-sur-Yon, commissioned to decorate the foyer of the Paris Opéra.

Georges Clemenceau (1841–1929) Statesman who was twice prime minister and drew up the Treaty of Versailles after World War I, born at Mouilleron-en-Pareds and buried near Mouchamps.

Benjamin Rabier (1864–1939) Artist from La Roche-sur-Yon, creator of the cheery Vache-qui-Rit (Laughing Cow) logo.

Jean de Lattre de Tassigny (1889–1952) Distinguished World War II soldier, born and buried at Mouilleron-en-Pareds.

Frédéric Mazzella (b1946) Vendée-born founder of BlaBlaCar, the world's biggest long-distance ride-sharing community. As of mid 2023, it had purchased Ouibus from SNCF and expanded to operate in 22 countries and had 100 million members.

The marriage, in 1152, of Eleanor of Aquitaine to Henri Plantagenêt, Duke of Normandy (who, two years later, became King Henry II of England) combined her dowry of western France with his existing lands in the north to bring around half of France into English hands. Their son Richard the Lionheart (Richard I of England) enjoyed hunting, and often stayed at Talmont, atoning for his foreign warmongering by providing funds for several abbeys, including that of Lieu-Dieu, at Jard.

More than a century later, after acceding to the throne of England in 1327, Edward III made a claim through his mother's line to the French crown. The resulting so-called Hundred Years War (it lasted for longer), sustained successively by Richard II, Henry IV and Henry V, made much of northern and western France into a battleground until 1453, when the French successfully won back all but the town of Calais.

By the mid 16th century the Vendée was a stronghold of many influential Protestants (*les Réformés*), which meant that the 36-year-long Wars of Religion that broke out in 1562 between Catholics and Protestants inevitably brought fresh devastation to religious buildings throughout the region. Eventually, Henri IV, who had been brought up a Protestant and converted to Catholicism on his accession, granted freedom of worship to the Protestants in 1598 through the Edict of Nantes, and the conflict came to an end. (The Edict was revoked a century later by Louis XIV.) Cardinal Richelieu, one-time Bishop of Luçon, and chief minister to Louis XIII between 1624 and 1642 (the period evoked in Alexandre Dumas's *The Three Musketeers*) saw the need to unite the whole of France – Catholic and Protestant – under one crown. To prevent strategic strongholds falling into Protestant hands, and to reduce the power of provincial dukes and princes, he ordered the destruction of many castles, including those of Apremont, La Garnache and Les Essarts.

The Wars of the Vendée After the Storming of the Bastille in 1789 and the Declaration of the First Republic in 1792, the power of the new regime created by the French Revolution was total. The nobility was abolished. Priests who refused to swear allegiance to the Republican government (rather than to the king, the previous head of the Church) were deported and replaced with 'loyal' ones. The names of towns and villages were changed from any with religious overtones (St-Gilles-sur-Vie, for example, became Port-Fidèle). Even the calendar was altered: Year I began on 22 September 1793; the 12 months (composed of three ten-day weeks) were renamed 'Vendémiaire, Frimaire, Brumaire...' and so on, while the days themselves were rebaptised 'Primidi, Duodi, Tridi, Quartidi...'. Moreover, the then-familiar measurements of *pieds* and *pouces* (feet and inches) were superseded by a new metric system.

Having previously endured the absolute power of the king, many of the urban middle classes embraced the new, revolutionary philosophies and the ideas of a world of greater justice. The labouring classes, too, welcomed the Declaration of the Rights of Man, and looked forward to the abolition of the taxes that they previously had to pay to the Crown.

However, new ideas permeated only slowly to the Vendée – then known as Bas-Poitou – more than 350km distant from Paris. In this rural region there was less social inequality than elsewhere: aristocrats were not as rich; tenant farmers were less poor; and priests were more revered in a religion that combined elements of local superstition with orthodox Catholicism. All in all, this was hardly fertile ground in which to plant and grow the seeds of the new revolutionary ideas.

Indeed, the Vendean peasants were appalled to find that the Revolution had removed their king (Louis XVI was executed in January 1793), forced on them new

1

DATE	FRENCH HISTORY	BRITISH HISTORY
EARLY TIMES		
7500–2500BC	Neolithic period *(Dolmens, menhirs)*	Neolithic period
4th century AD	Christianity reaches Poitou	Christianity in Britain
MIDDLE AGES		
AD486	Beginning of Merovingian period	Anglo-Saxon
751	Beginning of Carolingian period	Saxon kingdoms
987	Beginning of Capetian period	Ethelred II (Saxon),
	(Romanesque architecture, 10th–12th centuries)	then Danes, Saxons and Normans
1152	Henri Plantagenêt (Henry II of England) marries Eleanor of Aquitaine	From 1154 Henry II (Plantagenet)
	(Gothic architecture, 12th–15th centuries)	
1189–99		Richard Coeur-de-Lion (Richard the Lionheart, Plantagenet)
1337–1453	**Hundred Years War between France and England**	Edward III (Plantagenet)
1431	Death of Joan of Arc	Henry VI (Lancaster)
MODERN TIMES		
1515	Accession of François I (d1547) *(Renaissance architecture)*	Henry VIII (Tudor)
1562–98	**Wars of Religion in France**; destruction of many churches	Elizabeth I (Tudor)
1589	Accession of Henri IV of France (d1610) *(Classical architecture 1589–1789)*	Elizabeth I
1598	Edict of Nantes allowing Protestants freedom to worship	Elizabeth I
1610	Accession of Louis XIII (d1643) (1622, king fights Protestants near St-Gilles)	James I (Stuart)
1624–42	Richelieu prime minister (1627–28 siege of La Rochelle)	Charles I (Stuart)
1643	Louis XIV – 'the Sun King' (d1715)	Charles I
1685	Revocation of Edict of Nantes by Louis XIV; 400,000 Huguenots (French Protestants) flee abroad, many to England	James II (Stuart)

DATE	FRENCH HISTORY	BRITISH HISTORY
1774	Accession of Louis XVI	George III (Hanover)
1789	**FRENCH REVOLUTION**	George III
1792–1804	**First Republic**	George III
1793	Louis XVI guillotined 21 January	George III
1793–96	**WARS OF THE VENDÉE**	George III
1804–14	**First Empire**	George III
	Napoleon I (Bonaparte)	
	(1814 Napoleon exiled to Elba)	
	(Classical-style architecture and furniture,	
	resembling Britain's Regency style)	
1814–15	**First Restoration** Louis XVIII	George III
1815	Napoleon returns to power for	
	100 days (April–June), then banished	George III
	to St Helena	
1815	Louis de la Rochejaquelein attempts	George III
	unsuccessfully to reignite the royalist	
	cause in the Vendée	
1815–48	**Second Restoration**	
	Louis XVIII (d1824)	George III
1824	Charles X (exiled 1830)	George IV
		(Hanover)
1830	Louis-Philippe I (abdicates 1848 in favour	William IV
	of his grandson, the Comte de Paris)	(Hanover)
1832	The Duchesse de Berry, daughter-in-law	William IV
	of Charles X, attempts a rebellion in the	
	Vendée to place her son, the Duke	
	of Bordeaux, on the French throne	
1848–52	**Second Republic**	Victoria (Hanover)
1852–70	**Second Empire**	Victoria
	Napoleon III (Louis-Napoleon)	
	(Opulent architecture with wrought-iron	
	features; heavy, Victorian-style furniture)	
1870–1940	**Third Republic**	Victoria/Edward VII/
		George V
		George VI (Windsor)
1914–18	**World War I**	George V
1916	20,000 Vendean troops die	
	at Verdun	
1940–44	**World War II**	George VI
	France (including the Vendée) under	
	German occupation	
1947–58	**Fourth Republic**	George VI
		Elizabeth II (Windsor)
1958–present	**Fifth Republic**	Elizabeth II
		Charles III (Windsor)

priests loyal to the changed order, and that they were required to make payment to the Republican government of even higher taxes than had been due under the monarchy. Worse, the confiscated goods of the old Church and deported clergy were thought to be lining the pockets of the *bourgeoisie*, or middle classes, who had engineered for themselves the top administrative posts. Ignoring the new priests assigned to their churches, the Vendeans instead attended clandestine open-air Masses led by their own, rebellious, pre-Revolutionary clergy.

With that background of brooding discontent, the actual spark that ignited three years of horrific civil warfare was the Republican government's decision in February 1793 to raise a 300,000-strong army to defend France's borders against threatened invasion by neighbouring countries. The people of Bas-Poitou and surrounding départements refused to submit to formal conscription, leading to the arrival of Republican soldiers charged with drawing names of conscripts at random. Riots ensued, then in March the town of Machecoul saw the massacre of its Republican sympathisers. The 'Massacre of Machecoul' strengthened the resolve of the Republicans against the rioters but by the time they could respond, these smaller scale riots had grown into a broader counter-revolution.

The event generally considered to be the start of the wars proper was a similar stand against conscription, on 11 March 1793, by the people of St-Florent-le-Vieil on the River Loire, midway between Nantes and Angers (in what is now Maine-et-Loire département). The populace routed the '*Bleus*' ('Blues', or Republican troops, sometimes referred to as *patriots*), and captured their cannon, before calling upon a simple carter, Jacques Cathelineau, to lead them and others who joined the cause. He and former gamekeeper Jean-Nicolas Stofflet were 'working-class generals'; for the rest, the Vendean people prevailed on trusted local aristocrats to take command: François Athanase Charette de la Contrie, Louis de Lescure, Henri de la Rochejaquelein, the Duc d'Elbée; all names which have passed into local folklore.

After some spectacular early Vendean victories at Bressuire, Thouars, Fontenay-le-Comte and Saumur, and notably at Angers in June 1793, the '*Blancs*' ('Whites', or royalist Vendeans, also sometimes referred to by their opponents as *brigands*) seemed invincible. Their initial successes were partly due to the fact that they would disperse immediately after a battle, ghosting away to leave no tangible 'army' for the Blues to seek out and destroy. Initially ill-prepared, the Republicans were, however, soon reinforced by General Kléber's crack troops known as the 'Mayençais', who had been fighting on the German front. Vendean victory would soon turn to defeat at Nantes (where Cathelineau received mortal wounds). The Whites lost the town of Cholet, where Lescure was severely wounded. In search of hoped-for reinforcements from England (to where many of the French nobility had fled), the Vendée army then made a seemingly impossible dash northwards across the River Loire. (Here, before his death from wounds also sustained at Cholet, another leader, the Marquis de Bonchamps, earned his place in history by refusing to allow his Vendean troops to massacre their thousands of Republican prisoners.)

This exodus – known as the 'Virée de Galerne' – has, ever since, evoked a kind of 'Dunkirk spirit' in the region. Harried by the Blues, on 18 October 1793 the Vendeans ferried between 60,000 and 100,000 men, women and children north across the wide and treacherous river. Their aim was to capture a suitable port, perhaps Granville on the Cherbourg peninsula, or St-Malo in Brittany, ready to receive the expected English aid. During the epic journey the hungry, cold Vendeans marched some 200km north where they were joined by Breton guerrillas known as 'Chouans'.

In November, they laid siege to Granville, but without success. After a fruitless wait for help from England the Vendeans set off back towards the Loire. (Two years later, in 1795, William Pitt did eventually send forces, only for them to be cut down during an attempt to land on the Quiberon peninsula on the south coast of Brittany.) At Le Mans, 10,000 Vendeans were slain by the town's heavily armed Republicans. Tens of thousands more died in further combats, or from sickness and hunger. In December 1793, a few thousand managed to recross the Loire; many others, prevented from doing the same, fled west, where 6,000 fell victim to Republican troops in the forest of Savenay, west of Nantes.

Determined that such insurrection should never happen again, the Republican General Turreau gave orders that *colonnes infernales* ('fiery columns' of troops) should be sent to lay waste to every village and kill every remaining person in the département of Bas-Poitou – that would henceforth be renamed 'Vendée'. From early 1794 these death squads passed from village to village, burning, pillaging and massacring. At Les Lucs-sur-Boulogne, 564 people – women, children and old men – were shot as they knelt in church. At Les Sables-d'Olonne, blood from the guillotine ran thickly on to the town's golden sands. In Nantes, where even the 90 seconds required for this method of execution proved too slow, General Carrier instituted a more efficient method by drowning entire boatloads of prisoners in the River Loire.

The few surviving Vendeans returned home to find ruined houses, murdered families, and a reign of terror. For many months they continued their guerrilla warfare, among the gorse and bracken of the *bocage*. Charette and Stofflet signed peace treaties with the Republicans in 1795, though Charette continued to lead skirmishes against the Blues until his capture at La Chabotterie in March 1796; his execution followed, a few weeks after that of Stofflet.

Under a treaty drawn up by the Republican General Hoche in 1799, freedom of worship returned to France. Napoleon Bonaparte made supervision of the unruly Vendée less difficult, transferring the capital from Fontenay-le-Comte to La Roche-sur-Yon, in the geographical heart of the region. Here, he created a new town of straight, broad avenues, allowing rapid deployment of troops to quell future uprisings.

Although with the death of Charette the wars reached an end, a few further attempts were made to rekindle them. During Napoleon's brief return to power in 1815, Louis de la Rochejaquelein (brother of Henri) carried out an unsuccessful invasion near Croix-de-Vie. Some 17 years later the Duchesse de Berry tried to seize the French throne for her son, the Duke of Bordeaux – grandson of Charles X.

Debate still rages as to whether the uprising that cost so many lives was truly spontaneous or was engineered by landowners and priests reluctant to lose their power and fortunes. Some call the subsequent retribution on the Vendeans 'genocide'. Atrocities were, no doubt, perpetrated by both Vendean and Republican forces but, in the area where the memories live on, a certain amount of bias in the retelling of the stories is inevitable.

MORE RECENT TIMES Vast areas of pine and *chêne vert* (holm oak) were planted from the mid 19th century to anchor the shifting sands along the coast around St-Jean-de-Monts and north of Les Sables-d'Olonne. The coming of the railways in the 1860s helped to develop tourism around the ports of Les Sables and Croix-de-Vie, where a few fine examples of Victorian-period seaside architecture remain. When paid holidays for workers were introduced, the tourist industry received a further boost. Railways also provided a means of escape for many of the inhabitants of marshland farms, leading to a rural exodus around the end of the 19th century as young people flocked to the more lucrative work in towns. From the late 18th until the mid 20th century there were coal-mining and glass-making industries at Faymoreau, northeast of Fontenay-le-Comte.

The brooding silhouette of the occasional blockhouse reminds you that for more than four years of World War II the Vendée and other parts of the Atlantic coast were occupied by German forces. A Commonwealth War Graves Commission sign on the wall of a country cemetery usually indicates that it contains graves of Allied aircrew shot down over the Vendée while on bombing raids. Seen on the wall of a coastal cemetery – particularly around the Loire Estuary – it will probably denote the graves of some of the 3,000 (or more) British who drowned in June 1940 when the merchant ship *Lancastria* was sunk by enemy action in the midst of a massive evacuation operation from St-Nazaire. A visit to the Bunker museum in La Rochelle, or to the major sites in St-Nazaire, will provide some insight into the war period.

GOVERNMENT AND POLITICS

For administrative/political purposes, France is divided into 18 *régions*, each containing a number of départements, of which there are 95 in total across the whole country. The Vendée is département number 85, the high number being explained by the fact that originally numbers were ascribed to départements in accordance with where they appeared in the alphabet. The Vendée is part of the Pays de la Loire *région*, which also encompasses the départements of Loire-Atlantique, Maine-et-Loire, Mayenne and Sarthe.

ECONOMY

After tourism and services, the wealth of the département today is based on agriculture, which accounts for around 10% of the economy. This consists of beef and dairy cattle, pigs and poultry in the *bocage*, and cereal growing in the plain, together with sheep and cattle in the marshes, and early vegetables on the island of Noirmoutier. On the coast, fishing for sardines, tuna and sole provides some employment, while cultivation of oysters and mussels is prevalent. Manufacturing contributes around 7% through clothing and shoe-making, boat-building (Bénéteau Group), and the construction of agricultural machinery.

PEOPLE

Around 685,442 people lived in the Vendée in 2019, according to official statistics. To the cursory foreigner passing through the area, the typical Vendean may not appear to have much of a regional identity: they don't look different from anyone from elsewhere in France and they speak French. Of course, this is an area which has seen a healthy influx of people from other parts of France, perhaps for its climate or retirement or both, so many of the people you meet here may not be Vendean at all. Vendeans define themselves, however, through a strong connection to the land, *their* land, and in the coastal towns by their connection to the sea. In high summer, the coastal population is swollen with incomers to such an extent that you might be hard pushed to find many locals at all! The proportion of foreigners actually resident here is low, at around 2% compared with a French national average of more than 6%. On the islands, as might be expected, the inhabitants have micro-identities, proud of their island and referring semi-seriously to the mainland as *le continent*.

LANGUAGE

French is the only official language in France and is now spoken throughout the Vendée, with very few exclusively regional words or phrases still appearing in everyday use. For English-speakers, it is always said that the French are reluctant to talk in anything other than French, but while that may be true to some extent of the older generations, the influences of Hollywood and popular music means that young French people will happily converse in English if they can. If you can muster a few words in French yourself, even if only by way of greetings, it at least demonstrates some respect and shows that you recognise the fact that you are in France!

RELIGION

Roman Catholicism was once the state religion of France, starting with the conversion of King Clovis I in AD496. During the French Revolution of 1789, the relationship between the state and church was radically redefined. Secularism is now a core concept of the French Constitution. The principle of *laïcité* means that people are free to believe and practise any religion or not to practise at all, which has led to some friction over the years, particularly with religious symbols and clothing.

In 2021, the passing of the 'Upholding Republican Values' law, which was aimed at protecting French values, caused some conflict. Many civil society organisations felt that the law could fall disproportionately on minority religious groups. The most high-profile outcome of this law was the banning of abayas (loose-fitting, full-length robes worn by some Muslim women) which made headlines in many countries. Prior to this, the wearing of burqas, niqabs and other full-face coverings in public, was already banned.

The number of people identifying as Catholic (around half of the population) is slowly declining, with those citing no religion at all on the rise (51% of 18–59 year olds in metropolitan France said they had no religion in 2019–20). Given that devout Catholicism partially drove the counterrevolution, it isn't surprising that the Vendée has remained a bulwark against this broader trend and notes a higher number of practising Roman Catholics than in other regions of France.

Worshippers are always welcome to attend Mass (*la messe*) at Catholic churches – services are held on Saturday evening or Sunday morning (for times, see w messes. info/horaires). Protestant churches, or *églises réformées*, hold weekly services (in French), known as *cultes*, at Fontenay-le-Comte, Mouchamps and La Roche-sur-Yon; their churches are called *temples*.

Then there is the Anglican Church of All Saints, Vendée (w allsaintsvendee.fr), which covers the whole of the Vendée and which is part of the Church of England Diocese in Europe. Under the title of 'Congregations of All Saints, Vendée', regular services are held near La Mothe-Achard and near La Châtaigneraie, details are on the website, above.

The Association Vendée Maghreb offers daily prayers and services for worshippers at their mosque in La Roche-sur-Yon.

EDUCATION

La Roche-sur-Yon is home to the ICES (Catholic University of the Vendée), which is a private university of around 1,000 students. Courses are offered in law, history, English studies, biology, French and political sciences. Outside the Vendée, Nantes is the location of three public universities, while one of France's newest universities is based in La Rochelle.

CULTURE

LITERATURE Although the Vendée has produced its fair share of writers over the centuries, the French-language barrier inevitably means that Anglophones' awareness of them is limited, and few of the authors below have been translated into English. However, the works of **François Rabelais** (c1494–1553) are available in translation, notably his earthy tales of *Gargantua and Pantagruel* which are both funny and bawdy (the description 'rabelaisian' says it all!). More than 400 years later, and sharing with Rabelais a strong connection to Fontenay-le-Comte, the multi-faceted **Michel Ragon** (1924–2020) was actually born in Marseille but spent his early life in the south-Vendean former capital. He studied art, became a renowned essayist, and wrote novels such as *Les Mouchoirs rouges de Cholet* (*The Red Handkerchiefs of Cholet*) which, like many of his other works, concerns itself with the Vendée Wars. Although Belgian, **Georges Simenon** (1903–89) used his wartime experience of living in the Vendée to write some of his novels. (Simenon's time in the département was mired in controversy, with accusations of collaboration with the occupying Germans.) Vendean by birth, **Jean Yole** (born Léopold Robert, 1878–1956) took his pen name from the traditional marshland boat, the *yole*, and combined his writing with interests in politics and medicine. He wrote plays, essays and novels, the latter often portraying traditional, Vendean marshland life. Attributed to Yole is an inscription which can be seen on one of the windmills on the Mont des Alouettes (page 186): *'C'est le rôle de chaque génération de recueillir ce que la tradition détient de sages leçons d'énergies accordées, pour en ensemencer les réalités futures.'* ('Each generation should harvest the wisdom of the past and use it to sow the seeds of the future.')

Also born in the Vendée is prolific novelist **Yves Viollier** (1946–), whose works often describe aspects of the region: his 2011 book *La mer était si calme* (*The Sea was so Calm*) refers to Storm Xynthia, which had wreaked havoc on the Vendean coast the previous year (page 128).

ART The Vendée's landscapes have inspired painters as well as writers. Among the best known are **Paul Baudry** (1828–86), classical artist and portraitist, best known for his 30 frescoes commissioned to decorate the foyer of the Paris Opéra. The works of **Charles Milcendeau** (1872–1919) can be seen at the museum in his native Soullans (page 73). In Paris, he rubbed shoulders with such luminaries as Henri Matisse and Georges Rouault, and was a frequent visitor to Spain, but his subject-matter was usually drawn from the bleak *marais* around his birthplace. **Gaston Chaissac** (1910–64) was an exponent of *art brut*. A visit to the Abbaye Ste-Croix museum in Les Sables-d'Olonne, or to the Espace Gaston-Chaissac near Les Essarts, will give insight into the works of this innovative and bizarre artist who created works from broken doors, mattress-ticking and even cow dung!

Sculpture Twin Art Deco sculptors Jan and Joël Martel (both 1896–1966) were firmly rooted in the Vendée. Among their public works on view here are the moving war memorials of Olonne-sur-Mer and Les Clouzeaux; a panel in the garden behind Challans tourist office depicting traditional marshland dances; and an imposing monument to aviator René Guilbaud near Mouchamps.

MUSIC AND DANCE While the Vendée has no great recognisable musical tradition of its own, music often plays a part at the various festivals held (especially in summer) around the region. Throughout this book you will also find reference to events specifically dedicated to music of one form or another. The world-famous American Baroque-music maestro **William Christie** (1944–) is one of the Vendée's most famous residents, and occasionally conducts concerts in churches around Ste-Hermine. One of his protégés, **Hugo Reyne** (1961–) is director of a fine annual Baroque music festival held at the Logis de la Chabotterie (page 191). In another mood entirely, you may also be fortunate enough to catch a show-performance of the **Danse de la Brioche**, a folkloric dance often performed at weddings and involving a giant brioche being whirled around the room! The tradition is to offer a piece of this fluffy Vendean bread to the wedding guests as midnight approaches. Musical accompaniment will usually be provided by violin and accordion. Other folk dances can also be seen performed in period costume at Autrefois Challans (page 67) and other local festivities across the region.

ARCHITECTURE Typical architecture of the region includes the low, thatched *bourrines* of the Marais Breton, with their whitewashed walls; the rough stone-walled cottages with 'Roman' terracotta roof tiles redolent of the warm south; the taller, more solid limestone dwellings of the plain; and larger, often discreetly hidden country houses known as *logis*, such as that of La Chabotterie (page 191).

SPORT

Without any truly large cities, the Vendée itself lacks the population base to boast any major sports teams. To the north, FC Nantes play in the top French **football** division and in past years have won the title on eight occasions, most recently in season 2000–01. Nicknamed 'The Canaries', their past luminaries include Didier Deschamps and Marcel Desailly, both of whom won the World Cup with the French national team in 2008. In 2022, Nantes won their fourth Coupe de France, their first honour since 2001, but remain a little way off their glory days.

South of the Vendée, a new power emerged in the world of **rugby union** in 2016–17, as La Rochelle-based Atlantique Stade Rochelais ('ASR') came from almost nowhere to finish top of the French Top 14 league, within the regular season (though they then lost in the play-offs). They have gone on to win the European Rugby Champions Cup in 2022 and 2023. The heartland of French rugby has traditionally been much further to the south of the country, but with money injected by an entrepreneur, an unusually large proportion of French players and the third-lowest budget of any team, ASR have delivered a much-needed kick up the *derrière* of French rugby, which is overloaded with money and mercenary foreigners.

Perhaps the best-known sporting event associated with the area is the **Vendée-Globe** yacht race (page 112), which starts every four years from Les Sables. Nicknamed the 'Everest of the Seas,' this solo circumnavigation is probably the most challenging sailing competition in the world and draws huge crowds to the town.

2

Practical Information

WHEN TO VISIT

The Vendée generally enjoys considerably warmer weather than that of southern England, thanks to an oceanic climate with hot summers and mild, damp winters (page 4). Wind is a feature much of the time, providing welcome natural cooling in high summer and attracting watersports fanatics. Inland, incidences of extreme weather can occur, with occasional intense heatwaves (*canicules*) in summer and some frosty days in winter.

But weather is not the only factor determining the best time to come to the Vendée. Like many tourist hotspots in Europe, the region shows a huge spike in visitor numbers in July and August, with a peak during the French school holidays – particularly from around 14 July to 15 August. Visiting at this time has some 'pros', as *all* visitor attractions, tourist offices and restaurants will be open on most days. The 'cons' are that everywhere will be busy, with heavy traffic, a squeeze on parking (especially on the coast) and the challenge of finding a spot on the beaches. Accommodation prices during this time will also be at the top of the curve and advanced booking becomes essential. Other busy holiday times include Easter, the month of May with its large number of public holidays, and the half-term weeks leading up to Toussaint (at the start of November). Outside the peak periods, it can be surprisingly quiet, even in warm, sunny months such as June and September. Hiring a *gîte* or a mobile home on a campsite during these times can be less than half the cost of peak-time rental. Many accommodation options and visitor attractions will close for up to a month at some period between November and February, as their owners take a well-earned rest or carry out maintenance. These closures may vary from year to year, so visiting during this time requires careful checking or your choices can be limited. Apart from seaside and purely child-orientated activities, there is still plenty to visit in May and October, but if you are coming for a specific attraction, do check the relevant website in advance to ensure that it will be operating: opening hours may change from one year to another. Main museums and cultural sites are open – at weekends at least – almost all year.

HIGHLIGHTS

PASSAGE DU GOIS Pardon the pun, but a 'rite of passage' for visitors to the Vendée is to cross this 4.5km-long, part-cobblestone causeway across the seabed to the island of Noirmoutier. If you're on a day trip, be sure to first check the tide tables for the time of low water, then, as you drive, enjoy watching the locals take advantage of the sea's temporary absence to gather shellfish before visiting the island itself and later escaping via the bridge.

ÎLE D'YEU Take to the seas, and visit this island delight with its unique, peaceful ambience out of high season. Grab a bike on arrival to gently pedal past beautiful beaches at a true holiday pace. A sparkling jewel, not one to be missed.

PUY DU FOU If you like theme parks, you will love the incredible Grand Parc at Puy du Fou. And if you don't like them, two days here may be the aversion therapy needed to change your mind. With a stunning combination of Vendean history, jaw-dropping special effects, extraordinary creativity and innovation, it's unmissable – and if you can catch the Cinéscénie evening spectacular, all the better.

ÎLE DE RÉ Another drop of gold in the ocean, this island offers spick-and-span villages, delightful beaches for all tastes and activity levels, and enough historical sites to satisfy anyone with a thirst for the past.

MARAIS POITEVIN Away from the coast, but not from the water, the Marais Poitevin is a unique landscape of tree-lined canals, best seen by boat or canoe. Take your time here and enjoy the verdant scenery.

LA ROCHELLE This vibrant city deserves a place near the top of every Francophile's list. It's full of quirky museums and brimming with restaurants, historical buildings and elegantly arcaded shopping streets.

NANTES AND ITS MECHANICAL ANIMALS On the banks of the Loire, Nantes is an energising, creative and dynamic city…epitomised by the oversized mechanical elephant waiting to give you a ride!

CLISSON This picturesque town, just beyond the Vendée departmental border, is lined with beautiful Italianate architecture.

VENDÉE MILITAIRE Don't be deterred by the *'militaire'* in the name, because if you want to touch the area's identity, you need to unlock its history. Visit the Historial, the Refuge de Grasla and the Logis de la Chabotterie and discover their dark secrets.

VOUVANT Arty and beautiful, Vouvant is a delightful little fortified village that draws in the summer crowds. Wander the cobbles, visit the church, and soak up the legend of mythical Mélusine.

SUGGESTED ITINERARIES

The vast majority of summer visitors to the region will stay put for most of their holiday – being based on a campsite beside a perfect, sandy beach hardly encourages you to tour around. But if you want to see a bit more than sun, sea and sand, distances are relatively short and day trips to most inland points of interest are entirely possible. For dedicated tourers, here are a few suggested itineraries by car.

AN INTRODUCTION TO THE COASTAL HIGHLIGHTS (SEVEN DAYS) Assuming you enter the Vendée from the north, first spend some time in the northern *marais*, visiting the curious Port du Bec, before crossing the Passage du Gois causeway onto Noirmoutier island. After overnighting there, 'escape' via the bridge and meander down the coast to delightful St-Gilles for your second night. Les Sables-d'Olonne is your next stop, the heavyweight of the Vendean resorts. Here, stroll the promenade, do some shopping and don't miss the quaint fishing quarter of La Chaume. Next day, continue south to La Tranche and then on to L'Aiguillon-sur-Mer and the Pointe de l'Aiguillon. A slightly circuitous route next day takes you to La Rochelle, where you should spend two days soaking up the wonders of this compact, maritime town. To finish your coastal trip, cross the bridge to the Île de Ré where you can idle away time in any of its neat villages – for as many days as you can spare.

HISTORY AND WATERWAYS (SEVEN DAYS)   Again starting from the north, history fans can sate their appetite for knowledge with a couple of days in the Vendée Wars Country, visiting La Chabotterie, the Historial and the Refuge de Grasla – interesting, though perhaps not the most cheerful start to a holiday! So, now head east and be enthralled with two days (and a night) at the Puy du Fou. True, there's more history here, but so much fun to be had: it seems a shame to label its Grand Parc a mere 'theme-park.' Drive south, through Fontenay-le-Comte, to reach the Venise Verte ('Green Venice') to punt around gently on the tree-lined waterways of this inland wonder.

WEEKEND CITY BREAKS (TWO/THREE DAYS)   Flying into Nantes or La Rochelle gives you the opportunity to enjoy a city break in either. Whichever you choose, there is plenty to entertain and inform you: Nantes with its astonishing artistic creativity, La Rochelle with its rich maritime history.

TOURIST INFORMATION

As the world's most popular tourist destination, France has an enviable infrastructure to welcome its 90 million-odd annual visitors, and the Vendée with its endless beaches certainly plays its part. The département has nearly 50 tourist offices, although not all are open year-round and a few operate only in high season.

MUSEUM TIPS

A few tips on how to save time, money and to avoid frustration can be useful when visiting museums in the Vendée and France in general:

- If you're visiting more than one museum, ask at the tourist office or museum about any discount passes that might be available.
- In addition to any reduced charges mentioned in the text of this book, do ask about possible reductions for students, disabled visitors, unemployed or senior citizens.
- Some museums are free to everyone on the first Sunday of the month.
- Many museums in France are closed on Mondays (less often on Tuesdays), so plan your time accordingly.
- Nearly all museums and attractions are closed on 1 January, 1 May and 25 December.
- Do ask at the ticket office for any audio-guides or information handouts in English…even if they have them, they are not always spontaneously offered!
- Look out for European Heritage Days (Journées Européennes du Patrimoine), which take place each year in September (dates vary). Many places of interest offer free admission on these days, and have special events taking place (see w journeesdupatrimoine.culture.fr).

Endless brochures are produced, some in English, covering every possible activity. At these offices or tourism sites you often find a large revolving stand displaying a host of handy free cards, each describing – in both French and English – one of the 80 or so principal visitor attractions. The cards are updated each year and detail the address, telephone number, current opening times and admission charges, making it easy to pick and choose places you think will be of interest. Even better, each of these attractions is numbered, with the numbers marked on the official Tourist Board map – a great planning tool. For those who are map-averse, a satnav or GPS on your phone can be invaluable when touring the region.

When the offices are closed out of season, you can always try the *mairie* (mayor's office) of the nearest village. While the staff there are perhaps less likely to speak much English, they often have a stock of brochures relating to major attractions and can usually supply maps of local walks. Most villages also have websites with a *tourisme* tab, allowing you to find the necessary information, which is usually in French only. Throughout this book, where you see the word 'Mairie' as the first line of the address in the *Tourist information* section, this indicates that you should enquire at the mayor's office.

Vendée Tourisme e info@en-vendee.com; w in-vendee.com. The département's tourist board. For information on areas outside the Vendée, such as Nantes, the Loire Estuary, La Rochelle or the Île de Ré, see the relevant chapters.

TOUR OPERATORS

With no large resort hotels, the Vendée is not a traditional package-holiday destination, but there are still options for those who want someone else to organise their holiday for them, or who have a specific interest.

Biking France \ +33 (0)2 54 78 62 52; w biking-france.com. A long-established company, organising a variety of family-friendly routes in the region, including several holiday-length stretches of the Vélodyssée long-distance cycle trail.
Brittany Ferries \ + 44 (0)330 159 7000; w brittany-ferries.co.uk. A variety of holidays, combining ferry crossings with well-appointed self-catering cottages, campsites & a few hotels.
En Vendée Travel Agency \+33 (0)251 627 682; w in-vendee.com. A recently launched travel agency by Vendée Expansion, which can provide tailor-made packages for individuals & groups. Given their close links with the Vendée's tourist office, they have fantastic & up-to-date knowledge on everything that goes on in the region.
Travel Local w travellocal.com. A UK-based website where you can book direct with selected local travel companies, allowing you to communicate with an expert ground operator without having to go through a third-party travel operator or agent. Your booking with the local company has full financial protection, but note that travel to the destination is not included. Member of ABTA, ASTA.

RED TAPE

SHORT STAYS Citizens of Ireland and other EU countries do not need a visa to visit France; a valid passport or National Identity Card is currently sufficient. There is no 90-day limit on the length of stay, though there may be certain limitations imposed on citizens of some of the member countries who have recently joined the EU.

Citizens of the UK, United States, Canada, Australia and New Zealand and certain other countries can visit France as tourists for up to 90 days with a valid passport, and have no need of a visa.

It is possible to take one's pets to France on holiday, though it still needs a good deal of planning in advance – not least because the animal must be microchipped and vaccinated against rabies several weeks before your trip. It is imperative to understand the Pet Travel Scheme thoroughly and to follow it to the letter. For up-to-date information, look at the French Embassy website w uk.ambafrance.org for travel into France and the DEFRA site w defra.gov.uk for requirements about bringing your pet back into the UK.

Other important considerations are that you have checked with your intended accommodation that pets are welcome, and that you have not chosen a time of year when temperatures might be too high for the comfort of your pet – which may be used to a cooler climate. On many beaches, dogs are prohibited between 07.00 and 21.00 from June to September inclusive; double-check with the local tourist office, however, as this rule varies from one municipality to another.

Citizens of other countries visiting France will need to obtain a Schengen visa, valid for up to 90 days, which involves showing that you have sufficient funds and the necessary travel insurance. You should apply well in advance. Note that possession of a Schengen visa allows the holder to travel throughout the 27 Schengen countries during the period for which the visa is valid. Schengen visas cannot be extended.

To ensure that you are up to date with any changing requirements, those visiting France should check the 'Coming to France' section of the French Ministry of Foreign Affairs website (w diplomatie.gouv.fr).

LONGER STAYS Even if staying beyond 90 days, citizens of Ireland and other EU countries currently have no need for a visa, nor do they need a residence card (*carte de séjour*) provided they are living and working legally in France. Citizens of the UK, United States, Canada, Australia and New Zealand and most other countries will need a long-stay visa if staying in France for more than 90 days, whatever the purpose of the stay. You should contact your nearest French Embassy/Consulate well in advance of your trip if you require one, as the procedure can be very lengthy, and it is not possible to extend visas from inside France.

Those who hold a long-stay visa will need to obtain a *carte de séjour* from the office of the mayor (*mairie*) within eight days of their arrival in France.

EMBASSIES Details of French embassies and consulates around the world can be found at w embassy-worldwide.com/country/france. For those seeking consular assistance from their own countries while visiting France, most offices are based in Paris (though the USA is also represented in Rennes and Bordeaux). Details can be found at w embassy.goabroad.com/embassies-in/france.

GETTING THERE AND AWAY

BY AIR Although there are no international airports within the Vendée itself, the area is easily accessible through the nearby airports of Nantes (Aéroport Nantes Atlantique; w nantes.aeroport.fr) and La Rochelle (La Rochelle-Île de Ré;

w larochelle.aeroport.fr). A variety of airlines currently fly directly from several airports in the UK, and from Ireland, particularly during the summer. Flights from further afield such as the US or Australia will in most cases need to go via Paris Charles de Gaulle or another European airport. Check the relevant airport's website for the latest operators, or use a website such as Skyscanner (w skyscanner.net) or Google flights (w google.co.uk/flights) to keep up to date.

BY SEA Particularly for the many campers travelling from the UK and Ireland, taking the ferry or tunnel across the water to France and then driving down to the Vendée can be a practical and attractive option. If you are travelling as a family, it can also be cost effective and allows you to take as much luggage as your vehicle can hold. The shortest driving times can be obtained by taking the ferry to St-Malo in Brittany. Operators are listed below:

Brittany Ferries ✆ +44 (0)330 159 7000; w brittanyferries.co.uk. From the UK, sailings to St-Malo are from Portsmouth. There are also routes from Portsmouth to Caen, Le Havre & Cherbourg; from Poole to Cherbourg; & from Plymouth to Roscoff. From Ireland (✆ +353 (0)21 4277 801; w brittanyferries.ie), sailings are from Cork to Roscoff. Note that they also organise holidays to the Vendée (page 21).

Condor Ferries ✆ +44 (0)345 609 1024; w condorferries.co.uk. Operate sailings from Poole to St-Malo (via Jersey or Guernsey).
DFDS ✆ +44 (0)344 848 6090; w dfds.com. Sailings from Newhaven to Dieppe & Dover to Calais & Dunkirk.
Irish Ferries ✆ +353 (0)818 300 400; w irishferries.com. Sailings from Dublin Port & Dover to Calais.
P&O ✆ +44 (0)800 130 0030; w poferries.com. Dover to Calais.

BY TRAIN/TUNNEL For car drivers, the tunnel provides an alternative to sea travel. For foot passengers, an improved rail network to the region makes travelling by train a realistic alternative, though once in the region the options for getting about by public transport do somewhat hamper your flexibility.

Eurostar w sncf.com or w eurostar.com. Foot passengers can take the Eurostar service from London (St Pancras) to Paris or Lille-Europe, then connect through to Nantes for local or fast TGV trains (depending on your final destination) to Challans & St-Gilles-Croix-de-Vie, La Roche-sur-Yon, Les Sables-d'Olonne or La Rochelle. Total journey time will be between 6hrs & 8hrs; bear in mind that certain journeys require a change of station in Paris. For some journeys within France (eg: Paris to Nantes), it's sometimes worth looking at w ouigo.com, which offers very cheap fares on the French rail network. Be aware that their ticket prices vary a bit like airline tickets; you pay extra for luggage.
LeShuttle w eurotunnel.com. Folkestone to Calais (Coquelles), provides a frequent Channel crossing for cars & their passengers. Ticket price includes vehicle & up to 9 people; pets can travel with you, in your car.

HEALTH *with Dr Daniel Campion*

PREPARATIONS There are few health hazards in France and health care is excellent. It is wise to be up to date with routine vaccinations in the UK such as measles, mumps and rubella, and diphtheria, tetanus and polio. Visitors from the UK should always take their Global Health Insurance Card (GHIC), which can be obtained free from w nhs.uk/using-the-nhs/healthcare-abroad/apply-for-a-free-uk-global-health-insurance-card-ghic/. With this, you can claim some reimbursement of medical expenses under the reciprocal arrangement between Britain and France (see below). Travellers from other parts of the EU/EEA should continue to use the European Health Insurance Card (EHIC).

TRAVEL CLINICS AND HEALTH INFORMATION A full list of current travel clinic websites worldwide is available on w istm.org. For other journey preparation information, consult w travelhealthpro.org.uk (UK) or w wwwnc.cdc.gov/travel (USA). All advice found online should be used in conjunction with expert advice received prior to or during travel.

MEDICAL PROBLEMS
Insect and tick-borne diseases Since 2010, a number of outbreaks of **dengue fever** have occurred in parts of mainland France, mostly in the south. This virus causes a flu-like illness and a characteristic rash; rarely it can develop into a more serious illness. As of 2023, the daytime-biting *Aedes* 'tiger mosquito' – which can transmit dengue and other viruses – has spread to 71 *départements*, including the Vendée. Try to avoid bites if mosquitoes are around: wear clothes that cover your arms and legs and use a repellent containing DEET or icaridin on exposed skin. If you are walking in the spring and summer months, you should also be aware of ticks that may fall from overhanging branches or be hiding in the long grass. Ticks may carry Lyme disease and other infections. Make sure that you are wearing long trousers with socks and boots and a long-sleeved top when hiking in the spring and summer. Check yourself for ticks at the end of the day.

MEDICAL TREATMENT In order to be able to claim expenses with a GHIC or EHIC card (page 23), after consulting and paying the doctor or dentist, take the *feuille de soins* (medical treatment form) that you are given and hand it to the pharmacist with your *ordonnance* (prescription) form. The pharmacist dispenses the drugs (it is most important to keep any sticky labels from the boxes), and adds their details to the form. Gather together the form and sticky labels, your EHIC/GHIC and passport (or a photocopy of its important pages, if you are posting it). Take or send these to the nearest Caisse Primaire d'Assurance Maladie (CPAM), which are located at La Roche-sur-Yon, Challans, Fontenay-le-Comte, Luçon, Les Herbiers and Les Sables-d'Olonne. You should get quite a large percentage of your costs reimbursed. The offices at La Roche and Les Sables can arrange to hand over the cash, or at least a

TICK REMOVAL

Ticks should ideally be removed complete, and as soon as possible, to reduce the chance of infection. You can use special tick tweezers, which can be bought in good travel shops; or failing this, with your fingernails, grasp the tick as close to your body as possible, and pull it away steadily and firmly at right angles to your skin without jerking or twisting. Applying irritants (eg: Olbas oil) or lit cigarettes is to be discouraged as a means of removal since they can cause the ticks to regurgitate and therefore increase the risk of disease. Once the tick is removed, if possible douse the wound with alcohol (any spirit will do), soap and water, or iodine. If you are travelling with small children, remember to check their heads, and particularly behind the ears, for ticks. Spreading redness around the bite and/or fever and/or aching joints after a tick bite imply that you have an infection that requires antibiotic treatment. In this case seek medical advice.

cheque you can cash locally; otherwise, the system operates by sending a cheque to your home address in around six weeks. Note that neither EHIC nor GHIC cards are an alternative to travel insurance, and do not cover such health-related costs as medical repatriation or any private treatment, so it is still important to take out comprehensive travel insurance.

A pharmacist (*pharmacien*) can be consulted about minor ailments and will often discuss them with doctor-like gravity, binding up sprained ankles and dishing out reasonably strong medicines without the need for getting into the intricacies of the French health system. You do not, however, get reimbursed for this treatment.

For a minor beach injury, seek out the lifeguard post, where personnel should be trained in first aid. For a serious accident or illness, call 15 from a fixed phone for the SAMU (ambulances with doctors) or 18 for the *pompiers* (fire brigade). The *pompiers* also have ambulances and are trained in basic emergency medical care; they are often likely to be quickest on the scene if you are a long way from a town. From a mobile phone, dial 112 to reach any of the emergency services, and the operator will be able to pinpoint your position. Main hospitals are signposted with a red cross logo, either as (in ascending order of importance): CH (*centre hospitalier*); CHD (*centre hospitalier départemental*); CHR (*centre hospitalier régional*); or CHU (*centre hospitalier universitaire*).

There are Accident & Emergency departments (*urgences*) at: **Challans** (CH, Boulevard de l'Est, on the northeast corner of the inner ring road); **Les Sables-d'Olonne** (CH, on the D160, 4km northeast of Les Sables); **Ile d'Yeu** (CH, 17, Impasse Louise Raymond near Port-Joinville); and **La Roche-sur-Yon** (CHD, on the Cholet road at Les Oudairies, on the northeast side of town), which has satellite establishments in **Luçon** and **Montaigu**. Outside the Vendée, you will find *urgences* at **Nantes** (CHU Hôtel-Dieu, Place Alexis-Ricordeau, in the city centre); **St-Nazaire** (CH, Boulevard Georges Charpak, west of the centre); **Cholet** (CH, Rue Marengo, southwest of town); **Niort** (CH, 40 Avenue de Gaulle, south of the city); and **La Rochelle** (CH, Boulevard Joffre, east of the centre).

SAFETY

In respect of activities, safety rules and regulations are not always as stringently adhered to as they are in the United Kingdom. You are usually routinely issued with lifejackets or hard hats before canoeing, horseriding or karting jaunts, and bike helmets must be worn by the under 12s. Where given the choice of wearing bike helmets or not, French adults seem to choose not to, but tougher laws may follow soon. Safety arrangements at zoos, wildlife parks, lofty viewpoints and some amusement parks can still occasionally seem a bit casual.

As regards personal safety, street-crime rates are mercifully low. Nevertheless, upgrade your vigilance in crowded markets and lock valuables in the boot of your car. Seaside towns have their share of unruly summer visitors, but if you avoid dodgy nightspots and dark back streets you should be unaffected by them. As in major cities anywhere, it pays to be streetwise about money or valuables when visiting larger places such as Nantes or St-Nazaire.

Most people will be aware of the terrorist attacks which have struck France in recent years. Although these initially targeted Paris, the awful Bastille Day strike on Nice in 2016 showed that other towns are not immune, and it is now common to see armed police at airports or patrolling the promenades of seaside resorts. Visitors can play their part by looking after their belongings and staying vigilant. For the latest advice, do check the Foreign, Commonwealth and Development

Office website, **w** gov.uk/government/organisations/foreign-commonwealth-development-office. If you have a mobile phone, you should automatically receive updates from FR-Alert, France's alert system, which gives alerts via SMS to any major incidents of a natural, terrorist or technological nature.

Road safety is an issue for everyone, residents and visitors alike, with road deaths nearly twice the level experienced in the UK. See *Getting Around*, page 29.

EMERGENCY AND OTHER USEFUL NUMBERS

☏112 EC-wide, multi-lingual number for **all** emergency services,advisable when calling from a mobile (114 for hearing assistance)

From a landline, the individual ones are:

☏18 Fire (*pompiers*), who can also deal with medical emergencies
☏17 Police, or gendarmerie in rural areas
☏15 Ambulance (SAMU, or paramedics); be prepared, on answer, to press 1 for '*urgences*' (emergency); 2 for '*médecin*'(GP)
☏01 44 51 31 00 British Embassy (in Paris)

WOMEN TRAVELLERS

There should be no particular concerns for women visitors travelling alone in France. Take the same precautions as you do at home.

TRAVELLING WITH A DISABILITY

Parking spaces for disabled-badge holders are provided at tourist attractions and supermarkets. A blue 'Tourisme et Handicap' logo indicates hotels, restaurants or attractions accessible to wheelchairs, or with arrangements in place to help those with other disabilities.

Most beaches now have ramps leading down to them, and sometimes mats continuing a little way onto the sand. During July and August, several seaside resorts provide at their lifeguard stations free loan of beach-buggy-style wheelchairs (called 'Tiralo' or 'Hippocampe') to those visitors with limited mobility (*à mobilité réduite*, or *handicapé*). These allow bathers to be assisted right into the water. At the time of writing, towns (beach names in brackets) with these facilities include Noirmoutier (Les Sableaux), Fromentine, Notre-Dame-de-Monts, St-Gilles-Croix-de-Vie (Grande Plage) and Longeville-sur-Mer (Le Rocher). Further north, in Loire-Atlantique, top beaches for accessible fun include Pornichet, St-Marc-sur-Mer and St-Nazaire (Villès-Martin).

SENIOR DISCOUNTS

Slightly disappointingly, comparatively few visitor attractions offer discounts to senior citizens, though it's always worth enquiring when buying a ticket. Local train services offer a *'découverte sénior'* rate for over 60s (just ask when booking), with a reduction of 25% on off-peak fares. If you are going to do a lot of rail travel, it could be worth investing in a Carte Avantage Senior (€49 for a year at the time of writing) to obtain even greater reductions over the entire national rail network.

Wheelchair-using fishing enthusiasts are well catered for: many riverbanks and lakesides have specially designed pontoons jutting out over the water.

The traditional single-storey construction of many Vendée buildings means that museums are often on ground level only. Newer establishments are, of course, designed with accessibility in mind, often furnished with lifts and featuring accessible toilets. Older hotels and museums can still have daunting flights of steps. If in doubt, contact the venue for up-to-date information. '*Est-ce que c'est accessible aux fauteuils roulants?*' or '*Y a-t-il des toilettes pour handicapés?*' are useful phrases if you need to check wheelchair access or the existence of toilets for the disabled, and '*Avez-vous des chambres au rez-de-chaussée?*' to ask about ground-floor bedrooms.

The UK's **gov.uk** website (**w** gov.uk/government/publications/disabled-travellers/disability-and-travel-abroad) has a downloadable guide giving general advice and practical information for travellers with a disability (and their companions) preparing for overseas travel. The Vendée Tourist Board produces a wealth of useful information on its website (**w** in-vendee.com/tourisme-handicap), listing suitably adapted holiday cottages, B&Bs, restaurants and activities. There are quite literally hundreds of activities in the region that have received the 'Tourisme et Handicap' label, meaning that they are fully adapted for those with mobility limitations and other disabilities. Some of the major ones are:

- Cinéscénie du Puy du Fou (Les Épesses)
- Le Grand Parc du Puy du Fou (Les Épesses)
- Vendée Miniature (Brétignolles-sur-Mer)
- Zoo des Sables (Les Sables-d'Olonne)
- La Maison des Libellules (Chaillé-sous-les-Ormeaux)
- La Conserverie La Perle des Dieux (St-Gilles-Croix-de-Vie)
- L'Île aux Papillons (Noirmoutier)
- Le Château de St-Mesmin
- Biotopia (Notre-Dame-de-Monts)
- La Réserve Naturelle Michel Brosselin (St-Denis-du-Payré)

LGBTQIA+ TRAVELLERS

Same-sex marriage is legal in France. While there is no reason why LGBTQIA+ travellers should have concerns visiting this region, the Vendée is a fairly conservative place, particularly away from the coastal resorts. Discretion is always advisable in displaying public affection, whatever your sexuality. Although the actual content is fairly limited, the website **w** adheos.org purports to list LGBTQIA+ friendly establishments in the Vendée and Charente-Maritime, while **w** gayviking.com gives details of the same for Nantes.

TRAVELLING WITH KIDS

If ever a destination was set up beautifully for children, then surely it is the Vendée and its surroundings. This is particularly so on the coast, with dozens of child-orientated campsites and miles of gorgeous sandy beaches, many of them Blue Flag and many of which are supervised in July and August. But it's not all about building sandcastles: families can take advantage of waterparks, theme parks and endless kid-focused distractions by the sea. Inland, a pronounced feature of many historic sites is the effort that has been put in to make them user-friendly for younger visitors. Hence, as well as the stunning spectacles of Le Puy du Fou (page 182),

2

you will find castles with costumed actors, treasure hunts and medieval games for the little ones while parents soak up the history of the surroundings. The ages at which discounts for youngsters apply vary from site to site and family tickets are often available. When it comes to food (page 34), many restaurants offer children's menus, and there is usually a child-friendly pizzeria or crêperie in most towns.

WHAT TO TAKE

Apart from the necessary two-pin adaptor – which is hard to source once you're already in France – there is not much that the visitor needs to bring which cannot be easily bought in France. Campers and self-caterers who are also tea fanatics may wish to bring their own teabags, as the standard-issue French equivalent can be somewhat weak!

MONEY AND BUDGETING

The currency in France is the euro, made up of 100 centimes (or *centièmes d'euro*). Exchange rates for sterling and US dollars at the date of publication are given on page 2.

French banks usually open from Monday to Friday, between 09.00 and 16.00 in major towns. Some may close for lunch and some may open or close a bit later. They close for public holidays (page 40), sometimes from lunchtime the previous day. If a holiday falls on a Tuesday or a Thursday there is a tendency to join the day up to the nearest weekend by declaring the Monday or Friday as a holiday too (*faire le pont*) and thus they close for several days. However, as nearly every French bank has an ATM accessible 24/7, there is rarely a need nowadays for visitors to actually go to the counter. Most of these cashpoints have English-language options, too.

Using a PIN-protected, pre-loaded euro cash card, bought in the UK, enables you either to make a payment to a shop or restaurant while abroad, or to withdraw euros from a cashpoint, up to a daily limit or the amount you have put on it before leaving home. (You can also top these up online, during your stay.) Cash withdrawals with this type of card usually attract no transaction charges.

Credit cards such as Mastercard, Visa, American Express and Diners Club are widely accepted (particularly the first two, which are known as *cartes bancaires*) at petrol stations, motorway toll machines, supermarkets, hotels, mid- to upmarket restaurants and stores (though less so at small village shops, restaurants and cafés). Modern British cards with microchips now also work at France's automatic petrol pumps marked '24/24', and many of these have English-language instructions.

TIPPING Service is included in the bill for bars, hotels and restaurants, and indicated on the bill or menu by the words *prix nets*. However, people often leave something extra – even if it is just the small bits of loose change on the plate – if service was particularly good or if they are likely to return. Rounding up a restaurant bill by a few euros is fine, but there is certainly no expectation of a 10% gratuity. It is still customary to tip hairdressers and taxi drivers about 10% of the bill, and to press a coin or two into the hand of a guide after a particularly interesting tour.

COSTS AND BUDGETING For many visitors from the UK, prices in France will be similar to those at home. There are of course some specific differences, with wine and diesel fuel being cheaper than in the UK, while unleaded petrol and draught beer are more expensive.

Budgeting will depend largely on your accommodation choices. If you are camping, or booking hotels online, the chances are that you will be paying for this in advance. Campers and other self-caterers can expect to pay around the same for their supermarket shopping as they would at home; markets are vibrant places to buy fruit, vegetables, meat, cheese and fish, but in truth their prices are the same or even more expensive when compared with the large supermarkets.

Guide prices in euros are given below for a few items commonly purchased while on holiday. These relate to items bought in stores in an average-sized town, but you could certainly pay less if visiting a large supermarket, or easily pay double at a seafront grocer's in a resort town.

Bottle of water (1.5 litre)	€0.70
Bottle of beer (330ml)	€2.70
Loaf of bread	€1.50
Postcard	€1.50
Litre of petrol/diesel	€1.85/1.80

Based on two people sharing accommodation and other costs, and excluding any car hire, below is a rough guide *per person* to daily budgeting for accommodation, transport, food and entertainment, in high season.

Basic For those on a budget, you should be able to get by on around €80 per person, per day. This assumes using campsites or very basic hotels/B&Bs, breakfasting in a bar (café and croissant), taking advantage of a budget three-course lunchtime menu, filling your days with walking, sunbathing or other free activities and taking only a modest meal, or self-catering, in the evening. Out of high season, lower accommodation costs could reduce the daily spend per person to €55.

Comfortable Choosing between hotels of two or three stars, taking breakfast in the hotel, visiting a few museums or other attractions, enjoying a lunchtime *menu du jour* and an evening restaurant meal plus a bottle of wine means your daily spend should come to around €130 per person.

Luxury Staying in three-star-plus establishments with breakfast, with two good meals with wine per day at high-quality restaurants, and enjoying museums/attractions/trips, will put your spend at about €240 per person per day.

GETTING AROUND

BY BIKE For many visitors, cycling around the Vendée is a real treasure, with its flat landscape and hundreds of kilometres of cycle paths. The region is not well suited to those who are adrenalin junkies, but is certainly ideal for families, novices and those who perhaps haven't put foot to pedal for some time. You can bring your own bike strapped on to your car, or cycle it on to the ferry and pedal all the way down to the Vendée, or put your two-wheeler either on a plane or a train. For airlines' policies on accepting bicycles, contact the relevant carrier. Bikes can be carried on both Eurostar and SNCF trains, though conditions and charges apply: some trains allow free carriage, while others do not allow fully assembled bikes at all. A degree of pre-planning is needed therefore, but the relevant websites (page 23) give all the necessary information. The alternative is to simply arrive and hire a bike, which costs around €15 per day, with discounts for a week's or longer hire.

Whichever you choose, try to get hold of the 100-page booklet *Vendée Vélo*, produced by the Tourist Board. Updated annually, it contains dozens of itineraries between 4km and 76km in length, with grades of difficulty, maps, location of cycle hire and repair outlets and points of interest along the way. It is in French only, but still useful for non-French-speakers. Together with lots of other bike-friendly information it is also available on the Tourist Board website (page 21). Long-distance cyclists might fancy doing the Vélodyssée route, which runs for 1,250km from the ferry-port of Roscoff in Brittany to the Spanish border at Hendaye, in the Basque Country. The best bit is that 70% of it is undertaken on routes reserved for cycles, on cycle tracks or green ways (*voies vertes*). The section in the Vendée runs along the coast from Bouin in the north to L'Aiguillon-sur-Mer in the south.

BY CAR   If you plan to see much of this area in a condensed period of time, then taking your own vehicle or hiring one is the only practicable option. On the other hand, if you are intending to stay in one location for a beach holiday, and don't mind a bit of travel logistics to get there in the first place, a car may be unnecessary. Taking your own car to France requires awareness of some specific legal requirements.

What to take   You need to have the originals of the car's documents – registration document (plus a letter of authorisation from the owner if the vehicle is not registered in your name) and insurance certificate (or green card, if your insurer still provides one) – as well as your driving licence and passport in the vehicle whenever you are on the road. You can be stopped at any time for a random check, and it is an offence to be without these papers. (Major roads are particularly heavily policed around 17.00 each day and on Sunday afternoons.)

Your car must have a national identifier – ie: if it is registered in the UK it must carry a UK sticker rather than a GB one – and you must carry a warning triangle for use in case your car breaks down, plus a spare set of bulbs for your lights, as it is an offence to drive with any light out of order. Headlight beam converters or fitted headlight beam adjusters need to be in use to avoid blinding oncoming traffic. Headphones and headsets are not allowed to be worn by drivers or riders (this does not apply to integrated systems in motorcycle helmets). It is also compulsory for there to be at least one high-visibility vest *inside* the car (not in the boot) and to use it if you break down. Seat belts must be worn by all front- and rear-seat passengers. No child under ten may travel in the front seat (unless there is no rear seat in the vehicle, there are no seat belts or if the rear seats are already occupied by children under 10). Up until 2020, it was a legal requirement for drivers to carry a breathalyser in their car; this is no longer the case, but the alcohol limit is lower than it is in other parts of the world so it might not be a bad thing to invest in one. Finally, radar detectors kits for identifying mobile speed guns are not allowed and if you are found with one you'll likely open yourself up to a minimum €1,500 fine.

If you intend to drive through any large French towns or cities on your way to or from the Vendée, you may also need a Crit'Air sticker. These were introduced by the French government as a way of restricting traffic and reducing vehicle CO_2 emissions in large urban areas where air quality is poor. At the time of writing there were 11 Low Emission Zones (ZFE-m), which are listed on the Explore France website   (**w**   france.fr/en/holiday-prep/crit-air-anti-pollution-vehicle-sticker). You will need to display a Crit'Air sticker on your windscreen if you are driving in any of these places, and your vehicle may be refused entry to certain areas, or during specific times, depending on your vehicle's Crit'Air classification. This can be further complicated by ZPA (Zones de Protection de l'Air) restrictions, which are temporary measures activated if there is a peak in air pollution (for instance during a heatwave). You can apply for a sticker and find further details on the official Crit'Air website (w certificat-air.gouv.fr). The sticker costs between €3 and €6 depending on the classification of vehicle, and it's best to apply several weeks in advance. Drivers of vehicles caught without a sticker in a ZPA or ZFE-m will be fined up to €135.

Fines On-the-spot fines are common and a 'menu' of penalties can be found at w french-property.com/guides/france/driving-in-france/driving-offences. These range from a €17 parking fine through to minor speeding fines at €68, to immediate confiscation of your licence in more serious cases. Drink/drive limits, at 50mg per 100ml of blood alcohol are actually lower than those operating in England and Wales and random breath tests are carried out; you can have your licence withdrawn on the spot if tested positive. It is strictly forbidden to have any device that is capable of detecting speed cameras, even if it is switched off. Use of a mobile phone at the wheel, even hands-free, is also prohibited (though you will see plenty of drivers ignoring this law).

Road rules Although the old *priorité à droite* rule (by which any vehicle arriving from your right-hand side has the right of way) has been largely eliminated on major roads through the increased use of halt signs, there can still be instances when it applies. Always be on your guard in towns, glancing quickly at any road on your right to make sure there is a solid or a dotted line painted on it to halt emerging traffic. If not, you must cede priority! In villages, too, it can apply; look out for the X-shaped road sign on entering the village, which often means that the priority to the right rule applies throughout the village.

Another important thing to note is that if a French driver flashes their headlights at you they are not giving you the right of way – they are announcing that they are taking it for themselves.

Speed limits in France are 130km/h (81mph) on most motorways, reducing to 110km/h (68mph) in wet-weather conditions; 110km/h on dual carriageways, 100km/h (62mph) in wet weather; 80km/h (50mph) or often 70km/h (43mph) on other roads, 80km/h (50mph) and 60km/h (37mph) in wet weather. Where visibility is reduced to 50m, limits on all open roads reduce to 50km/h (31mph).

In towns and villages, the limit is 50km/h unless marked otherwise, from the moment you have passed the village's name-board, until you pass the crossed-out name on the way out – even if no speed limit is marked. In some town centres, the limit is marked down to 30km/h (19mph).

Motorway tolls Within the Vendée itself, tolls are levied on the A83 and A87 *autoroutes*, and you may also encounter toll roads in adjacent départements en route. UK credit cards with microchips can usually be used at manned and automatic motorway toll booths (without even having to type in your PIN), though bear in mind that you will pay a small transaction charge to your home bank for each use. Use cash if possible.

Fuel French petrol pumps offer two types of unleaded petrol and if you have an old car (roughly pre-2000) then you need to avoid at all costs the '95-E10' fuel, which is very common but which can damage engines and cause breakdowns. If in doubt, use the pumps simply marked '95' or '98', and avoid those marked 'E10'. Those needing diesel should use the pump marked '*gazole*'.

Parking In villages and small towns, as well as at non-resort beaches and for major events, parking is often ample and free. In the coastal resorts, it can be difficult to find a space in high season. You are not allowed to stop on the open road without pulling right off it onto a verge or pavement or into a layby. Where parking meters are installed, there is not much need for explanation – except to say, look closely at the times and days. A free period often covers protracted French lunchtimes in inland towns, while at seaside resorts, even Sundays and public holidays still require payment. If you're visiting out of season, read the instructions carefully as there may be no charge at all. In streets and car parks the system is often one of pay-and-display (*horodateur* or *distribueur*) – again, look at just what hours and days require payment. The third, and oldest-established, method of parking regulation is by cardboard parking disc in areas designated as *zones bleues*, indicated by street signs or by painted blue marks on the road. If you do not already own a parking disc (*disque de contrôle de stationnement*), you can usually pick one up at the nearest tourist office, supermarket, *mairie* or *tabac* (tobacconists) for a few euros. After dark, you should only park your vehicle facing the same direction as the flow of traffic in the lane nearest to you.

PUBLIC TRANSPORT If you are a fanatic of public transport and love logistics, you could get around the main towns in the Vendée using buses. The train can also be useful if you want to visit cities/towns like Nantes, La Rochelle, St-Gilles-Croix-de-Vie, St-Hilaire-de-Riez, La Baule and St-Nazaire. The rail network also reaches Les Sables-d'Olonne, La Roche-sur-Yon, Chantonnay, Pouzauges and Luçon, among others. To see the full network showing all stations served, or to see routes covered both by train and bus, take a look at the map (*carte de réseau*) at w ter.sncf.com/pays-de-la-loire.

Before you board any train, it is essential to validate your rail ticket by sticking one end of it in the yellow machine near the entrance to the platform – a process with the unlikely name of *compostage*. You must also do this when boarding a tram in Nantes (machines are inside each carriage).

Bus services are available between major towns and can be useful if you are staying mainly in one location but wish to make day trips to a few others. Visiting the Île de Ré from La Rochelle (page 206) is a good example; going to Noirmoutier from Nantes (page 59) would be another. Within major towns, such as Nantes or La Rochelle, the public transport system is generally very good.

MAPS Suitable for most visitors to France, the yellow-covered Michelin maps are excellent, and good value. To accompany this guidebook, the most useful of these will be No 316 (Loire-Atlantique/Vendée), which covers everything mentioned in these pages, including many of the major visitor attractions, from La Baule and Nantes in the north to La Rochelle in the south at 1:150,000 (1cm = 1.5km).

Slightly more detailed are the IGN (Institut Géographique National) 'Top 100' green series on the scale of 1:100,000 (1cm = 1km); No 131 (Nantes/La Roche-sur-Yon), No 132 (Cholet/Niort), and No 138 (La Rochelle/Saintes, and covering the Île de Ré) and will be most useful, depending on where you are based. For even more detail on an area you want to walk or to explore in depth, nothing beats the 1:25,000 (4cm = 1km) IGN 'Top 25' blue '*carte de randonnée*' series. IGN also produces a smaller-scale series at 1:250,000 (1cm = 2.5km), of which R11 covers Poitou-Charentes from Nantes to Poitiers and Limoges, its scope making it handy if you are touring by car over a wide area.

All are widely available in bookshops, Maisons de la Presse and large supermarkets in the Vendée area. The Michelin and IGN green series can also be found in good UK bookshops, while maps in the blue IGN series may be purchased from specialist travel bookshop Stanfords (7 Mercer Walk, Covent Garden, London WC2H 9FA; ✆ 020 7836 1321; w stanfords.co.uk) or direct from IGN at w ign.fr.

ACCOMMODATION

For peak times in July and August, booking well in advance is advisable and, indeed, often essential. A huge proportion of visitors to the Vendée choose to stay in campsites, which nowadays often entails renting a mobile home on a campsite rather than actually sleeping under canvas. Particularly out of season, this can be a very economical option. There are around 400 campsites in the area, and details of relevant websites can be found below. Despite its popularity, the region has none of the large, resort-style hotels that are found on the Mediterranean coast of Spain or Turkey, for example. Hotels are generally of the small, owner-managed type, some to a very high standard and with plenty of character, though you will find a few grander establishments just outside the Vendée in La Rochelle and Nantes. For would-be self-caterers who want something less communal than a campsite, there are plenty of holiday rentals available. Again, websites are detailed below.

CAMPING As well as the hundreds of classified campsites along the coast, the Vendée's interior is also well furnished with opportunities for camping. These can be anything from one- to five-star sites, but there are also more informal *campings à la ferme* (small sites on working farms). Many sites have swimming pools, plenty of activities for youngsters, on-site restaurants and shops; an increasing number of mobile homes have TV and Wi-Fi, which is sometimes at an extra cost. The extensive forests that sit just back from the beaches on many coastal sections provide the shade necessary to protect from the heat. Some specialised British tour operators offer luxury camping holidays in tents or mobile homes, while for independent campers the Tourist Board website (w in-vendee.com) details more than 370 sites. The **Caravan Club** (w caravanclub.co.uk) and the **Camping and Caravanning Club** (w campingandcaravanningclub.co.uk) also have useful information for campers and descriptions of some sites in the Vendée. If you want someone to do most of the organising for you, **Eurocamp** (✆ 01606 787125; w eurocamp.co.uk) is just one of the companies offering camping holidays in the region.

HOTELS, BED AND BREAKFASTS AND SELF-CATERING A number of hotels and B&Bs (*chambres d'hôte*) have been visited in the course of writing this guide and the best ones found are included with key facts and comments. There are, of course, many, many more. A list of Vendée hotels can be found on the Tourist Board website (page 21), while those under the **Logis de France** banner are viewable at w logishotels.com.

ACCOMMODATION PRICE CODES	
Prices based on a double room per night	
€€€€€	€150+
€€€€	€120–150
€€€	€100–120
€€	€80–100
€	below €80

Gîtes de France (w gites-de-france.com) has more than 400 self-catering rental properties on its site and **Clévacances** (w clevacances.com/en/) lists both hundreds of B&Bs and a bigger selection of rental properties. **Bienvenue au Château** (w bienvenueauchateau.com) features a few stylish B&B options housed in impressive country houses in the region covered by this guide. A quick mention also for **Alastair Sawday**'s excellent site (w sawdays.co.uk), which features a dozen or so carefully selected B&Bs and self-catering establishments in the Vendée region. Houses can also be rented through **Brittany Ferries** (page 21) and **Chez Nous** (w cheznous.com). **Interhome** (w interhome.co.uk) has more than 80 properties for rent in the Vendée, while **Cottages.com** (w cottages.com) also offers several self-catering units.

EATING AND DRINKING

You can eat very well in the Vendée, there's little doubt about that. Traditional local specialities are hearty peasant foods like cabbage, and the white haricot beans known as *mogettes* – that would be set to simmer slowly in the embers of the kitchen fire while a family toiled in the fields. With such a long coastline and active fishing industry, fish and shellfish are also an important part of the culinary repertoire. It's true that this is not the French département with the most refined, sophisticated food (although there are more than seven Michelin-starred establishments in the area and that number is growing), but the excellence of what you will find here relies on a number of high-quality raw ingredients and products that make the short journey from sea or land to the plate with not too much human interference. As you might expect, La Rochelle and Nantes offer a greater range of ethnic cuisine than you will find in the Vendée itself.

SHELLFISH When you buy fish and shellfish in a shop, don't hesitate to ask for advice on cooking. In particular, note that shrimps and prawns are usually sold ready-cooked (the little brown shrimps known as *crevettes grises* have much more flavour than their pretty pink cousins). Be careful when buying *langoustines* (salt-water crayfish) to check whether they are being sold ready-cooked (*cuites*) or raw (*crues*), as it's difficult to tell at a glance. If uncooked, they should be plunged into a large saucepan of well-salted boiling water flavoured with pepper and a little vinegar, brought back to the boil and then cooked briskly for just 3 minutes, before being cooled rapidly under cold water.

Crabs can be bought cooked, but most often are still clambering over one another, blowing bubbles, in the fishmonger's tray. The non-squeamish can steel themselves to place the creature in a large saucepan of cold water, heavily salted and flavoured with pepper and a bouquet garni of available herbs, then bring it to the boil and cook for 12 minutes per kilo (about 6 minutes per pound), before plunging

RESTAURANT PRICE CODES

Prices are based on the cost of a main course, per person

€€€€€	€25+
€€€€	€20–25
€€€	€15–20
€€	€10–15
€	below €10

the crab into cold water immediately when it is cooked. The only parts you should not eat are the fleshy, grey, finger-shaped gills and the stringy intestine. A pair of nutcrackers (or pliers, a hammer, or even – at a pinch – a couple of good, flat stones) is invaluable for cracking your way into the better-protected parts – try to buy some pointed metal shellfish-picks in a supermarket to dig out the best bits. Spider crabs (*araignées*) should be put into boiling water flavoured with a little cayenne pepper and cooked for 20 minutes per kilo (about 10 minutes per pound), then allowed to cool in the cooking water. If you can't face this, you can order cooked crabs or lobsters from a fishmonger at a day's notice.

FISH You can buy wonderful fish soup in large glass jars, to eat with a little spicy *rouille* sauce stirred in, and then sprinkled with *croûtons* and grated gruyère cheese. It's almost a meal in itself. Tuna (*thon*) is another regional speciality, especially on the Île d'Yeu, usually cooked lightly to leave it pink in the middle, unless you specify otherwise. In the Marais Poitevin, keep an eye open for eels (*anguilles*) on the menu, either to enjoy or avoid, depending on your taste. Sole is a local favourite in Les Sables-d'Olonne.

VEGETABLES Apart from the *mogette* and the Noirmoutier potato (page 36), other vegetables include a large variety of mushrooms which you can gather in forests and hedgerows. Chemists will identify them for you and advise on whether they can be eaten. On the whole it is probably safer to stick with those you can buy in the markets around October: chanterelles, ceps and horns of plenty (*trompettes de la mort*) look quite adventurous enough for most people.

CHEESE, BUTTER AND MILK Many artisanal cheeses can be found in the market halls of Vendean towns and villages. Even if you don't usually like goat's cheese it's worth trying one of the very fresh white ones, whose characteristic flavour is less pronounced. Among local cow's-milk cheeses is the region's oldest, Halbran, fairly hard and tasty. Look out for dairy stalls selling butter cut from towering yellow slabs – you buy it by the pound (*une livre* is the equivalent of 500g) or by the kilogram, and can choose from unsalted (*doux*), slightly salted (*demi-sel*) or salty (*salé*). Fresh milk is strangely hard to find, as the French are fond of the UHT or sterilised variety. You may find fresh milk hiding in the chiller cabinets, usually near creams and yoghurts. Red top is whole milk, blue top semi-skimmed, yellow top is unpasteurised farm milk, and green top a slightly fermented Breton favourite, *lait ribot*, rather similar to drinking-yoghurt. Cream is almost always the slightly sharp *crème fraîche*; if you want pouring cream, there are small cartons of *crème fleurette entière* that will whip fairly satisfactorily when chilled. There is no equivalent of British double cream.

DESSERTS Apart from brioche (page 37), other sweet treats include *flan maraîchin* (a pastry case holding an egg custard), *tourteau au fromage* (a zingy, black-domed cheesecake made from goat's cheese, nestling in a shallow pastry case, and tasting rather better than it looks), *fouace* or *fouasse* (a cross between cake and bread, firmer than brioche), and '*r'tournez'y*' – a delicious vanilla, hazelnut and wild strawberry ice-cream confection bearing the Vendée's hearts-and-crown logo, and sold in the best patisseries.

WINES You may not find many wines from the Vendée outside the area itself, but it is worth considering the steep slope that the département has ascended in a few

Here are ten Vendée specialities to look out for and suggestions of where to find them at their best.

OYSTERS (*HUÎTRES*) Oysters are available all along the Atlantic coast, but those from the Bay of Bourgneuf enjoy a particularly strong reputation. Noirmoutier island is another 'hotspot' and it was there that saw the appearance of the first oyster parks in the early 19th century. Usually of the long, knobbly *portugaise* variety, the shellfish are in season all year and are, to British minds, incredibly inexpensive. To open, attack the hinged end of the creature using one of the cheap, stubby blades with a special shield around the handle (available in supermarkets), avoiding getting flakes of shell mingled with the delicate flesh. Wrap your other hand in a tea-towel for protection!

THE NOIRMOUTIER POTATO (*LA BONNOTTE*) The island of Noirmoutier enjoys a microclimate that enables it to produce the first French new potatoes of the year – rather like Jersey Royals for the British market – as early as February. The sweet, fresh taste in early spring compensates for the slightly sorry sight of the island's fields shrouded in plastic wraps through the winter. Their arrival on the restaurants' menus is much anticipated.

BEANS (*MOGETTES*) The humble haricot bean finds an ideal environment for its cultivation in the Vendée. Introduced to the area by monks in the 16th century and in times gone by a staple of the local diet, it is still revered as an accompaniment to lamb – and even more so to *jambon Vendéen* (see below). To enjoy them at their best, they need to be soaked overnight, then simmered for an hour or two in water with no salt, just bouquet garni. Salt them only *after* they are cooked. You can stir in some crème fraîche after draining them. If this sounds too much trouble, there are some excellent, home-cooked versions bottled in glass jars, either plain or '*à l'ancienne*' (with tasty bits of bacon and carrot included), available in supermarkets. In late summer you sometimes see the new season's beans, called *demi-secs*, on sale still in their withered pods; these need no pre-soaking, and are supposed to be more digestible.

HAM (*JAMBON VENDÉEN*) After a long struggle, the ham of the region finally gained its spurs in 2014, being awarded the right to carry the IGP (Indication Géographique Protégée) label, the equivalent in some senses to the AOC awarded to fine wines. The region's sea salt (see opposite) and various spices are involved in the manufacturing process, which demands around three months of ageing before the ham can be eaten. Classically, it is served with another speciality, *mogettes* (see above).

MUSSELS You will not have to look hard to find mussels on the menus of the Vendée's coastal restaurants, usually served with a variety of delicious sauces. No surprise, as more than 5,000 tonnes are produced here each year, in an industry which has been going strong since a shipwrecked Irishman pioneered their cultivation on ropes, way back in the 13th century. L'Aiguillon-sur-Mer in particular is a renowned centre for these molluscs. If you are self-catering, note that they are always sold alive, and need to be well scrubbed and scraped, using a sharp knife to remove barnacles and any whiskery bits of 'beard'. Discard any that are not tightly closed. You can sometimes buy ready-scraped mussels (*moules grattées*), but you should still look them over carefully. To cook a kilo of mussels, heat 125ml of dry white wine with a chopped onion, a chopped clove of garlic, two teaspoons of chopped parsley, and some seasoning. When it is boiling, add the mussels, cover, and steam for 5 to 10 minutes until they open (throw out any that remain closed). Remove the mussels, and stir a little butter or cream into the juice before pouring it over them.

BRIOCHE Most people will be familiar with the soft, chewy, sweetish bread that appears on many a breakfast table across France and beyond. But it is the Vendée that is best known for these impossibly light and fluffy loaves. Though traditionally an Easter speciality, brioche is always served with coffee at midnight at local weddings. Every baker has their own version, though its origin is said to be in Vendrennes, near Les Herbiers. A variant is *la gâche*, which is denser but less sweet.

GARLIC BREAD (*PRÉFOU*) The Vendée's own garlic bread, or *préfou*, was originally used by the region's bakers to test the temperature of their ovens before baking the daily loaves. You can find it in *boulangeries* and supermarkets around the area, but Fontenay-le-Comte is the focal point for this simple delicacy which is often served hot *before* the main meal.

SALT (*SEL*) Many visitors dazzled by the saltpans along the coast, or on Noirmoutier island, will happily take home a souvenir bag of the 'white gold'. Sea salt – grey and chunky, known as *sel de mer* or *gros-sel*, and the finer, white *fleur de sel* that forms the first sparkling crystals on the surface of the saltpans – made the fortunes of the monasteries in the Middle Ages. At the time of Richard III, the Bay of Bourgneuf supplied 80% of the salt used in London. Today it is harvested, albeit on a smaller scale, with the same techniques in the salt marshes of Guérande, Bouin, Noirmoutier, St-Hilaire-de-Riez, Olonne and Talmont. Also grown in the same marshes – though looked on by the salt-makers as a weed – is the red, fleshy-leaved samphire (*salicorne*) that turns green when cooked and is sold, pickled, as a condiment, or fresh for brief cooking and use as a vegetable or in a salad.

SARDINES Fresh sardines are a real, yet inexpensive, treat. Sardine fishing may have declined on the Atlantic coast, but the industry based out of St-Gilles-Croix-de-Vie is still important to that town – look out for tins of premium 'vintage' sardines called *millésimées*. For the preparation of the fresh fish, gut and wash them well. If barbecuing, it is easiest to cook them in the bespoke metal contraption resembling a double tennis racquet, if you can lay your hands on one. Sprinkle them with olive oil and some coarse Noirmoutier sea-salt and grill for about 3 minutes each side (depending on thickness), then eat with something plain, like boiled potatoes or crusty bread, and butter.

CHALLANS CHICKENS (*VOLAILLES DE CHALLANS*) Once Challans was famous for its ducks, but now it's the chicken which is the town's culinary emblem. The region's farmers rear all manner of poultry, but it is the *poulet noir*, or black chicken, which is the standout bird nowadays. Take a trip to town on market day (page 66) and try some.

years to reach its much-coveted AOC (Appellation d'Origine Contrôlée) status. Despite Muscadet wine enjoying commercial acclaim and export success for many years across the 'border' in Loire-Atlantique, as recently as the 1970s the wines of the Vendée had to make do with lowly *vin de table* status. A decade later, and they had earned the right to label themselves VDQS (Vin Délimité de Qualité Supérieure), a step up the ladder, before eventually being accorded the AOC in 2011. Vendée wines are produced mainly around Mareuil (page 133), but also near the coast at Brem, as well as Vix, Pissotte and Chantonnay. Oenophiles can delight in touring these areas, indulging in wines that they cannot easily find elsewhere. A particular curiosity will be those created from the *négrette* grape, grown here and in only one other place in France. Reds, whites and rosés are all available. If truth be told, the finest of the wines produced in the area covered by this book are probably still from outside the Vendée itself, being the Muscadet de Sèvre-et-Maine (produced to the southeast of Nantes), particularly that which is bottled *sur lie* – left in the barrel on the lees, or sediment, to acquire a near-sparkling quality.

Among stronger local products are Pineau des Charentes, a fortified wine made from grape juice blended with cognac and drunk, chilled, as an aperitif; Troussepinette, a red aperitif flavoured with hedgerow fruits; and Kamok, a coffee-based liqueur distilled in Luçon.

On the Île de Ré, as well as local wines, you can enjoy the island's own cognac (page 206).

BEER Long live the revolution! No longer must French beer-drinkers and visitors confine themselves to drinking the mega-keg offerings of Stella Artois and Kronenbourg, while wistfully wishing for something more interesting. Craft beers have begun to make an impact in the region, as elsewhere in France – though it is mainly the bottled product which can be found at present. Micro-breweries are appearing in all sorts of places, the dreams of entrepreneurs or farmers looking to supplement their income. A pioneer in the region was Brasserie Mélusine, based in Chambretaud, which now brews 14 beers including an organic range, a beer aged in oak barrels and a white beer made with rose petals. If you're in the southern part of the Vendée, look out for the beers of Cibulle. The brewery's American Amber beer came first at the Bier Fest in Nantes. The island of Noirmoutier has its own craft beers, called 'La N'O' and available in six different varieties, while outside the département, the Île de Ré also has a range marketed under the label 'Ré'.

There are, of course, many more. When browsing the supermarket shelves or visiting bars or specialist stores, look for the words '*bière artisanale*' and you too can join this new French Revolution.

RESTAURANTS Lunch is hugely important in France, served between noon and around 13.30 or 14.00. Don't expect it to be served outside these times, however. Dinner rarely starts before 19.00 and service often finishes around 21.00. From Monday to Friday, most restaurants provide good-value, fixed-price menus at lunchtimes (and very occasionally on weekday evenings). These usually give the option of two or three courses, sometimes with wine and coffee included. Even top restaurants offer these daily menus, providing a good opportunity to sample gastronomic output at more affordable rates. If that's simply too much, most places offer a main-course-only option, a *plat du jour*. You can often eat well and more cheaply at small, family-run establishments – look around a market square, for example, for somewhere that looks popular, or ask the locals for advice. Many

Voted Gault & Millau's 'Best Chef of 2017', **Alexandre Couillon** is the boss of the now three-Michelin-star La Marine (page 60) on Noirmoutier island, which has joined an exclusive club as one of France's 29 best restaurants. He has a reputation for innovation and, happily for those with a lower budget, he also now has a less expensive bistro – La Table d'Élise (page 60) – next door to the main restaurant.

Based on the seafront in Brétignolles-sur-Mer, master chef **Jean-Marc Pérochon** uses local produce such as the famous chickens from Challans and fish plucked from the ocean (just a stone's throw away) in crafting his masterpieces at Les Brisants restaurant (page 103). You'll also find the humble white bean – the *mogette* – on his Michelin-starred menus.

In 2020, **Boris Harispe** at L'Abissiou in Les Sables-d'Olonne (page 108) joined the Michelin ranks; the restaurant that he runs with his partner, Mélanie Roussy, maintains a relaxed and friendly feel while delivering exceptional service on par with the outstanding dishes. Harispe is a close follower of the seasons with menus changing to reflect this. Of particular note is the attention to '*grande classiques*' such as *lièvre à la royale*, a combination that includes hare, foie gras and truffle and takes three weeks to prepare.

hypermarkets located on the edge of towns have reasonably priced self-service restaurants – though quality can be variable and ambience lacking.

While eating out at lunchtime is part of the fabric of everyday French life, dining out in the evening is more of an occasion, and prices are higher. Most restaurants will offer a variety of menus, from basic to gastronomic, as well as letting you choose à la carte.

For families, look out for the *menu enfant* (children's menu), and if all else fails, or if you are on a tight budget, you'll find a pizzeria or crêperie in most towns. The latter is a welcome import from Brittany, with crêpes (sweet) and *galettes* (savoury) served with a variety of delicious fillings.

For true local flavour, it's worth trying a *ferme-auberge*. These are real restaurants, rather than farmhouse kitchens, where at least half the food served has to be home-produced – so you're guaranteed fresh duck, lamb, foie gras, vegetables, or whatever is the farm's speciality. The owners always prefer you to book in advance, so that they have an idea of numbers.

VEGETARIAN AND VEGAN EATING n spite of those fantastic displays of vegetables in French greengrocers' shops and markets, vegetarians used to be poorly catered for in rural France. Restaurants could be a little stunned to be asked about vegetarian dishes and all too often would fob off anyone who did with the offer of an omelette. Today, however, many of the better restaurants might feature a vegetarian dish as a regular menu item, and of course those who don't mind eating fish will be spoilt for choice in this seafood-rich area. Otherwise you are probably looking at one of those ubiquitous pizzerias or crêperies. Vegans are still likely to find eating out more difficult, however. If you want to make sure a dish is suitable, you can use the sentence: '*Je suis vegan(e). Ce plat contient-il de la viande, du poisson, des crustaces, de la volaille, des oeufs, du miel, du lait ou des produits laitiers?*' ('I am vegan. Does this food contain meat, fish, shellfish, poultry, eggs, honey, milk or dairy products?') which should help narrow a menu down to what you're happy with.

The idea of buying organic foods has now taken a firm hold in the region, more so perhaps than in the UK. Look for the words *'bio'* or *'agriculture biologique'*, often showing a special, distinctive green-and-white 'AB' logo, indicating foodstuffs that conform to similar 'organic' regulations to those in the UK. Indeed, there are whole shops now dedicated to organic produce, with wines also to the fore of this growing movement and 'bio' beers similarly on the up. It's also worth knowing that there's a 'Label Rouge' (Red Label) designation indicating produce – from meat to melons – that has been farmed subject to stringent rules governing natural conditions and feeding. The phrase *'sans OGM'* on an item means the product contains no genetically modified organisms.

ALLERGIES For people with allergies, the French are beginning to mark products that might contain peanuts (*arachides*), though you have to read the small print carefully. *'Traces éventuelles d'arachide et autres noix'* means 'May contain traces of peanuts and other nuts'. Biscuits and other items containing *huile végétale* or *matière grasse végétale* may also contain peanut oil. However, some manufacturers now specify whether the oil used is the more universally friendly *tournesol* (sunflower seed), *palme* (palm), *colza* (oilseed rape) or *olive* (olive). If you have allergies then you can discuss these with your waiter, starting with the phrase *'Je suis allergique...'* Even better, print the relevant phrase on a card before you leave so they can read it clearly themselves and there won't be any mistakes.

PUBLIC HOLIDAYS

As well as the national holidays (*jours fériés*) listed below, each town and village celebrates its own localised festivals and events. Some of these are noted in the area chapters that follow.

Date	English name	French name
1st January	New Year's Day	Jour de l'an
March/April	Easter Monday	Lundi de Pâques
1 May	Labour Day	Fête du travail
8 May	VE Day	Fête de la victoire (Armistice)
39 days after Easter Sunday	Ascension	Ascension
50 days after Easter	Whit Monday	Lundi de Pentecôte (not universally recognised)
14 July	Bastille Day	Fête nationale
15 August	Assumption	Assomption de Marie
1 November	All Saints' Day	Toussaint
11 November	Armistice Day	Armistice de 1918
25 December	Christmas Day	Nöel

SHOPPING

The lunch hour is sacrosanct in France, and many shops, apart from large supermarkets and hypermarkets, close between noon and 14.00. Consequently, the lie-in-bed holidaymaker will find the mornings extremely short for shopping but, in contrast, the afternoons deliciously long as shops generally stay open until around 19.00. The smaller local food shops are usually open on Sunday mornings – as are some of the supermarkets in holiday areas – though almost everything is closed on Sunday afternoons. Good supermarket chains include Leclerc, Carrefour, Géant and Super/Hyper U, all usually located on the outskirts of towns, as well as Lidl, Aldi and a few Leader-Price. Bargain sports clothing and equipment are to be found at branches of Décathlon. The best places for smart city-centre shops are La Roche-sur-Yon, Les Sables-d'Olonne and Challans, plus Nantes and La Rochelle. Factory shops, or *magasins d'usine*, are popular, too, especially around Les Herbiers.

Junk-junkies should look out for *marchés aux puces* (flea markets), for *brocante* fairs or for *vide-greniers* (car-boot sales) where unusual holiday souvenirs can sometimes be found; tourist offices will have a list of dates in their area. Eagle-eyed car passengers can be instructed to look out for the many signs for *brocante* or *antiquités* in passing towns or villages (see below).

MARKETS Markets are usually morning-only events, finishing around noon or a bit later. In larger towns, often those with market halls, they are frequently held daily. At the entrance to most villages, you will see a sign indicating on which day the weekly market takes place. Sadly, in these days of hypermarket shopping the importance of markets is dwindling, and some are now very small; a few others take

ANTIQUES, BRIC-A-BRAC, FLEAS AND PLAIN OLD TAT

Many visitors to France spend happy hours browsing in antiques shops, picking through bric-a-brac or rummaging in car-boot sales. The Vendée certainly does not disappoint, providing plenty of opportunities to possess your own piece of French history. Look out for roadside signs advertising *antiquités* (antiques), *brocante* (bric-a-brac) or perhaps a forthcoming *vide-grenier* (car-boot sale). Although the differences between these three types of outlets are blurred, you are more likely to find something of real value at the first, something collectable at the second and something more quirky at the third. Often combining all three, and a regular feature particularly in high season, are the *marchés aux puces* (flea markets), which are usually weekend events. A useful place to research details of upcoming garage sales and flea markets is the BROCABRAC website (w brocabrac.fr/85). Much of the fun, of course, is in the hunt, rather than the eventual purchase, and beauty is in the eye of the beholder…

Grouped together under the banner Association Professionelle des Antiquaires et Brocanteurs de Vendée, the members of the département's professional body have shops, some listed below. Bear in mind that they are not open all the time – sometimes their owners may be out hunting for valuables themselves, so do phone ahead if you are making a special trip.

Aux Dauphins 9 Allée des Courlis, L'Aiguillon-sur-Mer; m 06 81 85 68 75
Coffineau 23 Rue Paul Doumer, La Roche-sur-Yon; m 06 29 27 8701
Didier Soulas 20 bis Rue Lafayette, La Roche-sur-Yon; 02 51 08 84 15. Specialising in 1950s & Art Deco.

Jouets des 4 D Dany Motsch 47 bis Rue des Halles, Les Sables-d'Olonne; 02 51 95 34 56. Specialising in old toys.
L'Estampille 4 Rue Jean Nicot, Les Sables-d'Olonne; 02 51 21 12 28

2

place in summer only, or on alternate weeks. Here is a day-by-day selection; entries in bold type are the most interesting; those in italics are held in summer only.

Sometimes market days and locations change, for instance if building works are going on. You can double check days and timings at w vendee-guide.co.uk/markets.htm.

Monday *L'Herbaudière* (Noirmoutier); Jard-sur-Mer; *Longeville*; *Merlin-Plage (St-Hilaire-de-Riez)*; *Olonne-sur-Mer*; *La Parée (Brétignolles)*; La Rochelle; *Les Sables-d'Olonne* (15 Jun–15 Sep).

Tuesday L'Aiguillon-sur-Mer; Brem; **Challans**; La Chaume; Le Château-d'Olonne; **Clisson**; Mortagne-sur-Sèvre; *Noirmoutier* (town); La Roche-sur-Yon; La Rochelle; Les Sables; St-Gilles; Sion; La Tranche.

Wednesday *Angles*; Croix-de-Vie; Les Épesses; Foussais-Payré; Les Herbiers; *Jard*; Luçon; Machecoul; *Merlin-Plage (St-Hilaire, afternoon)*; La Roche; La Rochelle; Les Sables; Port-Bourgenay; St-Jean-de-Monts; *La Grière (La Tranche)*.

Thursday Beauvoir; Brétignolles; Le Château-d'Olonne; *La Faute*; *La Guérinière (Noirmoutier)*; *Jard (harbour)*; La Mothe-Achard (first Thursday); Pouzauges; La Roche; La Rochelle; Les Sables; St-Gilles; St-Hilaire-de-Riez; Talmont.

Friday L'Aiguillon-sur-Mer; Brem; Challans; **Clisson**; Longeville; La Mothe-Achard (except after 1st Thursday of the month); Noirmoutier town; La Roche; La Rochelle (Place de Verdun, from 16.00); Les Sables; Ste-Hermine.

Saturday Bouin; Brétignolles; Challans; Le Château-d'Olonne; Coëx; **Croix-de-Vie**; *Fromentine*; **Fontenay**; **Guérande**; Les Herbiers; Luçon; Merlin-Plage; Montaigu; Pouzauges; La Roche; **La Rochelle**; **Les Sables**; St-Jean-de-Monts; *Talmont*; La Tranche.

Sunday *Angles*; Brétignolles; Le Château-d'Olonne; La Chaume; La Faute; *La Guérinière (Noirmoutier)*; *Maillé*; **Noirmoutier town**; Notre-Dame-de-Monts; La Rochelle; Les Sables; **St-Gilles**; St-Hilaire-de-Riez; St-Jean-de-Monts; St-Philbert-de-Grand-Lieu; Soullans; *La Terrière (La Tranche)*; **Vallet**.

ARTS AND ENTERTAINMENT

CASINOS French seaside resorts are, by tradition, well endowed with casinos. Far less exclusive than in the UK, they are welcoming establishments with a casual atmosphere, pleasant restaurants and bars open to non-players, as well as occasional evenings of entertainment. You need to be over 18 and to produce a passport or other photo ID to use fruit machines or gaming rooms, which open from 22.00 or 23.00 and close around 04.00 the next morning. Would-be roulette or blackjack players must pay the equivalent of several pounds to gain admission. You will find casinos at St-Jean-de-Monts, St-Gilles-Croix-de-Vie, Les Sables-d'Olonne (two), La Faute-sur-Mer, and also at La Rochelle, Nantes, Pornic and at St-Brevin-les-Pins.

CINEMAS The French are great moviegoers and most towns, even quite small ones, have cinemas, including an increasing number of multiplexes. However, with the exception of showings in a few Nantes cinemas such as the Katorza, near the Théâtre Graslin, and occasionally at the Concorde in La Roche-sur-Yon, films will always be in French (English-language ones being dubbed rather than subtitled), so entertainment value for non-French-speakers is restricted. The letters 'VO' (*version originale*) indicate that a movie is being shown in its original language, with French subtitles (though remember that the original language might be Swedish or Japanese!). Details are given in local newspapers (be sure you pick up the appropriate edition – a copy bought at some distance from your base may cover different towns from the one you are interested in).

In July and August a programme of free open-air film shows, known as Cinésites, is sometimes organised, with screenings after nightfall at castles and other venues. Locations are often selected to provide an appropriate backdrop, for example a tale of medieval swashbuckling might be projected alongside a ruined chateau of the period.

CONCERTS One of the most accessible forms of entertainment for non-French-speakers is music, and a look at the Vendée Tourist Office website (page 21) or individual town websites (as listed in the following chapters) will reveal a wealth of music and dance events in churches, auditoriums and even in the open air. Many of the historic places listed in this guide double up as music venues in July and August. For example, the Logis de la Chabotterie organises a festival of 17th- and 18th-century music in July and August; a free festival of chamber music is held at Luçon in July; and there is a fireworks and musical evening in July to celebrate Bastille Day in Cugand (w cugand.fr), near Clisson. Clisson itself, ornate and elegant, is also the unlikely venue for a huge heavy-rock festival (page 173) in June.

THEATRES Theatrical performances in France tend to rely heavily on words, and anyone with limited command of French may find them difficult to follow. There are traditional theatres at La Roche-sur-Yon, Luçon and Fontenay-le-Comte, and modern performance spaces at Les Sables-d'Olonne (within the tourist office complex), Challans, Les Herbiers and elsewhere. Outside the département you will find theatres at La Rochelle and at Nantes (where opera performances are also given between October and June at the Théâtre Graslin).

The best thing is to go for spectacle, and for this the night-time, open-air Cinéscénie at Le Puy du Fou (page 182) cannot be beaten. Other smaller son et lumière productions are performed at Olonne-sur-Mer and at Machecoul. Newer ones appear from time to time. They all tend to be popular, so book in advance through local tourist offices.

At Ascensiontide (usually May) and throughout July and August, at seaside towns from St-Brevin-les-Pins to La Tranche, some highly inventive street-theatre artistes are often engaged to give weekly, free open-air evening performances and concerts. Details can be found at w ladeferlante.com.

BEACHES France has many beaches which carry the Blue Flag ('Pavillon Bleu') indicating cleanliness and good water quality. Awards are given annually, so the list of those in the Vendée and the surrounding area changes from year to year. Recent recipients of the award include beaches – sometimes more than one – at Pornic, La Barre-de-Monts/Fromentine, Notre-Dame, St-Jean, Talmont, Longeville, La Tranche, La Faute, L'Aiguillon and Le-Bois-Plage-en-Ré. You can check out these and others on the French Blue Flag website w pavillonbleu.org.

Nudism is permitted on certain secluded beaches: Luzéronde, on Noirmoutier island, southeast of L'Herbaudière; La Grande Conche on Île d'Yeu; Les Lays at La Barre-de-Monts; Parée Grollier at Notre-Dame; Petit Pont-Jaunay, south of St-Gilles; Sauveterre, north of Les Sables; La Terrière, near La Tranche; and the Pointe d'Arçay beach at La Faute.

BOATING AND WATERSPORTS As you would imagine, more than 200km of coastline provides many opportunities to take to the sea, with opportunities for boat trips, including to the Île d'Yeu. Sailing, kayaking, windsurfing, kitesurfing, bodyboarding or balancing on a stand-up paddleboard are all possibilities as well. All coastal tourist offices and their websites have details of the many operators in their immediate area. The water-borne fun continues inland where guided canoe or traditional craft tours are available through open marshland in many locations such as Sallertaine and Maillezais. Canoes may also be rented on many of the Vendée's rivers, canals and lakes. Other inland opportunities can be found at Le Perrier, where you can be taken out on a punt-like *yole*; in the Marais Poitevin, where you can paddle your own flat-bottomed *plate* along tree-lined waterways in the 'Venise Verte'; or in the Parc naturel régional de Brière (page 243), north of St-Nazaire, where you can enjoy guided tours by traditional *chaland*. In addition, various vessels such as pedaloes, windsurfers, and rowing or sailing dinghies can be rented on inland lakes such as Apremont, Jaunay and Mervent.

CYCLING The Vendée claims to have the most cycleways of any French département. It is possible to cycle around its whole perimeter via almost 1,000km of linked circuits – though expect those on the east of the département to be a lot more hilly than the trails of the coast and marshes. You can download routes from w vendeevelo.vendee.fr. Hundreds of local cycle trails (*pistes cyclables*) and green ways (*voies vertes*) are signposted; tourist offices have details of them, as well as of bike hire (*location de vélos*) which can be found in nearly all coastal resorts.

One most unusual form of cycling is unquestionably the *vélo draisine*, a flat-bed wagon that runs along a disused railway line from Commequiers to Coëx (page 74), carrying four or five people, two pedalling and three resting (or perhaps shirking?).

DIVING If you have internationally recognised diving certificates, plus an official doctor's attestation that you are fit enough to undertake this sport, you can join local divers exploring wrecks off Noirmoutier or the Île d'Yeu. Enquire about *la plongée* (diving) at the relevant tourist offices.

FISHING
Sea fishing In season, boat trips may be taken from Les Sables-d'Olonne or from St-Gilles-Croix-de-Vie to fish for sea bass and mackerel. Fishing trips from the islands are also possible.

Shrimping and shellfish-collecting

At low water, it's fun to push a shrimping net through the shallows and rock pools or join the locals digging for cockles, clams and other shellfish. You need to consult tide tables to find the days with the highest figure in the column marked '*coefficient*' (a method of indicating extra-low and extra-high tides). *Coefficients* of more than 90 are best, giving the opportunity to scrabble on some of the more rarely uncovered sandbanks. The Pont d'Yeu, south of Notre-Dame-de-Monts, or the mudflats alongside the causeway leading to Noirmoutier island are popular spots, but keep an eye on the time, and stay away from any dubious outflow pipes as well as from commercial oyster beds or mussel posts. Official rules stress that you should not collect anything too tiny, nor harvest more shellfish than you can eat at a sitting.

Freshwater fishing

The Vendée's inland lakes and rivers yield bream, black bass, perch, roach, tench, pike, zander and carp. A few areas of the Haut-Bocage around Pouzauges, on the eastern side of the county, have trout rivers; marshland canals often harbour eels; while the sluggish lower reaches of rivers like the Vie contain more than their fair share of small catfish.

A one-week permit (*carte hebdomadaire*) can be bought online from the Associations de Pêche en France website (w cartedepeche.fr), allowing you to fish in all non-private waters of the Vendée and surrounding départements. These include rivers, and also areas on them where lakes have been created by dams. It is valid on seven consecutive days, at any time of year and costs €34. Day permits (*cartes journalières*) are also available from the same site, for €11.

Further information is obtainable from tourist offices, or from La Fédération de Pêche de Vendée (📞02 51 37 19 05; w federation-peche-vendee.fr, in French). Details of waterside cottages in the south Vendée, from L'Aiguillon-sur-Mer in the south to La Châtaigneraie in the east, including the marshlands of the Marais Poitevin, are available on the website of Sud Vendée Tourisme (w sudvendeetourisme.com).

There is also a growing number of fisheries where you can rent a rod and fish in a lake all day; ask at the nearest tourist office about '*pêche à la ligne*' or '*pêche à la journée*'.

'*Pêche Interdite*' means 'No Fishing'; ask if in any doubt about whether a stretch of water is included in the pass. Tackle and bait are on sale in sports and watersports shops and hypermarkets.

Traditional fishing

At the annual Fête des Pêcheurs around 15 August, visitors can accompany the fishers of Passay (page 230) as they cast their nets in the Lac de Grand-Lieu. This is a rare opportunity to see the centre of this large and mysterious lake that is now a nature reserve. Music and fireworks accompany the festival, and there are plenty of opportunities to sample freshwater delicacies such as eels, so it's not just for fishers.

GOLF

The Vendée has five 18-hole golf courses, situated at St-Jean-de-Monts, L'Aiguillon-sur-Vic (near Coëx), Nesmy (near La Roche-sur-Yon), Olonne-sur-Mer (near Les Sables-d'Olonne), and Port-Bourgenay (near Talmont-St-Hilaire). Golfers seeking further challenges nearby will find more courses at La Baule, Guérande, Pornic, Nantes, Cholet, Niort and La Rochelle. Golf clubs can usually be hired on the spot. Between May and September it is advisable to book in advance for the more popular courses like St-Jean and Port-Bourgenay. Green fees for 18 holes range from around €40 to €70 according to season, but several golf courses in the area are managed by the Blue Green company (w bluegreen.com/en), which

2

offers golf passes allowing you to play a selection of their courses in the Vendée and elsewhere at discounted green fees.

HORSERIDING There are many equestrian centres (*centres équestres*) in the region – enquire through local tourist offices. Style is often a bit more casual and 'wild western' than the British are used to. Most establishments provide hard hats (*bombes*), but it is as well to check this point first when booking a *promenade*, or ride.

SURFING The best surfing beaches lie between St-Gilles (Grande Plage) and Les Sables (Tanchet) – most notably those of Brétignolles (La Sauzaie) and Sauveterre – and between Longeville and La Tranche. There are surf shops at St-Jean, St-Gilles, Brétignolles, Les Sables, La Tranche and elsewhere.

TENNIS Many villages have a municipal tennis court or two, which can be booked by the hour, for a modest fee. Ask at the tourist office or *mairie*.

WALKING Although the lack of hilly terrain may deter some walkers (and may encourage others!), the Vendée can be discovered on foot. All tourist offices and many *mairies* (mayor's offices) have details of local walks and reasonable maps. The Vendée county council produces a fantastic guide of coastal and inland walking routes called ' Vendée Rando', which is available for download at w vendee.fr/guide-vendee-rando. While it is in French, the routes and place names are easy to understand with a limited grasp of the language. A quick look on the shelves of big French supermarkets in the area will usually reveal a guidebook or two of walks. If you are organised enough, you can download many walking maps from local tourist office websites before leaving home.

Long-distance walks The IGN map 903 shows all the Grande-Randonnée (long-distance footpath) routes in France and is available from w themapcentre.com. Grande-Randonnée footpaths in the Vendée, waymarked with red-and-yellow signs, include GR36, GR364, GR Pays Entre Vie et Yon and GR Pays de la Côte de Lumière.

Local walks You can, of course, walk shorter sections of any of the above Grande-Randonnée routes. In addition, almost every village has a network of signposted footpaths leading to its main beauty spots and places of interest. Maps are usually given on large panels in village car parks, or are available from local tourist offices and *mairies*.

Balades GPS Tourist offices near the mainland side of the Noirmoutier bridge have pioneered walking circuits in the coastal pine forest, for which visitors rent a special, hand-held satnav gadget. Other tourist offices have begun to offer these, too. You do need a good knowledge of French to get the most out of them though.

OPENING TIMES

Lunch is usually served between noon and 14.00 with dinner starting at 19.00 and served through to 21.00 or later. Restaurants tend to close on Sunday evenings and Mondays. Patisseries open earlier and stay open throughout the day, except for lunch.

Shops are usually open six days a week Monday to Saturday, from 09.00–noon and 14.00–19.00. Many, especially in smaller towns close at lunchtime.

Times seem to vary substantially at the Post Office, or La Poste – even in some cities they may only open for a couple of hours each day, so it's good to check on the internet beforehand.

MEDIA AND COMMUNICATIONS

TELEPHONE To call a French number from within France, you simply dial the ten digits of the number. To call a French number from outside France, dial 00 for international access, then 33 for the country code, then the number omitting its initial zero. To call a number outside France from inside, dial 00 for international access followed by the country code for the place you are calling (44 for the UK, 353 for Ireland, 1 for the USA), and then the number you require, but omitting its initial zero.

MOBILE PHONES Since 2017, when roaming charges were scrapped within the European Union, EU citizens travelling within the EU have not been charged extra for calls, text messages or internet when outside their home countries. For UK citizens post-Brexit, a few mobile providers still offer free roaming voluntarily – but check with your operator before going. Similarly, in respect of data, certain providers have a cap on your usage, so it is worth checking with your provider pre-departure to avoid running up an unwanted bill.

Once in France, to ring a French number you just dial its ten digits. However, anyone wishing to call *your* mobile from within France (from a landline or mobile) must treat yours as a foreign (ie: a UK, Irish, USA, etc) number, dialling the access and country code (see above) first and then dropping your mobile's initial zero.

To dial a UK number (including a UK mobile – even if you know it, too, is in France), you must treat it as a foreign one, ie: dial 00 44 followed by the UK number without the initial zero. (This may require amendment of numbers stored in your mobile's memory.) Anyone calling your mobile from the UK, however, just dials your normal mobile number as if you, too, were in the UK.

INTERNET France is up to speed with everyone's frantic need to be permanently connected and nearly all hotels, B&Bs, self-catering units and even many campsites now offer Wi-Fi (pronounced '*wee-fee*' in French), usually free of charge but still occasionally at an extra cost. Many cafés also have free Wi-Fi for customers, and even if they do not display the symbol, it is often worth asking. Otherwise, you can use the Vendée's excellent Wi-Fi hotspots, which are often marked with a red-and-white logo and generally located adjacent to tourist offices, or outside some focal points such as a *capitainerie* (harbourmaster's office). These are free to use for local tourist information, but there is sometimes a small daily fee for wider surfing. You are welcome to connect inside the tourist offices themselves, where Wi-Fi is always free of charge.

If you don't have internet accessible via phone or computer, a few towns still have internet cafés; otherwise, the local library or *médiathèque* will often have a terminal you can use for a euro or two. Ask about these at the tourist office or the *mairie*.

NEWSPAPERS English newspapers are occasionally available in good newsagents such as Maisons de la Presse in large towns and, increasingly, in village shops in the most tourist-friendly or expat-inhabited areas. Usually they are one day old, but in summer you sometimes find the current day's paper on sale.

The main local daily newspaper is the broadsheet *Ouest-France* (with several local editions, so make sure you get the right one). As well as international and national news, it carries invaluable pages of local snippets to interest the French-reading holidaymaker: cinema and exhibition listings, weather maps, details of local fêtes, scandals, accidents and other indispensable trivia.

POST OFFICES In major towns and cities, post offices are open Monday to Friday until around 17.00 or 18.00. On Saturdays, they open until noon. Surprisingly, even small villages still cling on to their post offices, although these may not be open every day. You may also find that a '*point-poste*' has been incorporated into the village's general store. For stamps for the UK, ask for '*timbres-poste pour le Royaume-Uni*'. Postage stamps are also obtainable from tobacconists (*tabacs*) – although they often do not know the rates for overseas mail.

CULTURAL ETIQUETTE

We do joke about it, but history tells us that the relationship between the British (particularly the English) and the French has not always been the most comfortable one. We refer to them as 'frogs' while they call us '*rosbifs*' (roast beefs) and neither term is one entirely of endearment. There are certainly profound differences in mentality and philosophy, which can cause friction and misunderstandings, though this is probably exaggerated. Most French people are charming and welcoming, and your holiday should pass without any problems.

Language is an obvious barrier, but the famed unwillingness of the French to speak English is becoming a thing of the past. To the extent that it still exists, it is probably confined to older generations. Certainly, the under 30s – brought up on the influences of Anglophonic popular music and Hollywood films – are very keen to demonstrate their knowledge of English, wherever possible.

Saying a heartfelt '*bonjour*' to the owner of a shop or restaurant when entering will certainly endear you to them and ensure good service thereafter; saying '*merci*' or '*au revoir*' on departure is also the norm in France. Failure to observe these little rituals can mark you out as ignorant or rude.

Visitors from Britain need to show patience when waiting to be served in shops. The local person in front of you may be deeply engaged in social chit-chat with the cashier, oblivious to your growing impatience. '*Vive la différence!*' you need to say, and keep smiling is what you need to do, as someone pushes in front of you to ask a 'quick question'.

A handshake on meeting someone is always expected; don't be surprised to also see people kissing each other lightly on the cheek, though this is not necessarily a custom you are expected to copy.

TRAVELLING POSITIVELY

There are a range of ways that you can give back to the region. One of the best of these is simply through the purchase of local goods and produce. While in St-Gilles-Croix-de-Vie, why not visit local sardine producers and purchase a range of delicious offerings to eat there or take away. If you are heading to the coastal areas, do visit the salt producers or the many oyster and mussel shacks such as in Noirmoutier. Les Fiefs Vendeens wines are available direct from the vineyard or in many local restaurants and there are plenty of art galleries and artisan shops selling local goods. Weekday and weekend markets, of which there are plenty, are another fantastic way of supporting this wonderful area.

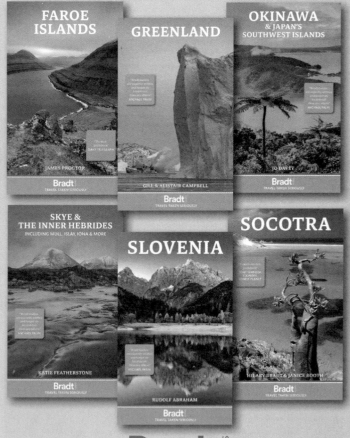

Part Two

THE VENDÉE

3

Northwest Vendée and the Islands

Just inland from the busy coastal resorts, the chequer-board fenland of the Marais Breton-Vendéen is criss-crossed with tamarisk-fringed canals. There may be little in the way of elevation, but the abundance of water and characteristic single-storey, white-painted houses ensure that there is plenty to catch the eye. While the seaside resorts lure the summer crowds, the busy Tuesday market in the marshland capital of Challans provides a weekly highlight all year round. In July and August, the action heightens even further as the town steps back a century to stage four extra, highly enjoyable traditional fair days.

Flat marshes can indeed hide some surprising treasures. Each summer the small village of Sallertaine becomes a centre for craft shops, while the surrounding countryside still contains some of the pretty, thatched cottages known as *bourrines*. Near Soullans, a pair of these old houses contain paintings by Vendean artist Charles Milcendeau, who lived here a hundred years ago. A variety of attractive, more sophisticated villas overlook the sea at Sion and at St-Gilles-Croix-de-Vie.

Across the water, two sun-soaked islands wait to be explored: the rugged Île d'Yeu can be reached only by boat; the balmier isle of Noirmoutier is accessible by bridge or, more romantically, by causeway across the bed of the sea – at low tide, of course. This chapter starts at Bouin in the north, then covers Challans and places of interest to its north (including Noirmoutier), then continues southwards – and offshore – to end with the Île d'Yeu.

BOUIN

Full of narrow lanes and ancient houses, unspoiled Bouin is now firmly famous for its oysters. But the village originally made its fortune from salt-making – in the 15th century it supplied 80% of London's saline requirements. The riches from this precious commodity were enough to endow the impressive church with three magnificent Baroque altarpieces.

The oyster fishers who work at nearby Port du Bec, Port des Champs and Port des Brochets produce around 12,000 tonnes a year of the precious molluscs. The rich mud of the bay provides ideal conditions for fattening the baby shellfish, which are then laid out underwater in openwork plastic sacks. On reaching maturity, after four years, they are collected and purified in tanks here before sale. In early August the oysters are celebrated, with the **Les Gobeurs d'Huîtres** festival, when competitors have to swallow three-dozen of them in the shortest possible time.

Bouin no longer has its own tourist information office; instead see Beauvoir-sur-Mer (see opposite).

WHERE TO STAY AND EAT

Domaine le Martinet (23 rooms) Pl du Général Charette; ☎02 51 49 23 23; e contact@domaine-lemartinet.com; w domaine-lemartinet.com; ☉ Apr–Oct only. Quiet hotel in an attractive 18th-century house, combining old-world charm with modern facilities. Free Wi-Fi, parking, seasonal outdoor pool. Acclaimed restaurant (☉ closed Mon, Tue lunch & Sun eve; €€€). €€€€

Gratt'huîtres 31 Port des Brochets, 4km northwest of Bouin; ☎02 51 54 24 26; ☉ Apr–mid-Sep lunch & dinner daily, May–Jun Wed–Sun only. Trendy quayside oyster bar, offering panoramic views from a 1st-floor deck. Opening hours are changeable, so phone in advance. €€€

SHOPPING

La Rose des Vents Quayside, Port des Brochets; m 06 84 87 93 53. A small white building, next to the bridge, this shop sells oysters, salt & souvenirs – typical of many in the region.

WHAT TO SEE AND DO

Port du Bec Quaint and characterful, the rickety-looking wooden jetties make this the most picturesque of Bouin's little oyster harbours, which has also been nicknamed 'the Chinese port'. Brightly painted boats lie alongside, loaded with lobster pots and their colourful, fluttering pennants. There's tremendous activity about 2 hours after low tide as the fishers return from their expeditions into Bourgneuf Bay, and you have to be nimble to dodge the ancient tractors that reverse at high speed down to the water's edge to drag in the trailers of oysters. Watch out too for the motorhomes!

BEAUVOIR-SUR-MER

Despite its name, this little town 16km northwest of Challans is no longer 'on sea' but well and truly stranded 3km inland. For a vivid impression of where the waters must once have been, glance south across the low-lying marshland as you approach the town from Challans.

In Beauvoir, take a moment to visit the 12th- to 14th-century church of St Philbert – indeed, if you drive in from Challans through the centre of the village, the D948 practically thrusts you in through the north door on a tight double bend. Markets here occupy Thursday mornings. Each June, **Les Foulées du Gois** is a spectacular running event on the nearby causeway, with the best of the 1,500 competitors having to race the incoming tide. The **Foire aux Moules** is the August mussel festival.

If you plan to cross the causeway to Noirmoutier – an unforgettable experience – continue along the same road, following directions for 'Le Gois', and you will see large signs with worrying graphics of semi-submerged cars and – more helpfully – times of low tide when you can safely drive along this submersible roadway. *'Prochaine basse mer à…'* is also displayed in neon and translates as 'next low tide due at…'

TOURIST INFORMATION

Office de Tourisme 9 Rue Charles-Gallet; ☎02 51 68 71 13; w gochallansgois.fr; ☉ 09.30–12.30 Tue, Thu & Fri

WHERE TO EAT AND DRINK

Le Relais du Gois Route du Gois; ☎02 51 68 70 31; w relaisdugois.com; ☉ Jul–Aug 10.00–22.00 daily, Jun & Sep closed Mon–Tue eve & all day

Wed, Oct–May closed Tue eve & all day Wed. While a few eating & drinking places cluster around the end of the causeway, this is the one with the

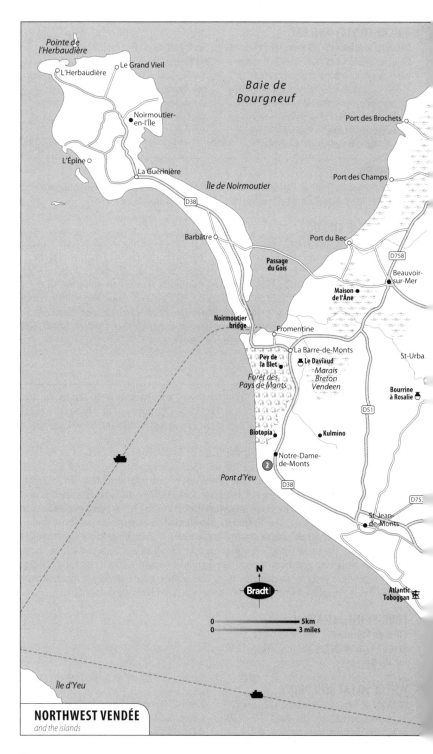

Pointe de l'Herbaudière

Le Grand Vieil

L'Herbaudière

Baie de Bourgneuf

Noirmoutier-en-l'Île

Port des Brochets

L'Épine

La Guérinière

Port des Champs

Île de Noirmoutier

D38

Barbâtre

Port du Bec

D758

Passage du Gois

Beauvoir-sur-Mer

Maison de l'Âne

Noirmoutier bridge

Fromentine

La Barre-de-Monts

St-Urba

Pey de la Blet

Le Daviaud

Marais Breton Vendeen

Forêt des Pays de Monts

Bourrine à Rosalie

D51

Biotopia

Kulmino

Notre-Dame-de-Monts

②

Pont d'Yeu

D38

D753

St-Jean-de-Monts

N

Bradt

0 ————— 5km
0 ————— 3 miles

Atlantic Toboggan

Île d'Yeu

NORTHWEST VENDÉE
and the islands

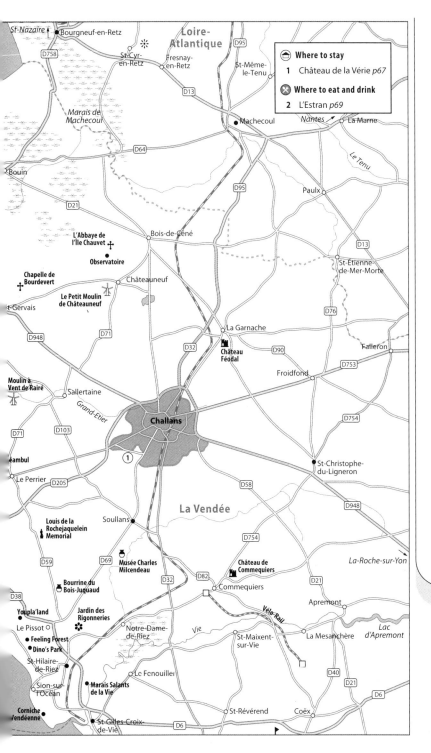

Where to stay
1   Château de la Vérie *p67*

Where to eat and drink
2   L'Estran *p69*

St-Nazaire

Bourgneuf-en-Retz

Loire-Atlantique

D758

St-Cyr-en-Retz

Fresnay-en-Retz

St-Même-le-Tenu

D95

D13

Nantes

La Marne

Marais de Machecoul

Machecoul

Le Tenu

D64

Bouin

D95

Paulx

D21

D13

Bois-de-Céné

St-Étienne-de-Mer-Morte

L'Abbaye de l'Île Chauvet

Observatoire

Chapelle de Bourdevert

Châteauneuf

D76

Le Petit Moulin de Châteauneuf

t-Gervais

La Garnache

D948

D71

D32

Château Féodal

D90

Falleron

D753

Froidfond

Moulin à Vent de Rairé

Sallertaine

D754

Grand-Étier

Challans

D71

D103

éambul

St-Christophe-du-Ligneron

Le Perrier

D205

D58

La Vendée

D948

Louis de la Rochejaquelein Memorial

Soullans

D754

D59

D69

Musée Charles Milcendeau

Château de Commequiers

La-Roche-sur-Yon

Bourrine du Bois-Juquaud

D32

D82

Commequiers

D21

Apremont

D38

Youpla'land

Jardin des Rigonneries

Vélo-Rail

Lac d'Apremont

Le Pissot

Feeling Forest

Notre-Dame-de-Riez

Vie

St-Maixent-sur-Vie

La Mesanchère

Dino's Park

St-Hilaire-de-Riez

Le Fenouiller

D40

D21

Sion-sur-l'Océan

Marais Salants de la Vie

D6

Corniche Vendéenne

St-Gilles-Croix-de-Vie

D6

St-Révérend

Coëx

best view. The morbid can watch the traffic to & fro, wondering if anyone will get caught by the tide. A good spot for a drink or to sample local seafood. €€€€

WHAT TO SEE AND DO

Maison de l'Âne (On the D948, 1km west of Beauvoir; ☎ 02 51 93 85 70; w lamaisondelane.com; ☺ Apr–Jul 10.30–18.00 Wed–Sat, changing to 10.30–18.00 Mon–Fri & Sun during school holidays; Jul–Aug 10.00–18.30 Mon–Fri & Sun; Sep 10.30–18.00 Wed–Sat; €6/4/free adult/child/under 2s, family tickets available, donkey rides on site €2.50) You probably wouldn't believe there could be 25 different types of donkey, but at this fenland farm you can meet them all, from the small, grey Provençal variety to the large, shaggy *baudet du Poitou*; from the Egyptian white

---

PASSAGE DU GOIS

A drive either to, or from, Noirmoutier island along this part-cobblestone causeway edged with seaweed and glistening with sea water is a magical experience – particularly on a moonlit night. Until 1971 the 4.5km causeway, passable just twice a day either side of low water, was the only access to Noirmoutier, except for a passenger ferry from Pornic. Its dog-leg route is studded with sturdy poles and platforms that provide windswept sanctuary for anyone caught out by the rising waters; if you return for a look at high tide, you can see why they might be necessary!

Nature and tides are merciless, and the road has a history of being damaged and destroyed by storms. You should treat this phenomenon with the greatest respect. Tide tables (*horaires des marées*) are available from tourist offices in the area to indicate safe crossing times, which vary each day. Times are also published in local papers and shown on huge roadside panels on both sides of the causeway, supplemented with flashing signals of warning once the tide begins to rise. Cross only within 90 minutes either side of low water (*basse mer*, or *marée basse*), and never park on the causeway itself, which is wide enough for just one lane of traffic in each direction. For the 3 hours that bridge the low tide, there is an extraordinary amount of activity, as the locals drive off onto the occasional hard area of seabed to take advantage of extra-low tides (indicated by the highest figures in the column of the tide tables marked '*coefficient*'). They scrabble in the mudflats for cockles and clams, or search out oysters and other shellfish, accompanied by tractors to haul the catch to dry ground. At the island end of Le Gois, signboards give information about the birdlife and the causeway, which was visited by the 1999, 2011 and 2018 Tour de France cycling events.

Allow plenty of time to cross at peak periods (summer Sunday afternoons, and throughout July and August); it can be a bit worrying to find yourself stuck in a traffic jam, beginning to fret about the rising tide. The handsome bridge near Fromentine now provides alternative – if less exciting – road access. For the return to the mainland, follow the signposts to *Sortie de L'Île* or even occasionally '*continent*' – either *par le pont* (by the bridge) or *par Le Gois* (by the causeway).

Of course, you may wonder why, in this digital age, an electronic barrier is not installed at each end of the passage, linked to a computer somewhere which has the tide times programmed into it…ah, but that would take all the fun out of things, wouldn't it?

to the Berry black. Children can stroke them, and enjoy donkey rides. You can see the females being milked at 15.00 each day, and even buy ass's-milk soap in the shop. Goats, pigs and peacocks ensure that this is a children's firm favourite. There's no café, so bring a picnic.

Chapelle de Bourdevert (On the D59, 4km east of Beauvoir) At a country crossroads stands an enchanting little chapel dating from the 12th or 13th century, said to have been built by two sailors in gratitude for surviving a shipwreck in the days when the sea lapped against this spot. It's rarely open, but if it is, step inside to see – hanging on either side of the ornate altar – a collection of babies' shoes placed there by parents who come and pray to the Virgin to guide their children's first steps. (Even if closed, you can peek through the back door to admire the chapel's simplicity). A few waymarked walks begin from the car park behind the chapel.

ÎLE DE NOIRMOUTIER

Barely a kilometre off the coast, this long, thin island is a massive draw for summer visitors, with its population swelling 15-fold in July and August. It connects to the mainland by a short bridge from Fromentine and, at low tide only, by 'Le Gois', the 4.5km causeway (see opposite) that is a tourist attraction in its own right – one of the wonders of France.

Thanks to its microclimate, Noirmoutier produces the first yellow pompoms of mimosa in the dark depths of February, delectable early potatoes served at the smartest tables in France, and a tremendous harvest of seafood – particularly conger eel, sole, squid and oysters. Salt and *salicorne* (marshland samphire) are other island specialities and it now has its own artisanal beer, called 'N'O'.

The island's economy once depended to a great extent on salt production, and you can still see the rectangular drying-pans (especially around L'Épine) where sea water is allowed to evaporate, leaving crystals to be raked up into little white pyramids. A blue-signposted 'Route de l'Île' leads motorists and cyclists around the lanes and past low, whitewashed houses to such pretty villages as Le Vieil, La Blanche and Bois de la Chaise. Do fall in love with the island, but not head-over-heels, as property prices are disconcertingly high.

The colourful, animated port of L'Herbaudière on the north coast is a centre for fishing, yachting and – more recently – gastronomy, since Alexandre Couillon's waterfront La Marine restaurant (page 60) has been elevated to three Michelin stars. At Bois de la Chaise (sometimes written 'Chaize'), a wooded area on the northeast coast where grand 19th-century villas line sandy tracks among forests of holm oaks, the air in February is heavy with the perfume of mimosa; its sheltered beach of La Plage des Dames – distinctly Breton in atmosphere, with a row of neat beach huts – is so popular in high summer that parking is impossible (better to go by bike or on foot). Watersports are on offer there, too. La Guérinière, on the south coast (bypassed by the superhighway that connects the bridge with the island's capital), is an attractive village strung out seemingly forever along the old main road of the island and full of shops selling beach balls, shrimping nets and other traditional holiday equipment.

The island's capital is Noirmoutier-en-l'Île, a trim, pretty place with smart shops and restaurants along its quayside and surrounding the stalwart 12th-century castle. The street on the south side of St Philbert's church leads into the Banzeau district, one of the most attractive parts of town, full of narrow lanes and whitewashed fishermen's houses that are now chic retreats for Parisians.

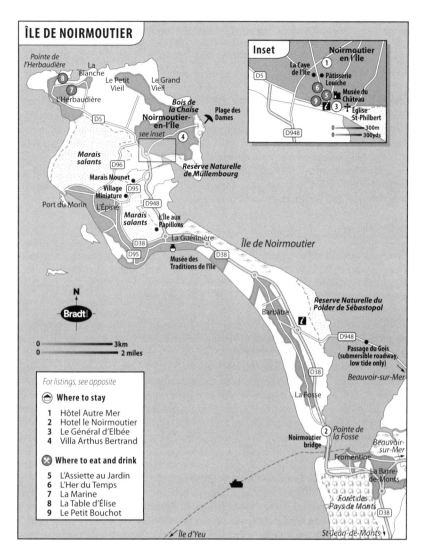

ÎLE DE NOIRMOUTIER

Pointe de
l'Herbaudière
La
Blanche
Le Petit
Vieil
Le Grand
Vieil
L'Herbaudière
Bois de
la Chaise
Noirmoutier-
en-l'Île
see inset
Plage des
Dames
D5
Marais
salants
D96
Reserve Naturelle
de Müllembourg
Marais Mounet
Village
Miniature
D95
Port du Morin
L'Épine
D948
Marais
salants
L'Île aux
Papillons
La Guérinière
Île de Noirmoutier
D38
D95
D38
Musée des
Traditions de l'Île

N

Bradt

0 ————— 3km
0 ————— 2 miles

Reserve Naturelle du
Polder de Sébastopol
Barbâtre

D948
Passage du Gois
(submersible roadway,
low tide only)
D38
Beauvoir-sur-Mer
La Fosse

Inset
Noirmoutier
en l'Île
La Cave
de l'Île
Pâtisserie
Louiche
Musée du
Château
Église
St-Philbert
D5
D948
0 ————— 300m
0 ————— 300yds

Noirmoutier
bridge
Pointe de
la Fosse
Beauvoir-
sur-Mer
Fromentine
La Barre-
de-Monts
Forêt des
Pays de Monts
D38
Île d'Yeu
St-Jean-de-Monts

For listings, see opposite

⌂ **Where to stay**
1 Hôtel Autre Mer
2 Hotel le Noirmoutier
3 Le Général d'Elbée
4 Villa Arthus Bertrand

✕ **Where to eat and drink**
5 L'Assiette au Jardin
6 L'Her du Temps
7 La Marine
8 La Table d'Élise
9 Le Petit Bouchot

One word of warning: the island's shape and road system make Noirmoutier-en-l'Île something of a traffic bottleneck. In July and August the number of vehicles attempting to enter the town – especially when low tide has lured thousands of extra visitors across the causeway – can create impossible hold-ups on the main approach road. On such days, it is better to investigate the sleepy charms of Barbâtre on the south shore, or the excellent museum at La Guérinière (page 62) nearby, or to visit L'Épine, and Port du Morin to the northwest. Even better, ditch the car and hire a bike. If you are good enough at navigating to take the byways, you can skirt the west side of Noirmoutier town and explore the two parts (Le Grand and Le Petit) of the smart north-coast village of Le Vieil. Tranquil out of high season, the island sees plenty of activity in summer. The **Régates du Bois de la Chaise** are classic boat races which bring extra energy to the Plage des Dames, in early August.

GETTING THERE AND AWAY **Car drivers** can access Noirmoutier either at low tide on the D948 across the Passage du Gois or at any time by the D38 past Fromentine and over the bridge. Just before entering Noirmoutier-en-l'Île, look out for the 'Gratipark' sign off to the left. You can park here for free, but even with 400 spaces, it fills up quickly in season.

Half-a-dozen **buses** (route number 13) leave Nantes railway station daily, arriving 1 hour 40 minutes later at the bus station in Noirmoutier-en-l'Île. The same number make the return journey. On the island, the bus stops at Barbâtre and La Guérinière. A full timetable can be found at w paysdelaloire.ter.sncf.com.

GETTING AROUND In high summer, free **buses** take beachgoers from Noirmoutier-en-l'Île to the sands at Bois de la Chaise, Le Vieil and L'Herbaudière (w ville-noirmoutier.fr).

With 80km of cycle tracks, **cycling** is very popular, with bike hire available in all the main towns; most hire companies offer free breakdown assistance. Weekly rates are around €50 for a non-electric bike. Both companies listed are in the capital, Noirmoutier-en-l'Île, and offer roughly the same services.

Cycles Charier 23 Av Joseph Pineau; ✆02 51 39 01 25. Children's bikes, adult on/off-road & electric bikes. Adult bikes from €14/day. Helmets & child seats available, delivery possible. Open all year.

L'Île à Vélo 12 Rue du Boucoud; ✆02 51 35 97 76; e lileavelo@orange.fr; w lile-a-velo.com. Same range & prices as for Cycles Charier.

TOURIST INFORMATION Both of the following branches of the Île de Noirmoutier tourist office (w ile-noirmoutier.com) are fully equipped to provide details of accommodation, bike hire and water- and land-based activities.

Barbâtre Rue du Polder; ✆02 51 39 80 71; ⊕ Apr–Jun & Sep 09.30–12.30 & 14.00–18.00 daily, Jul–Aug 09.00–13.00 & 14.00–19.00 daily, Oct–Mar 09.30–12.30 & 14.00–17.30 Mon–Sat

Noirmoutier-en-l'Île Rue du Général Passaga; ✆02 51 39 12 42; ⊕ Apr–Jun & Sep 09.30–12.30 & 14.00–18.00 daily, Jul–Aug 09.00–13.00 & 14.00–19.00 daily, Oct–Mar 09.30–12.30 & 14.00–17.30 Mon–Sat

WHERE TO STAY *Map, opposite*
A comprehensive list of all the available accommodation options is listed on the tourist office website (page 21), with everything from campsites through B&Bs to Noirmoutier's top hotels. Despite the island's popularity, there are no high-rises to spoil the skyline.

Le Général d'Elbée (25 rooms) 2 Pl d'Armes, Noirmoutier-en-l'Île; ✆02 51 39 10 29; e contact@ generaldelbee.fr; w generaldelbee.fr. After a recent takeover & a thorough renovation, probably the island's swishest address – albeit at a price. In an 18th-century town-centre house, you'll find a spa, heated pool & high standard of interior decoration. There are 6 different categories of room available – all are smart. The hotel added a trendy new cocktail bar a few years ago, along with a terrace where you can enjoy views across the estuary. Free Wi-Fi. €€€€€

Villa Arthus Bertrand (18 rooms) 9 Allée de Chaillot, Noirmoutier-en-l'Île; e contact@ villa-arthusbertand.com; w villa-arthusbertrand. com. One of the island's most exclusive hotels, this former chateau is set behind high walls & nestled amid an extensive wooded park. High ceilings, wood floors & warm colours give it a welcoming, relaxed feel, despite the grandeur of the building. The hotel offers a swimming pool, spa, free Wi-Fi, private parking, outside terrace & restaurant along with a 'mini-club' for children to give the adults time off to relax. €€€€€

Hôtel le Noirmoutier (14 rooms) 57 Rue de la Pointe, Barbatre; **e** contacthotel@lenoirmoutier.fr; **w** lenoirmoutier.fr. At the southern end of town as you arrive on the island via the bridge, is this converted stable block located down a quiet lane & on the beach. Newly opened in 2023, the hotel has a friendly, family feel. It has been refurbished to a high standard with interior colours that reflect the coastal environment around it. There are sea views from every room. The hotel offers private parking, restaurant, bike hire & swimming pool. **€€€€**

Hôtel Autre Mer (27 rooms) 32 Av Joseph Pineau, Noirmoutier-en-l'Île; ℡ 02 51 39 11 77; **e** contact@autremerhotel.fr; **w** autremerhotel.fr. Just north of town on the road to Bois de la Chaise, a decent, renovated mid-range option with free Wi-Fi & private parking. **€€€**

✕ WHERE TO EAT AND DRINK *Map, page 58*

The island is something of a gastro destination. Although the centre of Noirmoutier town has the biggest choice, don't forget to explore behind the castle area, where a number of chic and classy dining options present themselves. The kingpin of cuisine, however, is at the northern tip of the island: the three-Michelin-starred La Marine. In early spring, look out for the *bonnotte* – the much-revered Noirmoutier potato – on restaurant menus.

La Marine L'Herbaudière, 5km northwest of Noirmoutier town; ℡ 02 51 39 23 09; **w** alexandrecouillon.com; ⏱ 12.15–13.15 & 19.15–20.15 Wed–Sat. This is the only restaurant in the Vendée to carry 3 Michelin stars. Culinary wizard Alexandre Couillon works hard to source the highest quality ingredients with the fish coming from the local fish auction on the island & the vegetables from his own garden. The tasting menu follows the seasons & ensures that this has remained the island's top address. If you're having one holiday splash-out, this is the place – but it's a big splash! You may also need to book months in advance. **€€€€€**

L'Assiette au Jardin 9 Rue du Robinet, Noirmoutier-en-l'Île; ℡ 02 51 54 93 95; **w** lassietteaujardin.fr; ⏱ 19.30–21.00 Tue–Sun, noon–13.30 Sat & Sun. A bright, easy-going setting near the castle with a sunny outside terrace & a beautiful menu of seasonal, local produce. **€€€€**

La Table d'Élise L'Herbaudière, 5km northwest of Noirmoutier town; ℡ 02 28 10 68 35; ⏱ 12.15–14.00 & 19.15–21.00 Wed–Sat. Taste Alexandre Couillon's cooking more accessibly & at a fraction of the price of La Marine (see left). **€€€**

Le Petit Bouchot 3 Rue St-Louis, Noirmoutier-en-l'Île; ℡ 02 51 39 32 56; ⏱ 10.00–13.35 & 17.00–21.00 Thu–Mon. Popular restaurant close to the castle, with simple but cosy interior & open-air courtyard for summer evenings. Good value. **€€€**

L'Her du Temps 18 Grande Rue, Noirmoutier-en-l'Île; ℡ 02 51 39 09 28; ⏱ noon–14.00 & 19.00–21.00 Tue–Sat, noon–14.00 Sun. Sublime savoury galettes & sweet crêpes to die for, in this central, straightforward location. **€€**

SHOPPING In the island capital, Noirmoutier-en-l'Île, a stroll along the pedestrianised Grande Rue will introduce you to the best options, with a number of good-quality outlets. A Thursday bric-a-brac market unfolds in the Place St-Louis in summer months, while a swarm of white vans arrives on the main square on market days – Tuesday (1 Apr–30 Sep), Friday and Sunday (24 Jun–2 Sep) – to set up their stalls. The dark building in the centre of the Place de la République is the venue for delicious foodstuffs.

Other market days on the island include: Monday (1 Jul–31 Aug), L'Herbaudière; Wednesday, Barbâtre; Thursday and Sunday (1 Jul–mid-Sep), La Guérinière; and Saturday, L'Épine. As usual, some of these fizzle out around lunchtime.

La Cave de l'Île 19 Grande Rue, Noirmoutier-en-l'Île; ℡ 09 81 67 95 54; ⏱ 10.00–17.00 Mon–Sat, with longer hours in high season. There are a few good wine shops in town, but Lionel & Benjamin sell their wares with humour amid chaos. Island beers & aperitifs, too. English spoken.

Pâtisserie Louiche (formerly Plaisirs et Saveurs) 28 Grande Rue, Noirmoutier-en-l'Île. Buy crunchy 'St Philbert' biscuits from this patisserie on the main street that has recently celebrated 100 years of operations.

WHAT TO SEE AND DO

Beaches Noirmoutier can claim more than a dozen beaches, with the ones nearest to the main town being the busiest in summer. For relative peace and quiet, head instead for those around L'Épine, though the Plage des Dames at Bois de la Chaise is better suited for little ones to swim, having a gentle slope and being supervised in high season.

Église St-Philbert (Noirmoutier-en-l'Île; free) Beneath the tall church that lies just north of the castle, and accessible from near the side of the main altar, is an 11th-century crypt that holds the empty tomb of St Philbert (sometimes called St Philibert), who founded a monastery on the island in AD674. Because of repeated Viking invasions, the saint's remains were removed by his followers to St-Philbert-de-Grand-Lieu (page 231) and, later right across France to the abbey of Tournus in Burgundy, leaving just one vertebra and a rib to be venerated in the Vendée. Press the button for a taped explanation of the church's history (in French), with musical accompaniment. Philbert is credited with converting the population to Christianity and boosting the island's commercial development.

Musée du Château (Pl d'Armes, Noirmoutier-en-l'Île; ✆02 51 39 10 42; w ville-noirmoutier.fr/transitions/le-chateau; ⏱ Jul–Aug 10.00–19.00 Wed–Mon, Sep 10.00–12.30 & 14.30–18.00 Wed–Mon; €8/5/free adult/under 15s/under 6s; pick up English-language info with your ticket) The imposing, dry-moated castle in the centre of the island's capital is visible from afar across the flat landscape. Its combination of fairy-tale turrets and macho walls has meant that it has starred in a number of films, such as Robert Bresson's 1974 movie *Lancelot du Lac*. Owned in 1347 by England's Edward III, and later by the Black Prince, its turbulent history includes being attacked in turn by the English, Spanish, Dutch and French, as well as by 18th-century Vendée rebels and Republicans. Truly multi-purpose, it served as a prison for insurgents of the Paris Commune in 1871, as a centre for internees in World War I, as a victualling centre for the occupying forces during World War II, and as a place to contain German prisoners after the Liberation.

Several flights of steep stone steps lead to various levels containing well-displayed archaeological remains; navigational equipment, maps and souvenirs; and memories of local history – including the bullet-ridden chair in which the Vendean general the Duc d'Elbée was shot, in January 1794, by Republican troops in the square outside the castle gates. Temporary exhibitions are sometimes organised in the upper rooms, before a final flight of wooden stairs leads to a windswept outdoor walkway with fantastic 360° views across the island and beyond. A notice by the ticket office tells you how far you can see from the top (*Author note*: 24km on the day of my visit).

Village Miniature (Route de Noirmoutier, L'Épine; m 06 81 21 69 88; ⏱ Apr–Aug 10.00–19.30 daily, Sep 14.00–18.30 daily; €7/4/free adult/under 13s/under 3s) A vision of France in miniature, from Alsace to Provence, made by Jean-Christophe Fouasson – clearly a man with a passion. Constructing his detailed model houses at a scale of 15cm to the metre, he has created in this small plot a Pyrenean farmhouse, a Loire chateau, a thatched Breton cottage and dozens more – including, of course, some whitewashed Vendean houses. Small children might find it hard to obey the 'don't touch' signs but, in compensation, there is a playground to enjoy and jigsaws to complete. It would suit younger children, but older ones might be bored. You can bring a picnic; drinks and ice creams are available in high season.

Musée des Traditions de l'Île (Pl de l'Église, La Guérinière; ✆ 02 51 39 41 39; ⊕ early Apr–mid-Jun & mid-Sep–mid-Nov 14.00–17.30 Tue–Sat, mid-Jun–mid-Sep 10.00–12.30 & 14.00–17.30 Tue–Sat; €5/3/free adult/under 17s/under 6s) Collect an English-language handout at reception to visit this charming small museum beside the church of La Guérinière, showing the islanders' activities and way of life linked to fishing, salt production, farming and the manufacture of linen in the early 20th century. Everything from rowing boats to wedding dresses is displayed in a series of rooms, several of them arranged to show typical interiors of island homes.

L'Île aux Papillons (ZA des Mandelliers, 5 Rue de la Fassonnière, La Guérinière; ✆ 02 51 35 77 88; w ile-aux-papillons.com; ⊕ Apr–May 14.00–19.00 daily, Jun–Aug 10.00–19.30 daily, Sep 14.00–19.00 daily; €9.40/6.90/free adult/under 12s/under 3s) Artfully arranged pathways lead through a covered enclosure where hundreds of butterflies – some gigantic – flutter freely about your head and settle on the tropical plants growing around about you. Information boards are in French and English. Peering into a glass case, you can watch others struggling from their chrysalises to join the fun, and there's an interesting video, with English subtitles, to tell you about their life cycle. There is also an aviary dedicated to a colourful group of lorikeet parrots.

Resérve Naturelle de Müllembourg You can start at the castle in Noirmoutier town for a nice walk down to the jetty leading southeast from the town quay towards the site of Fort Larron, with panoramic views across the mudflats to the right and the Marais de Müllembourg salt marshes on the left. In winter you should see ducks, geese and small waders; in spring and summer plenty of avocets, egrets and redshanks, especially around the time of high tide. The site is very exposed, so wrap up warmly in winter; take drinks and sunhats in high summer. Further south, next to Le Gois, birds also favour the island's other protected area, the Polder de Sébastopol and there may be guided bird-spotting trips in high season – ask at the tourist office.

The beaches and harbours cycle ride A circuitous cycle route across the north of the island will take you from the Bois de la Chaise in the east to the Port de l'Herbaudière, via the historic centre of Noirmoutier-en-l'Île and the castle museum. The ride is around 19.2km and should take roughly 2 hours if you follow the blue icons that mark the route. That said, the route is not as well marked as it could be and taking a map is essential – the directions can be found in the 'Carte Touristique booklet' produced by the tourist office, which you will find on their website (page 21) or at most bike hire venues . Bicycles are easy to hire on the island (page 59) and an electric bike will make the journey a breeze.

Marais salants Some of Noirmoutier's 130 or so salt-makers (known as *sauniers*) welcome visitors to their saltpans where they demonstrate the process of producing salt crystals through the evaporation of sea water by wind and sun, and sell some of their output. The annual cycle of cleaning and reshaping the clay squares in March, letting in the first sea water in May, harvesting salt from mid-June to early September and then flooding the whole thing to protect it from the vicissitudes of winter is hard work, and the *sauniers* don't often attain their target of a tonne of salt for each individual *oeillet*, or saltpan. Heavy rain is catastrophic, as it dilutes the brine and sets

the process back several stages. Visits are usually free…but they would appreciate it if you bought some salt. Mid-June to early September is best, around the L'Épine area. Each salt pan has its own little hut, with 'Sel' painted on the side.

One operation where the friendly husband-and-wife owners speak good English is Marais Mounet (on the right-hand side of the road that joins Noirmoutier-en-l'Île to L'Épine, before the Village Miniature; m 06 01 71 17 50; w seldenoirmoutier. com; ⊕ Apr–Nov). They produce around 40 tonnes of the so-called 'white gold' from their business.

Boat trips to Île d'Yeu (Rue de la Pointe, Pointe de la Fosse, Barbâtre; ☏ 02 51 60 14 60; w compagnie-vendeenne.com; ⊕ Jul–Aug only, see website for departure dates & times; return fares: €41.90/35/29.50/22.70/6 adult/concessions (over 60, disabled, student)/under 19/under 14/under 4, single trips also available) Departing from Pointe de la Fosse, in the south of the island near the bridge, high-season day trips are possible to the more remote Île d'Yeu, just in case Noirmoutier is not proving 'insular' enough for you. There is free parking near to the departure point; note no bicycles are allowed on board, so hire them on Yeu (page 83).

LA BARRE-DE-MONTS AND FROMENTINE

Forest walks and cycleways wind through the perfumed pine woods that hold the shifting sands in place near the village of La Barre-de-Monts, northwest of Challans. Here, on the mainland side of the Noirmoutier bridge, look out for the strange wooden, canalside *pêcheries*. These are simple cabins from which dangle contraptions that look like giant spiders, with square nets strung between the tips of their 'feet', which are winched down into the water as the tide rises, to catch unwary fish swimming in from the sea. Keep an eye open, too, for the last of the marshland *bourrines* – the small, mud-walled, thatched cottages that were homes for the poorest farming families. For beaches most suitable for child-friendly swimming, try the west-facing ones to the southwest of the Noirmoutier bridge.

Next to La Barre, Fromentine is a sprucely kept place by the sea, with a few hotels and many more campsites. It sports a charming beach in the shadow of the Noirmoutier bridge. As the main port for transporting passengers, vehicles and cargo to the Île d'Yeu, an island lying 25km offshore (page 80), it also has an impressive ferry terminal, the Gare Maritime.

The beachfront promenade, lined with an assortment of small villas, is pedestrianised, so by car you could easily pass it by. Park in a side street (meters or pay-and-display parking) and walk through one of the sandy alleyways between the houses to reach the shore where the 1920s and 30s seafront villas range in style from Art Deco to frankly fake Arabian. Sadly, others were sacrificed during World War II to make way for the ugly lookout posts and gun emplacements of Hitler's Atlantic Wall.

Some forlorn vestiges of that era emerge from the waters from time to time. On 8 August 1944, four German minesweepers took refuge in the narrows here, but were spotted, attacked and sunk by Allied aircraft. At low tide, sections of their rusty hulks can still be seen close to the island.

TOURIST INFORMATION
Office de Tourisme Pl de la Gare, Fromentine; ☏ 02 51 68 51 83; w paysdesaintjeandemonts. fr; ⊕ Apr–mid-Jul 10.00–12.30 & 14.00–18.00

Mon–Sat, mid-Jul–end Aug 09.30–19.00
Mon–Sat, 10.00–12.30 Sun

WHERE TO EAT AND DRINK

Les Navigateurs 2 Av de l'Estacade, Fromentine; 📞 06 56 86 37 31; ⏰ Jul–Aug 08.00–20.00 Mon, Tue, Thu & Sun, 08.30–21.00 Fri & Sat. In a handsome seafront building with a large terrace, tuck into tasty *croque monsieurs* (toasted cheese-&-ham sandwiches), or more substantial, elaborate dishes. €€€

Côte et Café 3 Av du Phare, Fromentine; 📞 02 51 49 46 69; ⏰ 08.00–21.30 Fri–Tue. Situated not far from the seafront, a good-value brasserie-style place with standard fare served inside or on the terrace. €€

WHAT TO SEE AND DO

Le Daviaud: Écomusée du Marais Breton-Vendéen (Signposted off the D38C & D22, 5km south of Fromentine; 📞 02 51 93 84 84; w ledaviaud.fr; ⏰ early Feb–early Apr 10.00–18.00 Tue–Fri, early Apr–late Jun 10.00–19.00 Tue–Fri, 14.00–19.00 Sat–Sun, late Jun–mid-Sep 10.00–19.00 Mon–Fri, 14.00–19.00 Sat–Sun, mid-Sep–early Nov 14.00–18.00 Tue–Fri & Sun; adult/under 18s/under 6: 4 Feb–7 Apr €5/3.50/free, 8 Apr–17 Sep €10/7/free, 18 Sep–5 Nov €7/4.9/free) A modern entrance building welcomes you to this eco-museum, and the tour begins with some talking heads (translated into English) recounting their connections with the marshland terrain. Outside, you can wander through the marshes, perhaps surprising a heron or a goat, meet a giant Breton horse and visit the several rebuilt *bourrines* (traditional thatched houses) which either have original furniture, agricultural machinery or show cinema-screen-sized videos of traditional dancing.

Wandering the marshes is relaxing and recent investment in renewing this place has been well worthwhile. Alongside working saltpans are interesting descriptions of the region's salt industry. From July to mid-September there could be afternoon demonstrations of traditional crafts such as basket-weaving, or punting in flat-bottomed *yoles* (formerly the only form of transport through the flooded marshland in winter). To take in the whole of the site could require a good couple of hours – and a fair amount of walking on wooden walkways. There's not much shade, so take protective clothing in hot weather. Binoculars might be useful to help spot the birdlife.

Pey de la Blet (Route de la Rive, off the D38, 1.5km southwest of La Barre; free access at all times) In a land as flat as this, getting above the treeline is a rarity. Here, you can eyeball passing birds from a wooden platform, level with the tops of the pines, and enjoy a magnificent 360° view out towards the Île d'Yeu or inland across the marshes. You can park under the trees, cross the cycle track, and start climbing the 144 wooden steps to the tower at the top. Exhausting!

Île d'Yeu trips (Compagnie Yeu-Continent, GareMaritime, Port-Fromentine; 📞 02 52 32 32 32; w yeu-continent.fr; ⏰ year-round, see website for detailed departures; return fares: €45/31.60/24.70/8.70 adult/under 18s/under 13s/under 4s; fares are slightly cheaper if booked more than 1 month ahead) Fromentine is one departure point for excursions to the beautiful Île d'Yeu (page 80), 25km offshore. (Other boats leave from St-Gilles, page 79.) Fast *vedettes* convey foot passengers across, usually in around half an hour. If you're hoping to park while you visit the island, make sure you arrive in good time to deposit your car at Compagnie Yeu Continent's free car park about 15 minutes' walk away from the terminal. Directions can be found on their website.

Balade GPS (Rentable from the tourist office in Fromentine, page 63; €9/6 full/half day; returnable deposit or passport required) As an enjoyable family outing, you can rent a special GPS that will guide you on a 7km tour of discovery in the forest, though you do need a good knowledge of French.

BOIS-DE-CÉNÉ

A few ancient houses dating from Renaissance times add to the attraction of this village 10km north of Challans. The restored 14th-century church contains Romanesque pillars with interesting stone carvings on the top – including some depicting the Seven Deadly Sins (you may wish to cover the children's eyes for the saucier ones).

For tourist information, see Challans (page 67). With no recommendable places to refresh yourself in or near this small village, Challans is also the best place to retreat for lunch, or buy ingredients for a picnic to bring with you.

WHAT TO SEE AND DO
L'Abbaye de l'Île Chauvet (Signposted off the D28 Châteauneuf–Bois-de-Céné road; w festivalîlechauvet.fr; ⊕ Jul–mid-Sep 14.00–18.00 Sun–Fri; €5/free adult/ under 10s) The site of this ancient abbey, just to the west of the village, was indeed once a small *île*, or island. Take the D28 Châteauneuf road and then turn right across marshes drained by the monks who lived here. A short woodland path leads from the grassy car park to the romantic ruins of the abbey church. Founded by Benedictines in 1130, it was much damaged by the English in 1381, taken over in 1679 and renovated by monks of the Camaldoli order, and later abandoned following its destruction by the Republicans after the French Revolution.

A low Romanesque doorway admits to the roofless chancel. To its south stands the fairly intact refectory building with, on its first floor – beneath magnificent original oak beams – a small museum. Its eclectic collection includes rough-hewn statues of saints, a few lace headdresses, engravings of other abbeys in the area, and an account of the coded signals used by monks during their mealtime silence to ask for milk, water, wine or a knife. Downstairs, seated on hard, monastic-style benches in the low-ceilinged *cave aux moines*, you can see a romantic video about the abbey, accompanied by Gregorian chant. A festival takes place here in August, with concerts and other events – see the website for dates and details.

Observatoire (Off the D28, take the road signposted to the abbey – see above; free access at all times) The small, thatched wooden observatory overlooking the marshland near Île Chauvet Abbey has an information board (in French only) about the migrating species of birds that you might see nearby. Just a field away is a platform installed to encourage storks to nest. If you train your binoculars on it, you might be lucky enough to see some during spring or summer.

Le Petit Moulin de Châteauneuf (Châteauneuf, 3km southwest of Bois-de-Céné) The sails of this windmill, built in 1703, provided power right up until 2016, when the Vrignaud family ceased operations after seven generations of milling. Sadly, it's now just a photo stop – though a very picturesque one. You can still imagine its slatted sails straining and groaning in high winds like the sails of a ship at sea.

LA GARNACHE

Clustered around the ruins of its medieval castle, this village 6km northeast of Challans was for four centuries an important feudal stronghold and the base of a regional government.

3

It was near La Garnache that the future Vendean leader Charette was living when, in 1793, he was dragged from his bed by local peasants, who insisted that his naval experience made him ideally suited to lead them in their revolt against the Republican army (page 12). Given his eventual sticky ending, he may wish that he'd turned over and gone back to sleep. On a lighter note, the local culinary speciality here is *le Garnachoix* goat's cheese.

For tourist information, see Challans (see opposite).

✖ **WHERE TO EAT AND DRINK** Those who don't want to splash out on the delights on offer at Le Petit St Thomas can head to the Crêperie du Château just over the road.

Le Petit St Thomas 25 Rue de-Lattre-de-Tassigny; ☏ 02 51 49 05 99; **w** restaurant-petit-st-thomas.com; ⏲ noon–14.00 & 19.30–21.00 Wed–Sat, noon–14.00 Sun. This smart, yet welcoming restaurant opposite the castle is just the place for a special occasion, with elegant décor & even more elegant food & service. It is not a cheap experience, but it won a Michelin Bib Gourmand award in 2023 (indicating good value for money) & you won't be disappointed. €€€€

Crêperie du Château 1 Rue de Challans; ☏ 02 51 60 19 89 ; ⏲ noon–14.00 & 19.00–21.00 Tue & Fri–Sat, noon–14.00 Wed. Run by 2 elderly ladies, this quaint café sits at the entrance to the Château Féodal. Cakes & cold & hot drinks are served along with delicious crêpes. In the summer there is a medium-sized terrace outside & inside you will find further seating along with a table of secondhand tea sets to peruse & possibly purchase while you wait. €€

WHAT TO SEE AND DO

Château Féodal (Route de Nantes) Under new ownership since 2022 and closed to the public at the time of writing, this ruined 13th- to 15th-century stronghold was built by the lords of La Garnache, then partially destroyed in 1622 at the behest of Louis XIII and further still under the Revolution, which has left just the 12th-century keep and two vertical slices of the castle's round stone towers. Sadly the rooms of the keep are no longer viewable but the ramparts and the remains of the defences conjure up at least some of the castle's history and are still visible from the street nearby.

Chapelle de la Victoire (Route de St-Christophe; ☏ 02 51 93 11 08; ⏲ 09.00–18.00 daily; free) The stocky stone chapel at the east end of the village, with its elegant little spire, was built to commemorate a naval battle at faraway Lepanto in 1571 that resulted in a decisive Christian victory over the Ottomans. The building was restored in 1712.

CHALLANS

As the '*capitale du canard*', or 'duck capital', this pleasant inland market town was once to France what Aylesbury was to England, and you will find many duck-related dishes on local menus. Formerly reared in enormous numbers in the surrounding marshes, these birds have now been overtaken by the free-range black chickens (*poulet noir*) and guineafowl (*pintade*). Bristling with cafés and smart shops, the town of Challans is particularly renowned for its terrific market on Tuesday mornings. From the countryside around, shoppers come to stock up on fresh fish, vegetables, cheese and other produce in the covered food hall; outside, hundreds of stalls fill the streets and squares with local colour and offer clothes, farm equipment, gadgets and even live poultry. (On Friday and Saturday mornings, the food hall is open on its own.) For local treats, search out menus

AUTREFOIS CHALLANS…LA FOIRE (w autrefoischallans.com) On four Thursdays in July and August (dates vary, see website) the clock is turned back to 1910, and more than 1,000 locals dress up in turn-of-the-last-century costume. The men sport blue denim smocks and heavy clogs, or traditional marshland garb of black close-fitting trousers and short, matador-style jackets with jaunty small-brimmed hats. The women wear pretty lace *coiffes* or the face-shading white bonnets known as *quichenottes* (supposedly a corruption of the English 'kiss not' – a name said to date from the time of English occupation during the Hundred Years War) that were a common sight until 40 years ago. Horse-drawn carts clatter through the streets, children re-enact schoolroom scenes, farmers trade ducks and chickens, and old folk spin, weave, strip kernels from corncobs and indulge in old-fashioned diversions like *l'aluette* (a boisterous card game) or *palets* (a riotous contest involving metal discs thrown at a board). There's food, music and an old-time wedding parade.

LES PUCES LIGNERONNAISES (St-Christophe-du-Ligneron; ⏲ 3rd Sun July & 2nd Sun Aug 07.00–19.00; nominal admission charge) This vast open-air flea market is held twice a year on a village sports ground 9km southeast of Challans. Around 200 stalls offer many happy hours of treasure hunting among chests of huge, monogrammed linen sheets, racks of old picture postcards, and displays of furniture, glass and bric-a-brac.

with duck, black-feathered chicken and *flan maraîchin* (pastry case filled with egg custard).

TOURIST INFORMATION
Office de Tourisme 1 Rue de l'Hôtel de Ville, Challans; ☏ 02 51 93 19 75; w gochallansgois.fr; ⏲ 09.30–12.30 & 14.00–17.30 Tue–Wed & Fri, 09.30–12.30 Thu & Sat

WHERE TO STAY AND EAT
Château de la Vérie [map, page 54] (21 rooms) Off the D69, 3km southwest of Challans; ☏ 02 51 35 33 44; e info@chateau-de-la-verie.com; w chateau-de-la-verie.com. Roll down the tree-lined driveway & feel like lord or lady of the manor at this regal old country house, where nymphs & statues await your arrival. Each room is different, decorated in classical style. Renowned restaurant (not cheap! €€€€), swimming pool & tennis. Sumptuous grounds surround the property. B/fast inc. €€€€€
Au P'tit Farphadet 53 Rue Gambetta; ☏ 02 51 49 02 93; ⏲ noon–14.00 Mon, Tue & Thu, noon–

14.00 & 19.15–20.30 Wed, Fri & Sat. Well worth the short walk from the town centre. Chic dining room, outdoor terrace, super value & great food. Children's menu. A family business that deserves support. €€€
Delicafé 13 Rue Gobin; ⏲ 08.30–18.30 Tue–Sat. You can choose from any of the traditional cafés around the market, but this modern place provides a peaceful alternative – & coffee in all sorts of hot & cold creations, well above average in quality. Good-value b/fasts. €

SALLERTAINE

At one time an island, delightful Sallertaine village sits on a rocky outcrop overlooking the flat landscape of the Marais Breton. Formerly a busy centre to which farming families would travel by flat-bottomed boat on Sundays to attend

Mass, the village is now a permanent home for a dozen artisans and attracts further artists and craftworkers in the summer months. Their whereabouts are indicated by a large wall plaque by the bus stop: some quirky old bicycles, placed around the village, carry messages offering you encouragement as you seek them out.

You can take a canoe trip on the canals around the 'island', or follow a signposted walk into the countryside in the footsteps of 'Jean Nesmy', the fictional hero of a 19th-century novel by celebrated writer René Bazin. In 1899, Bazin used the village and its surroundings as the setting for *La Terre qui Meurt* (*The Dying Land*), in which he painted a poignant image of the pressures on rural life brought about by the drift from the land at a time of encroaching industrialisation.

Celebrations of the artisans' skills take place across three or four Mondays in late July/early August with the Nocturnes, encompassing a craft fair and street entertainment. Early August is also the time for the village antiques fair.

TOURIST INFORMATION
Office de Tourisme Mairie, 38 Rue de Verdun; 📞 02 51 35 51 81; w sallertaine.fr; ⏁ 13.30–15.30 Mon–Fri, 09.30–noon Sat

---

✕ WHERE TO EAT AND DRINK
La Cantine du Chêne Vert 6 Pl de la Liberté; 📞 02 28 17 63 81; ⏁ Jul–Aug (check website as hours vary), Sep–Jun noon–14.00 Tue–Thu, noon–14.00 & 18.30– 23.00 Fri–Sat, plus every 3rd Sun of month. With a butcher turned chef in the kitchen, this place prides itself on serving good quality local meats alongside traditional, homemade dishes. The décor is welcoming & warm, with walls dotted with colourful paintings – appropriate for Sallertaine – & there's a large,

pleasant terrace on which to relax. €13 will buy you the plat du jour that includes 2 courses, making this a well-priced gem in the heart of the village. €€€
Le Marais Gourmand 2 Rue du Pelican; 📞 02 51 93 13 02; w restaurant-lemaraisgourmand. com; ⏁ noon–14.00 Mon–Fri, noon–13.30 Sun. Centrally located with a constantly changing menu on offer (so check the website) at various prices. Small terrace at rear. €€€

WHAT TO SEE AND DO
L'Île aux Artisans (Around the village centre; w lileauxartisans.fr; ⏁ extended exhibitions Jul–Aug, see website for details) Around a dozen artisans exhibit year-round, but each summer some of the village's older buildings are transformed into pop-up shops and studios for potters, woodturners, furniture restorers and other craftspeople who sell everything from wooden toys to weather vanes. In November and December, Sallertaine's ancient church (see below) hosts four popular Arts d'Hiver weekends, where artisans exhibit in the run-up to Christmas.

Église Romane (Place de la Liberté; 📞 02 51 35 51 81; ⏁ Jul–Aug) A witch's-hat-type spire crowns the village's 12th-century church, replaced by the newer, bigger church on the main square in 1910. It was saved in the nick of time from total destruction in 1915 by the intervention of René Bazin (see above). Its interior has undergone recent restoration, to reveal traces of medieval wall paintings lying beneath the layers of whitewash.

La Route du Sel (49 Rue de Verdun ; 📞 02 51 93 03 40; w laroutedusel.com; ⏁ Jul–Aug 09.00–19.00 daily, other months by pre-arrangement; a variety of guided packages available, see website for booking & prices) Renting a two-person canoe and paddling for an hour or so on the 'Salt Route' around the former island of

Sallertaine gives a real marshlander's feel for the flat Marais Breton. An assortment of longer, guided trips includes outings featuring magical dawn journeys, with breakfast, hearing the awakening wildlife of the marshes; trips with a convivial barbecue lunch, or a candlelit barbecue under the stars; a jaunt in a ten-person canoe to the nearby Moulin à Vent de Rairé (see below); and a guided marshland walk of 2 hours, taking in local places of interest. It can be scorching on hot summer days, so take hats and suitable clothing.

Moulin à Vent de Rairé (Off the D103 St-Urbain road; \ 06 37 77 69 57; w moulin-a-vent-de-raire.com; ⊕ Apr–end Sep 14.00–18.00 daily; €4.50/2.50 adult/child) The enthusiastic and entertaining miller takes visitors up rickety wooden staircases to visit three floors of this working windmill – built in 1555, and claimed to have been in continuous use since. The view across the marshes from the top-floor window, regularly interrupted by the wood-slatted sails creaking past, is breathtaking – though anybody with small children in tow will need to watch out for the flailing machinery and narrow, open stairs. Visits are only by guided tour, which is done in French with English translation. There's a café and gift shop, too. Leaflets are available to clarify the explanations and demonstrations.

La Bourrine à Rosalie (Le Robinet, on the D119, south of Sallertaine; m 06 32 52 09 23; ⊕ Apr, May, Jun & Sep 14.30–18.30 daily, Jul–Aug 10.30–12.30 & 14.30–18.30 daily; €5/3/free adult/under 19s/under 6s) Nestling in the marshes is this reed-thatched, two-roomed cottage, inhabited until 1971 by the doughty old lady whose photograph hangs on the wall inside. The simple, white-painted interior gives an (albeit slightly sanitised) image of the hard life in one of these isolated marshland farms, far from any road, in which beds needed long legs to stay above winter flood waters and electricity was not installed until 1961. Neat labels explain the origins and purposes of items on display. Outside, typical of these rural homesteads, you'll find a small orchard, a few ducks and a donkey.

NOTRE-DAME-DE-MONTS

A seaside village 6km south of the Noirmoutier toll bridge and just north of the better-known resort of St-Jean-de-Monts, this reputedly has the finest-textured sand on the Vendée coast. As you can guess from the 'sails' adorning its traffic roundabout, Notre-Dame is firmly orientated towards 'windy' themes. You can try dinghy sailing, windsurfing and sand yachting at the Pôle Nautique, near the north end of the beach. An unusual Jardin du Vent (page 70) has been created in and around an old windmill – there's even a wind festival (Festival à Tout Vent) every July.

In calmer mode, the resort also lays on free concerts and street-theatre performances for summer visitors, and leisure- and pleasure-seekers can find places to have a go at quad biking or mini-golf. Market day is Sunday.

TOURIST INFORMATION
Office de Tourisme 6 Rue de la Barre; \ 02 51 58 84 97; w paysdesaintjeandemonts.fr; ⊕ opening times change monthly see website for details

◀ WHERE TO EAT AND DRINK
L'Estran [map, page 54] 55 Rue de St-Jean (on the D38, south of town); \ 02 51 58 86 48; w restaurantlestran.com; ⊕ Jul–Aug 10.00–13.45 & 18.30–20.30 Thu–Sat, 10.00–13.45

3

Wed & Sun; for other months, see website. With a focus on shellfish, but plenty of other choices, too – steak, rabbit, fish & a good range of desserts. Children's menu, & menus translated into English. €€

WHAT TO SEE AND DO

Jardin du Vent (29 Rue Gilbert-Cesbron; ☎ 02 28 11 26 43; w jardinduvent.fr; ⏰ Apr, May, Jun & Sep 10.00–noon & 14.00–18.00 Tue–Fri, 14.00–18.00 Sat–Sun, Jul–Aug 10.00–19.00 Tue–Fri, 14.00–19.00 Sat–Sun; free to visit, check website for prices for guided tours & workshops) There's no missing the collection of triangular sails twirling in the breeze on top of a restored windmill that raises its head above the town centre. Inside, a new exhibition each year takes a different wind-related theme; once you emerge into the grounds an ingenious series of devices to enjoy includes wind chimes, machines that blow bubbles or puff fragrances, colourful kites and windsocks, and an unusual sail-powered roundabout. Some English-language information is available from the ticket office, though it might not quite tie up exactly with the exhibits – a knowledge of French is helpful here.

Biotopia (50 Av de l'Abbé Thibaud, 1km north of Notre-Dame; ☎ 02 28 11 20 93; w biotopia.fr; ⏰ early Apr–late Jun 14.00–18.00 Wed–Mon, late Jun–mid-Sep 10.00–19.00 Wed–Sun, 14.00–19.00 Sat–Sun, mid-Sep–early Nov 14.00–18.00 Wed–Sun; €7/4/free adult/under18s/under 6s) This small visitor centre in the pine forest delivers an ecological message through interactive displays and guided tours. There is a short video that provides a day in the life of the plants and animals living in the dunes. There is also the option to hire an iPad that allows you to discover 3D animals hiding on a table, and which can also be used on a marked nature trail to provide further information on the plants and wildlife that you might stumble across in the woods and dunes.

Kulmino: Salle Panoramique (La Croix, Route du Perrier (D82), 3km east of Notre-Dame; w kulmino.fr; ⏰ early Apr–late Jun 14.00–18.00 Wed–Sun; late Jun–mid-Sep 10.00–19.00 Mon–Fri, 14.00–19.00 Sat & Sun, mid-Sep–early Nov 14.00–18.00 Wed–Sun; €5/4/free adult/under 18s & students/under 6s) Nothing makes you feel more gnat-like than standing beneath this 73m-high *château d'eau*, or water tower. And nothing is better for making you realise how flat this countryside is than to enjoy the panorama from the top! Water from here has flowed through a 17.6km pipeline to supply the neighbouring Île d'Yeu since 1961. A lift takes you up to a louvre-shaded glass hall where loudspeaker points offer lengthy (20-minute) lectures in French, English, German – or even the local *patois*, or dialect – on the local landscape and traditions. Outside, fixed binoculars and orientation plaques help you make the most of this magnificent viewpoint over the Marais Breton-Vendéen. You could probably take an hour to visit; choose a clear day to get the best views of the marshes, the coast, the Île d'Yeu and the isle of Noirmoutier.

Pont d'Yeu (Just off the D38, south of Notre-Dame: look out for the signpost on your right & follow the right-hand fork) Not, alas, a bridge to the Île d'Yeu, this natural phenomenon is just a rocky spit of land 50m wide and several kilometres long, heading in that direction. Lying to the south of Notre-Dame's main beach, it is uncovered only at the lowest low tides. (In the current tide tables, look for the days with the highest figures in the *coefficients* column.) Legend says that St Martin wanted to evangelise the people of the Île d'Yeu but could find no boat to take him there. In exchange for the soul of the first Christian to use it, the Devil offered to build a path across, and the saint accepted – on condition it was completed before cockcrow. Satan's crew set to work, plying the local cockerel with alcohol to buy extra time – but the confused bird crowed even earlier than usual, so the route was never finished.

ST-JEAN-DE-MONTS

Compared with its coastal near-neighbours, St-Jean-de-Monts is a high-rise giant that – for better or worse – ticks all the resort boxes. On the seafront, apartment blocks are almost fully shuttered even in May and June, but in high season the masses arrive and the shades come up. Across the wide esplanade with its welcome free car parking, marvel at a generously proportioned beach of perfect sand that stretches as far as the eye can see. It's not surprising that St-Jean bills itself a 'Station Kid', reflecting its desire to ensure that youngsters are well catered for. In season, teenagers scoot along the seafront on rollerblades or propel themselves on four-seater quadri-cycles, while younger children enjoy roundabouts, beach swings, slides and inflatables, or pedal old-fashioned metal pony carts on the sands. With countless bars, fast-food restaurants, discos and a casino, the place has all the trappings necessary to accompany a good beach holiday – there is no lack of night-time entertainment either.

Anyone looking for sporty pursuits will find sand yachting at the northern end of the beach, zip-wires in the forest, plus golf, tennis, riding and archery and the Océabul indoor leisure pool on the seafront. Details of all these can be found at the spacious tourist office in the resort's conference centre, which also hosts regular high-quality art exhibitions.

But the 8km of flat, beautiful sands remain the resort's main attraction. For those seeking the heart of the original fishing village of St-Jean, now half a mile inland, search out the lovely market hall as well as the attractively restored church with its 17th-century bell tower and pointed wooden-tiled spire. Market days are Wednesdays and Saturdays, daily in July and August.

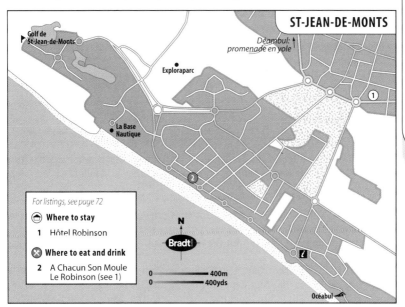

ST-JEAN-DE-MONTS

Golf de
St-Jean-de-Monts

Déambul:
promenade en yole

Exploraparc

La Base
Nautique

1

2

N

Bradt

For listings, see page 72

⊖ **Where to stay**
1 Hôtel Robinson

✕ **Where to eat and drink**
2 A Chacun Son Moule
   Le Robinson (see 1)

0 ———— 400m
0 ———— 400yds

Océabul

TOURIST INFORMATION

Office de Tourisme 67 Esplanade de la Mer; 📞02 72 78 80 80; w paysdesaintjeandemonts. fr; ⏰ opening times change each month – see website for details. Hook up to the free Wi-Fi here (no code required) or you can access it at 20 hotspots around town.

 WHERE TO STAY AND EAT *Map, page 71*

St-Jean is not top-heavy with large hotels and the food is centred around 'fast'. Some good exceptions are listed below.

Hôtel Robinson (52 rooms) 28 Bd du Maréchal Leclerc; 📞02 51 59 20 20; e infos@ hotel-lerobinson.com; w hotel-lerobinson. com; ⏰ closed Dec–Jan. St-Jean has a number of hotels but this Logis de France establishment is possibly the best, particularly given its recent upgrade. Rooms have AC, satellite TV & free Wi-Fi; facilities include a decent heated swimming pool, jacuzzi & gym. Popular with British golfers, discounts on green fees offered. Family-run, it also has an excellent restaurant (see below). €€€

Le Robinson At Hôtel Robinson, see above. High-quality meals served in the restaurant of the above hotel, near the town centre. In fine weather, diners can make use of the large terrace; the interior is smart & the choice is better than most. The 'vegetarian' menu offers mackerel & eggs. €€€€

A Chacun Son Moule 22 Esplanade de la Mer; m 06 67 45 07 42; ⏰ Apr–Sep noon–13.45 & 19.00–20.45 Tue–Sat, noon–13.45 Sun. A clever play on the saying '*A chacun son goût*' or 'each to his own taste', this seafront option is one for the mussel lover. Slightly quirky, but the bivalves are served up with a choice of delicious sauces accompanied by a generous helping of crispy home-cut chips. €€

SPORTS AND ACTIVITIES

Golf de St-Jean-de-Monts Av des Pays-de-la-Loire, near northwest end of beach; 📞02 51 58 82 73; w golfsaintjeandemonts.fr. This 18-hole links course by Yves Bureau – 9 holes among pine trees, 9 alongside the sea – is rated as one of the best in western France. 18 holes: €81/59 high/low season.

La Base Nautique Av de l'Estacade; 📞02 51 58 00 75; w labasenautique.fr; ⏰ 09.00–12.30 & 14.00–18.00 Mon–Sun. If it's watersports you want, go no further. Kayaks, stand-up paddleboards, sailing & kitesurfing equipment are all available here, as well as lessons. Availability of specific activities varies across the year; check the website or phone for details.

Océabul Pl de l'Europe, Esplanade de la Mer; 📞02 28 11 00 00; w vert-marine.com; ⏰ year-round daily but times vary – see website; swimming only: €6.75/5.20/free adult/under 12s/under 3s, extra charges for use of hammam & sauna. An indoor swimming pool, with sauna, hammam & various activity classes.

WHAT TO SEE AND DO

Exploraparc (Route de la Parée Jésus, near golf club; m 06 44 36 04 83; w exploraparc.com; ⏰ Apr–Oct, see website for full details; from €24/22/19/15/13 per activity adult/under 14s/under 10s/6–7 yrs/3–5 yrs) Whirrings, whizzings and whoops of joy fill the air in the fragrant pine forest. Energetic folk of all ages don harnesses and helmets, and are given detailed safety instructions before climbing up into the trees and embarking on one of several circuits – colour-coded to show difficulty – varying between 1m and 12m above the ground. Other activities can be found here too, such as laser-tag, escape games and virtual reality amusements. Not for very young children, nor for the fainthearted. Advance booking advisable.

Déambul (6 Pl de la Rochejaquelein, Le Perrier, 7km west of St-Jean on the D753; 📞02 55 51 58 03; ⏰ Jul–Aug departs 10.00, 11.00, 14.00, 15.00, 16.00 & 17.00 Mon–Fri, 10.00 & 11.00 Sun, booking essential; €5/free adult/3–5 yrs) A guided

30-minute trip through the open marshland in a *yole*, a traditional flat-bottomed boat, poled along the narrow canals 6km northeast of St-Jean. The return leg of the journey is taken in a *calèche* (horse-and-cart), making a 2-hour outing in all. Commentary is in French.

SOULLANS

This large village on the frontier of the marshes and the hillier *bocage*, 6km south of Challans, was the birthplace of one of the Vendée's best-known painters, Charles Milcendeau (1872–1919), who cut his artistic teeth by sketching the customers at his father's café on the market square. One of Milcendeau's works, *La Flagellation*, hangs in the local church.

TOURIST INFORMATION
Office de Tourisme   15 Pl Jean Yole; ☏ 02 51 35 28 68; w paysdesaintjeandemonts.fr; ⊕ Jul–Aug only

WHERE TO EAT AND DRINK
Le Gabion   10 Pl Jean Yole; ☏ 02 51 68 03 53. Good lunchtime choice, with generous portions, choice of starters & mains. Close to the tourist office, this represents good value. Booking advisable, little English is spoken. €€€

WHAT TO SEE AND DO
Musée Charles Milcendeau (84 Chemin du Bois-Durand; ☏ 02 51 35 03 84; w musee-milcendeau.fr; ⊕ early Apr–late Jun & late Oct–early Nov 14.00–18.00 Wed–Sun, late Jun–mid-Sep 14.00–19.00 Mon–Sun; €5/4/free adult/under 18s & disabled/under 6s) Partially created from two *bourrines*, this charming museum lies deep in the heart of the countryside, 3km south of Soullans. It is devoted to two of the village's most celebrated inhabitants: the painter Charles Milcendeau (1872–1919), whose home this was, and his contemporary Léopold Robert (1878–1956) – a doctor and, later, writer and politician. Under the pseudonym 'Jean Yole', Robert published many books in praise of the Vendée, and is commemorated here by a small collection of photographs and objects, and a biographical film.

A bright, air-conditioned, state-of-the-art gallery houses dozens of portraits of Milcendeau's family and neighbours – exactly the sort of ruddy-cheeked country folk you still see in the markets today – as well as atmospheric domestic scenes and some dramatic, wintry views of the flooded land that surrounded his marshland home. (If you have driven across parched August pastures to get here, you may feel he went a bit over the top in some of these, but February's rains often produce the same effect today.) Cleverly shaped windows frame the landscapes outside almost like those within. Tablets are available to borrow during your tour, but it is probably enough to admire the paintings and watch the films – which have an English-language option on show. One concentrates on the life of Milcendeau, his love affair with Spain and the influences his visits had there on his work. There is also a 20-minute film about Jean Yole, a worthy, but less visual subject.

The painter's bedroom-cum-studio in the second house is a total contrast to the modernity in the first. In place of whitewash, Milcendeau covered the walls with stylised birds, cats and flowers in vivid blues and yellows, arranged stuffed pigeons at the windows and reshaped the doorways in Moorish style – all in an attempt to imbue his damp cottage with the sunshine and colour of his beloved Spain.

The quiet village on the edge of the *bocage*, 9km southeast of Challans, was, until the end of the Middle Ages, a centre of considerable feudal power – as testified by the remains of its small stone fortress. Visitors flock to Commequiers today to enjoy a fun family outing on the Vélo-Rail (see below), an imaginative re-use of an abandoned section of railway track. Market days are Wednesdays and Saturdays.

The restaurant at the station previously provided proper French cuisine but has now closed, and with little to recommend in terms of a replacement, visitors are advised to look to the nearby towns of Apremont (page 100) or Coëx (page 101) for food and drink.

TOURIST INFORMATION There is no permanent tourist office in Commequiers. In high season (Jul–Aug) there is a tourist information point at the Château de Commequiers; in low season, contact the St-Gilles-Croix-de-Vie Tourist Office (page 79).

WHAT TO SEE AND DO
Château de Commequiers (Off the D754, just north of the village centre; w amisduvieuxchateaudecommequiers.com; free access at all times) The eight handsome – though crumbling – round towers of the stone castle (terminally damaged in 1628 on the orders of Cardinal Richelieu) give these ancient ruins the appearance of the very best kind of sandcastle. It is all brought colourfully to life once a year, in August, for the village's Fête Médiévale. The rest of the year, you can download the LegendR VR app (€5). Created by the local tourist office, which has worked hard to make the site more engaging, the app provides visitors with a more interactive experience, highlighting points of interest and providing a view of the castle as it would have been in the 15th century. There is also a children's playground and a colourful display that maps the castle's history, and it makes a great place for a picnic.

Vélo-Rail (Route de St-Gilles (D754); ☎ 02 51 54 79 99; w velorail-vendee.fr; ⊕ Apr–Nov, exact dates & times vary, consult website; advance booking essential; from €29 per wagon; journey takes around 1hr 45mins) Lively children can work off surplus energy by pedalling their parents through the countryside on rattling flat-bed wagons (known as *draisines*) along 9km of disused railway line. Each wagon can take two adults and two children (three if they are little). Everyone sets off in convoy at fixed times, with strict instructions to maintain a 50m gap between each four-person vehicle (allow even more space when the rails are wet). Good written instructions in English are shown to customers at the departure point. The rural route takes in level crossings and small viaducts, and gives views of the River Vie. Take cold drinks and snacks to fuel the pedallers en route. It's good fun, and fortunately there is now a turntable at the far end, so there's no longer any need to lift the 80kg wagons off the rails when it's time to turn around for the homeward journey! In the high season's heat – perhaps thankfully for tired legs – the route is 2km shorter.

Well-endowed with dunes, pine trees, a rugged rocky shoreline and a multitude of neighbouring beaches that stretch far to its north, this little town lays claim to being one of the Vendée's earliest coastal resorts. Modern St-Hilaire encompasses a tranquil town centre far from the waves, a forest which is a favourite with joggers, walkers and cyclists, the marshland village of Notre-Dame-de-Riez and the more dramatically sited clifftop resort of Sion-sur-l'Océan. Sheltered among the trees north of town are dinosaur parks, zip-wires, waterparks, mini-golf and all the essential child-friendly add-ons to a beach holiday. A modest population of around 11,500 swells in summer to 150,000. Aside from the recent seaside buildings, there are still a few attractive seafront villas dating from the 1880s, and St-Hilaire's 17th-century church contains several religious paintings by local artist Henry Simon, who lived and worked here. Markets take place on Thursday and Sunday; there's a vintage car rally on Easter Monday.

TOURIST OFFICE

Office de Tourisme 21 Pl Gaston-Pateau; \02 51 54 31 97; w payssaintgilles-tourisme. fr; ⏲ Mid-Sep to the end of May 09.30–12.30 & 14.00–18.00 Mon–Sat, Jun & 1st half Sep 09.30–12.30 & 14.00–18.30 Mon–Sat, 10.00–12.30 Sun, Jul–Aug 09.30–13.00 & 14.00–19.00 Mon–Sat, 10.00–13.00 & 16.00–18.30 Sun. An additional information kiosk on the Av de la Pège (D123) is open in high season (⏲ early Jul–late Aug 10.00–12.30 & 16.00–19.00 Mon–Sat).

WHERE TO EAT AND DRINK

Pilours 6 Av de la Corniche; \02 21 76 03 85; w pilours.fr; ⏲ noon–22.00 Mon–Sun. One of the pricier restaurants in town, though its decked open terrace with views over the Atlantic Ocean can't be beaten. The fish-themed interior reflects the menu & fresh fish is served daily. €€€€

201 Forest Avenue 201 Av de la Forêt, Sion sur l'Océan, St-Hilaire-de-Riez; \02 51 60 82 01; w 201forestavenue.fr; ⏲ noon–14.00 & 19.00–21.15 Tue–Sat, noon–14.00 Sun. Despite having a rather Hollywood name & sharing its building with a 10-pin bowling alley, this is an upmarket option

with a large, chic dining room overlooking the sea. Good value during the week, pricier menus at the w/end. €€€

Le Lamparo 221 Av de la Corniche; \02 51 55 01 83; w restaurant-lamparo.fr; ⏲ Apr–Jun & Sep–Dec 12.15–14.00 & 19.15–21.00 Thu–Mon, Jul–Aug 12.15–14.00 & 19.15–21.00 Mon–Sun, Jan–Mar 12.15–14.00 & 19.15–21.00 Mon, Thu, Fri & Sat. Choice of menus, towards the upper end of the price scale, using local produce from land & ocean. €€€

WHAT TO SEE AND DO

Corniche Vendéenne As an antidote to the endless sandy beaches, the shoreline at Sion, 2km west of St-Hilaire centre, rises to provide the northernmost cliffs of the Vendée, and some breakaway rock-stacks known as the 'Cinq Pineaux' (Five Pine Cones). The small beaches among the cliffs are crowded in summer but provide a series of sheltered coves to protect out-of-season visitors – and, above the aptly named 'Trou du Diable' (Devil's Hole), deliver some dramatic effects of wind and water surging upwards through a rock arch for those who brave the autumn gales. On the landward side of the road, the purpose-built apartments are somewhat anodyne, though the odd turreted turn-of-the-century edifice harks back to grander days.

Atlantic Toboggan (42 Av des Becs, near Merlin-Plage, on the D123; \02 51 58 05 37; w atlantic-toboggan.com; ⏲ mid/late Jun–end Aug 10.30–19.30 daily; €25/20/free adult/under 12s/under 3s, if entering park after 16.00, price is €17 all ages) Whether you (or more likely, your children) favour the 'Kamikaze', the 'Black Hole' or one of the other many different water chutes (*toboggan*, in French, means slide), this family aqua park, 7km northwest of St-Hilaire and just back from the

Plage des Becs, makes a great day out. It has a total of five 15m-long waterslides, plus pools, pedaloes, playgrounds and picnic spots, and a huge wave pool (listen for the siren that tells you when the waves are going to start breaking). A rarity, in that swimming shorts *are* accepted here (no need for Speedos). Drinks and snacks are available, or you can bring your own picnic.

Bourrine du Bois-Juquaud (L47 Chemin Bois Juquaud; ✆ 02 51 59 94 07; w sainthilairederiez.fr/la-bourrine-du-bois-juquaud; ⊕ early Apr–Jun 14.30–18.30 Tue–Sun, Jul–Aug 10.30–18.30 Mon–Fri, 14.30–18.30 Sun, Sep 14.30–18.30 Tue–Sun; €6/4/free adult/under 18s/under 6s, guided tours also available – see website for details) Now an eco-museum, this picturesque limewashed cob-built cottage and its outbuildings, 4km north of St-Hilaire, are among the last witnesses of a vanished way of life. Before being able to see it 'in the flesh' you are directed towards a 15-minute film (in French) that uses an interview between children and a guide to explain traditional construction techniques. An adjacent room in the visitor centre has computer screens on which you can call up descriptions in French and English of local architecture, artists and traditions. (On request at the ticket desk, further English-language information is available.)

Once in front of the reed-thatched cottage itself, you can appreciate the primitive building materials and the simple, self-sufficient life of the farmers who, in 1818, constructed the house with their own hands. Its two rooms were inhabited until 1967, still without electricity or running water. The traditionally furnished living room looks out onto a neat vegetable garden. There are occasional demonstrations of dancing, threshing, weaving or butter-making.

Feeling Forest (Av de la Parée Préneau; ✆ 02 51 35 72 61; w feelingforest.com; ⊕ Apr–Sep, see website for detailed opening hours and prices) This is one of the popular treetop amusements, with aerial trails at six levels of difficulty featuring scrambling nets, zip-wires and climbing walls (minimum age 3 years; tough training shoes essential). There is also mini-golf (€5).

Louis de la Rochejaquelein Memorial (Les Mattes – sometimes written Les Mathes – signposted off the D59 6km northwest of St-Hilaire) A simple stone cross in a cluster of trees marks the place where the Vendean general Louis de la Rochejaquelein fell, rallying his troops, on 4 June 1815. Brother of the great Vendean leader Henri de la Rochejaquelein (page 12), he had landed from England a few days earlier and embarked on a short-lived attempt to revive the royalist cause and drive Napoleon's forces from the marshes. A thousand soldiers from each side once faced one another on this sandy terrain; today, a series of information boards laid out along the forest path detail the events that led to the death of the General.

Youpla'land (17 Chemin de la Conge; m 07 83 16 13 35; w youplaland.com; ⊕ Apr–Jun & Sep check website for hours, Jul–Aug 10.30–19.30 daily; free/€9/free: adult (accompanying child)/children over 90cm in height/under 90cm) Suitable for those under 14, this space full of inflatables is somewhere your cherished offspring can bounce around for an hour or two. Also on site are child-friendly quad bikes and boats (extra charge, helmets provided), among other attractions. Drinks and snacks available; safety notices are in English.

Dino's Park (63 Av de la Faye; m 06 16 63 27 47; w dinos-park.com; ⊕ Apr–mid-Sep – consult website for detailed hours; €13/8.50/free adult/under 12s/under 4s)

Who said dinosaurs are dead? In this part of the forest, more than 30 still move and roar, causing delight among younger visitors. You can dig for bones, or (at extra cost) enjoy a treasure hunt with a prize at the end, take part in cave painting or try some archery. Information is helpfully translated into English. Drinks and snacks available. Not accessible with pushchairs or wheelchairs.

Marais Salants de la Vie (Marais de l'Étoile, 81 Route du Sel, on the D38 1km south of St-Hilaire; m 06 81 97 39 84; ⊕ May, Jun & Sep contact by phone to find out the schedule, Jul–Aug 10.00–noon & 14.30–18.00 Mon–Fri, 14.30–18.00 Sun, plus English-speaking tours 10.00 Wed; €6/4/free adult/under 18s/under 6s, good English-language brochure with your ticket) Though the last *salines* ceased commercial production in the 1970s, salt has been produced around St-Hilaire since the 7th century. Among the modern enthusiasts who have revived some of the saltpans, Anthony Oger has laid out his *oeillets*, their square pools twinkling in the sun, around a big black sloping-sided *salorge* where the finished salt is stored.

He explains how he lets sea water arrive in a holding basin, then allows it to flow through an ever-descending series of shallow basins while its water content is evaporated by wind and sun. (An English leaflet is available at reception.) Flicking and swirling his long wooden rake, Oger gently drags out the harvest of crystals forming on the surface of the shallow water – first the delicate white *fleur de sel*, then below this the grey grains of *gros sel*. In autumn water is let in to cover all the *oeillets* through the winter; in spring they have to be carefully reshaped for a new season.

Jardin des Rigonneries (2 Route de la Marzelle à l'Oisson, off the D69, 1km northeast of Le Pissot; m 06 37 97 78 86; w lejardindesrigonneries.fr; ⊕ mid-May–mid-Aug (varies slightly each year): May 15.00–19.00 Tue–Sun, Jun–Aug 10.30–12.30 & 15.00–19.00 Tue–Sun; €6/free adult/under 12s) Well hidden away in the marshes, 3km north of St-Hilaire, is this surprisingly luxuriant garden, now 30 years mature. Though quite an open situation, the sandy soil supports dahlias and buddleias, marguerites and artichokes, and ponds full of water lilies and flag irises. Try and visit in May or June for the unbelievable displays of roses, which scramble, tumble and ramble over frames and hedges. There's a sandy little playground for children, too.

ST-GILLES-CROIX-DE-VIE

A pair of attractive seaside towns – now municipally merged (since 1967), with a single unwieldy '*portmanteau*' name – stand on opposite sides of the River Vie as it meanders into the ocean. Croix-de-Vie on the north bank and St-Gilles-sur-Vie on the south both maintain an active fishing industry and a long tradition of sea bathing, as evidenced by some attractive 19th-century seaside villas.

Overlooked by a cylindrical former lighthouse called the Tour Joséphine, trains from Nantes terminate conveniently alongside Croix-de-Vie's harbour and main street. The town is renowned for sardines and anchovies, and for its large canning industry (trade name 'La Perle des Dieux'). Real connoisseurs will find these in the company's shop on the pedestrianised Rue du Général de Gaulle, where the pricey prize are the cans of *sardines millésimées*. These are vintage sardines, to be laid down and lovingly turned from time to time over the years so that the fish are evenly imbued with oil. (Along the same street, the hum of refrigerators may tempt you to choose an ice cream from the many outlets with a vast array of flavours on offer.) Not to be outdone by its neighbour, Croix-de-Vie's market comes to the Place

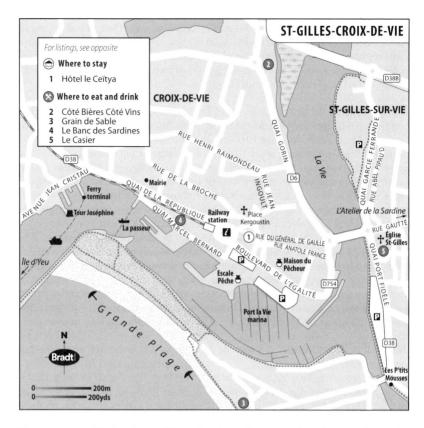

For listings, see opposite

🛏 **Where to stay**

1 Hôtel le Ceïtya

❌ **Where to eat and drink**

2 Côté Bières Côté Vins
3 Grain de Sable
4 Le Banc des Sardines
5 Le Casier

CROIX-DE-VIE

ST-GILLES-SUR-VIE

RUE HENRI RAIMONDEAU

QUAI GORIN

La Vie

QUAI GARCIE FERRANDE

RUE ABEL PIPAUD

Ferry terminal

Mairie

RUE DE LA BROCHE

RUE JEAN INGOULT

D6

L'Atelier de la Sardine

RUE GAUTTÉ

AVENUE JEAN CRISTAU

QUAI DE LA RÉPUBLIQUE

Tour Joséphine

QUAI MARCEL BERNARD

Railway station

Place Kergoustin

RUE DU GÉNÉRAL DE GAULLE

RUE ANATOLE FRANCE

Église St-Gilles

La passeur

Île d'Yeu

BOULEVARD DE L'ÉGALITÉ

Maison du Pêcheur

QUAI PORT FIDÈLE

Escale Pêche

D754

Port la Vie marina

D38

Grande Plage

N

Bradt

Les P'tits Mousses

0 ———— 200m
0 ———— 200yds

Kergoustin on Wednesday and Saturday. As well as providing those sardines, the sea is also the background to the town's other claim to fame as the headquarters of Bénéteau, one of the world's biggest yacht manufacturers. Its seahorse logo can be seen on many of the boats in the Port-la-Vie marina.

A small ferry (*passeur*) takes foot passengers on a 2-minute boat journey across the harbour mouth in summer, giving quick access from the town to the northern end of the Grande Plage – avoiding some of the parking problems encountered on the south side of the river. The little boat leaves from the quay, just across the railway line from Croix-de-Vie's *mairie*.

Across the river, at St-Gilles-sur-Vie, stands an attractive old church (in the tower of which one of Napoleon's generals was killed in 1815, during the second Vendean uprising). Now, the thrice-weekly market sets up around it, on Tuesdays, Thursdays and Sundays. Along the quay, the Quai du Port-Fidèle, restaurants jostles shoulders for your business – you're spoiled for choice. This is also the side of the river for the Grande Plage, aptly named and a lovely stretch of beach; choose your time carefully, though, as it can become impossibly crowded in summer when an incoming tide compresses sunbathers onto an ever-narrowing ribbon of sand.

On both sides of the river, a series of bollards bear blue information plaques on the towns' industrial and maritime heritage, with brief biographies of 15th-century navigator Pierre Garcie-Ferrande, 19th-century adventurer Narcisse Pelletier, local artists Henry Simon and Charles Atamian, and many others. At Whitsuntide (May/June), the St-Jazz-sur-Vie jazz festival is held in town.

TOURIST INFORMATION

Office de Tourisme Place de la Gare; ☎ 02 51 55 03 66; w payssaintgilles-tourisme.fr; ⏰ Sep–Jun 09.30–12.30 & 14.00–18.00 Mon–Sat, Jul–Aug 09.30–13.00 & 14.00–19.00 Mon–Sat, 10.00–13.00 & 15.30–19.00 Sun. You can hook up to Wi-Fi here…but also look out for the marked lampposts around town, indicating that you are in one of the many Wi-Fi hotspots.

WHERE TO STAY *Map, opposite*

Hôtel le Ceïtya (22 rooms) 47 Rue du Général de Gaulle; ☎ 02 51 55 01 13; e contact@hotel-leceitya.com; w hotel-leceitya.com. A cool chic place & very central. All rooms with AC, free Wi-Fi, TV with international channels, private bath or shower. Most have soundproofing – make sure you get one of these, as it can be noisy out front. Serves good-quality coffee on its terrace. **€€€**

WHERE TO EAT AND DRINK *Map, opposite*

Grain de Sable 60 Av de la Plage; ☎ 02 51 55 30 97; ⏰ noon–14.00 & 19.00–21.00 Tue–Sat, noon–14.00 Sun. Just off the Grande Plage, this popular restaurant offers a refined menu with seasonal cuisine. The kids' area in the corner gives it a family feel & while the interior is up to date, try to book ahead so that you can take in the sea views from a table on the terrace. **€€€**

Le Casier 15 Pl du Vieux-Port; ☎ 02 51 55 01 08; w lecasier.com; ⏰ mid-Feb–mid-Dec noon–14.00 & 19.00–22.00 daily. You'll need to reserve here in the season: it's small, with a few outdoor tables great for people-watching, especially on market days. Food is carefully prepared, though unpretentious. **€€€**

Côté Bières Côté Vins 3 Bd Georges Pompidou; ☎ 02 28 12 96 56. At first glance, this looks like a wine & spirits warehouse, but enter this bar/ off-licence/venue to have a coffee, an early snifter, or browse the huge range of beer & wines. A good place to find Vendée wines & local craft beers. Tapas-style sharing plates of charcuterie, sardines & cheeses will help to absorb the liquid delights. Occasional music, plus a terrace looking out over the river towards town. **€**

Le Banc des Sardines On the quay, between the railway tracks & the fishing port; w le-banc-des-sardines.fr; ⏰ Apr–Aug noon–14.00 & 19.00–20.30 Wed–Mon, Sep noon-14.00 Wed–Mon. A bit out of the way, but worth the hunt. A basic sardine shack run by a cheerful team, serving sardines, fish of the day & rillettes. Those with hunger pangs can finish with a plate of biscuits. Very fresh, very good value. Eat 'in' (though all tables are in the fresh air) or take-away. **€**

WHAT TO SEE AND DO

Boat trips to the Île d'Yeu (Compagnie Vendéenne) ☎ 02 51 60 14 60;

w compagnie-vendeenne.com) Between April and September, a passenger ferry makes the 65-minute crossing from Croix-de-Vie to the Île d'Yeu. The tourist office (see above) also has details of half-day and whole-day excursions on a *vieux gréement* (an old, sail-powered fishing boat), or sea-fishing trips on more conventional craft.

Maison du Pêcheur (22 Rue du Maroc; m 06 45 57 54 86; ⏰ Apr–Sep 14.30–17.30 Wed–Sat; €3/1.50 adult/child) A tiny, brilliantly whitewashed house in one of Croix-de-Vie's oldest streets, just across from the tourist office, is furnished with items typical of a Vendée fisherman's home in the 1920s. As the whole place measures only about 35m², it doesn't take long to visit its two rooms and backyard; don't miss the intricately laundered *coiffes* (starched headdresses), which girls had to wear to keep their good reputation. Also note the sepia photographs of sail-powered sardine-fishing boats.

In an extra room at the side, among old photographs of the sardine boats of yesteryear, you can read the curious tale of a discovery allegedly made at nearby Brétignolles in 1908. On finding a large barrel washed up on the beach, the villagers bored a hole in it and tasted the contents – a delicious amber-coloured liquid. Keen to take it home, they began to load the barrel onto a cart when it fell and broke open, not only spilling the fluid but revealing a pickled orangutan that had been en route for a museum! (A stuffed ape in a glass case adds spice, though not much veracity, to the story.)

Escale Pêche (53 Quai Marcel Bernard; ☎02 28 17 79 88; w escalepeche-vendee. fr; ◷ see website for opening times; €7/€4 adult/child) This new museum takes you behind the scenes of sea fishing in St-Gilles. The tour starts with a film where local fishers share their stories – some of which are very moving – followed by a tour of the interactive displays where you can learn about different fishing techniques and also experience a fish auction. Guided tours are available.

Les P'tits Mousses (Port Miniature, Av de la Cour St-Laud; m 06 84 92 89 97 ; w les-ptits-mousses.fr; ◷ Apr–mid-Sep – check website for hours as they vary; pedaloes from €16 for 2 people, canoes or stand-up paddleboards from €19 pp) Unsupervised children over 12, parents and supervised youngsters can have a great time manoeuvring miniature ferries, tugs, tankers and fishing boats on the quiet waters of the Jaunay river, a stone's throw from St-Gilles' Grande Plage. There are also pedaloes, stand-up paddleboards and canoes for hire.

L'Atelier de la Sardine (1 Chemin des Gabelous; ☎ 02 51 55 68 08; w laperledesdieux.com; ◷ mid-Apr–Sep 10.00–13.00 & 14.30–18.30 daily, Feb– Mar & Oct 10.00–13.00 & 14.30–18.30 Wed–Sat; access to the shop & museum is free) The town's best-known canning enterprise gives visitors a chance to learn about the catching and conserving of sardines, one of St-Gilles' specialities. A staff member gives a brief talk in French, before a short but excellent English-subtitled film takes you through the niceties of the industry, by way of a series of interviews with those involved. There is an interactive museum in the back with audio guides available. A tasting of vintage sardines presented like fine wines then follows, perhaps enhanced with orange-infused oil or other exoticisms. Allow an hour in total, after which you can, of course, buy any products which take your fancy.

Cycle up to the heights and along coast There is plenty of cycling to be done here and the Tourist Office can provide you with a handy brochure 'Á Vélo' which lists some options. For a short but scenic ride from town with a brief lunch stop at Pilours (page 75), you can head northwest out of the Tourist Office and take the road up past the quay and into the older and enviable 'Belle Epoque Villas' in St Hilaire de Riez, stopping at a viewpoint on the way to take in the Grande Plage. You'll find the restaurant a little further on, where an outside terrace allows you to enjoy refreshments with views over the Atlantic Ocean. The more adventurous can follow this with a dip at the Plage des Bussoleries before returning to town.

ÎLE D'YEU

Time seems to have stood still on this picturesque island, 23km² of pure bliss that lie less than an hour off the coast to the west of St-Gilles-Croix-de-Vie. Few cars travel the gorse-lined lanes, and the island's houses, often topped with pretty weathervanes and shuttered in gentle colours, seem bleached by the thousands of hours of sunshine that beat down on them.

Bicycle is king along the quays of the island's capital, Port-Joinville, though challenged by Renault 4s and Citröen 2CVs, cars of yesteryear that dare to push

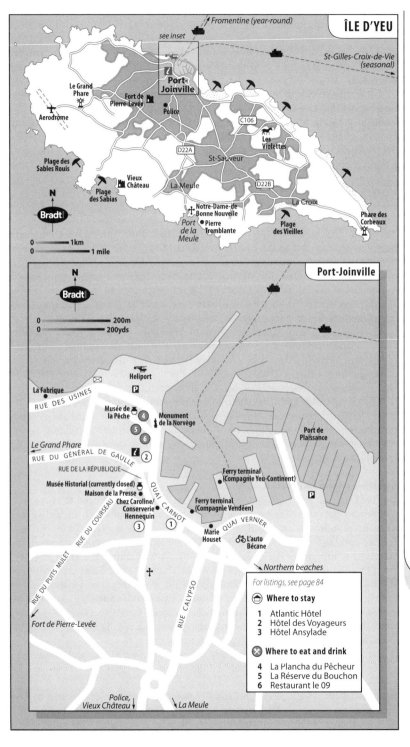

ÎLE D'YEU

Fromentine (year-round)

see inset

St-Gilles-Croix-de-Vie (seasonal)

Port-Joinville

Le Grand Phare

Fort de Pierre-Levée

Police

Aerodrôme

C106

Les Violettes

D22A

St-Sauveur

Plage des Sables Rouis

N

Vieux Château

Plage des Sabias

La Meule

D22B

La Croix

Notre-Dame-de-Bonne Nouvelle

Port de la Meule

Pierre Tremblante

Plage des Vieilles

Phare des Corbeaux

Bradt

0 — 1km
0 — 1 mile

N

Bradt

Port-Joinville

0 — 200m
0 — 200yds

Heliport

La Fabrique

RUE DES USINES

Musée de la Pêche

4

5

6

Monument de la Norvège

Le Grand Phare

RUE DU GÉNÉRAL DE GAULLE

2

Port de Plaisance

RUE DE LA RÉPUBLIQUE

Musée Historial (currently closed)

Maison de la Presse

Chez Caroline/ Conserverie Hennequin

3

1

Ferry terminal (Compagnie Yeu-Continent)

Ferry terminal (Compagnie Vendéen)

QUAI CARNOT

Marie Houset

QUAI VERNIER

L'auto Bécane

RUE DU PUITS MULET

RUE DU COURSEAU

Northern beaches

RUE CALYPSO

Fort de Pierre-Levée

Police, Vieux Château ↓

La Meule ↓

For listings, see page 84

🛏 **Where to stay**

1 Atlantic Hôtel
2 Hôtel des Voyageurs
3 Hôtel Ansylade

✖ **Where to eat and drink**

4 La Plancha du Pêcheur
5 La Réserve du Bouchon
6 Restaurant le 09

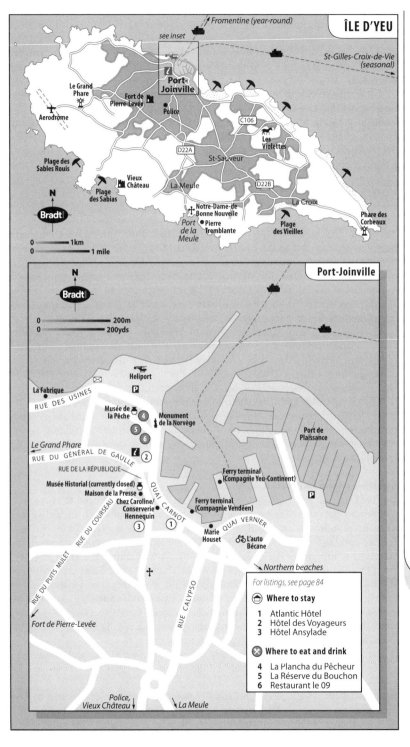

gently through the hordes of bronzed, bicycled summer residents towing shopping trailers behind their two-wheeled transport. In Rue de la République, the narrow shopping street just one block back from the seafront, even bikes are frowned on, and pedestrians have it to themselves. In July and August, the market takes place daily.

The northeast side of the island is full of sheltered, sandy beaches for swimming and picnicking. On weekdays off-season, take your pick and you may have the sands to yourself. More dramatic features will be found on the wild, rocky south coast: the 40m-high Grand Phare, a lighthouse built in the 1950s; the caves on the Sables Rouis beach; the ruins of a feudal fortress (the Vieux Château); the pretty fishing harbour of Port de la Meule overlooked by the tiny, whitewashed chapel of Notre-Dame-de-Bonne-Nouvelle, to the east; a Toytown-sized harbour on the western edge of the sandy Plage des Vieilles; and, in the village of St-Sauveur at the centre of the island, an attractive Romanesque church – one of the oldest in the Vendée – founded in the 6th century by St Martin of Tours. Among several Neolithic monuments is an enormous, rat-shaped stone, the Pierre Tremblante, balanced above a cliff to the east of Port de la Meule, which will move if pressed firmly in a particular spot.

In 1945, the 90-year-old Marshal Pétain, who headed France's pro-German Vichy government during World War II, was incarcerated in the gloomy Fort de Pierre-Levée (page 85) after his death sentence for treason was commuted to life imprisonment. He died six years later, and is buried in the island's cemetery.

Yes, there are points of interest here to fill your days, but the perfect experience on this island pearl is to grab a bike and pedal gently, your nostrils filling with floral scents, then pine, perhaps a hint of wood-smoke, then flowers yet again. If you can linger longer than a day, the island will grab hold of you, massaging you into a slower pace of life, one that is all too rare, all too necessary.

At Ascensiontide (around May), in even-numbered years, the island holds a flower festival, while in odd-numbered years there is a festival of the sea. If you're looking for culinary specialities, try the tuna, the *patagos/palourdes* (clams) served with cream sauce, *morgates* (squid), *tarte aux pruneaux* (prune tart) or *Min-Min* (prune-and-butter sweets).

GETTING THERE AND AWAY

By boat   Unless you can afford a chopper (see below), you'll need to take a boat journey to get here. Taking a car is possible, but complicated, expensive and virtually pointless to an island so small. Instead, check the companies' websites for car-parking information and leave your motor behind. Foot passengers can travel the 45 minutes to Port-Joinville year-round with **Compagnie Yeu-Continent** from Fromentine (Gare Maritime, Fromentine; \02 52 32 32 32; w yeu-continent. fr). Bikes can be carried if pre-booked, but the extra fare is not cheap (€28.80 return). Services are also operated by **Compagnie Vendéenne** (\02 51 60 14 60; w compagnie-vendeenne.com) from Noirmoutier's La Fosse (45mins, Jul–Aug only), and from Fromentine (45mins, Mar–Nov) and St-Gilles-Croix-de-Vie (60 mins, Mar–Sep). They do not accept any types of bike.

Return tickets with either company cost around €42/30/24, adult/under 18s/ under 12s. Pre-booking, which can be done online, is advised.

By helicopter   Helicopter flights from Fromentine heliport are operated by **Oya Hélicoptères** (Route de La Barre-de-Monts, Beauvoir-sur-Mer; \02 51 59 22 22; w oya-helico.fr; €120/90/50 adult/under 12s/under 2 one-way). They also offer a variety of excursions for small groups. For all these, you need to book a few days ahead in the peak season.

GETTING AROUND

By bus Bus lines connect Port-Joinville to all the major beaches and points of interest, with two routes running infrequently throughout the year. Additional bus lines and increased frequency occurs in the French school holidays (mid-July to end August). Tickets can be bought from the tourist office (see below) or Maison de la Presse in Port-Joinville (single journey €2/1.50/free adult/child/under 5s); pick up a timetable from the tourist office.

By bicycle This is not a destination for competition road cyclists, nor for off-road adrenalin junkies, but leisure cyclists who are happy with upright, city-cycles will be in their element. If you contemplate a day exploring the island, take a good map (it's surprisingly easy to lose your bearings); consider buying sandwiches and drinks in Port-Joinville, or on the mainland before you set off, as there is a severe lack of places for snacks on the way. In off-season, take your pick from the many outlets, but advance booking is advisable in July and certainly in August. Most enterprises will include helmets, though the French seem averse to wearing them. They're compulsory for under 12s. Make sure you use the locks provided, as theft is not unknown. You will need to leave your ID/passport or cash as deposit. Some hire companies will accept your return ferry ticket. There are several companies near the ferry terminal – look to your left as you disembark – plus one directly in front of the tourist office.

L'auto Bécane 8 Rue de la Chaume, Port Joinville; \02 51 58 73 67, 02 51 58 70 42; e bonjour@autobecane.com; w autobecane.fr. A variety of bikes for hire (3- or 21-speed, off-road) plus electric ones at extra cost. They have their own maps, with estimated times marked for each journey stage, good to know if you're catching the ferry home. For the less energetic, scooters & cars, too.

On foot The GR80 walking route takes you around the island, a total distance of 30km, so doable in a day if you are a speedy walker and don't get distracted, but too long to finish and return by ferry the same day. Better to split the circuit over two days, staying overnight in Port-Joinville and using the buses to get back to town at the end of day one and pick up where you left off, on day two. The tourist office also has a map with details of shorter walks, many of them loops. Take provisions with you from Port-Joinville, as there is very little to sustain you when you're out of town.

By train Well, it's not quite a traditional train, but like many self-respecting French holiday destinations, the island can offer **Le Petit Train** (m 06 07 99 91 92; w petittrain-iledyeu.fr; ⊕ Apr–Sep daily – check website for departure times; €15/8/free adult/under 12s/under 4s) land-train to take you around without you making any effort. The 2-hour circuit begins and ends at Port-Joinville and visits the west coast and Port de la Meule.

TOURIST INFORMATION

Office de Tourisme Rue du Marché, Port-Joinville; \02 51 58 32 58; w ile-yeu.fr; ⊕ Oct–Mar 09.00–12.30 & 14.00–17.30 Mon–Sat, Apr–Jun & Sep 09.00–12.30 & 14.00–18.00 Mon–Sat, Jul–Aug 09.00–13.00 & 14.00–19.00 Mon–Sat, 09.30–13.00 Sun. If you're getting off the ferry, make a beeline here first to beat the queues.

🏠 WHERE TO STAY   *Map, page 81*

If campsites dominate on the mainland, here self-catering properties are very much to the fore. Hotels are neither particularly numerous, nor strong in quality, reminiscent of those French establishments of 30 years gone. Charm, yes, but luxury? No. Nevertheless, you should book well in advance for July and August, as they sell out quickly. If you're staying for more than a few nights, consider renting an apartment or villa: the island's website (**w** yeu-island.com) is bilingual and allows you to see details on all hotels, B&Bs, holiday homes and campsites, at a glance.

Atlantic Hôtel (17 rooms) 3 Quai Carnot, Port-Joinville; ☎02 51 58 38 80; **e** atlantic-hotel@orange.fr; **w** hotel-yeu.com. If you like quaintness (for which read 'old-fashioned') then this fits the bill. 3 stars seem a bit generous, perhaps. A true relic of the bygone, but great harbour views from some rooms will allow you to enjoy the to & fro of all the boats. TV, free Wi-Fi, all with bath or shower. Not suitable for those with limited mobility. **€€€€**

Hôtel des Voyageurs (20 rooms) 10 Quai Carnot, Port-Joinville; ☎02 51 58 36 88; **e** hotelvoyageuryeu@wanadoo.fr; **w** hotelyeu.

com. Probably the better of the harbour-front hotels, scoring points on both comfort & price. Don't expect luxury & you won't be disappointed. All have private bath & TV, free Wi-Fi. Ask for a sea view, though it will cost you more. Pleasant b/fast room, bar downstairs. **€€€**

Hôtel Ansylade (15 rooms) 18 Rue Gabriel Guist'hau, Port Joinville; ☎02 51 58 35 59; **e** hotel.ansylade@orange.fr; **w** ansylade.fr. Being away from the harbour means lower prices. The standard is similar, & there's a choice of private or shared bath. The former have AC. One room adapted for those of limited mobility. **€€**

✕ WHERE TO EAT AND DRINK   *Map, page 81*

As well as the listings below, most eating establishments on the island can be found in Port-Joinville, within a few hundred metres of the tourist office and along the harbourfront.

La Plancha du Pêcheur 13 Pl de la Norvège, Port-Joinville; ☎02 51 59 11 15; ⏲ noon–14.30 & 19.00–22.00 daily. Overlooking the sea, with fresh, well-cooked seafood & fish. **€€€**

La Réserve du Bouchon 3 Rue de la Chapelle, Port-Joinville; **m** 06 88 22 31 43; ⏲ Apr–Nov 11.00–14.00 & 17.00–02.00 daily. In a smartly painted building 100m from the tourist office, a great place to unwind. Less formal than some,

it does good b/fasts, brunches & offers free Wi-Fi. **€€€**

Restaurant le 09 9 Rue Georgette, Port Joinville; ☎02 51 26 01 61; ⏲ noon–13.30 & 19.15–21.30 Mon & Thu–Sun, noon–13.30 Wed. Attentive, friendly service, a peaceful courtyard & – of course – carefully prepared & beautifully presented food are the ingredients which combine to make this one of the island's best dining choices. **€€€**

SHOPPING   Port-Joinville has plenty of interesting little outlets to poke around in, especially along the port and the pedestrianised streets behind.

Chez Caroline/Conserverie Hennequin
Quai Carnot; ☎02 51 58 38 16; **w** conserveriehennequin.com. Well, the salt may be from the mainland, but the tuna & other canned & bottled fish are preserved right here on the island. The Hennequin family has gone from catching fish to preserving it, as the generations have changed. Also stocks fish soups, seafood cassoulets & the local craft beers.

La Fabrique 14 Rue des Usines; ☎07 72 21 26 62; **w** lafabriqueyeu.com; ⏲ open Feb–Nov, check website for exact times. To be in this association of almost 30 artisans, you must live & work on the island. The result? A super collection of crafts, arts & cards – perfect souvenirs to remind you of your time here in paradise.

Marie Houset 17 Quai de la Mairie; **m** 06 24 22 40 40; **e** mariehouset@yahoo.fr. Of course, different art appeals to different tastes, but Marie's stylish island & fish themes will surely find favour with most. If the shop's not open, some of her works can be found at La Fabrique.

SPORTS AND ACTIVITIES
Les Violettes Chemin des Violettes, Les Sapins; ☏02 51 58 74 00; e centreequestre@lesviolettes.fr; w lesviolettes.fr; ⊕ open all year round. Rides on the beach for experienced riders, & in the forest for all levels. Shetland ponies available for the youngsters. Lessons are also possible. Rides from €25.

WHAT TO SEE AND DO
Musée de la Pêche (7 Quai de la Chapelle, Port-Joinville; ☏02 51 59 57 21; w ile-yeu.fr; ⊕ mid-Apr–Jun & Sep 10.00–12.30 Tue–Sat, Jul–Aug 10.00–12.30 Mon–Sat plus afternoons if it's raining; €8/3.50/free, adult/under 16s/under 5s) A fascinating glimpse of the fishing industry on which the island's economy has depended for centuries. The museum was originally created in 1898 as an Abri du Marin, a place where sobriety among sailors could be encouraged. A 20-minute video – very visual, even for those who don't understand much of the French commentary – explains the rigours of the fishers' lives. Up in a first-floor room are models of different types of craft – some raised on solid plastic 'water' so that you can see the lines, nets or lobster pots beneath. The island's important tuna-fishing industry is represented by models of the sail-powered 'dundees', bristling with large tuna-fishing rods. In 2017, there were still 28 fishing boats operating from Port-Joinville, of which eight were deep-sea vessels.

Monument de la Norvège (Quai de la Norvège, Port-Joinville) A sombre granite monument near the northern end of the waterfront commemorates a terrible tragedy. On 26 January 1917, the Île d'Yeu lifeboat went to the aid of an open boat carrying seven survivors from a Norwegian ship torpedoed off Spain a few days earlier. Having picked up the starving sailors, the lifeboat crew found a contrary tide made a return to harbour impossible. They anchored a mile off the coast to wait for it to turn, but the anchor rope broke and the helpless craft was blown northwest by icy winter winds. After three days in glacial conditions the boat reached the coast of Finistère, in Brittany, but five Norwegians and six of the 12 islanders had perished from cold and hunger.

Musée Historial (Rue de la République, Port-Joinville; ⊕ closed for renovation, reopening date unknown – currently viewable from the outside only) This strange old house, near the tourist office, was the home of Marshal Pétain's wife in the late 1940s during her husband's imprisonment. Previously it exhibited a series of dioramas showing the island's history from prehistoric times, via the Vieux Château in its medieval heyday, to the brief arrival from England in 1796 of the exiled Comte d'Artois, who the Vendeans hoped would lead them in a new uprising against the Republicans. The tragic tale was recalled of the Norwegian sailors (see above) in 1917, and there was a precise re-creation of Marshal Pétain's damp stone prison cell in the citadel (see below). At the end, you entered a tightly shuttered room crammed with souvenirs of Pétain, recalling his once-brilliant military career. Most bizarre here, was to see the former marshal's clothes and gloves laid out on a bed, just as if he were still wearing them.

Fort de Pierre-Levée/La Citadelle (1km southwest of Port-Joinville; free) Head south from Port-Joinville, up through a forest of holm oaks to this gloomy fortress in which the elderly Marshal Pétain was held for six years after World War

II. Pétain is buried in the island's cemetery a little further east. Surrounded by green bushes, his grave backs onto the roadside wall and faces in the opposite direction to all the others. The fort nowadays is used as premises for local associations such as the kayak club.

Vieux-Château (South coast, 3km southwest of Port-Joinville; ⊕ Apr–Sep guided tours from 11.00, last tour at 16.30; €6/2, adult/child; Jul–Aug self-guided tours possible between 13.30 & 14.45; €2) The remains of the 14th-century fortress, 1km northwest of Port de la Meule, seem to grow from the rocks themselves. Built during the Hundred Years War, the fort changed hands several times between the French, the Spanish and the English. Guided tours take place regularly each day in summer; be prepared to wait outside for the previous one to finish. It's a rugged place, full of steps and ruined walls, so visitors need to be nimble.

Le Grand Phare (Route de l'Aérodrôme; ⊕ Apr–Jun & Sep 10.30–13.00 Mon-Fri, 10.30–12.30 & 14.00–17.00 Wed, 10.30–12.30 Sun, Jul–Aug 10.30–12.30 & 14.00–18.00 daily; €4/2/free adult/under 18s/under 7s) Built as recently as 1951, this 40m-high lighthouse replaced a previous one constructed after a shipwreck in 1827 but which was destroyed in 1944.

Port de la Meule A delightfully scenic little southern-coast harbour, accompanied by one solitary restaurant and flanked by characterful fishers' huts. A good stop-off if you're on a round-island walk or cycle tour.

4

La Roche-sur-Yon, Les Sables-d'Olonne and the Bas-Bocage

Long before sunbathing had been invented, Richard the Lionheart was probably the first Briton to appreciate 'holidaying' in this popular area – though he came for the hunting rather than for the beaches. He would barely recognise it now, but today's many British visitors can follow vaguely in his footsteps, day or night, amid the ruins of his fortress at Talmont. For them and countless others, however, it is the endless golden sands stretching along this part of the Vendée's coastline which are the main lure. Top of the league for resorts is Les Sables-d'Olonne; large, lively and providing good shopping, eating, culture and entertainment, even for those venturing to the Vendée out of season. Right next door, La Chaume oozes character, refusing to cede any respect to its larger, glitzier neighbour. In this central coastal region, distractions for the young and young-at-heart take the form of theme parks, aquaria, a zoo and much more – more than enough, certainly, to fill a fortnight's break.

Away from the coast and its modernity, in among the gently rolling landscape that constitutes the Bas-Bocage, Avrillé is an area rich in prehistoric traces, while among the other inland villages, picturesque Apremont with its lake, ruined Renaissance castle and steep, narrow streets is a favourite with families. At the centre, administratively and (almost) geographically, lies La Roche-sur-Yon, truly Napoleonic in its grid-system layout and firmly established as the departmental capital. Our chapter starts there, then covers the sites to the south before sweeping up anticlockwise through the interior and running down the coast from Brétignolles-sur-Mer in the north to St-Vincent-sur-Jard in the south.

LA ROCHE-SUR-YON

After the Wars of the Vendée, Napoleon Bonaparte wished to create a new base to control this unruly département, having decided that the existing capital of Fontenay-le-Comte was too far from the centre, and in 1804 picked on the small village of La Roche-sur-Yon. Demolishing much of the old part (though a corner of it can still be seen around Place de la Vieille Horloge), he created a 'new town' of Classical-style buildings and die-straight streets around the central parade ground, from which radiated avenues designed to give 20,000 soldiers instant access to any trouble-spots. Modestly, he called it 'Napoléon'. With the ever-changing status of France over the next 66 years the town's name was altered no fewer than seven times, reverting finally to that of the original village in 1870. (However, 'Napoléon-Vendée' – the name the town bore under Napoleon III at the time the railway

Kulmino

D71 D103 **Challans** D754

D51

Déambul
Le Perrier

St-Christophe-
du-Ligneron

D205

D753

D58

La Vendée D948

Louis de la
Rochejaquelein
Memorial

Soullans

Exploraparc St-Jean
de-Monts

D59

D754

Océabul

D38

Bourrine du
Bois-Juquaud

Musée Charles
Milcendeau D32

Château de
Commequiers

Atlantic
Toboggan

D69

D82

Commequiers

D21

Youpla'land

Jardin des
Rigonneries

Apremont

*Lac
d'Apremont*

Le Pissot

Notre-Dame-
de-Riez

Vélo-Rail

Vie

Feeling Forest

Dino's Park

Vie

St-Maixent-
sur-Vie

La Mesanchère

St-Hilaire-
de-Riez

Sion-sur-l'Océan

Le Fenouiller

D21

Stèle de
Brionni

Marais Salants
de la Vie

St-
Révérend

Coëx

Chapelle
Notre-Dames
de Garreau

Île d'Yeu

Corniche
Vendéenne

St-Gilles-Croix-
de-Vie

D6

La Chapelle-
Hermier

Marti

L'Aiguillon-
sur-Vie

Givrand

Jaunay

La Chaize-
Giraud

*Lac de
Jaunay*

D38

D12

Landevieille

D12

La Sauzaie

Vendée
Miniature

St-Julien-
des-Lanaades

Brétignolles-sur-Mer

D40

Brem-sur-Mer

D55

La Parée

Parc des
Dunes

L

Plage de la
Normandelière

Menhir de
la Crulière

D32

Atlantic Lézard
Surf School

La Corde

Vairé

D

Menhir de la
Conche Verte

D80

D38

D87

Champclou

Île-d'Olonne

**ATLANTIC
OCEAN**

Olonne-
sur-Mer

D80

Château de
Pierre-Levée

Les Salines

D949

L'Aubraie

**Les Sables-
d'Olonne**

Château
d'Olonne

La Chaume

Abbaye St-Je
d'Orbes

Puits d'Enfer

Aquarium
de Vendée

Port Bourg

⌂ **Where to stay**

1 Domaine de Brandois *p99*
2 Le Gîte de la Pommeraie *p98*

✗ **Where to eat and drink**

3 La Cabane *p104*
4 La Guinguette de Piquet *p94*
5 Les Brisants *p103*

N

Bradt

0 ——————— 5km
0 ——————— 3 miles

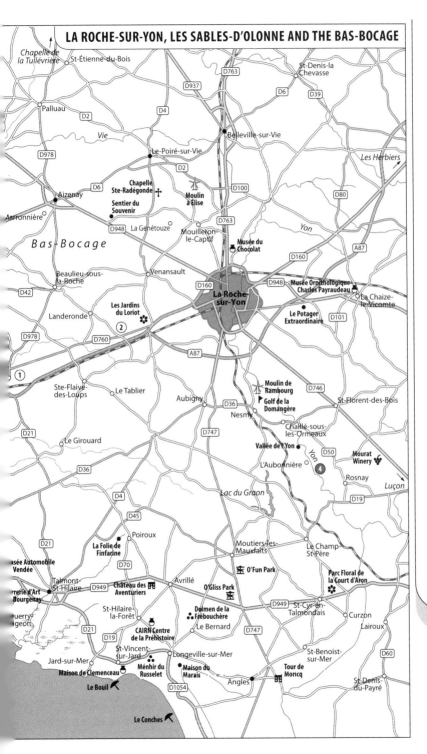

LA ROCHE-SUR-YON, LES SABLES-D'OLONNE AND THE BAS-BOCAGE

Chapelle de la Tullévrière
St-Étienne-du-Bois
D763
St-Denis-la-Chevasse
D937
D6
D39
Palluau
D2
D4
Belleville-sur-Vie
Vie
D978
Le-Poiré-sur-Vie
Les Herbiers
D2
Aizenay
D6
Chapelle Ste-Radégonde
Moulin à Élise
D100
D80
Sentier du Souvenir
Aarronnière
D948
La Génétouze
Mouilleron-le-Captif
D763
Yon
A87
Bas-Bocage
Musée du Chocolat
D160
Beaulieu-sous-la-Roche
Venansault
D160
La Roche-sur-Yon
D948
Musée Ornithologique Charles Payraudeau
La Chaize-le-Vicomte
D42
Les Jardins du Loriot
Le Potager Extraordinaire
D101
Landeronde
(2)
D978
D760
A87
(1)
Ste-Flaive-des-Loups
Le Tablier
Aubigny
D36
Moulin de Rambourg
Golf de la Domangère
D746
St-Florent-des-Bois
D21
Nesmy
Chaillé-sous-les-Ormeaux
D747
Vallée de l'Yon
D50
Mourat Winery
Le Girouard
L'Aubonnière
Yon
(4)
Rosnay
D36
Luçon
D4
Lac du Graon
D19
D45
Poiroux
D21
La Folie de Finfarine
Moutiers-les-Mauxfaits
Le Champ-St-Père
Parc Floral de la Court d'Aron
usée Automobile Vendée
D70
O'Fun Park
Talmont-St-Hilaire
D949
Château des Aventuriers
Avrillé
O'Gliss Park
rerie d'Art Bourgenay
Dolmen de la Frébouchère
D949
St-Cyr-en-Talmondais
Curzon
uerry-geon
D21
St-Hilaire-la-Forêt
Le Bernard
D747
Lairoux
D19
CAIRN Centre de la Préhistoire
St-Vincent-sur-Jard
Longeville-sur-Mer
St-Benoist-sur-Mer
D60
Jard-sur-Mer
Maison de Clemenceau
Ménhir du Russelet
Maison du Marais
Tour de Moricq
St-Denis-du-Payré
Le Bouil
D1054
Angles
Le Conches

arrived in the 1860s – is still etched indelibly into the stone above one of the station platforms.) A signposted Circuit Napoléon leads you on a 2.5km perambulation around some of the most obvious sights. Horse-drawn carriage rides cover much the same route during the summer.

The lack of interesting nooks and crannies that the grid layout imposed helped to earn La Roche the unenviable description of 'about the dullest town in France' from the 19th-century travel writer John Murray. That seems a bit harsh: it's certainly not pretty, yet it is trying hard and has points of interest for the persistent. A witty fountain of oil drums now makes a splash in front of the theatre; the few old buildings around Place de la Vieille Horloge have been restored. A real focal point are the strange, fun mechanical animals that occupy the Place Napoléon, with the central statue of the man himself on horseback seemingly supervising proceedings.

Famous sons of the town include artist Paul Baudry (1828–86), who decorated the foyer of the Paris Opéra and was born on the street that now bears his name. If you ever eat Laughing Cow cheese, you have probably stared at the work of another La Roche citizen, Benjamin Rabier (1864–1939), who designed the original Vache-qui-Rit logo. Rabier is actually better known in France as the creator of Gédéon, a sort of Gallic Donald Duck, whose cartoon exploits gripped the nation in the 1920s and 30s.

The principal shopping area in the centre is the semi-pedestrianised Rue Georges-Clemenceau, where the usual 'High Street' names can be found, including a branch of Galeries Lafayette. The 'quartier des halles', or market area, to the southeast of the Place Napoléon has been under construction for a number of years and at the time of writing was reaching its completion. Currently, the market is held every day except Monday and Wednesday, in the indoor hall opposite the tourist office. A few words of warning for drivers: remember the very low (30km/h) speed limit in the town centre, and avoid La Roche's many bus lanes (particularly tricky around Place Napoléon). For a bit of peace in the town centre, the Place François Mitterrand is home to a well-tended and colourful garden and is flanked by the handsome préfecture building.

Having recently moved to a new location on the western outskirts of the city, the impressive gardens and oversized legumes of Le Potager Extraordinaire are well worth a visit.

TOURIST INFORMATION
Office de Tourisme 7 Pl du Marché; ☎02 51 36 00 85; w ot-roche-sur-yon.fr; ⏰ 10.00–18.00 Mon–Sat; exact times vary from year to year, see website

✕ WHERE TO EAT AND DRINK
Brasserie Le Beurre Zinc 10 Rue de Verdun; ☎02 51 09 90 42 ; ⏰ daily. At the time of writing this restaurant was still the Bistrot du Boucher & in the process of moving to its new name of Le Beurre Zinc. Hearteningly, the intention is to continue to produce simply cooked steaks, poultry & fish in the brasserie style; good-value lunch menu, & its central location ensures it's popular with local office workers. €€€

Le P'tit Marais 24 Rue des Halles; ☎02 51 48 56 81; ⏰ noon–14.30 Tue, noon–14.30 & 19.30–23.00 Wed–Sat. From a short menu, choose between 1, 2 or 3 courses at this small, neat restaurant in the town centre. Children's menu. Cheaper at lunchtime. Excellent steak usually features. €€

SHOPPING
Gelencser 2 Rue Maréchal Joffre, off Pl Napoléon; ⏰ closed Sun afternoon & Mon. La Roche's gourmets stock up on a delicious selection of chocolates & cakes in this smart town-centre shop. The company also runs the Musée du Chocolat (page 92).

L'Arbre à Sucre 12 Rue Jean Jaurès; 🕻09 81 18 32 51; w larbreasucre.fr; ⊕ closed Sun afternoon.   Delicious artisan chocolates & 16 flavours of melt-in-the-mouth macarons.

WHAT TO SEE AND DO

Place Napoléon/Les Animaux de la Place (Pl Napoléon; ⊕ free access to view at any time, closed Jan; animals can be operated mid-Mar–mid-Jun 10.00–18.00, mid-Jun–early Sep 10.00–19.00, early Sep–mid-Mar 10.00–18.00) The tourist office leaflet will tell you that these mechanical beasts are from the Napoleonic era and were recently rediscovered during city renovations. Nonsense – the tongue is firmly in cheek! Nevertheless, children will love pulling the levers to operate the giant mechanical frogs, the dromedary, crocodile, hippo and others which inhabit the ornamental pools in the main town square. In this fast-paced digital age, it's a refreshing change to see pneumatically and hydraulically powered machines still causing such pleasure. The square itself contains thousands of plants, and there's a café at one end, while the huge St Louis church, with its Greco-Roman columns dominates the other side. Even Napoleon's statue is dwarfed by this, the biggest religious building in the Vendée. The square is a relaxing place…but watch out for the town buses, which all depart from here.

Haras de la Vendée (120 Bd des États-Unis; 🕻02 51 37 48 48; w sitesculturels. vendee.fr; ⊕ early Apr–early May 10.00–12.30 & 14.00–18.00 Mon–Thu, 14.00–19.00 Sat & Sun, Jul–Aug 10.00–19.00 daily; €9/7/free adult/under 25s/under 12s) The Conseil Général, or county council, has taken over this one-time national stud – one of the largest in France – founded by Napoleon in 1843 to breed horses and mules for his army. Today its roomy boxes are home to around 50 horses and ponies – from draught animals to classic riding horses, and from Shetland ponies to thoroughbred trotters. There are 45-minute guided tours (no extra charge) of this immaculately groomed city farm, explaining how the animals are exercised, shod, mated and generally cared for. Although they're in French, you can pick up English-language information to assist you when you buy your tickets. You are free to wander around and watch various equestrian shows; these may include displays of the curious bareback-riding discipline known as *voltige*, and demonstrations of training horses in near-circus tricks. Allow a good couple of hours at least, if you're a horse-lover. Regular evening shows (with separate admission charge, see website) combine music, dressage and fairy-tales with dramatic riding skills.

Musée de La Roche-sur-Yon (17 Rue du President de Gaulle; 🕻02 51 47 48 35; w larochesuryon.fr/musee; ⊕ 13.00–18.00 Tue–Fri, 11.00–18.00 Sat & Sun; free) Plans are afoot for a new museum in 2028, which will be housed in a building overlooking Place Napoléon. Until then the city's museum is being hosted in the former Malreaux school. There are three rooms, a gallery and a mezzanine level. Among the collection you'll find paintings by the artists Paul Baudry (1828–86) – a native of the town itself – and illustrator Benjamin Rabier, famous for the 'Laughing Cow' ('La Vache qui rit') design found on the ubiquitous cheese portions. Temporary exhibitions are held each year which vary in theme.

Maison Renaissance (Pl de la Vieille Horloge; 🕻02 51 47 48 35; ⊕ Jul–Aug 15.00–18.00 Mon–Sat; closed on public holidays; free) On the corner of the oldest square in town is an elegant Italianate house dating from 1566, which contains displays devoted to the growth of La Roche from a humble village to the focal

4

point of the Vendée in the aftermath of the Vendée Wars. It also has a section on one of the region's most innovative sons, visionary aircraft designer René Couzinet (1904–56). It is open for guided tours for a short summer period.

Musée du Chocolat (38 Rue Paul Émile Victor; \02 51 24 22 44; w chocolats-gelencser.com; ⊕ Jun 10.00–19.00 Tue–Sat; Jul–Aug 14.00–19.00 Mon, 10.00–19.00 Tue–Sat; Nov–Jan closed; for other months see website; €6.50/4/free adult/under 13s/under 6s) This family concern in the north of La Roche has 60 years' experience of making delicious sweet treats. Pleasingly, all the information is translated into English, tracing the origins of chocolate and its introduction to Europe by Spanish conquistadors. During working hours (⊕ 10.00–16.00 Tue–Sat), you can watch production through a glass window. On the way round, you can use the plastic tokens included in the ticket price to extract various chocolates from dispensers. A gift shop awaits you at the end, but the delicious odour accompanies you all the way round! If you only want to taste or buy, you could visit the Gelencser shop in town (page 90).

Musée Ornithologique Charles Payraudeau (Mairie, 4 Rue des Noyers, La Chaize-le-Vicomte, 10km east of La Roche; \02 51 05 70 21; ⊕ 09.00–noon & 14.30–16.30 Wed–Fri; €3/free adult/under 18s) This museum to the east of La Roche displays about 2,000 stuffed birds – from sparrows to spoonbills – that were left to the village of La Chaize-le-Vicomte by a 19th-century naturalist, a native of the town. The numbers may be overstated, but are you *really* going to count? They are all neatly labelled and given coloured codes showing which can legally be shot!

Le Potager Extraordinaire (Route de Beautour, Curzais, 6km east of La Roche sur Yon; \02 51 46 67 83; w potagerextraordinaire.com; ⊕ Jul–Aug 08.30–23.00 daily; Nov–Mar closed; for other months see website; €14.50/9/3/free adult/student/under 15s/under 5s) Revamped and now relocated to a 7ha plot there is even more going on here than before. Staged and dramatic garden rooms are brilliantly interwoven with an impressive display of gardening prowess. Every cucurbitaceous plant (marrow, pumpkin, squash, gourd, etc) you could imagine is here, among other rare plants – more than 1,500 different varieties in all, including the twisted Devil's Claws and the bulbous Turban Squash – plus 300 different tomatoes (even blue ones!). A meandering path leads past a series of themed plots: decorative, organic, prickly, perfumed, medicinal, poisonous and tropical. Signs (mostly in French) prompt you to touch or smell. The tomato and gourd tunnels are arguably the main attractions. Regular guided tours are led by enthusiastic staff, who often suggest how to cook their favourite vegetables; afterwards you can buy whatever's in season and take it home to try for yourself. The season culminates with the **Incroyables Légumes** at the end of September, when French gardeners bring their huge vegetables from far and wide to be judged here. Size and weight are everything in each category, from 'longest gourd' to 'fattest squash'. If you are a fan of flowers, it's best to visit between mid-July and mid-August, but vegetable-lovers should choose mid-August onwards. A fantastic children's park can be found near the exit, complete with life-sized hot air balloon and slides. There is also a restaurant here serving snacks alongside freshly cooked dishes using products from the Potager gardens.

Les Jardins du Loriot (60 Chemin de la Tour, La Mancelière, near Venansault, 10.5km southwest of La Roche; \02 51 40 35 41; w jardinsduloriot.fr; ⊕ early

May–1st Sun Oct 14.30–19.00 Tue–Sun; €9/5/free adult/under 13s/under 5s) These delightful Asian-orientated gardens, laid out around a lake, are full of rustling bamboos and Chusan pines. In total, there are more than 2,500 plant varieties on view. Features include a Japanese bridge, pagoda and water-driven sculptures that accentuate the mood; winding paths take you from darkness to light, and from greenery to banks of flowering hydrangeas, accompanied by sounds of croaking frogs and trickling water. Inspiration comes from Bali, Java and elsewhere. A photographic exhibition commemorates the visit to southeast Asia by Vendée politician Georges Clemenceau (pages 8 and 196) in 1920.

To get there, exit the A87 at junction 33 and take the D760 towards La Mancelière. Turn right after the caravan showroom and follow the signs.

NESMY

Since the 13th century, local clay deposits have sustained a pottery industry at this village 6km south of La Roche-sur-Yon. The council has even seen fit to include a red pottery jug on Nesmy's colourful coat of arms.

Nearby Aubigny, 4km west of Nesmy, has put itself on the tourist map for its unlikely feat of having an incredible number of outsized objects listed in the French *Guinness Book of Records*. Commissioned for an annual Festival des Records that the village held from 1983 to 1992, many of these are on public display (page 94).

For tourist information, see La Roche (page 90).

WHERE TO EAT AND DRINK
Le Bel'Arôme 5 Rue St-Laurent, Aubigny, 4km west of Nesmy; 02 51 98 08 74; w le-bel-arome. fr; noon–13.30 & 19.00–20.30 Tue–Thu, noon–13.30 & 19.00–21.00 Fri, 19.00–21.00 Sat, 19.00–20.30 Sun. Excellent pizzas, with a variety of inventive flavours – including fresh raspberries when in season. A welcoming staff, a nicely renovated building. €€€

SPORTS AND ACTIVITIES
Golf de la Domangère On the D85, 3km north of Nesmy; 02 51 07 65 90; w bluegreen.fr. This 18-hole course by Michel Gayon is laid out around a smart clubhouse, which is open to all for lunch. It's part of the Blue Green golf network, which sells golf passes letting you play a variety of different courses across France & other countries.

WHAT TO SEE AND DO
Poterie de Nesmy (23 Rue Georges-Clemenceau; 02 51 07 62 57; w poteriedenesmy.fr; 10.00–noon & 14.00–18.30 Mon–Sat, Feb–Sep also 15.00–18.00 Sun) Monsieur Charpentreau's family has been working Nesmy's village-centre pottery (formerly known as Vieille Poterie) non-stop since 1857. During World War II, the pottery never stopped working, even hosting the village schoolchildren in its attic as the school had been requisitioned by the Germans. Inside the rickety buildings, the clay-spattered workshops are a hive of industry on weekdays. A pleasant, spacious shop sells the hand-turned, hand-painted products that range from simple flower-decorated plates, candlesticks, jugs and dishes to traditional 60-litre salt-glazed storage jars suitable for a lifetime's supply of gherkins – with some more bizarre items in between. A descriptive leaflet is available in English.

Moulin de Rambourg (Off the D85, 2km northeast of Nesmy; 02 51 06 03 15 (Maison des Libellules); Jul–Aug 13.00–19.00 daily; €3/2/free adult/student &

under 15s/under 6s, discounts apply if you also visit the Maison des Libellules, see opposite). This large restored, stone-built watermill standing beside a ford across the River Yon, is well signposted from the village centre. A series of panels outside explain the workings of the mill (which ceased commercial activity in 1981). In the summer months, you can take a guided tour of the interior (involving a good many steep wooden steps) to see how the 4.5m-diameter waterwheel turned the stones to grind corn, and how the flour was then graded in a large sieve known as a *bluterie*. It's a pretty spot, with picnic places and waterside footpaths; in summer, you can rent canoes from the adjacent campsite (€10/hr, €15/2hrs).

Espace des Records (Zone Parc de Loisirs de la Tournerie, Rue Jules-Verne, Aubigny, 4km west of Nesmy; ☎02 51 98 77 90; ☼ Apr–Jun & Sep 14.00–18.00 daily, Jul–Aug 10.30–noon & 13.30–18.00 daily, Oct–12 Nov 14.00–17.30 Sun; €5/3/free adult/under 12s/under 6s) A museum of giants: this curious collection of more than 90 huge objects includes vastly oversized skittles, a coffee grinder, a grandfather clock made of 280,000 matches, a 3.1m-high spinning wheel, a 3.8m-long clothes peg and a 10.5m-diameter replica of Maurice Chevalier's straw boater. The criterion is that everything must be functional, however enormous the scale. Though you may wonder why anyone bothered, you cannot help admiring the makers' skill. It's particularly child- and wheelchair-friendly, with English brochures available.

CHAILLÉ-SOUS-LES-ORMEAUX

One of the best-kept secrets of the Vendée is the valley of the River Yon. From Chaillé-sous-les-Ormeaux (Chaillé Under the Elms; 14km southeast of La Roche-sur-Yon) south to Le Champ-St-Père, narrow lanes run either side of the river – though they provide motorists with barely a glimpse of this picturesque stretch of water. However, there are several pretty riverside spots off the D101 on the west side of the water (follow signs to the 'Vallée de l'Yon'), especially l'Aubonnière, where a footpath takes you along the riverbank. On the east side, off the D50, look for signs to Piquet, where you can park beyond the *guinguette* (see below) and walk down a steep slope to the roofless remains of a 19th-century waterside mill, its jagged, top-floor window openings giving it the appearance of a ruined castle.

TOURIST INFORMATION
Office de Tourisme Mairie; 13 Rue de la Mairie; ☎02 51 34 92 43; w rivesdelyon.fr; ☼ 09.00–12.30 & 14.00–17.30 Wed

✕ WHERE TO EAT AND DRINK
La Guinguette de Piquet [map, page 88] Coteau de Piquet, near Le Tablier off D50, 6km southeast of Chaillé; ☎02 51 46 73 52; w laguinguettedepiquet.com; ☼ Apr, May, Jun & Sep noon–14.00 Fri, noon–14.00 & 19.00–21.00 Sat & Sun, Jul–Aug noon–14.00 Wed, noon–14.00 & 19.00–21.00 Thu–Sun. A rustic open-air bar & restaurant. This family-run eatery has updated its menu with a move away from the grilles & crêpes that received mixed reviews to focus instead on more traditional cuisine. It is locally sourced where possible, by Luca, an Italian chef who has managed to put his own twist on many of the recipes. The live entertainment has remained, however, which is what makes this place stand out. High summer sees Sat evening accordion nights with dancing (inside or out) plus a full schedule of concerts ranging from rock to jazz, Irish, manouche & Edith Piaf tributes. €€€

SHOPPING

Domaine des Jumeaux 30 Rue de la Marie; m 06 75 41 19 34; e domainedesjumeaux@yahoo. fr; ⊕ 10.00–13.00 & 14.30–17.00 Mon–Fri. At the shop of this small winery, you can taste some of their wholly organic products & buy them if you like. Reds, rosés & whites are all available, with no added sulphites. Some wines are made from the rare *négrette* grape, which can only be found in the Vendée & near Toulouse.

WHAT TO SEE AND DO

Maison des Libellules (9 Pl de l'Église; ☎ 02 51 06 03 15; w destination-larochesuryon.fr; ⊕ Easter hols, Jun & 1st half Sep 14.00–18.00 Sun–Fri, May 14.00–18.00 Sun & hols, Jul–Aug 10.30–19.00 Mon–Fri, 14.00–19.00 Sat, Sun & hols; €5/3.50/free adult/under 18s & students, limited mobility/under 4s) A timeline at floor level leads visitors from the formation of the stars 13 billion years ago through evolving plant and fish life, the age of dinosaurs and the development of civilisation, to local legends of *farfadets* (elves) and the giant Gargantua, miraculous springs, chaotic granite boulders and everything that makes up the geology of the lovely Yon Valley (see below). There are buttons to press and drawers to open, and a good 20-minute film (in French only) about the surprisingly predatory *libellules* (dragonflies), from which the centre takes its name. You could spend an hour or more here, if you take in the film and the adjoining wildlife-friendly garden, but note that the dragonflies themselves only appear around the pond when the weather is warm, but not *too* hot – so seeing real ones can be a bit of a lottery.

Vallée de l'Yon (L'Aubonnière, off D101, 5km southeast of Chaillé) Park by the picturesque stone Logis de l'Aubonnière – now a youth hostel – and walk down a leafy path to find some dramatic waterside scenery. In the 19th century the rapid current created by the steep descent of the River Yon between here and Luçon was harnessed to provide energy for tanning, fulling, paper-making and other industries. Granite boulders are strewn along the narrow valley where the Yon rushes past little ruined watermills, tumbling over weirs and swirling around islands and alder trees. To the left is a large weir; to the right a longer path leads to the old mill at Piquet and the strange hollow-scooped rocks in the water called 'giants' cooking-pots'. Some parts of the bank are pretty steep, particularly if you walk to the right, so hold securely on to any small children.

LE POIRÉ-SUR-VIE

This picturesque village perched on a rocky outcrop northwest of La Roche-sur-Yon is clustered around a central square overlooked by one or two well-preserved Renaissance houses dating from 1613. Among the artistic features here are a wonderfully baroque altarpiece in the church and, across the square, a wall decorated with a huge painting of a wedding, created by distinguished local 'naïve' artist Raphaël Toussaint (b1937).

Le Poiré is the hub of a large network of footpaths (maps available from the tourist office). During autumn rambles, you may see strange piles of vegetation stacked to dry around single poles in the fields. These will be the plants of the ubiquitous *mogettes*, the white haricot beans that appear on so many menus – often accompanying local gammon. In July and August, the new season's beans are on sale still in their pods. Known as *demi-secs*, these can be cooked without any preliminary soaking and the town's Nuit de la Mogette festival on 14 August celebrates the much-cherished bean.

If you take the D4 towards Les Lucs, you pass two interesting country houses (neither of them open to the public). At the Château de Pont-de-Vie, 1km north of Le Poiré, General Charette spent a few nights as a prisoner after his capture near La Chabotterie (page 191) by Republicans on 23 March 1796. Some 2km further north, the Château de la Métairie has its own tragic links with the Vendée Wars: three daughters of the Vaz de Mello family, who owned the house in the 18th century, met their deaths at the guillotine in 1793.

For tourist information, see Aizenay (see opposite).

✖ WHERE TO EAT AND DRINK
Crêperie du Moulin à Élise On lakeside, by Moulin à Élise; ☎02 51 06 42 86; ⊕ Mon–Sat lunch & Fri–Sat eve (Jul–Aug Thu–Sat eve). Crêpes, galettes (savoury pancakes), plus meat & salads, giving you the excuse to linger in this great location. May do 'off-menu' vegetarian options. €€€

WHAT TO SEE AND DO
Église St-Pierre (Off market square) Dating from 1826, Le Poiré's church contains some ancient treasures, including a 13th-century figure of Christ above the door of the tower; a 1655 carved stone *pietà*; and a dazzlingly restored 17th-century altarpiece. The magnificent organ above the nave weighs 13 tonnes. It was built in 1896 by E and J Abbey, sons of renowned English organ builder John Abbey (1785–1859), and installed here in 1982.

Moulin à Élise (On the lakeside, 250m southwest of Le Poiré; ☎02 51 31 61 38; ⊕ Apr–Oct guided visits 15.00–18.00 Sun; free) The village's beautiful 19th-century watermill, restored between 1988 and 1991, is an outpost of Le Poiré's tourist office during July and August. This attractive spot, at the far end of the lake off the D6, is worth a visit even outside that time, for its signposted footpaths, children's playground (across the bridge), picnic tables and cosy little restaurant/crêperie (see above). Guided tours of the mill interior are sometimes available, showing the waterwheel, the grain hopper and the millstones. A few waymarked walks begin from the mill; nearby there's a pleasant park and an excellent indoor swimming pool.

Chapelle Ste-Radégonde (Signposted from the D4, 1km north of La Genétouze) In the depths of the countryside 3km south of Le Poiré, stands a small chapel dedicated to a 6th-century saint who was once a Queen of France. According to legend, Radégonde was fleeing from her cruel husband, King Clotaire, when she came across a peasant sowing oats and besought him not to tell anybody that she had passed that way. He agreed, whereupon the seeds he had sown germinated instantly, springing up high enough to hide the fugitive. Her pursuing husband, witnessing this miracle, recognised the hand of God, and abandoned his chase. The chapel door is generally locked, but the setting is picturesquely wooded; you can walk down a sunken lane to the stream that runs below and join a circuit of local footpaths (map available from the *mairie* of La Genétouze).

AIZENAY

Situated on the edge of a 228ha forest 16km northwest of La Roche-sur-Yon, the pleasant little town of Aizenay is easily pinpointed on any map of France as it usually sits on the centre fold. The woods in the area conceal some interesting finds, including the poignant Sentier du Souvenir, remembering an American bomber crew shot down in World War II (see below). The forest is criss-crossed with signposted walks, and is home to large wildlife species such as roe deer and wild boar.

TOURIST INFORMATION
Office de Tourisme 2 Av de la Gare; ☏ 02 51 31 89 15; w tourisme-vie-et-boulogne.fr; ⏰ 10.00–12.30 Tue, 10.00–12.30 & 14.30–17.30 Wed–Sat

WHERE TO STAY AND EAT
Château de la Marronnière La Marronnière, off D978, 1km south of Aizenay; m 06 25 02 00 55; e resa@chateauvendee.com; w chateauvendee. com. B&B rooms in 18th-century country house, set in spacious grounds. Large garden & pool, free bikes & table tennis. Free Wi-Fi throughout. B/fast inc. €€€€

La Sittelle 33 Rue du Maréchal Leclerc; ☏ 02 51 34 79 90; ⏰ 12.15–13.30 & 19.15–20.30 Thu–Mon. Elegant & popular place between the tourist office & town centre. Classic dishes are orientated towards 'rural' fare (foie gras, game, etc). €€€€

SHOPPING
Pâtisserie Angélus 9 Rue du Maréchal Foch, by church; ⏰ 08.00–13.00 & 14.30–19.00 Wed–Sat, 08.00–13.30 Sun. Irresistible cakes, sweets, handmade chocolates & homemade ice creams.

WHAT TO SEE AND DO
Piste Cyclable Aizenay is at the centre of the smoothly tarmacked cycle route (also popular with rollerbladers) that links Coëx (page 101) with the county town of La Roche. It meanders for 15km in either direction through peaceful countryside, along the path of the old railway line. Sadly, there was nowhere to hire bikes in Aizenay at the time of writing, so bring your own.

Sentier du Souvenir (4km southeast of Aizenay; ⏰ free access at all times) On the eastern fringe of the forest, a moving memorial commemorates five members of a US bomber crew who died when their Flying Fortress crashed into a field in March 1944. Among the trees, modern aluminium shards have been artfully placed, bearing the tale (in French) of the survivors – three of whom were captured, with two escaping to Spain. (One of the airmen was caught only because a German soldier decided to relieve himself in the very ditch where the poor American was hiding.) You can still see the crater resulting from the explosion when the bomb-laden fuselage hit the ground. The place has an atmosphere all of its own, as if the incident has only just happened. There's also a 5km walk in the woods, starting from this point.

To get there from the D948 La Roche-sur-Yon road, turn north on the D100A, signposted towards La Genétouze. The concealed car park is on the left, 200m after some new industrial units.

Stèle de la Brionnière (2km off the main D6, 6km southwest of Aizenay; signposted) Another reminder of the region's role in World War II, this granite monument on a quiet country lane marks the spot where on 11 August 1943 a consignment of arms was parachuted to local Resistance members, some of whom were captured and sent to their deaths in Buchenwald and other camps. A 2015 memorial to diarist Anne Frank, by Vendean artist Henri Gueguen, has been erected next to it.

ST-ÉTIENNE-DU-BOIS

This village 19km northwest of La Roche-sur-Yon still has a few Renaissance houses clustered around its church – opposite the rather incongruously modern *mairie*. Local footpaths begin down the hill behind the church, near the *lavoir*, or washing-place. If you've an hour to spare, the Sentier du Coteau – through woodland and across an ancient bridge made of megalithic stones – makes a delightful walk. This is an area known for its Gros-Plant wines.

There are no restaurants in this small town, so head north to Legé or east to Les Lucs-sur-Boulogne (page 191) to find something to eat.

TOURIST INFORMATION
Office de Tourisme Mairie, 2 Pl de l'Église; ☏ 02 51 34 52 11; w stetiennedubois-vendee. fr; ⏰ 09.00–12.30 & 14.00–17.30 Mon–Tue, 09.00–12.30 Wed–Fri, 09.00–noon Sat

WHAT TO SEE AND DO
Chapelle de la Tullévrière (On the D94, 5km northeast of St-Étienne; ⏰ usually during daylight hours; free) In a rural hamlet stands a tiny chapel, reconstructed in 1835 on the site of an earlier building of 1794 where the Abbé Ténèbre, one of the rebel priests, celebrated Mass during the Wars of the Vendée (page 9). Within the simple interior, two stained-glass windows depict clandestine religious services of the time. On the wall is a memorial to 22 local martyrs – men, women and children who were slaughtered on 1 March 1794 as they attempted to hide from a Republican death squad. Large glass cases illuminate automatically to display a chalice, a statue of an angel and a priest's surplice said to have been made during the Vendée Wars by local women from their wedding dresses. The rather bizarre modern statue outside represents the Abbé Ténèbre (1742–1822), who was arrested in 1798 and deported by the Republicans to Guyana. There he endured five years of terrible hardship before being allowed to return to continue his ministry in the Vendée village of Vairé.

BEAULIEU-SOUS-LA-ROCHE

This picturesque village, clustered around a tree-shaded square, bills itself as a 'Village of Arts' and has become a focus for artisans and craftspeople. It is also famous for its three-day Christmas market, always held on the first weekend of December. As well as an artist's studio and antiquarian bookshop, the village centre has a bookbinder, picture framer, candle-maker, potter and jewellery maker. The Café des Arts exhibits paintings by locals, and even the colourful night-time illumination of the church spire seems like a spectacle.

TOURIST INFORMATION
Office de Tourisme Mairie, 4 Pl du Marché; ☏ 02 51 98 80 38; w beaulieusouslaroche.fr; ⏰ 13.30–17.30 Mon–Fri

WHERE TO STAY AND EAT
Le Gîte de la Pommeraie [map, page 88] (cottage) La Pommeraye, Landeronde, 7km southeast of Beaulieu-sous-la-Roche; m 06 03 22 14 75; w gitelapommeraie.com. A large cottage with 3 good-sized bedrooms, terrace, pool, Wi-Fi & garden. B/fast inc. €€€€

Café des Arts 2 Rue de la Poste; ☏ 02 51 98 24 80; ⏰ noon–13.30 & 19.30–21.00 Tue & Thu–Sat, noon–13.30 Sun. Not too many options in town, but this attractive little place – a true restaurant, not a mere café – opposite the church serves excellent food, received a Michelin Bib Gourmand & hosts exhibitions by local artists. €€€€

WHAT TO SEE AND DO

Cour des Arts The archway on the south side of the square leads to a pretty courtyard containing an antiquarian and secondhand (French) bookshop, a jewellery workshop, a bookbinder's *atelier*, and the studio of artist Régis Delène-Bartholdi. Throughout the rest of the village, various other quirky studios and shops complete the picture.

Féerie des Santons (Pl de l'Église; ☎02 51 98 23 80; w feeriesantons.fr; ⊕ Dec–mid-Jan & Jul–Aug 14.00–18.30 daily; €7/3/1/free adult/under 15s/under 10s/under 3s) Twice a year, more than 700 charming little figurines (*santons*) enliven a selection of model villages that evoke Provence, the Vendée, snow-covered mountains, and the sand-filled Sinai Desert, among others. The character changes from room to room, with magical lighting effects, and takes on a Nativity theme around Christmas when the village's renowned market also comes to town.

Église de Landeronde (Landeronde, 4km southeast of Beaulieu; ⊕ daytimes) The small, squat 11th-century church of this nearby village is known for its decorated altarpieces and painted wooden sculptures (look for that of plague-sufferer St Roch, accompanied by the faithful dog that brought the saint food during his self-imposed isolation).

LA MOTHE-ACHARD

This large village lies midway between La Roche-sur-Yon and Les Sables-d'Olonne, its standout feature being its picturesque 1920s iron-and-glass market hall. Among local curiosities are Château-Gaillard, an eccentrically battlemented former presbytery in the village of Le Girouard, 6km southeast of La Mothe, and a couple of stone wolves that – appropriately – stand guard outside the *mairie* of Ste-Flaive-des-Loups (St Flavia of the Wolves), 5km to the east.

TOURIST INFORMATION

Office de Tourisme 56 Rue Georges-Clemenceau; ☎02 51 05 90 49; w achards-tourisme.com; ⊕ Oct–Mar 10.00–12.30 Tue, Thu & Sat, 10.00–12.30 & 14.30–17.30 Wed & Fri; Apr–Jun & Sep 10.00–12.30 & 14.30–18.00 Mon–Fri, 10.00–12.30 Sat; Jul–Aug 10.00–12.30 & 14.00–18.30 Mon–Sat, 10.00–12.30 Sun & hols

WHERE TO STAY AND EAT

Domaine de Brandois [map, page 88] (39 rooms) La Forêt, off D760, 1km east of La Mothe; ☎02 51 06 24 24; w domainedebrandois.com. Small, 4-star chateau-hotel with surprisingly modern décor, AC, TV & free Wi-Fi. Rooms in main house are plusher & more expensive; a dozen 3-star motel-style rooms around the orchard cost less. Can also organise horseriding. The restaurant, La Cantine (⊕ noon–15.00 Mon–Fri; €€€€€) offers high-quality dining with a modern twist, thanks to a much-travelled Welsh chef, & is the place for a high-end treat, given the thumbs-up by locals. €€€€

WHAT TO SEE AND DO

Le Grand Défi (40 Rue de l'Étoile, St-Julien-des-Landes; ☎02 51 98 79 02; w grand-defi.com; ⊕ Jul–Aug 09.00–20.30 daily, Nov–end Mar closed; for other months see website; tree-top trails €11.50–23.50, according to age, paintball from €17–40, according to age & number of shots, other activities from €6.50, multi-activity tickets available; advanced booking recommended in high season) Just 15 minutes from the coast, this popular adventure park open even in wet weather provides a range of fun activities for youngsters. Think laser and explorer games, zip wires, disc golf, pony rides, paintball and farm animals. Activities are colour-coded to show what age they suit; phone ahead outside peak season, or check website for opening times.

APREMONT

Proud of its status as a *petite cité de caractère*, or 'specially charming village', Apremont clings in picturesque fashion to the rocky sides of the Vie Valley. Its skyline dominated by the church and the romantic remains of a Renaissance castle, it also lays claim to a reservoir which offers an inland beach and a variety of water-based activities. A brochure from the tourist office outlines an interesting walking trail, backed up by information panels at strategic points, telling the village's history in French and English. Around Rue des Bretons, to the south of the river, a few imposing mansions line the narrow streets; on the north side, smaller houses stagger up a steep slope alongside the church. A dam, or *barrage*, signposted east of the bridge, has created the 'lake', which at 170ha is the largest in the Vendée. Hot days draw in swimmers, paddlers, boaters, fishers and those wishing to try artificial water-skiing.

TOURIST INFORMATION
Office de Tourisme Pl du Château; ☎02 51 55 70 54; w tourisme-vie-et-boulogne.fr; ⊕ Apr–Sep. Located inside the castle walls.

✖ WHERE TO EAT AND DRINK
Le Relais de Apremont 14 Rue Georges-Clemenceau; ☎02 51 55 70 22; ⊕ 09.00–15.00 & 19.00–22.00 Thu–Sat, 09.00–15.00 Wed & Sun. Down below the castle, with a spacious terrace & large interior, pleasant enough & very good value – especially at lunchtime. €€

SPORTS AND ACTIVITIES
KS Wakepark Rue du Barrage, at the Lac d'Apremont; m 06 20 09 18 41; e ks.waterpark@ gmail.com; w kswaterpark.fr; ⊕ Apr–Nov 10.00–20.00 daily by reservation, Jul–Aug 11.00–20.00 daily. Just outside town, there are a few places by the lake where you can hire stand-up paddleboards, electric boats, kayaks, pedaloes & fishing boats. Here at KS, you can also practise your water-skiing towed behind a teleski. From €20/hr, min age 7 yrs.

WHAT TO SEE AND DO
Château d'Apremont (Pl du Château; ☎02 51 55 70 54; w tourisme-vie-et-boulogne.fr; ⊕ early Apr–early Jul & Sep 13.30–18.00 Tue–Sun, early Jul–Aug 10.00–19.00 Mon–Fri & 14.00–19.00 Sat–Sun; €7.50/4/free adult/under 18s/under 5s) Pick up an English-language leaflet and map with your ticket. Two towers and a chapel remain of the fine castle built in 1534 by Admiral Philippe Chabot de Brion on the site of an earlier stronghold. A childhood friend of the French King François I, the admiral had accompanied François to his summit meeting with England's King Henry VIII at the Field of the Cloth of Gold 14 years earlier. On 17 April 1622, the young King Louis XIII is said to have slept here after defeating a Protestant army at Riez. The castle later fell into disrepair and in 1733 was partially demolished.

The chapel contains a copy of the Rouleau d'Apremont, a long scroll bearing a fascinating 16th-century pictorial survey of the River Vie from the sea up to Apremont. You can also see an ingenious light show, which uses visual trickery to tell the story of Philippe Chabot (English commentary available). There are occasional special events, involving mime, music and dance in the castle grounds, in July and August.

You can climb the castle's east tower via a series of empty rooms, looking out over the village's rooftops, until you reach the magnificent network of wooden beams that supports the pointed roof. (Recorded commentary and descriptive leaflet in English.) Back at ground level, follow signs to the *voûte cavalière*, a steep indoor ramp cut into the rock. Grand visitors arriving by boat, below, would be conveyed up this dark slope on horseback and emerge, dazzled by daylight, into Chabot de Brion's then-glorious formal gardens.

Another interesting feature, half-buried beneath a corner of the garden, is the *glacière*, or ice-house – a Renaissance-style refrigerator hewn into the rock where winter ice would have been stored to preserve food in hotter months, or even to create chilled desserts. It still provides some welcome cool air on hot days.

Château d'Eau and Muséographie sur l'Eau (Rue du Château d'Eau; ☎02 51 55 70 54 (tourist office); m 09 67 81 27 93 (Jul–Aug only); ⊕ 2nd week Jul–Aug 13.00–18.30 Sun–Fri; €4/3/free adult/under 18s/under 7s) In the flat terrain, the Vendée never misses an opportunity to get you some altitude. Let yourself be whisked by lift up Apremont's 80m-high *château d'eau*, or watertower (built in 1966), for a stupendous view over the town, westward to the sea and islands, and eastward towards the plain and distant Haut-Bocage. Choose a clear day, and take binoculars and a map for an interesting exercise in orientation. You can also learn a bit about water here: the tower supplies the whole northwest region of the Vendée.

COËX

Coëx (correctly pronounced 'kwex', rather than 'coh-ex') lies at the far end of the Vélo-Rail line from Commequiers (page 74), and off a 30km cycleway from La Roche-sur-Yon, along the route of an old railway line. Market day is Saturday and there is an antiques fair here in April, while jam is celebrated with its own festival in September. The village is also known for the Carnaval de mi-Carême, a large carnival held in the middle of Lent, which draws thousands to watch giant decorated floats parade through the streets. The nearby waters of the Lac du Jaunay provide a venue for walking, some excellent fishing, and a few watersports – but strictly no swimming. The Jardin des Olfacties, a scented garden behind the church, is a pleasant place to take a picnic or a gentle stroll.

For tourist information, see St-Gilles (page 79).

WHERE TO EAT AND DRINK
Auberge du Jaunay Le Pré, La Chapelle-Hermier; ☎02 51 34 68 20. In a super location, an attractive cottage looking down over the lake of the same name. Booking advisable in high season, especially if you want an outside table – which everyone does! €€€

SPORTS AND ACTIVITIES
Golf des Fontenelles Route de Coëx, D6, L'Aiguillon-sur-Vie, 3km west of Coëx; ☎02 51 54 13 94; w bluegreen.fr. An 18-hole course designed by Yves Bureau, open to visitors & very popular

with the British. It has full facilities, including a restaurant open to all. About €70/28 per round, high/low season; see website for prices which are dynamic based on how busy it is, & also for details of weekly pass options.

WHAT TO SEE AND DO

Lac du Jaunay Just south of Coëx you'll find this picturesque 125ha lake, strangely invisible from the surrounding road network but well known to fishers. Leaving town heading east, then turning south onto the D21 and right again onto the D42, first look out for the sign to 'Observatoire'. Following this road to its end, you come to a small car park and a wooden walkway leading to an observation post. The local birds are identified on a signboard in French and English. You are likely to see some moorhens paddling about, though sightings of kingfishers or the European otter, both said to frequent this place, are rare. It's a charming place; pike and perch might bob up and a croaking of frogs may accompany your visit. Retracing your steps to the main road and continuing along the D42, the next turn takes you past the Camping le Pin Parasol, giving you great views down over the waters, before the road crosses the lake and reaches the tree-lined La Baudrière. It has something of the atmosphere of a seaside fishing hamlet. There are picnic tables, and in July and August you can rent canoes and pedaloes here. There's a 12km footpath around the whole lake, signposted by yellow waymarks; to walk the easier half, set off anticlockwise from La Baudrière and return there via the nearby road bridge over the lake. Back on the D42, the next turn takes you down to Le Pré, where there are watersports in high season and the Auberge du Jaunay (page 101), also open in high season.

Chapelle Notre-Dame de Garreau (On the D42 between Chapelle-Hermier & Martinet, 6km southeast of Coëx) The unusual 16th-century chapel near the banks of the Jaunay River is the site of a pilgrimage on the first Sunday of September each year. A panel on the south side of the river tells the legend of a knight returning from the Crusades, who prayed to the Virgin for help as he was almost swept away trying to cross it. The large boulder nearby is said to have risen from the water, enabling him to reach the bank, and is supposed still to bear the hoof-print of the knight's horse.

ST-RÉVÉREND

If you approach this small village, 8km east of St-Gilles-Croix-de-Vie, from the direction of Coëx, you'll notice two significant landmarks. One is a giant watertower, painted with beach and golfing scenes by an artist who must have had a good head for heights; the other is St-Révérend's 19th-century windmill, its white sails rotating gently above the treetops.

TOURIST INFORMATION

Office de Tourisme Mairie de St-Révérend, Rue Maréchal de Lattre de Tassigny; 02 51 54 61 11; w mairie-saintreverend.fr; ⏱ 08.30–12.30 Mon–Thu, 14.00–18.30 Fri

WHAT TO SEE AND DO

Moulin des Gourmands (Rue René Bazin; 02 51 60 16 72; w moulin-gourmands. fr; ⏱ Apr–Jun & Sep 14.00–18.00 daily, 1st w/end Jul–end Aug 10.00–12.30 & 13.30–19.00 daily, check website for opening times outside these months; €6/3/free adult/under 12s/under 5s) Handsomely restored and with its sails turning merrily, this windmill, dating from 1842, is an imposing sight. As you climb its 36 steep steps, the miller describes the whole process – from sowing the field of corn you pass on the way in, to using the emerging flour in the bread oven and the crêperie that you can stop at before you leave. To the accompaniment of the rhythmic tick-tack of the *barbouilleur*, indicating the rotation speed of the 2m-diameter millstone, the *meunier* demonstrates how he controls the slatted sail area by pulling levers from inside, and points out sketches of the mill and of a miller's donkey, drawn on the walls by a long-forgotten predecessor. A gift shop and crêperie are on site.

BRÉTIGNOLLES-SUR-MER

A cheerful seaside atmosphere pervades this village, with shops selling buckets, spades, bodyboards and other holiday paraphernalia. The market comes to town on Thursdays and Sundays, plus Tuesdays in high summer. La Parée beach has something for everyone: sandy enough for digging and sunbathing, it is also full of interesting-shaped pebbles and, at low tide, good rockpools. There's also an enjoyable mini-golf along Avenue de la Plage, good waves for surfers at La Sauzaie, to the north, and an attractive beach at La Normandelière, to the south, popular with wind- and kite-surfers and with seaside bars, a sailing school, and rockpools at low tide. Visitors in wheelchairs can borrow a 'Tiralo' (page 26) at the beach's shallow sea-water lake.

For tourist information, see St-Gilles (page 79).

WHERE TO STAY AND EAT

Les Brisants   [map, page 88] 63 Av de la Grand'Roche, 2km southeast of centre; ☎02 51 33 65 53; w lesbrisants.com; ☉ 12.15–14.30 & 19.30–21.00 Wed–Sun. Sea views from airy dining room, with Michelin-starred cuisine; menus strong on fish & seafood. Not inexpensive, so save it for a special occasion. Also hotel rooms (€€€). €€€€€

Bistrot des Halles   1 Pl des Halles; ☎02 53 81 92 21; ☉ 09.00–14.30 Mon–Tue & Sun, 09.00–20.30 Thu–Sat. Much gentler on the wallet, this central place near the church is justifiably popular, especially for its 3-course lunch menu. Tasty fresh food & well presented. €€€

WHAT TO SEE AND DO

Vendée Miniature (50 Rue du Prégneau, Les Morinières, 1.5km northwest of Brétignolles; ☎02 51 22 47 50; w vendee-miniature.fr; ☉ Apr–May & Sep 14.00–18.30 daily, Jun–Aug 10.00–19.00 daily, 26 Dec–7 Jan 14.00–18.30 daily; €11/6.50/free adult/under 13s/under 5s) This collection of exquisitely detailed model houses, churches, windmills and farms from 1900 were painstakingly created from wood, tiles and local stone by Yves Aubron, a former cabinet-maker. There's an introductory video, in French, before an L-shaped circuit takes you past a tiny world complete with shops, café, school, station, smoking chimneys and working steam engine, peopled by 650 characters – accompanied by the sounds of bells, birds and family festivities (a helpful English translation is available). On your tour, you may suspect a power cut, as every 10 minutes an owl hoots and darkness falls momentarily over the scenes, to end with a cock-crow announcing a new dawn. Special raised steps allow children to get a good view – though it's strictly 'hands-off', so make sure they are not tempted to touch anything. As an example of the work that has gone into this minor masterpiece, more than 80,000 tiny replica tiles have been hand-cut to cover the roofs.

BREM-SUR-MER

Though now a kilometre from the sea, this pretty village 15km north of Les Sables-d'Olonne was formerly, as its name implies, a seaside port. It may seem strange to think of salt breezes wafting over vineyards, but Brem is also now a respected centre of wine-making. More than a dozen growers produce reds, whites and rosés – once served, it is said, at the table of Cardinal Richelieu, and today marketed under the Fiefs Vendéens label. If you're trying to find some seaside that's off the beaten track, try the wonderfully wild Havre de la Gachère, an area of sand dunes and beach 3km south of Brem that became the village port in the 11th century as the sea receded. For a delightfully chilled experience, kick back or take to the waters at La Cabane, a bar in the middle of the marshes. Market-lovers should visit Brem on Tuesdays or Fridays in high season.

For tourist information, see St-Gilles (page 79).

✖ WHERE TO EAT AND DRINK

Les Genêts 21 bis Rue de l'Océan; ✆ 02 51 96 81 59; ⏰ 12.15–13.15 & 19.30–21.00 Wed–Sat, 12.15–13.15 Sun. Obtaining a Michelin star in 2017, this converted old mansion houses the culinary creation of Amélie & Nicolas Coutand (previously of the 3-starred Troisgros in Le Bois sans Feuilles), where regional ingredients take centre stage. They're so local, in fact, that vegetables come directly from the cottage garden. €€€€

La Cabane [map, page 88] Chemin de la Ch'noue, off the D80, south of Brem; ⅿ 06 76 70 04 60; ⏰ Jul–Aug 11.00–23.00 Thu–Sun. Whether you want to sunbathe, down some oysters & a craft beer or 2, or perhaps take to the inland waterways on a stand-up paddleboard or in a canoe, you can't do much better than this delightful spot mid-marshland. Just off the main road, yet firmly off the tourist track. There's plenty of birdlife, too, or you could choose to take a fishing trip. €€

SHOPPING

Christian Bourcereau La Corde, 2km east of Brem, signposted off the D38; ✆ 02 51 90 50 77, phone ahead to ensure he's open – he often has exhibitions in Paris & elsewhere. Fine earthenware & porcelain, with an emphasis on Japanese techniques, made using a wood-fired kiln. His products are elegantly displayed at his showroom in this picturesque hamlet. One for the specialists.

SPORTS AND ACTIVITIES

Atlantic Lézard Surf School Plage des Dunes 1, between Brem & Brétignolles; ⅿ 06 83 61 13 07; ℮ contact@lezardsurfschool.com; ⓌⓌ lezardsurfschool.com; ⏰ Mar–Nov depending on tides & conditions. With more than 25 years' experience & based on one of the surfers' favourite beaches, this surf school is a good choice for all levels. In high season, they run 8 group lessons per day & rent boards, stand-up paddleboards & necessary wetsuits. English spoken.

WHAT TO SEE AND DO

Église St-Nicolas-de-Brem (Rue du Prieuré) On the northwest side of Brem, you come across a real delight: the remains of a Romanesque church built in 1020 by monks from St Martin's monastery, near Tours. Just the central one of the three original naves survives from the destruction by Protestants during the Wars of Religion. The carvings above the west door are thought to show St Nicholas, surrounded by sculpted acrobats and other figures; on the south wall, fire-breathing serpents intertwine above a small window. At night, illuminations bring a ghostly quality to the place. Entering through the low north doorway you find a simple, whitewashed interior with fragments of 12th-century frescoes, revealed in the early 1980s beneath layers of paint. On the left is a Crucifixion; on the right, three women at Christ's tomb.

Parc des Dunes (Rue de l'Écours, at the side of the D38, 500m northwest of Brem; ✆ 02 51 90 54 29; Ⓦ parc-des-dunes.com; ⏰ early Apr–Jun 11.00–18.30 Wed–Sun,

Jul–Aug 10.30–19.30 daily, early–mid-Sep 11.00–18.30 Wed–Sun; €12/free over/ under 90cm in height) This excellent, slightly old-fashioned yet ever-expanding amusement park is perfect for active two- to ten-year-olds, who can spend all day in boats and ball-ponds, on roundabouts and bobsleighs, bouncing on inflatables or trying out pedal go-karts, aquaslides and mini-golf. Most notices are in English as well as French and good advice is posted as to which rides suit which age group. Play is not supervised, so keep an eye on your children as their safety is your responsibility. Take a picnic (there are lots of places to sit), plus drinks, sunhats, swimwear ('Speedo' style, not swimming shorts) and towels.

Dolmens and menhirs Some 5,000 years ago, Neolithic people were busy raising stones and building tombs here. Northwest of Brem, off the D38, is a small dolmen on the lane leading to La Normandelière beach. Other prehistoric stones include the Menhir de la Crulière (signposted north of the D54, 2km east of Brem), and the Menhir de la Conche Verte (on the GR364 footpath in the forest of Olonne, 3km south of Brem).

LES SABLES-D'OLONNE AREA

In 2019 the commune of Olonne-sur-Mer was merged with Les Sables-d'Olonne and is now known as the Les Sables-d'Olonne Agglomération, making it the second most populated municipality in the region after La Roche-sur-Yon. You could be forgiven for finding the names of the individual towns and villages misleading. Île-d'Olonne, at the northwest tip of the group, is no longer an island; Olonne-sur-Mer, lying due south, is now stranded 2km from the sea; and at Château-d'Olonne, to the southeast, there is little sign of a chateau. (Les Sables-d'Olonne, on the other hand, spreading out to the south and west of these three, has no shortage of sable.) Les Sables-d'Olonne is listed first followed by Olonne-sur-Mer, which covers the remaining quarters of Île-d'Olonne, Olonne-sur-Mer and Château-d'Olonne.

LES SABLES-D'OLONNE The outskirts of Les Sables, with some healthy, modern industrial and retail units, can make you feel you are entering a city, perhaps the first since you got off the plane in Nantes or at La Rochelle. But this is a leisure playground, by far the ritziest seaside resort in the Vendée. Les Sables offers a vast and gently shelving beach of ultra-manicured sand, backed by the long, busy promenade known as Le Remblai. On the other side of the spit of land is an active port lined with many good restaurants. Between the two lies an area of narrow streets full of old houses and interesting shops, somewhere to find a bit of welcome shade on a summer day. Here, too, are the witty shell murals adorning the walls of the area called Ile Penotte (page 109) and the animated market of Les Halles Centrales.

The dazzling glass building on Le Remblai houses the tourist office, plus a theatre, disco, restaurant and one of the town's two casinos. Across from it is an open-air, heated salt-water swimming pool, ideal if you don't want to brave the ocean. On summer evenings lively street performers entertain passers-by in front of the pavement cafés, and concerts are also sometimes organised in the nearby Jardin du Tribunal. In the daytime, you can stroll the beach and choose your activity level, from hiring a deckchair and sunbathing, to swimming or sailing.

Shoppers will enjoy the pedestrianised streets to the east and north of Notre-Dame-du-Bon-Port, around Les Halles; small children would probably prefer to dig in the sand or play on the little roundabouts in Place de la Liberté – the gardens near the *hôtel de ville* (town hall), just to the east of the Muséum du Coquillage.

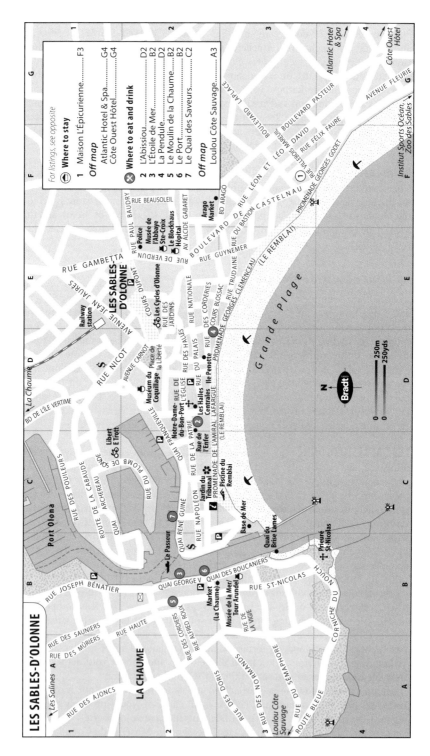

LES SABLES-D'OLONNE

For listings, see opposite

Where to stay
1 Maison L'Épicurienne.............F3

Off map
Atlantic Hotel & Spa..............G4
Côte Ouest Hôtel.................G4

Where to eat and drink
2 L'Abissiou.........................D2
3 L'Étoile de Mer..................B2
4 La Pendule......................D2
5 Le Moulin de la Chaume......B2
6 Le Port............................B2
7 Le Quai des Saveurs...........C2

Off map
Loulou Côte Sauvage............A3

LA CHAUME

Les Salines

Port Olona

Grande Plage

Railway
station

LES SABLES-
D'OLONNE

0   250m
0   250yds

106

If you fancy a trip out to sea – for a simple jaunt around the bay, an opportunity to fish for mackerel to take home for supper, or to spend a few hours on board a working trawler – various possibilities are available, with details through the tourist office.

Historically, driving near the seafront of Les Sables, with its unforgiving one-way system, was no fun in summer, and parking could be a problem. For the last few years, however, parking in the town centre has been forbidden. Instead, you can now park at the entrance to town and catch one of the free 'les Marinettes' buses that run to the main beach and the pedestrian quarter around the market, or Halles Centrales

For those who want to spend a whole day here – there's enough to detain and entertain you – an even better tip is to arrive early (around 08.00–09.00) and drive around to the oldest part of town – La Chaume – on the opposite side of the harbour entrance where you can park quayside all day for free. Then, start with a bracing walk along the jetty out beyond the Prieuré St Nicolas, which will give you the best view of Les Sables' Grande Plage and the buildings behind it.

Continue with a coffee at the L'Étoile de Mer (page 111), usually full of some quirky local characters and one of several cafés beside the departure point for *le passeur* ferry. Here, hop on board for the shortest boat trip of your life and start your exploration of Les Sables. Although now one town, Les Sables and La Chaume were once separate, and in the heads of some old-timers, their identities are very firmly different: some Chaume residents tease the 'Sablais' about the relative youth of their town, claiming that the 'Chaumois' are '1,000 years ahead' of their 'bourgeois' neighbours.

Getting around   Visiting Les Sables is all about strolling the promenade, engaging in beach- or sea-based activities or enjoying the shops around the market. You will need to take the ferry or bus between Les Sables and La Chaume, however. The small **Le Passeur ferry** [106 B2] (✆ 02 51 96 81 00; ⊕ Jul–Aug, 07.00–01.00 daily, Jun, Sep & Easter hols 07.00–22.00 Sun–Thu, 07.00–midnight Fri, Sat & the days before the hols, Oct–May 07.00–20.00 Mon–Thu, 07.00–22.00 Fri, 08.00–22.00 Sat, 08.00–20.00 Sun & hols; €1.10 (single)/free adult/under 6s) scuttles back and forward, with a journey time of 2 minutes. In high season, two other shuttles run: one from Port Olona to town and the other from the Base de Mer to Quai du Brise Lames. Half-a-dozen **bus** lines connect Les Sables with La Chaume, as well as letting you access all other points of interest in town.

There are several places to hire a **bike.** The tourist office has all the details, or try Libert E Trott [106 C1] (8 Quai Ernest de Franqueville; ✆ 06 44 68 44 50; ⊕ 10.00–18.00 Mon–Tue & Thu–Sun; €10 p/hr).

Tourist information
Office de Tourisme   [106 C2] 1 Promenade Wilson; ✆ 02 51 96 85 85; w lessablesdolonne-tourisme.com; ⊕ Apr–Jun & Sep 10.00–12.30 & 14.00–18.00 daily, Jul–Aug 09.30–19.00 daily, Oct–Mar 10.00–12.30 & 14.00–18.00 Mon–Thu & Sat, 14.00–18.00 Fri. Outside office hours, you'll find the lists of hotels, bike hire, etc, displayed in the window. If you're a would-be walker or cyclist (or even kayaker), pick up the office's booklet 'Balade & Vous', which describes a number of circuits; although in French, they are reasonably easy to follow.

Where to stay   Note that prices escalate shockingly every four years for the November departure of the ultra-challenging Vendée Globe around-the-world yacht race, with the latest one taking place in 2024. Even if you *can* afford it at those times, you may still have to book two years in advance!

True, it's the Vendée Globe which keeps Les Sables at the forefront of the yachting world. But you don't have to wait four years for some maritime fun and games, as there is usually something with a nautical theme occurring every summer. Few of the main races take place annually, but there are enough of them that you're likely to be there when at least one of them is. The big ones are the Golden Globe Race (based on the original 1968 Sunday Times around the world race where crews go without GPS or other electronics on board), the Solo Maître CoQ, the 1000 Milles, the Mini-Transat, the Vendee Arctique and the New York-Vendée Les Sables.

There is also the Vendée Va'a Polynesian festival, which has become a set date in the town's annual calendar. The focal points of this event are the *pirogue* races, with teams of six rowers taking part in gruelling competitions that cover up to 50km and 4 hours out in the ocean. Taking part are local oarspeople, rowers from the Basque Country, Marseille and, of course, from Polynesia. There is a Polynesian village, dancers on the beach and music to accompany the arrival of the oarspeople. An exhausted member from each team has to run up the sand to the finishing line after their rowing stint.

The festival takes place over three or four days around Ascensiontide, in May, so dates very slightly from year to year.

Côte Ouest Hôtel [106 G4] (97 rooms) Route du Tour de France; 02 51 21 77 77; w hotel-coteouest.com. Entering the reception you could be forgiven for thinking that you've just stepped on to a 1930s ocean liner. This is a 4-star hotel with all the accompanying amenities. The restaurant has panoramic views of the sea & forests & comes with a highly recommended buffet lunch on Sun, where a feast of fruits de mer, lobsters & incredible desserts are offered in quantity. Wi-Fi, TV Fitness & Wellness Club. €€€€

Maison L'Épicurienne [106 F3] (5 rooms) 9 Rue Villebois Mareuil; m 06 71 84 89 37; e contact@ maisonlepicurienne.fr; w maisonlepicurienne. fr. Delightfully situated just 30m from the Grande Plage, beautifully styled & run by a charming couple, this is an excellent address. Rooms are all individually decorated, all have private bath, AC, TV & free Wi-Fi. A 2-night minimum stay is required in high season, booking in advance is advisable. €€€€

Atlantic Hotel & Spa [106 G4] (34 rooms) 5 Promenade Georges Godet; 02 51 95 37 71; e info@atlantichotel.fr; w atlantichotel. fr. Situated across the road from the beach, this is a 4-star hotel that has well laid-out rooms in calming colours, with some of the more expensive options offering sea views. Sgls, dbls, trpls & a family suite, each with TV. There is a good restaurant at the hotel with views of the beach, plus a pool, spa & free Wi-Fi. €€

✖ Where to eat and drink

L'Abissiou [106 D2] 81 Rue des Halles; 09 86 36 42 29; e contact@labissiou.fr; w labissiou.fr; ⊕ Jul–end Aug 19.30–21.00 Tue–Sun, end Aug–Sep noon–13.30 & 19.30–21.00 Wed–Sat, noon–13.30 Sun; see website for times in other months & for making reservations. Tucked away a few streets back from the main promenade & beaches, the pink façade provides a warm welcome to this new establishment, which has been received with glowing reviews & a recent Michelin star. Run by Mélanie & Boris, who met at the 3-star Michelin restaurant La Villa Madie in Cassis, the restaurant specialises in seasonal, locally sourced, gourmet-styled dishes. You can choose from 2 tasting menu options, the 4-course 'Euphotic' & the 7-course 'Depth'. This is a truly culinary experience with a huge amount of effort & thought being put into each dish by Boris in the kitchen & delivered with charm by Mélanie as front of house. €€€€

Le Quai des Saveurs [106 C2] 10 Quai René Guiné; ☎ 02 51 23 84 91; w lequaidessaveurs.net; ⏰ noon–13.30 & 19.30–21.00 Mon–Tue & Sat–Sun, 19.30–21.00 Fri. Along a gastronomic quay, where you're spoiled for a choice of restaurants, this one is the standout. Great food, though not the cheapest; you should enjoy your minor splurge here. €€€€

La Pendule [106 D2] 67 Promenade Clemenceau; ☎ 02 51 95 05 63; ⏰ Jan–mid-Nov noon–15.00 Mon, noon–18.00 Wed–Thu & Sun, noon–21.00 Fri–Sat. 20 years old & still serving excellent crêpes & galettes on the seafront, plus omelettes & a few fish & meat options. Wash them down with a glass of cider. Good value, given its prime location. €€€

Shopping

Les Halles Centrales [106 D2] (⏰ Jul–Aug 08.00–13.00 daily, Sep–Jun 08.00–13.00 Tue–Sun) You enter the lovely glass-&-brick-built market hall from Rue du Palais, on the seaward side of the building, arriving at 1st-floor level where small farmers sell their produce on Wed & Sat. From here, an escalator carries you down to the ground floor where you find a terrific selection of colourful food stalls loaded with glistening shellfish, heaps of golden *mirabelle* plums (in season), gleaming mountains of butter, & fragrant bunches of fresh vegetables & herbs. A little oyster bar lurks in the corner – you can have as few as 3 of them for €4 with a glass of Muscadet, a good option.

Arago Market [106 F2] (27 Boulevard Arago) There's another morning market on Tue, Fri & Sun (daily for food), with extra outdoor stalls for clothing etc, in the Arago district.

Sports and activities

Base de Mer (Sports Nautiques Sablais) [106 C3] Promenade Joffre; w sportsnautiquessablais.com. For those who want to brave the Atlantic (rather than the tame Lac de Tanchet), here you can take lessons in sailing, windsurfing & other watersports. It's situated at the west end of the Remblai promenade. Bookings & enquiries can be made via the website.

Institut Sports Océan [106 G4] 1 Promenade Kennedy; ☎ 02 51 95 15 66; w institutsportsocean. com; ⏰ 09.00–noon & 14.00–18.00 Mon–Fri. Take to the Lac de Tanchet, choosing between sail,

stand-up paddleboard or kayak. You can opt for lessons or, if already experienced, rent a craft & practise on your own. It's great for beginners, away from the waves. Some instructors can give lessons in English.

Piscine du Remblai [106 C3] Promenade de l'Amiral Lafargue; ☎ 02 51 23 53 00; ⏰ Jul–Aug 10.00–19.30 daily, other months reduced hours. If the ocean looks a bit cold, avail yourself of this seafront heated swimming pool, also with hammam & jacuzzi. €6.90/5.60/free adult/under 16s/under 3s.

What to see and do

Grande Plage [106 D3] A beach with something for everyone and in summer, it seems that everyone is right here on the sands. Long, flat and wide, it slopes gently and disappears at high tide. But between high waters, it is a great people-watching venue, a place to relax or indulge in beach games and frolics. At its southern end, a cluster of rocks breaks through, interrupting the sands and inviting youngsters to search among its many pools.

Rue de l'Enfer [106 D2] This tiny street, which runs between Rue des Halles and Rue de la Patrie, a few blocks west of the central market hall, is reputed to be the narrowest in France (and was once the narrowest in the world, holding a 1986 Guinness World Record). You'll need to breathe in to squeeze along it – at the bottom, the walls on either side hardly allow for the width of an average person's shoulders.

Ile Penotte [106 D2] (Rue d'Assas) Among the quirkiest features of Les Sables is an ever-extending series of shell murals created by Danielle Aubin – a resident of one of the little streets just behind the seafront promenade. Near the beachside clocktower take a street called Rue Travot, head inland for 50m then take the first street on the right, Rue d'Assas. Facing you is a splendid representation of Neptune; along both sides of this and adjacent streets is a variety of further decorations made from mussel, scallop, cockle and limpet shells. Look up, look down, and look around corners – some are in the most surprising places.

Muséum du Coquillage [106 D2] (8 Rue du Maréchal Leclerc, at eastern end of fishing harbour; \02 51 23 50 00; w museumducoquillage.com; ⊕ Jul–Aug 10.00– 19.00 daily, Feb–Jun & Sep–Dec 14.00–18.00 Mon, 10.00–12.30 & 14.00–18.00 Tue–Sun; €9/8/6/free adult/under 18s/under 12s/under 4s) More than 50,000 shells of all kinds, from familiar winkles and sea-urchins to the colourful, speckled and exotic produce of the South Seas inhabit this private museum, one of only two shell museums in France. They are beautifully presented in glass cases, mostly with chatty descriptions (in English as well as French).

Musée de l'Abbaye Ste-Croix (MASC) [106 E2] (Rue de Verdun; \02 51 32 01 16; w lemasc.fr; ⊕ opening times are based on school holidays, see website for details; €5/3/free adult/student/under 18s) This delightful museum and gallery of modern art occupies one wing of a 17th-century building that was formerly a Benedictine convent. Temporary exhibitions fill the first floor throughout the year, while a collection of mixed-media Surrealist works by Romanian artist Victor Brauner (1903–66) occupies much of the ground level. The permanent collection also includes a couple of charming pictures of Les Sables in the 1920s by Albert Marquet (1875–1947) and a large selection of colourful collages and paintings by Gaston Chaissac (1910–64; page 195), an exponent of *l'art brut*. Under the ancient beams of the attic is a marvellous collection of local costume, model ships and items relating to the fishing industry, including some wonderful naïve paintings of boats by local fishermen-turned-artists Paul-Emile Pajot (1873–1929) and his son Gilbert (1902–56).

Le Blockhaus Hôpital [106 E2] (Rue de Verdun; \ 02 51 32 80 12; w blockhaus-sables.com; ⊕ Apr–Sep 10.00–19.00 daily, Oct–Mar 10.00–18.00 daily; €9/6.50/free adult/under 13s/under 5s) This forbidding concrete bunker on the busy traffic intersection next to the Abbaye Ste-Croix museum is a fantastic place to learn about life in the Vendée under German occupation. An excellent 15-minute documentary about the outbreak of World War II (with English subtitles) shows the changes imposed on this peaceful seaside resort: the fluttering of swastika flags over the promenade; the building of German defences on the sands; the arrival of 20,000 refugees; the rationing of food; Marshal Pétain's orders to collaborate with the invaders; attacks by British and American naval and air forces; the work of the Resistance; and, finally, the liberation of the town in September 1944. As Les Sables lay midway between the still-German-held pockets of St-Nazaire and La Rochelle, the town became strategically important for the Allies from this point.

After the film, you follow a route through 20 rooms, some with original equipment for purifying air or generating electricity, others with stern-faced dummies in scenes depicting typical activities from the time when this was a German hospital; there are also glass cases with everyday items from the period, wall panels of amazing wartime photographs, and so much fascinating information that you will never be able to read everything in one visit. (English translation of it all has not been possible, but you are given an information sheet bearing an outline explanation of each scene.)

Watch your step as you go, because you'll be so intent on taking everything in that you could easily stumble on some of the uneven thresholds between rooms. Virtual tours are also available in both English and French (see website for details).

Zoo des Sables [106 G4] (Route du Tour de France; 📞 02 51 95 14 10; 🌐 zoodessables.fr; 🕐 Feb–Mar 13.30–18.30 daily, Apr–Jun & Sep 09.30–19.00 daily, Jul–Aug 09.30–19.30 daily, Oct–Nov 13.30–18.30 daily; €18/14/free adult/under 11s/under 3s) Beyond the southernmost end of the Remblai, some 2km from the town centre, lies a well-laid-out and cared-for zoo in a tree-filled park alongside the River Tanchet, with a collection of reptiles, exotic birds, big cats, squawking parakeets, anteaters and other animals – 350 species in total. Free-roaming monkeys swing down from the trees to investigate the rubbish bins among the rose bushes and fragrant frangipani trees, and otters and penguins splash about in pools – glass-sided, so you can watch their underwater antics. Feeding times are posted at the gate. It's very family-friendly, with ramps for pushchairs, lots of picnic spots, and notices telling you that the ducks love popcorn (children can buy small bags of it to feed to animals). Free parking nearby.

La Chaume A sailors' and fishers' village of days gone by, La Chaume has its own sense of identity, an independent spirit that you can tap into during time spent in the quayside bars. Wander away from the quay and enjoy the peace of the quaint streets around the church. It has its own morning market, too, on Tuesdays, Thursdays and Sundays – from Tuesday to Sunday in July and August. You can drive around to La Chaume on the boulevard that passes the north side of Port Olona marina, or arrive by the tiny ferry. Towering over the market is one of the town's most distinctive pieces of architecture – the square-sided Tour d'Arundel that still serves as a lighthouse. La Chaume's other major landmark is the pointed spire of the church – a few blocks inland from the quay. Alongside it, a few trompe-l'oeil paintings have transformed several once-dreary blank walls to add some humorous views of the town.

🍴 Where to eat and drink
Le Port [106 B2] 24 Quai George-V; 📞 02 51 32 07 52; 🕐 10.30–15.00 Mon–Tue, Thu & Sun, 10.30–15.00 & 19.00–22.30 Fri–Sat. Traditional restaurant, with the midday *menu du marché* short on choice but long on value. 1st-floor tables have a view over the harbour. €€€€

Loulou Côte Sauvage [106 A3] 19 Route Bleue, La Chaume; 📞 02 51 21 32 32; 🕐 noon–13.30 & 19.15–20.30 Wed, Fri & Sat, noon–14.00 Thu & Sun. Unprepossessing from the street but fabulous sea views & good food within. €€€€

L'Étoile de Mer [106 B2] 33 Quai George V, La Chaume; 🕐 06.30–01.00 daily. With a great people-&-boat-watching spot by the ferry quay, the characters of La Chaume gather here of a morning to smoke, drink coffee & exchange gossip. Do join them. Occasional boisterous music on summer w/end evenings & regular karaoke parties. A great ambience. €€

Le Moulin de la Chaume [106 B2] 55 Rue du Dr Canteteau; 🕐 06.00–19.30 Mon–Wed & Fri–Sat, 06.00–19.00 Thu, 06.00–14.00 Sun. Queues form at this excellent bakery to buy the many different & tasty breads, some sold by the kilo. €

What to see and do
Port Olona [106 B1] (Capitainerie, or harbourmaster's office, Le Port du Vendée-Globe; 📞 02 51 32 51 16) More than 1,000 yachts are moored in this busy marina

near the north end of La Chaume, with shops, bars and restaurants and, frequently, live music during the evenings.

The port hits the headlines every four years as the start and finish of the single-handed, non-stop, around-the-world sailing race known as the Vendée-Globe, held most recently in 2024. The event, dubbed 'the Everest of the seas', has given rise to some nail-biting exploits by British competitors (Ellen MacArthur 2000/01; Mike Golding 2004/05; Samantha Davies 2008/09; Alex Thomson 2016/17). The winner usually accomplishes the gruelling circumnavigation in about 75 days. Early November is the time it begins; for three weeks beforehand you can visit the pontoons to see the yachts before they set off. The arrivals, spread over about six weeks from late January, draw enormous crowds keen to give their favourite a hero's welcome.

Musée de la Mer/Tour d'Arundel [106 B3] (Pl Maraud; m 07 68 51 65 37; w oceam.org; ⊕ May–Sep 10.30–12.30 & 15.00–18.00 daily; museum & tower (combined) €5/3/ free adult/under 15s/under 5s, museum or tower (individually) €3/1.50/free) Scale models, naval objects, plans and documents are on show – though slightly lacking in explanation – inside this 12th-century former chateau. The small museum downstairs is devoted to nautical matters and to La Chaume's rich fishing history. You can also read a little about the local sailor-turned-pirate, the bloodthirsty 'Nau l'Olonnais', who mercilessly tortured his victims in the Caribbean and was himself eaten by cannibals in 1671. If you can face the climb to the top of the adjacent Tour d'Arundel, you can enjoy a seagull's-eye view of Les Sables.

Prieuré St-Nicolas [106 B4] (⊕ during exhibitions, times & admission charges vary) This beautifully restored Romanesque church and one-time fort stands in a commanding position on the point, overlooking the ocean and the entrance to Les Sables harbour channel. It's open to the public throughout the year for exhibitions and concerts, which are held in the summer, giving you a chance to view the austere stone interior.

Les Salines [106 A1] (120 Route de l'Aubraie, D87A, L'Aubraie, 2.5km north of La Chaume; ℡02 51 21 01 19; w lessalines.fr; ⊕ Apr–Jun & Sep–end Oct 09.30–noon & 14.00–18.30 Mon–Fri, 14.00–18.30 Sun; Jul–Aug 09.30–19.00 daily; Nov–Mar 14.00–17.00 Mon–Fri; ticket office closes 90mins before times given; boat trip & salt 'adventure' trail €24/14/free adult/under 13s/under 3s, salt 'adventure' trail only €15/11/free) There are two parts to this salt-based attraction: the Parc d'aventure du sel, an open-air trail that takes you on a self-guided tour of the salt-making process, and Balades en bateau, a guided boat trip. The **Parc d'aventure du sel** trail takes about an hour to walk, winding along bumpy mud paths and rustic steps. On arrival, you are given the times of live salt-making demonstrations, and a rather inadequate English booklet with translations of recorded commentaries you will encounter.

The visit starts with a great view over the extensive salt marsh below; however, working out where to go from here is a bit of a puzzle. French-speakers will learn quite a bit from viewing a 7-minute film in the video room about the techniques of the *saunier* (salt-maker) as he lets sea water flow into his shallow basins and then, after weeks of evaporation, skims off the delicate white *fleur de sel* and rakes in the chunkier, grey *gros sel* beneath.

However, the trail overall is a bit of a disappointment. Relying almost entirely on panels with written descriptions in French only, plus occasional commentary points, it tells the story of salt manufacturing, beginning with the Romans' use of heat to evaporate the grains from sea water 2,000 years ago. You read of the unpopular salt tax (*la gabelle*), introduced in France in 1340 and maintained here for more than six centuries. In a wooden ship-like structure, you learn about Les Sables' once-great cod-fishing industry off distant Newfoundland, for which huge amounts of salt were required to preserve the catches until their sale, months later on their return to France.

Tying in with the times of the boat trips, there are demonstrations by a present-day *saunier*. Flourishing a long-handled, rake-like *simouche*, he skims crystals from the surface of the glittering saltpans, and explains (in French) the system of sluices that allows the salt water in to dry off slowly from the sun and wind. Today, about 100 *oeillets* – the square pans in which the sea water evaporates – remain of the 30,000 that were once worked here; from June to September, each *oeillet* can produce around 100kg of salt (depending on how much rain hinders the process). There are a few rather perilous games en route to entertain children, and in the summer season they might get to gather up a handful of salt crystals to take home after the demonstration, but the admission charge seems nonetheless ridiculously high.

The **Balades en bateau** boat journey, downriver to the edge of Les Sables (a 1½-hour return trip), gives a chance to hear (in French, with written English translation on request) the history of the town and its fishing and salt industries. The marshes here were full of saltpans till 50 years ago; today fish farming has taken over much of the same area. There's no shade on board, so take sunhats, and garments with sleeves in hot weather. On your return, you are given a demonstration of salt harvesting by a *saunier* and may then tour the Parc d'aventure described above, making a 2½-hour experience in all.

On an adjacent site, you can rent canoes for €12 for the first hour, or stand-up paddleboards for €16, from La Terrasse des Salines (w laterrassedessalines.fr).

OLONNE-SUR-MER Olonne-sur-Mer, a former commune of the Vendée, is now a quarter of Les Sables-d'Olonne Agglomération, having merged in 2019 alongside Château-d'Olonne, Île-d'Olonne, Vairé, Sainte-Foy and St Mathurin. As well as beach entertainment, activities here include birdwatching, go-karting, golf, tennis and canoeing.

For tourist information, see Les Sables (page 107).

Where to stay and eat The town is not overendowed with good restaurants. If you don't fancy splashing out at the Cayola, you will find a couple of pizza parlours in the town centre. Alternatively, head down the road to Les Sables with its good choice of places to dine (page 108).

Longère des Olonnes (4 rooms) 58 Route des Maraîchers; 📞02 51 04 34 81; w longeredesolonnes.com. Coolly modern *chambres d'hôte*, accommodating up to 4 people, in a low-rise building set around a pool. TV, free Wi-Fi & fridge. B/fast inc. €€€€
La Villa St Jean (19 rooms) 45 Prom Edouard Herriot; 📞02 51 22 00 69; w lavillasaintjean.com. On the beach with sea views from 17 of the 19 pleasant rooms & a fantastic restaurant serving

local food with a seasonal menu. TV, free Wi-Fi. B/fast inc. €€€
Le Cayola 76 Promenade de Cayola (D32B coast road), Château-d'Olonne, 7km southeast of Les Sables; 📞02 51 22 01 01; w le-cayola.com; ⏰ noon–14.00 Tue–Thu & Sun, noon–14.00 & 19.30–21.30 Fri–Sat. Superbly sophisticated clifftop restaurant, in romantic setting overlooking the bay. Booking strongly advised. Beware: you could spend a small fortune here! €€€€€

4

Le Manoir de la Mortière Rue Eugène Nauleau. Opening in 2024, so no chance to review at the time of writing. However, this new restaurant will be set in a medieval manor & is the latest creation from Marjorie & Nicolas Ferré of Le Quai des Saveurs local fame, who have an ambition to offer gastronomic excellence. We expect good things.

Sports and activities

Golf des Sables d'Olonne Allée de la Pierre-Levée, 2km southeast of Olonne, near the large D760 roundabout; 📞02 51 33 16 16; w golfdessablesdolonne.com. There are plenty of water features on this 6,063m course, designed by Bruno Parpoil. Green fee €70/45 high/low season for 18 holes.

What to see and do

Musée des Traditions Populaires (30 Rue du Maréchal Foch, 500m west of church; 📞02 51 96 95 53; w memoiredesolonnes.wixsite.com/musee-traditions; ⊕ Apr, Jun, Sep & mid-term hols 14.30–17.30 Mon–Fri, Jul–Aug 15.00–18.30 Mon, Wed & Fri, 10.00–noon & 15.00–18.30 Tue & Thu; €4.50/2/free adult/under 13s/under 6s) This charming museum of local costume, customs and way of life is laid out in six rooms of a 19th-century school building in the centre of Olonne. It includes agricultural and woodworking tools and some lovely local *coiffes*, or headdresses, plus amusing relics from the early days of the area's seaside-holiday industry. An unexpectedly large collection of French World War I memorabilia has been deposited by a local resident, whose father died in the trenches. In the entrance hall, look for a chunk of rock from Le Veillon beach that bears the footprint of a dinosaur. English information sheet available at reception.

Château de Pierre-Levée (2km southeast of Olonne; 📞02 51 90 75 45; ⊕ son et lumière show, 5 days in Aug; €20/17/10 adult/child, student, disabled/under 12s) Although this pretty stone house, modelled on the Trianon chateau at Versailles, is only rarely open to the public, you can get a good view of it from the road that leads to Olonne golf club. Better still, in early August some 200 local residents take part in an excellent son et lumière presentation in the grounds, telling the history of the house and of the surrounding area – speak to the local Tourist Office for details.

Observatoire d'Oiseaux (Champclou, near Île-d'Olonne, signposted off the D38, 2km north of Olonne; 📞02 51 33 12 97; w adev-asso.fr; ⊕ accessible at all times mid-Jun–end Aug, see website for other times; free except when an ornithologist is present, which is 19–30 Jun 09.00–13.00, Jul–Aug 09.00–13.00 & 16.00–19.00; €4/2.50/free adult/under 19s/under 8s) At this simple, wood-built birdwatching post, visitors can look out over Île-d'Olonne's old salt marshes, home to France's second-largest colony of avocets. In fact, it was in an effort to conserve this species that a protected area here was created. At times there will be friendly members of the LPO (the French organisation which protects birds) with high-powered telescopes and bird books; otherwise take your own binoculars and bird book to help with identifying the curlews, stilts, spoonbills and other wading birds that take up temporary residence in this wetland. Huge migrating flocks pass by in March/April and August/September and more than 200 species have been recorded here. After your visit, you can continue into Île-d'Olonne, then take the D87 across the marshes to La Chaume.

Puits d'Enfer (On the D32B, 3km south of Château-d'Olonne) About 2km southeast of Les Sables, the coastline turns to water-eroded cliffs and gullies, where spray is driven up like geysers on stormy days, earning the site its name of 'Hell's Well'. (Be careful not to stray near the edge in fierce weather conditions.) This was the site of a gruesome discovery in February 1949, referred to as '*la malle sanglante*' ('the blood-soaked trunk'), when a laundry basket containing the body of an elderly Parisian, murdered by his housekeeper, was found at the bottom of the cliff.

Abbaye St-Jean-d'Orbestier (On the D32A, 3km south of Château-d'Olonne) The solid vestiges of this 12th-century abbey stand on a windswept point just back from the sea. Half-hidden by some institutional buildings, the church is currently under restoration, but with walls and roof now safe it has become a centre for cultural events and acts as a venue for summer films, plays, exhibitions and concerts.

TALMONT-ST-HILAIRE

A former port of great charm nestles below the impressive remains of a medieval castle that once belonged to the powerful Princes of Talmont and, between 1152 and 1204, to the English crown. A little less ancient, up the hill behind the castle, stand some beautiful old, creeper-covered mansions.

Port Bourgenay, an area above the cliffs 5km southwest of Talmont, contains a traffic-free holiday development and sporting complex, as well as a golf course (page 116). Down on the waterside beyond a turreted castle (today belonging to a religious order), is a sailing school, and a marina, with cafés, restaurants and yacht-orientated shops. Talmont's market day is on Thursday.

TOURIST INFORMATION
Office de Tourisme 11 Rue du Château; ✆02 51 90 65 10; w destination-vendeegrandlittoral.com; ⊕Apr–Aug 09.30–12.30 & 14.00–17.30 Mon– Tue, 09.30–12.30 Wed–Fri; Oct–Mar 09.30–12.30 Mon–Wed & Fri–Sat; for other months see website

WHERE TO EAT AND DRINK
Greenhouse Bourgenay Golf Club; ✆02 51 23 35 45; w greenhouse-restaurant.fr; ⊕ noon–15.00 Mon–Thu, noon–15.00 & 19.00–22.00 Fri–Sat, noon–15.00 Sun. Green velvet-clad chairs & dark wood flooring give this upmarket establishment an English private members club atmosphere while the cuisine remains staunchly French in style. Its location at the golf club means you can also enjoy views of the course. Leave your putter at home & enjoy the regular concerts & live music that take place Fri & Sat nights. €€€€

La Plage Plage du Veillon; ✆02 51 90 31 45; ⊕ Apr–Sep 10.30–22.00 daily. Inspired by the bars of Ibiza, this is the place for enjoying a drink on the beach according to the locals, but don't be deterred by the crowds. A wide range of cocktails, wines & local beer compete with mussels, burgers, steaks or the fish of the day, which is sourced from the Sables-d'Olonne auction a few kilometres away. You can round your meal off with a huge range of ice creams for dessert. €€€

Le Relais Talmondais 13 Rue du Château; ✆02 51 60 90 86; ⊕ Sep–Jun noon–14.00 Tue–Sat, Jul–Aug noon–14.00 Mon–Sat. With the castle towering over its outdoor tables, this is a good place to relax, before or after your chateau visit. Midday menus are great value, making it popular – booking advised, especially in summer. Food is beautifully presented. €€€

Les Loups de Mer 310 Av de la Plage; ✆02 51 22 22 08; ⊕ noon–14.00 Tue–Thu & Sun, noon–14.00 & 19.00–21.00 Fri–Sat. A bright interior & some outdoor tables at this pleasant place on the D4A by the campsite. Delicious desserts complement a fairly short main-course menu. Children's options & toddlers' play area. €€€

SPORTS AND ACTIVITIES

Golf de Port Bourgenay Av de la Mine, Port Bourgenay, 6km southwest of Talmont-St-Hilaire; ☎02 51 23 35 45; w bourgenaygolfclub.com. An 18-hole, par-72 seaside course designed by Pierre Thevenin. It also has an 18-hole, par-54 pitch-&-putt course, ideal for beginners.

WHAT TO SEE AND DO

Château de Talmont (Pl du Château; ☎02 51 42 81 00; w chateaudetalmont.com; ⏰ early Apr–early Jul 10.30–18.00 daily, early Jul–Aug 10.30–19.00 daily, Sep 10.30–18.00 daily, late Oct–early Nov 10.30–12.30 & 14.00–18.00 Tue–Sun; high season €14/9/free adult/under 13s/under 5s, low season €7/5/free) Richard Coeur-de-Lion (the English King Richard the Lionheart, son of Henry Plantagenet of England and of his French wife, Eleanor of Aquitaine) spent a good deal of time hunting in the neighbouring forests and was responsible for building Talmont Castle. The imposing ruins you see today are for the most part 12th century; the castle was much fought over during the Wars of Religion, and reduced to its present state in 1628. On your approach to the castle, you'll be put in the mood by some piped medieval music. From the top of the keep there are marvellous views over the town, countryside, marshes and sea – it's a long way up, and you'll welcome the breeze at the top. During the Heritage Days in September there is a programme of medieval events – including some in English – with costumed performers encouraging visitors to try archery or calligraphy, watch knightly ceremonies, ride a pony or learn medieval board games (instructions in English) or dances. (On other days, you go around the castle at your own pace.) Between April and November there is also the option of taking part in the Escape Game (can be booked in advance; from €23), where you play a team of archaeologists tracking down the treasure of 12th-century members of the Order of the Templars. A small café selling drinks and crêpes is situated inside the grounds and there's a gift shop. In June, in odd-numbered years, the castle is the venue for the town's medieval festival (see website for details).

Musée Automobile de Vendée (Route des Sables-d'Olonne, D949, 6km west of Talmont; ☎02 51 22 05 81; w musee-auto-vendee.com; ⏰ Apr–May & Sep 10.00–noon & 14.00–18.30 daily, Jun–Aug 10.00–19.00 daily; €16/8/free adult/under 13s/under 5s) More than 150 immaculately presented vehicles – mostly French, of course, but a few Italian, German and US marques – contribute to the iconic smell that mingles rubber, leather and petrol at this museum. Well labelled in English, the exhibits date from 1885 to the 1970s. Among them are such makes as De Dion-Bouton, Bugatti and Hispano-Suiza, plus a selection of horse-drawn carriages, bicycles and motorbikes, and beautiful old posters advertising glorious cars of the past. French classics include a Citroën DS and a Traction Avant. The collection comes more up to date with Maseratis and Ferraris and there's that French peculiarity, the three-seater Matra Bagheera. British cars? See if you can spot the Lola…and the British Leyland contribution.

Verrerie d'Art de Bourgenay (Rue des Forges, off the D4A, Querry-Pigeon, 5km southwest of Talmont; ☎02 51 32 71 42; ⏰ Jul–Aug 10.00–noon & 14.30–19.00 Mon–Fri, other months telephone for information; free) Since taking on this glass-blowing studio in 2009, Stéphanie and Valérien have filled it with some great creations. There is a real air of performance about the twisting and caressing of the molten glass accompanied by rock music (!) but the skill (and soft hands) required is at times truly breathtaking. The shelves in this converted barn are full of vases, lamps and figurines for sale – some quite reasonably priced, given the craftsmanship involved.

Aquarium de Vendée (Av de la Mine, Port Bourgenay, 5km southwest of Talmont; 📞02 51 32 30 00; w aquarium-vendee.com; ⏰ Sep–Jun 10.30–12.30 & 14.00–18.00 daily, Jul–Aug 09.30–19.00 daily; €15.80/13.80/11.80/free adult/under 18s/under 13s/under 3s) Talmont's aquarium presents a series of 120,000-litre tanks arranged around three big halls showing underwater scenes from the Seychelles to Haiti, plus a reconstruction of a mangrove swamp. Take your time visiting, though, as you soon come to the end, and would be hard-pushed to spend more than an hour here. There are colourful tropical fish everywhere, sharks in the lagoon area, and a variety of rays in the tank representing the Celebes Sea (Indonesia). Feeding time, with (French) commentary is at 15.30 (July and August 10.45, 11.30, 15.15 & 16.15); most, though not all, information boards are translated into English. There's also a café and gift shop.

JARD-SUR-MER

A charming small seaside resort 20km southeast of Les Sables-d'Olonne, Jard-sur-Mer houses a pretty harbour for up to 500 boats, plus three sandy beaches, a Monday market day and many attractive villas half-hidden among pine woods. The port is overlooked by the Conchette windmill, one of nine mills that ground corn in the area a century ago. Among some delightful walks is the 5km Circuit du Payré, starting 1km beyond the turning to the Abbey of Lieu-Dieu, which leads along clifftops and past wind-twisted holm oaks to the mouth of the Payré River.

TOURIST INFORMATION
Office de Tourisme Pl de la Liberté; 📞02 51 33 40 47; w destination-vendeegrandlittoral. com; ⏰ Apr–Jun 09.30–12.30 & 14.00–17.30 Mon–Wed & Fri, 09.30–12.30 Thu & Sat; for other months see website

WHERE TO EAT AND DRINK
Le Canoa 39 Rue des Sables d'Or; 📞02 51 96 91 34; ⏰ Jul–Aug 10.30–15.00 & 18.00–23.00 Wed–Mon. Right on the sand, this is a true beach bar with great cocktails, stunning plates of fish & delicious ice cream sundaes with a choice of fruits. €€€€

Le Kou-Dé-Ta 30 Rue Morpoigne; 📞02 51 33 44 55; w kou-de-ta.com; ⏰ noon–14.30 & 18.00–02.00 Mon–Tue & Fri– Sun, 18.00–02.00 Thu. By the roundabout in the town centre; choose from lobster, fish or meat dishes in this popular place. Children's menu & some excellent cocktails are plus points. €€€

Crêperie du Moulin 9 Rue du Commandant Guilbaud; 📞02 51 20 18 65. A standard crêperie, down by the sea. A favourite with families for its delicious crêpes & savoury galettes. €€

La Coussoussière d'Hocine 31 Rue de l'Océan; 📞02 51 96 81 58; ⏰ 10.00–13.30 & 17.00–20.30 Thu–Sun. A take-away-only option, popular with self-caterers & campers. Delicious, but you need to order the night before. €€

WHAT TO SEE AND DO
Église Ste-Radégonde (Pl Sully; ⏰ guided tours Jul–Aug 10.30 & 12.30 Tue & Thu) Jard's Romanesque church is dedicated to a one-time Queen of France (page 96). Fortified in the Middle Ages, and sacked by Protestants in 1568, it has many interesting features, including a Renaissance-style chapel, added in 1573. The church is often locked, so your best opportunity to see the interior is around the time of a service – on Saturday evening or Sunday morning – or on one of the tourist office's guided tours, in summer.

Maison de Clemenceau (St-Vincent-sur-Jard, 2km southeast of Jard; 📞02 51 33 40 32; w maison-de-clemenceau.fr; ⏰ mid-May–mid-Sep 10.00–12.30 & 14.00–18.30

Tue–Sun, mid-Sep–mid-May 10.00–12.30 & 14.00–17.30 Tue–Sun; €8/free adult/under 18s & under 26s if EU nationals/French residents) As soon as you see this enchanting low-built cottage on the sands you can understand why Georges Clemenceau (pages 154 and 196) chose this spot for his retirement in 1919. After his momentous work on the Treaty of Versailles, the peace settlement at the end of World War I, the fiery politician withdrew here to write his memoirs at his desk overlooking the sea. The interior is full of books, clothes, furniture and objects, as if the 'Tiger' (as he was affectionately known) had just left it to go out for a stroll round his beloved garden. His friend the Impressionist painter Claude Monet is reputed to have given him some ideas for its design, though rabbits have the upper hand today. Other dignitaries to visit 'Le Tigre' here included the young Hirohito (later to become Emperor of Japan). The tiles in the kitchen were a gift from workers at Longwy, in Alsace, in gratitude for their province being returned to France in 1918; the kitchen clock stands fixed at the time that Clemenceau died in his Paris apartment. A 20-minute video precedes the guided tour; good English notes are available. You can also download the new augmented-reality Sky Boy app, which plays four different scenes as Georges Clemenceau himself invites you to various rooms in his house.

AVRILLÉ

Its large number of prehistoric remains have earned the area around Avrillé, 23km east of Les Sables-d'Olonne, the nickname of 'the Carnac of the Vendée' (after the famous megalith-rich site in Brittany). More than 20 dolmens and 100 menhirs are scattered around the area. Behind Avrillé's *mairie* is one of the largest standing stones in France – even Asterix's muscular sidekick, Obelix, would have found shifting the 7m-high 'Ménhir du Camp de César' a challenge. The CAIRN centre (see opposite) gives you an idea of how such stones were moved and raised.
On a more modern note, the town hosts a large craft fair in mid-July.

TOURIST INFORMATION

Mairie 2 Av du Général de Gaulle; ☎ 02 51 22 32 22; **w** avrille85.fr; ⏲ 14.00–18.00 Mon, 08.00–noon Tue & Thu, 08.00–noon & 14.00–18.00 Wed & Fri. Alternatively, you can visit **w** destination-vendeegrandlittoral.com for details.

WHERE TO EAT AND DRINK

Le Ménhir 14 Av du Général de Gaulle; ☎ 02 51 95 61 94; ⏲ noon–14.00 Mon, Tue & Sun, noon–14.00 & 19.00–21.00 Fri–Sat. Occupying a lovely stone building & serving excellent cuisine. Summer specials include lobster & mussels; grills are another speciality. **€€€**

WHAT TO SEE AND DO

Château des Aventuriers/Château de la Guignardière (Route des Sables-d'Olonne, D949, 1km west of Avrillé; ☎ 02 51 22 33 06; **w** chateau-aventuriers.com; ⏲ castle: early Apr–mid-Jun 11.00–20.00 daily, mid-Jun–early Jul 10.00–20.00 daily, early Jul–early Sep 11.00–20.00; see website for details on park & other castle opening times; €24/19 adult/under 12s) Such a remarkably well-preserved Renaissance stately home as this is a rare sight in the Vendée. La Guignardière was built in 1555 by Jean Girard, who held an important post ('Master of the King's Bread'!) in the court of the French King Henri II. Having been occupied during the Wars of the Vendée by Republicans, the chateau escaped destruction in the post-Revolutionary conflicts.

Today, its 'Parcours Historique' (50-minute guided tour – in English as well as French) takes you from vaulted cellars to beamed attics, by way of furnished *salon* and bedrooms, panelled dining room, and a granite staircase pierced with occasional holes through which defenders could shoot at attackers below.

Outside, there are three well-designed and well-run new trails, available in English, where visitors can follow pirate- and dinosaur-themed routes, as well as an augmented reality 'murder mystery'. If these aren't enough, there's also an escape room-style haunted house where you work as a team to solve puzzles, lift a curse and escape (under 10s aren't allowed). Self-guided tours around the chateau are possible; get a brochure with your ticket. Younger children are also catered for with a Western City that provides playgrounds, bouncy castles and Cowboys and Indians horse exhibitions during the summer months (Mon & Fri, see website for timings). You could easily spend the day here.

CAIRN Centre de la Préhistoire (St-Hilaire-la-Forêt, 3.5km southwest of Avrillé; 02 51 33 38 38; w cairn-prehistoire.com; ⊕ Jul–Aug 10.30–19.00 daily, for other months see website; €8/7/free adult/under 15s/under 5s) About 80% of the Vendée's prehistoric sites are to be found in the five villages around St-Hilaire-la-Forêt, so this is a good place to start. At this archaeological Neolithic research centre, you can try lighting fires with two sticks, making jewellery from shells, polishing stone axes, making primitive pots, or weaving in the style of our early ancestors. In July and August, visitors are given the opportunity to try one or two such crafts, or to help with erecting a standing stone, constructing a cairn, or daubing mud on the walls of a Neolithic-style building. There are two exhibition rooms to take in first – one using models to show techniques of raising standing stones; the other devoted to a temporary exhibition on some Neolithic theme. A multi-media presentation about prehistoric times follows (try and sit close to the screen to read the English subtitles). Things come to life outside, with the hands-on experiences that are both fun and enlightening. Some of the enthusiastic guides speak English and an English-language leaflet comes with your ticket.

Dolmen de la Frébouchère (Off the D91, 4km southeast of Avrillé; free access) Follow signs into the countryside north of Le Bernard to the Vendée's largest prehistoric burial chamber. In spite of some incongruous pink gravel that has been spread around to prettify the area, the mighty structure – its top slab weighing 100 tonnes – remains an awe-inspiring sight.

La Folie de Finfarine (Chemin des Écoliers, Poiroux, 6km northwest of Avrillé; 02 51 96 22 50; w finfarine.fr; ⊕ Jul–Aug 10.30–19.00 daily, for other months see website; €10/6.80/free adult/under 16s/under 4s) In the centre of nearby Poiroux is the 'bee-centric' visitor centre of a forest park designed to give a feeling for the ecology of woodland and its flora and fauna. It's a low-key sort of place, to be sampled slowly, appreciating its eco-friendly woods and ponds; watching the 10-minute film on a wraparound screen that charts the life of a bee; dressing up to navigate a giant hive; enjoying the quiz sheet about the life of Bizzbee the bee; trying out the small maze of holm oaks; and watching bee-keeping demonstrations by robot-like figures in the Miellerie. You learn about old country remedies, too (slugs' slime with sugar for a cold; flowers to help you sleep; ginger as an aphrodisiac). English translations are provided.

Indoors, cutaway trees show the inside of oak, poplar and cherry; you can sniff the essence of each tree type (slightly confusingly, the French word *essence*

4

in connection with trees means 'species'), and lift blocks of different woods to test their relative weights. It's pleasantly shady in hot weather, and there's a small children's playground – made of wood, of course. There's also a café and gift shop.

MOUTIERS-LES-MAUXFAITS

The pride of this ancient village 21km south of La Roche-sur-Yon, on the road to La Tranche, is its unusual 18th-century market hall, whose Roman-tiled roof rests on an intricate structure of solid oak beams and no fewer than 41 stalwart stone columns. The historic atmosphere of the village centre is accentuated by the collection of old houses clustered around the market, alongside the well-preserved Romanesque church of St-Jacques. This 12th-century building was familiar centuries ago to travellers en route to Santiago de Compostela. In recognition of those times, Moutiers has incorporated a pilgrim's scallop shell into its present-day town emblem.

At the Lac du Graon, 5km northeast of Moutiers, summer visitors can sail, fish or rent boats. A kilometre south of town, the Bois Lambert is the venue for the early-August **Fête du Cheval** (w lafeteducheval.com), an equestrian one-day event, plus horse-driving competitions, country dancing and music. To the northwest, in St-Avaugourd-des-Landes, the **Fête du Folklore et du Sanglier** is a 'wild boar' festival which also involves international folk dancing and a gigantic 'Gallic' dinner where up to 2,000 are fed each year. It is held on 15 August.

For tourist information, see Jard-sur-Mer (page 117).

✳ WHERE TO EAT AND DRINK You can grab snacks and light meals inside O'Gliss and O'Fun parks (see below), if you are spending a day there.

Le Champ de Foire 43 Rue des Sables;
☏02 51 98 91 67; ⏰ 09.00–14.30 Mon–Fri.
A lunchtime option, just west of the town centre.

Food is traditional, service is professional & the atmosphere is welcoming. Best to arrive before 13.00 for lunch; it can get busy. €€

WHAT TO SEE AND DO

O'Gliss Park (Le Pont Rouge Route de la Tranche Le Bernard; ☏02 51 48 12 12; w oglisspark.fr; ⏰ late-Jun–early Sep 10.00–19.00 daily; €35.90/27.90/16/free adult & over 11s or over 1.5m in height/under 11s & seniors/3–4yrs/under 3s) A full-tilt waterpark with wave machine, giant waterslides and all the trimmings. Although located inland, it's well worth the trip if this is the kind of thing that keeps your kids entertained. There's a 'beach area' and snack bars, or you can bring in your own picnic, if you prefer, to eat in designated areas. There's little information in English, but many of the young staff members speak English and are able to help. Unusually for France, swimming shorts *are* permitted here, so no need to pack your Speedos, gentlemen.

O'Fun Park (Le Bois Lambert, Le Bernard, Moutiers-les-Mauxfaits; ☏ 02 51 48 12 12; w ofunpark.fr; ⏰ Apr–late Sep, see website for hours; prices from €35.90/25.90/19.90 adult & over 11s or over 1.5m in height/under 11s & seniors/3–4 yrs; 1-day & 2-day passes available; in high season, advanced booking advised) Previously known as the Indian Forest, this is a brilliant place to take children and teenagers, guaranteed to give them (and adults, too) thrills aplenty. The 20ha forest site echoes to the clicking of harness clips and whoops of joy as kids master the various challenges. Treetop trails are colour-graded according to difficulty; as well as zip-wiring through the forest, youngsters can enjoy a water jump, paintballing, bungeeing, climbing a wall, orienteering or riding a mechanical bull; 3–11-year-olds will be happy with pony rides, bouncy inflatables and a shady, 18-hole mini-golf course. Gloves and harnesses are provided; tough shoes should be worn for the tree-top activities (make sure you have no keys, money, etc, in your pockets before starting out). Children under nine must be accompanied by a participating adult on all activities.

It gets very busy in high season, and you should arrive as early as possible to avoid the lengthy queues to get in; for the tree-top adventures, you may also have to wait up to an hour for the next 2-hour session to start. For those who can't bear to tear themselves away, there are even wooden tree-houses (*cahutes nichées*) to rent overnight. Strangely, safety information is not displayed in English, though there are usually English-speaking staff available to help. At the time of writing, a Wild West-style hotel (O'Tel Park), which will be kitted out with stagecoaches and prairie houses in a rural setting, is under construction with an opening date planned for summer 2024.

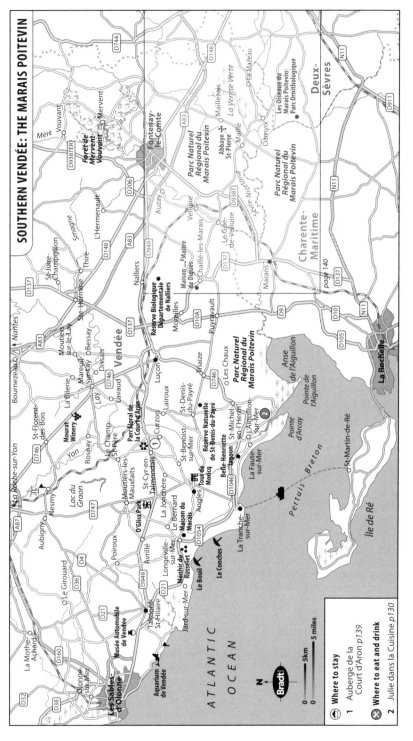

SOUTHERN VENDÉE: THE MARAIS POITEVIN

5

Southern Vendée: the Marais Poitevin

A narrow coastal strip, a huge expanse of open fenland or 'dry marshes', and a captivating area of 'wet marshland' bearing the name of La Venise Verte, or 'Green Venice': these three elements combine to form the Marais Poitevin, or Poitou Marshes, that occupy nearly all the terrain of the southern Vendée. It is the second-largest wetland in France (after the Camargue).

On the coastal strip, La Tranche-sur-Mer is renowned for its beaches, sunshine and watersports and has long revelled in its reputation as a popular holiday destination. Along with the neighbouring resorts of La Faute and L'Aiguillon-sur-Mer, it provides the ideal location for those seeking a relaxing time on the sands, and offers enough leisure attractions within easy striking distance, perfect for days when doing nothing proves to be just too much.

Inland, nearly 50,000ha of land reclaimed from the sea constitute the dry marshes, by far the biggest part of the Marais Poitevin Natural Park. If you're looking for distractions from the flatness of this treeless landscape, just head northeast to the wine village of Mareuil, or visit Luçon – a dignified town with a cathedral that has for centuries been the seat of the bishops of the Vendée. Birdwatchers will revel in the numerous species on view at St-Denis-du-Payré.

But while the coastline and the inland towns of the dry marshes certainly have their attractions, the flagship feature of this southern part of the Vendée is the area known as the Venise Verte, or 'Green Venice', which spills over the Vendean border and shares its delights with the two neighbouring départements of Charente-Maritime and Deux-Sèvres. No-one coming to this region should miss a trip to this, the most famous area of what is France's second-largest humid zone. This carefully preserved green and leafy part of the southern marshlands is full of picturesque villages, which together with numerous canals and cycleways play their part in luring around 1.5 million visitors to the Marais Poitevin every year. Here, you can travel by boat or bike among a maze of tranquil, tree-shaded waterways – a wonderful antidote to the frenzy of everyday life.

Note that some of the places listed in this chapter, although inland, are in reality only a short drive from the seaside, so a minor detour from the coast will let you access them. For those wishing to stray outside the departmental boundaries to continue their 'Venetian' experience, we suggest a few other places to visit in the non-Vendean Venise Verte.

THE SOUTHERN COAST

From north to south, the southern Vendean resorts exist on a well-established menu of sand and sea, quiet in off-season, their populations swollen in summer with holidaymakers eager to lap up their indisputable charms.

LONGEVILLE-SUR-MER A thick band of pine forest shelters the sandy beaches that lie 2km southwest of Longeville. Set slightly inland, it is a village of whitewashed cottages clustered around a solid 12th-century church, with a regular market day on Friday, plus additional days in high summer.

Longeville is a place for active sports: sand yachting, canoeing, horseriding, forest walks and cycle trails. The vast open space of Les Conches beach, to the south, draws surfers – especially for its renowned go-to spot 'Bud-Bud', and for the nearby surf schools. Further north, the aptly named Plage du Rocher (rock beach) is good for rockpools at low tide, as well as for quantities of fossils down near the water's edge; it is also a focus for sand yachting. Most northerly of Longeville's beaches is Le Bouil, which offers sailing, mini-golf and cycle hire. Both Les Conches and Le Rocher are supervised in high season, but not Le Bouil. An enjoyable, non-beach day for children could be spent at the excellent Château des Aventuriers (page 118), just 6km north, at Avrillé.

Tourist information

Office de Tourisme 2 Pl de la Liberté (Pl de l'Église); 02 51 33 34 64; w longevillesurmer. com; ⊕ Jul–Aug 09.00–13.00 & 14.00–18.30 Mon–Sat, 09.30–12.30 Sun & hols; Sep–Mar 09.00–12.30 & 14.00–17.30 Mon–Fri, 09.00–12.30 Sat; Apr–Jun 09.00–12.30 & 14.00–17.30 Mon–Sat. Leaflets detailing a number of waymarked walks are available.

✗ Where to eat and drink

La Mariennée 4 Chemin des Roulettes; 02 51 33 41 73; ⊕ noon–14.00 & 17.00–22.30 Thu–Tue. In a new location just around the corner, & now providing a large outside terrace, with an eclectic mix of knick-knacks decorating the interior. Some dishes here have a distinctly Asian influence, but even if you don't like spice, you'll find something to please you at this pleasant, popular place near the Plage du Bouil. Burgers & pizzas for the children. €€€

Le Blue Bay 10 Pl de la Liberté; 02 51 33 31 48; w restaurant-lebluebay.fr; ⊕ noon–14.00 & 19.00–21.00 Mon & Wed–Sun. A new name (previously Restaurant les Sports) but very much the same place. It still serves beautifully presented food. Very popular so advance booking advised. Great-value midday meals, Mon–Fri. €€–€€€

Sports and activities

Manu Surf School Plage des Conches; m 06 72 92 04 51; w manusurf.com. Based on Les Conches beach, with more than 20 years' experience & English-speaking instructors, Manu surfs all year, but their beach office is only open mid-Jun to mid-Sep. They also rent stand-up paddleboards & surfboards. Lessons from €35.

Ocean Players Plage du Bouil; 07 832 52 00 34; e contact@oceanplayers.fr; w oceanplayers. fr; ⊕ Apr–Sep 14.00–18.00 Sat–Sun, w/days on demand. Catamarans, windsurfers & kayaks to rent. They also run a sailing school & provide yoga sessions. From €15/hr for a paddleboard.

What to see and do

Maison du Marais (La Pépière, Chemin du Pont; 02 44 41 04 92; ⊕ May–Jun & Sep 13.00–17.00, Jul–Aug 09.00–17.00; boat, max 4 people: €25, canoe, 2–3 people: €20) Hire a canoe or rowing boat to set out on a 5km/2-hour circuit exploring the marshland. Information boards along the route explaining flora and fauna enhance the trip.

Walking and cycling trails Among the many woodland footpaths is an entertaining *parcours de santé*, or fitness trail, known rather off-puttingly (for the

Anglophone, at least) as CRAPA – short for Circuit Rustique d'Activité Physique Aménagé. It's on the D105, just south of the turning for Le Rocher beach, with some 30 sturdy obstacles to walk along, jump off or climb over. There's also a 13km mountain-bike (VTT, in French) circuit to the east of Longeville village. Maps of many waymarked routes, ranging from 1km to 10km, are available from the tourist office.

Prehistoric stones A number of Neolithic remains dot the area, including Longeville's own standing stone – the 'Pierre qui vire', or 'stone that turns' (also known as the Ménhir du Russelet) – located off the Chemin du Russelet, about 1km southwest of the village. Local legend claims that it spins around at midnight: have a few glasses of wine before you visit to increase your chances! There are many more menhirs and dolmens around Le Bernard (page 119), 2km northeast of Longeville; you could rent a bike and set out to explore them all.

ANGLES It's surprising to find a theatre in a town so small, perhaps, but any such surprise is trumped by the primitive bear sculpture that peers down from above the west door of the ancient church – undoubtedly the main curiosity of this attractive village. According to local folklore, the beast was a dangerous animal that abducted and ate the village's youngest and most beautiful maidens. A holy man managed to tame the *malabête*, as the animal was known, turn it to stone, and place it in this elevated position where it could do no further harm.

If that is not strange enough, then a neighbouring village provides another bizarre sculptural feature to rival that of Angles. At St-Benoist-sur-Mer, 4km to the northeast (and, despite its name, at least 10km from the sea), the tiled roof of the church is crowned by the figure of a rabbit, placed there as a joke by the original monastic builders. Look closely and it's – yes – smoking a pipe!

Tourist information
Office de Tourisme Pl du Champ de Foire; 02 51 97 56 39; w visitangles-vendee.com; ⏰ Jul– Aug 09.30–13.00 & 14.00–18.30 Mon–Sat, 09.30–13.00 Sun & hols

Where to eat and drink Close to the church, visitors will find a few choices for dining, with Racine possibly being the top pick.

Racine 7 Sq Docteur Pierre Provost; 02 51 27 97 84; ⏰ 12.15–14.00 & 19.00–21.00 Thu–Sun, 12.15–14.00 Mon. A smart, intimate little restaurant opposite La Trattoria, providing an upmarket alternative with a seasonal menu of dishes bordering on the artistic. For seafood lovers, the scallops with cauliflower purée & truffle oil is a must. €€€

La Trattoria 32 Rue Nationale; 02 51 97 58 41; ⏰ 10.00–13.30 Wed, 10.00–13.30 & 18.00–20.45 Thu & Sun, 10.00–13.30 & 18.00–21.00 Fri–Sat. Difficult to miss with its baby-blue shutters & prominent signage. Serves simple, freshly prepared meals at affordable prices. €€

What to see and do
Tour de Moricq (Moricq, 2km east of Angles; ⏰ viewable from exterior at all times, occasional guided tours, in French, in Jul–Aug; information from the tourist office, see above) Marooned in the marshland, at the eastern end of the village of Moricq, rises a majestic isolated square tower built in the 15th century, on what was then the coast, to defend the mouth of the River Lay. The port of Moricq silted up four centuries later, and the tower fell into disrepair. Now partially renovated, it can be viewed from the outside. If on a guided visit of the empty interior, you can look

up inside to see monumental fireplaces still clinging to the walls at the different levels. At certain times, you may also be able to visit the nearby Octroi, 1km to the south. This handsome building, constructed on an arch over the water, served until 1948 as a local tax-collecting office.

LA TRANCHE-SUR-MER With ten beaches, over 13km of sand and dozens of campsites, it's no surprise that La Tranche is both a popular family resort as well as a paradise for surfers and windsurfers. The influx of youthful summer visitors swells the population from its usual 2,700 to nearly 100,000. Entering town in the off-season, you seem to take a bewildering amount of time to reach the centre as you are directed around a series of one-way streets. There is good reason: the road system is geared towards coping with those high-summer crowds when the 1,500 free parking spaces become somewhat inadequate. With just its out-of-season inhabitants, the town can seem strangely empty.

During World War II, many of La Tranche's buildings were brutally razed to improve sightlines for the defence of the German submarine base at La Rochelle. Despite the necessity of much subsequent rebuilding, the curious visitor can still find picturesque side streets lined with former fishermen's cottages. As parking can be difficult in high season, bikes are useful for visiting the town centre; dedicated cycle trails lead through the forest to the west, or across the marshes to the east.

What the town lacks in museums and other touristic sites, it makes up for in sporting activity, and if you are not already an expert, there are surfing and windsurfing schools with friendly instructors to coax beginners or fine-tune already acquired skills. Pick up the Plan des Plages (beach map) from the tourist office, as it details all watersports providers. The less sporty will find shady walks in the forest of holm oaks and fragrant pines to the west of the town, and plenty of temporary summer entertainments such as amusement parks, paintball, concerts, circus and street theatre to fill the days and evenings (plus spectacular firework displays on the national holidays of 14 July and 15 August). In addition, the high season witnesses two antiques and bric-a-brac fairs, and the annual **Raid La Tranche/Île de Ré** race for windsurfers (and, more recently, kitesurfers) from the town out to the island of Ré, 12km offshore. Regular markets are on Tuesday and Saturday, with an extra Wednesday one in high season.

If you want to escape the seaside activities, you can take a boat trip south to the Île de Ré, or even as far as the famous Fort Boyard. Drive northwest, beyond the flat marshland, to look for prehistoric stones around Le Bernard, or for summer family fun at the chateaus in Avrillé and Talmont, or the O'Fun and O'Gliss activity parks at Moutiers; go northeast to look around the shops and cathedral at Luçon; or travel east to Maillezais and the peaceful 'Green Venice' marshland. Historic La Rochelle in the Charente-Maritime département is worth a day trip; it's only about 30km as the seagull flies, though reckon on twice that distance by road.

Tourist information

Office de Tourisme Rue Jules Ferry; ☎ 02 51 30 33 96; **w** latranchesurmer-tourisme.fr; ⏱ 09.00–13.00 Mon–Sat, also 15.00–17.00 during school hols. Friendly & efficient, they have a useful map of parking options to dispense, & a map of cycle routes, as well as all the usual information.

 ## Where to stay

Les Dunes (45 rooms) 68 Av Maurice-Samson; ☎ 02 51 30 32 27; **e** info@hotel-les-dunes.com; **w** hotel-les-dunes.com; ⏱ late Mar–early Oct. In a town with surprisingly few hotels, this is one of the best. 3 different standards of room, some with sea view. Family rooms also available. All with free Wi-Fi, TV with international channels. Pool, sauna, solarium, fitness room, free private parking. Restaurant on site. Pleasant management. €€€–€€€€€

Résidence Belle Plage (12 apts) 41 bis Rue Anatole France; 📞02 51 28 78 62; e contact@ residencebelleplage.com; w residencebelleplage. com. For weekly rental or w/end stays, modern, spacious, luxury apartments with kitchen, large living space, & bedrooms to cater for 2–8 people. Superb location, all units with sea view, some with huge terrace. Free Wi-Fi, TV & private parking. Expensive in season, but attractive off- & mid-season prices. Also hotel rooms without kitchen. €€€–€€€€€ (weekly).

🍴 Where to eat and drink

Côté Bistrot Pl Capitaine Bigot; m 06 10 56 07 47; ⏰ 12.15–14.00 & 19.15–21.00 Tue–Sat, 19.15–21.00 Sun. A seafront favourite just south of the town centre, this chic, modern establishment serves up great steak, seafood & good burgers. €€€

Les Fondus de Popote 26 Av Maurice Samson; 📞09 51 61 93 19; ⏰ noon–13.30 & 19.00–21.00 Wed–Sun. A rustic interior is accompanied by a warm & cosy atmosphere that is more reminiscent of the mountains than perhaps a seaside restaurant. As the name suggests, they specialise in traditional mountain cuisine, with many dishes such as the raclette & giant Tomahawk steaks designed for sharing. The menu also features classics such as moules marinières & an impressive wine list. €€€

Phare West 25 Av de la Plage; 📞02 51 30 48 76; ⏰ Feb–Oct noon–14.00 & 19.00–21.00 Tue–Fri & Sun, noon–14.00 & 19.00–21.30 Sat. On the pedestrian street leading off the square, a friendly place, specialising in mussels in a variety of sauces, also salads, meat dishes & a daily fish special. Free Wi-Fi. €€€

Bar Starfish 34 Av Maurice Samson; 📞02 51 30 16 93; ⏰ 15.00–23.00 Mon–Wed & Sun, 15.00–midnight Fri, noon–midnight Sat. Hard to miss at the top of town with its bold blue frontage. During the day it can be a quiet meeting place for families to share coffees & crêpes, while in the evening it becomes a thriving sports bar regularly hosting live music events. €€

What to see and do

Boat trips (Croisières Inter-Îles, Route de l'Embarcadère; 📞 05 46 50 55 54; w inter-iles.com; €31.50 adult return price) In July and August, you can hop on a boat for an away-day on the lovely Île de Ré – the island whose flat silhouette is visible on the horizon (page 205). At its ultra-chic little capital of St-Martin you can rent bikes to explore the island further, or simply enjoy the quayside shops. A different day trip can take you to the much more distant Île d'Aix, passing the famous Fort Boyard, followed by a few hours ashore in La Rochelle.

LA FAUTE-SUR-MER Set on a sandy peninsula between the sea and the River Lay, 23km southwest of Luçon, La Faute – like its neighbours – has successfully resisted the high-rise developments that mar so many of today's seaside resorts elsewhere.

Its 12km of beaches, its forest footpaths, and its much-vaunted microclimate attract a host of summer visitors; in July and August the village's population rises

XYNTHIA, AN UNWELCOME VISITOR

La Faute and L'Aiguillon have recovered well since the tragic events of February 2010, when a severe storm named Xynthia came calling in the middle of the night. It was an unpleasant reminder of the power of the sea and the fragility of the Vendée's relationship with it. La Faute suffered worst when Xynthia struck, with many lives lost and hundreds of houses destroyed.

The sea wall, which dated from the time of Napoleon, was breached by relentless waves reaching 7.5m. The quaint single-storey dwellings of the seaside towns were ill-designed to combat the flood, and with waters rising quickly to over 2.5m, many inhabitants drowned in their sleep.

The French Government ordered the destruction of over 800 damaged Vendean houses following the disaster. In the aftermath, it was shown that corruption had led to building permits being granted on unsuitable land, vulnerable to flooding, and jail sentences followed for the guilty.

Now the sea wall has been rebuilt and normality has been restored, a peace enabled by the sacrifice of many residents who were subject to enforced evictions from areas deemed to be at risk of future inundation.

from 1,000 souls to more than 40,000. Luckily, there is room for all on the golden sands – though reaching the beach can require a hike over the dunes. Market days are Thursday and Sunday, between April and October. Quirkily, the town holds a roller-blade festival in June. But La Faute also has a story to tell, having had to rebuild itself since it was overwhelmed by a vicious storm in 2010 (see above). Visitors today will be blissfully unaware of its recent tragedy.

Tourist information

Office de Tourisme Rond-Point Fleuri; ✆02 51 56 45 19; w sudvendeelittoral.com/infos-pratiques/notre-office-de-tourisme; ⊕ Oct–Mar 10.00–12.30 & 14.00–17.00 Fri; Apr–Jun & Sep 09.00–13.00 Mon–Tue & Sun, 10.00–12.30 & 14.00–17.30 Wed–Sat; Jul–Aug 09.30–13.00 & 14.30–18.30 Mon–Sun

✕ Where to eat and drink
A quick stroll along Avenue de la Plage will let you browse the menus of most of La Faute's dining choices.

Le Cul de Poule 29 Av de la Plage; ✆02 51 27 12 13. Across the roundabout from the tourist office. Looking a little tired these days but a pleasant enough place with good, fresh produce. €€

Sports and activities

Centre Nautique Municipal Plage des Bélugas; ✆06 03 20 61 24; e centrenautique@laiguillonlapresquile.fr; w charavoile.net; ⊕ Jan–Mar on Plage des Bélugas, Mar–Nov on Plage des Amourettes; times for yachting depend on low tide, see website. This centre hires out stand-up paddleboards, kayaks, Hawaiian pirogues & sand yachts, offering either lessons or straightforward rental. Lower age limits apply. Prices vary, but include €55 pp for 3hrs in a sand yacht.

Kitesurf Vendée m 06 26 78 89 70; e kitesurfvendee@gmail.com; w kitesurfvendee.fr. Operating courses year-round from halfway along the Pointe d'Arçay peninsula (though not with a permanent office there, so contact in advance is advisable), the operation offers full instruction in shallow waters. No English-speaking instructors at present, though this may change. Courses from €130.

What to see and do

Beaches   Among La Faute's beaches, the **Grande Plage** is overlooked by the casino, which has a restaurant and bar open to all – not just to gamblers. The **Plage des Bélugas** has an area given over to sand yachting, and another for trampolining and various children's entertainments. **Plage des Chardons** is backed with pine woods that offer welcome shade in summer. All beaches have matting paths leading down to the sands, making life easier for pushchairs and wheelchairs, and Tiralos (page 26) to help people with disabilities enjoy a bathe. Further down, there's a naturist beach near the end of the Pointe d'Arçay. Parking can be difficult in peak season; the beaches and casino have pay-and-display spaces. It's slightly easier – and free – nearer to the forest.

Birdwatching   The **Belle-Henriette lagoon**, cut off from the beach to the north of the casino, attracts terns, grebes and occasional spoonbills in summer, as well as migrating redstarts and wagtails among the 234 bird species recorded here. (For mammal-lovers, the European otter is also present.) At the other end of La Faute, the southern tip of the **Pointe d'Arçay** is a strictly protected nature reserve, a staging post for thousands of wading birds at migration times. Now known as the **Rade d'Amour** ('Harbour of Love'), near the end of the point, this area makes use of land once given to oyster farming but now thoughtfully returned to nature. Equipped with boardwalks, viewpoints and information panels, it explains the ecology of this important wetland. Standing proudly in splendid isolation is the oyster farm's workshop, renovated and looking as though it's still in use. Push a button to hear a short audio about the farmer's life (in French only). A leaflet from the tourist office will show you how the peninsula has advanced into the sea over the years: in the early 18th century, it hardly existed at all. A variety of terns, gulls and other seabirds, plus perhaps a hobby or buzzard, provide interest for birdwatchers.

L'AIGUILLON-SUR-MER   The most southerly of the Vendée's seaside resorts, L'Aiguillon was in times gone by a trading port at the mouth of the River Lay where ships were loaded with cargoes of cereals cultivated on the reclaimed land of the *marais desséché* – the 'dry' marsh, or open fenland to the northeast. Now, L'Aiguillon Bay is one of the largest shellfish-producing areas of France and oyster- and mussel-farming are still the livelihoods of many who live in the whitewashed cottages and keep their boats alongside the spindly wooden jetties. Legend has it that, in 1255, a shipwrecked Irishman named Patrick Walton was the first to try planting a stake in the water and encouraging mussels to grow on it. Today, at low tide, thousands of these *bouchots* are revealed standing in the mud, each holding a rich crop of shellfish.

An artificial lake on the waterfront provides the town's opportunity for swimming; if you prefer the real thing, with ocean waves, you'll discover fine-sand beaches at neighbouring La Faute. Other diversions include free evening entertainment in the peak summer months, with spectacular firework shows on 14 July and 15 August. During those same two months you can visit the bay's oyster beds; spend a day at sea on a *vieux gréement* (traditional sail-powered wooden boat); or sign up for a group outing with a French guide to try shrimping in the shallows, *surf-casting* (fishing from the beach), or *pêche au carrelet* (catching fish by lowering a square net into the water from a bridge). Information and reservations are available through the tourist office. L'Aiguillon's markets take place on Tuesday and Friday, with an additional Wednesday one in summer.

Just along the D44, beside the Hôtel du Port, is a house bearing a plaque proclaiming it to have been the setting for one of crime-writer Georges Simenon's novels *La Maison du Juge* (*Maigret in Exile*). The creator of Inspector Maigret lived at various places in the Vendée and neighbouring Charente-Maritime during the 1930s and 40s, and set several of his novels in the area. Early in World War II, Simenon was appointed High Commissioner for Belgian refugees, charged with organising accommodation and jobs for thousands of his less fortunate countrymen fleeing the Nazi invasion of Belgium.

Tourist information

Office de Tourisme   Av Amiral Courbet; ☎ 02 51 56 37 37; w sudvendeelittoral.com; ⏲ Oct–Mar 09.30–12.30 Mon–Tue, Fri–Sat & hols; Apr–Jun & Sep 09.30–12.30 Mon & hols, 09.30–12.30 & 14.30–17.00 Tue & Fri–Sat; Jul–Aug 09.30–18.30 Mon–Sat, 09.30–13.00 & 15.30–18.30 Sun & hols

✗ Where to eat and drink

Julie dans la Cuisine   [map, page 122] 86 Route de la Pointe, on the D46C, towards the Pointe de L'Aiguillon; ☎ 02 51 56 27 67; w julie-dans-la-cuisine.fr; ⏲ noon–14.00 Tue–Thu & Sun, noon–14.00 & 19.00–21.30 Fri–Sat. A bright, modern place offering top-notch mussels (of course), meats, fish, burgers & salads & a variety of menus, including a bargain menu at lunchtime & a children's one. Booking advisable. €€€

Shopping

Aux P'tites Puces   Bd des Courlis; ☎ 02 51 56 46 97; ⏲ 10.00–noon & 14.30–18.00 Tue–Sat. If you're in search of fabric or a bag of buttons, or just about anything else, visit this one-time haberdashery store now turned into something of a bazaar. You'll almost certainly buy something!

What to see and do

Église St-Nicolas   (Rue du Général Leclerc) If you can tear yourself away from sea and sand, L'Aiguillon's tall, white 1930s-built church is worth a visit. Unusually, the top windows are semicircular, making their exuberant stained-glass starbursts look like firework displays. The large model boat on display once hung from the rafters as a focus for inhabitants' prayers for the safety of their fishermen. A moving war memorial lists the 80 Aiguillonnais who failed to return from the trenches of World War I, with details of where they fell.

Pointe de L'Aiguillon   (⏲ free access at all times) A long spit of land juts out into L'Aiguillon Bay, bordered by a concrete dyke that protects the hard-won fields from the sea. At the town end of the wall, various outlets advertise mussels and eels for sale. The road alongside the route affords views eastward to the wind-carved cliffs of La Dive – a former island, standing a dizzy 15m above the flat lands – and, to the south, of the bridge linking La Rochelle with the low-lying Île de Ré. The wall beside the road has undergone significant strengthening over the last few years and it blocks the outlook on the seaward side, but at various points you can clamber up primitive steps to see the mussel posts stretching away to the horizon at low tide.

When you finally reach the furthest point – often windy – the mudflats of the shallow Anse (or bay) de L'Aiguillon are visible to the east. Now a wildfowl reserve of national importance, they provide a haven for avocets and other waders. Between September and November nearly half a million migrating birds pass this way – in greatest numbers just after sunrise. Volunteers from the Ligue pour la Protection des Oiseaux (LPO; a French equivalent of the RSPB) are there to count them, and to organise guided visits. Birdwatching information is available from the LPO (☎ 02 51 46 21 91; w vendee.lpo.fr) or from L'Aiguillon tourist office (see above); there are also a few information panels at the Pointe itself.

An attractive enough town in its own right, Luçon is also the commercial centre of the neighbouring wine-growing area.

LUÇON So effective are its bypasses that Luçon and its 10,000 inhabitants are quite easy to miss. Avenues leading to the heart of this charming old town, at the junction of the plain with the southern marshes, are lined with artfully trained trees, their green or copper-coloured foliage trimmed into leafy arches. The heart of the town is dominated as much by a crazily designed concrete water-tower near the Champ-de-Foire (built in 1912 to supply a regiment of dragoons garrisoned in the town) as by the elegant 85m spire of its cathedral.

Luçon's most famous inhabitant was the future Cardinal Richelieu, who arrived in 1606 as the region's bishop and declared the place to be 'the filthiest and most unpleasant in France'. (Don't worry: things have changed!) The town suffered a great deal at the hands of the Huguenots during the Wars of Religion but, as a Republican stronghold, emerged relatively unscathed from the later Wars of the Vendée.

Immaculately well groomed today, Luçon's streets are lined with substantial two-storey houses of white stone and organised into a complicated one-way system. If you want to stop and look around, it's best to leave the car in the huge car park opposite the cathedral and explore the quaint side streets on foot.

The main shopping areas are Rue Georges Clemenceau, heading north from the cathedral, and Rue Président de Gaulle, leading west. There is a covered market hall behind the cathedral, and a tourist office near the *hôtel de ville*; markets here take place on Wednesdays and Saturdays.

Tourist information
Office de Tourisme Pl Édouard-Herriot; 📞 02 51 56 36 52; w lucon.fr; ⏰ 09.30–12.30 & 14.00–18.00 Tue–Fri

➤ Where to stay *Map, page 132*
Au Fil des Saisons (6 rooms) 55 Route de la Roche; 📞 02 51 56 11 32; w aufildessaisons-vendee.fr. A well-run, smart hotel with a good restaurant (see below) & a garden. Flat screen TVs & Wi-Fi access. €€€

➤ Where to eat and drink *Map, page 132*
Au Fil des Saisons 55 Route de la Roche; 📞 02 51 56 11 32; w aufildessaisons-vendee.fr; ⏰ lunch & dinner Tue–Fri, dinner Sat & lunch Sun. There's an upmarket feel to this excellent, understated restaurant north of the town, but prices are good for what you get. Choose between inside, conservatory or terrace; a variety of menus on offer, with more than a dash of creativity in the presentation. €€€€

L'Ardoise Gourmande 52 Rue Clemenceau; 📞 02 51 56 35 10; ⏰ noon–13.45 Tue–Wed, noon–13.45 & 19.45–21.30 Thu–Sat. Highly recommendable, coolly modern place, on north side of town centre. *Menu du jour* is good value. €€€

Pain 'ssionnément Gourmand 7 Rue du Président de Gaulle; m 06 72 54 15 81; ⏰ 07.00–13.30 & 15.30–19.00 Tue–Sat, 07.00–12.45 Sun. Opened in the spring of 2023, this new patisserie already swells with local clientele. The interior is clean & sharp with glass counters adorned with a glistening array of freshly baked goods. The business is run by a husband & wife team; Simon gives a welcoming smile to each customer & Alison is a magician in the kitchen. The chocolate éclairs are out of this world. €€

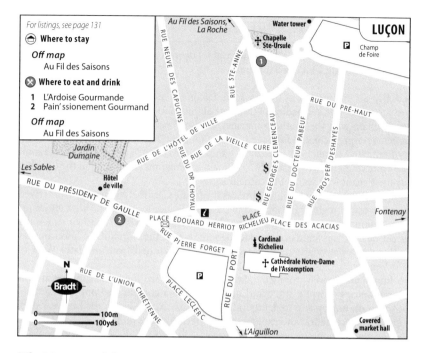

For listings, see page 131

🛏 **Where to stay**

Off map
   Au Fil des Saisons

❌ **Where to eat and drink**
1 L'Ardoise Gourmande
2 Pain'ssionement Gourmand

Off map
   Au Fil des Saisons

What to see and do

Cathédrale Notre-Dame de l'Assomption (Pl Richelieu; ⏰ 09.00–noon & 14.00–17.00 daily, Mass: 19.00 Sat, 11.00 Sun) Richelieu, who in his youth was bishop here from 1606 to 1622, gave Mass beneath the graceful spire and soaring white columns of the cathedral, and is reputed to have preached from the painted wooden pulpit now kept in the north aisle. In a mixture of architectural styles, the interior features Romanesque carved faces of humans and animals alongside 17th-century stone garlands. The monumental organ was made by the celebrated 19th-century organ builder Aristide Cavaillé-Coll and presented to the town by Emperor Napoleon III. The cathedral is linked on its south side to the bishop's palace by a beautifully preserved 16th-century cloister.

Jardin Dumaine (Access via Rue de l'Hôtel-de-Ville or Allée St-François; free) This shady green oasis in the town centre is well hidden behind the *hôtel de ville* (town hall). Inside its 4ha, you can stroll along gravel paths (definitely not on the grass!), among formal borders, collections of interesting trees and shrubs, and an avenue of giant 150-year-old yew hedges (from which waft strains of recorded music in summer). There is a pretty, Victorian-style bandstand for open-air concerts. Youngsters love the topiary animals on the north lawn that recall the fables of La Fontaine – mostly familiar to British children, as the 17th-century French writer cribbed them from Aesop. On 14 July (Bastille Day), the garden is illuminated by paper lanterns for an evening procession and dancing.

Chapelle Ste-Ursule (Rue Clemenceau; 📞 02 51 56 36 52; ⏰ Jul–Aug 14.30–18.00 Mon–Sat; free) The austerity of the white-walled chapel, in a former convent, is softened by a decorative altarpiece and an astonishing 33m-long wooden ceiling entirely covered with 17th-century paintings of cherubs and musical instruments (to avoid dizziness, it's best to sit down to look at them). A plaque on the end wall records the sad fate of the convent's nuns during the Vendée Wars; 11 of them died in the town's prison.

MAREUIL-SUR-LAY AND SURROUNDS As the Lay River makes its way from east to west, it's crossed by the busy D746 trunk road that bowls from north to south through this small wine-producing town. Mareuil is dominated by the chunky spire of its austere Romanesque church and by a beautifully restored 16th-century castle. Nevertheless, it may be the products of the nearby vineyards, rather than the buildings, that tempt you to stop here.

The village of Rosnay, 5km to the west, is reputed to have the highest wine output (not consumption!) per head of population in France, with almost 10% of its nearly 600 inhabitants said to be wine producers. A signposted Route des Vins (Wine Route) leads to many of them and the Mareuil tourist office stocks a free *Guide de la Route des Vins* leaflet, complete with map and opening hours, listing nine vineyards offering *dégustations* (tastings). (If you are thinking of buying wine, take enough cash with you, as small producers may not accept credit cards.) In early August, the Les Vignerons en Fête festival allows local producers to showcase their wines and offer tastings.

About 6km northeast of Mareuil, the peaceful village of Moutiers-sur-le-Lay has a central square overlooked by several superb *maisons bourgeoises* (large houses), and a part-Romanesque church. From around the 5th century AD a community of monks lived here (*moutier* means monastery), while a former priory, just off the square, was once the residence of the bishops of Luçon.

Tourist information

Office de Tourisme 17 Rue Hervé-de-Mareuil;
☎ 02 51 97 30 26; w paysmareuillaisvendee.com

Where to stay

Château Brédurière (7 Rooms) La Brédurière, 5km north of Moutiers sur le Lay; m 06 34 96 44 11; w chateau-brediere.com. A historic building set in a 17th-century vineyard that still produces its own wine. There are 3 stunning & rather grand rooms in the castle itself. Outside, safari-style lodges are available in a wilder setting that provides sweeping views of the surrounding landscape, a good choice for those looking for a self-catering option (only available for the full week during high season). Onsite, there is a good restaurant, heated outdoor pool & a wellbeing centre. Dog owners also welcome. €€€€€

Where to eat and drink

L'Aubraie 6 Rue du Pont Eiffel, Péault; ☎ 02 51 97 78 74; w laubraie.com; ⊕ Mar–Jun & Sep–Oct noon–14.00 Wed & Sun, noon–14.00 & 19.00–21.00 Tue & Fri–Sat; Jul–Aug noon–14.00 & 19.00–21.30 Tue–Sun. Although the food (salads, mainly meat dishes – little for fish-lovers or vegetarians) lacks a bit of finesse, the large terrace & riverside location beside Gustave Eiffel's bridge are enough to make this a good option. The high points on the menu are the generously portioned desserts. Children's menu. €€€

La Vache à Lay 88 Rue Echallard; ☎ 02 51 28 41 19; w lavachealay.fr; ⊕ lunch & dinner daily. In a rather functional-looking building, nevertheless the food is fine if unsophisticated. Choose from a variety of sharing platters, burgers & a daily fish dish. Occasional theme evenings – such as country & western – may dictate whether you visit...or not. Children's menu. €€€

Maison Desamy 2 Rue Hervé-de-Mareuil; ☎ 02 51 52 69 43; ⊕ noon–14.00 & 19.30–21.00 Tue & Thu–Sat, noon–14.00 Wed. Created by Simon Bessonnet, previously Alexandre Couillon's deputy at the acclaimed La Marine in Île de Noirmoutier (page 60). This smart little Michelin-starred restaurant is situated directly next to the Mourat wine merchants & beneath the gaze of the restored 16th-century castle. Serving exquisite meals with high-quality ingredients sourced from the region. Very reasonably priced given the provenance of the chef & highly recommended. €€€

What to see and do

Mourat Winery (Route de La Roche-sur-Yon, 2km north of Mareuil-sur-Lay; ☏ 02 51 97 20 10; w vignobles-mourat.fr; ☉ 09.30–12.30 & 14.00–19.00 Tue–Sat) A beautifully presented winery shop, featuring the full range of reds, rosés and whites – including some organic products – from the Mourat family, owners of the village's magnificent chateau and among Mareuil's best-known wine producers. Contact at least a day in advance if you want a winery tour (€40 inc tasting & a picnic with wine), which can be arranged in English; you can choose to go on foot or rent either a bicycle or an electric car (€40 pp plus additional €25 charge for the car). But if you just want to shop, you will be equally welcome. In July and August, you can also visit the Mourat shop in Mareuil town, set in a gorgeous stone building – a former toll house – alongside the bridge (2 Pl Circulaire; ☉ 09.30–12.30 & 14.00–19.00 Mon–Sat). Enthusiastic staff at either location will discuss the finer points of the wines, and pour some for you to taste.

Église de Dissais (Dissais, off the D19, 2km east of Mareuil, opposite cemetery; ☉ Jul–Aug, on request – contact tourist office, page 133; free) A 12th-century church in the Mareuil countryside has been restored as a memorial to 7,500 combatants who lost their lives during the Vendean army's three unsuccessful attempts to take the nearby town of Luçon from the Republicans in June, July and August 1793. Ring in advance and the tourist office will open it up for you. A 13km waymarked walking trail starts from the church.

Pont de Lavaud and parachute memorial (Lavaud, on the D50, 4km southwest of Mareuil) Lavaud's simple iron bridge, restored in 2013, was designed by none other than the great engineer Gustave Eiffel in 1866, to carry traffic on chunky pillars across the River Lay. Some 300m to its west, a tall granite stone commemorates the first Allied parachute-drop of arms to Vendean Resistance workers, on 14 July 1943. The poetical coded message '*Pourquoi me réveiller au souffle du printemps?*' ('Why awaken me at the first breath of spring?') transmitted via the BBC from London, alerted the *résistants* to the arrival of the precious consignment, which they hastily concealed in the house beside the present monument. Note that the monument is on a sharp bend, so park at the Aubraie restaurant and walk along the road – caution required.

Château de Bessay (Bessay, 6km east of Mareuil; ☉ Jul–Aug, times vary so contact tourist office – page 133; free; tours are guided and by appointment only) This magnificent Renaissance tower is attached to a private, traditional *logis*, or country house. After watching a short slideshow (in French) about the building's history, you climb via a series of big empty rooms (Henri of Navarre, future King Henri IV of France, slept in one on 10 January 1589) to the *chemin de ronde*, or sentry-way, around the bell-shaped roof. Pierced by holes through which defenders could aim muskets at invaders, this walkway offers panoramic views over the surrounding countryside. In the grounds, a 16th-century dovecote lined with 3,200 nesting holes gives an idea of how many pigeons might have once been needed to feed staff and family.

Musée Terre d'Antan (La Billerie, off the D48, 10km northeast of Mareuil; m 06 70 00 40 60; w tourismelandes.com; ☉ 10.00–noon & 14.30–18.00 Mon, Wed & Fri; €6.50/3.50 adult/child) This museum dedicated to the agriculture of yesteryear is spread over eight rooms, in the barns and outbuildings of a farm. As well as tractors and harvesters, you'll find implements for barrel- and clog-making, miller's and blacksmith's tools, plus a 1930s' schoolroom.

STE-HERMINE
Today's motorways and bypasses mean you can easily miss this small town on the edge of the plain, straddling the River Smagne 12km northeast of Luçon. Visitors arriving from the west, via the D948 almost have the impression of falling off the wooded *bocage* on to a carpet of fields that roll away to the horizon like a billowing ocean. Where the road meets the D137, the junction is dominated by a rugged World War I memorial featuring the politician Georges Clemenceau (pages 117, 154 and 196) and several *poilus* – the affectionate nickname for French soldiers of 1914–18. Ste-Hermine's other small treasures are scattered through the rather straggling town: they include a handsome, privately owned chateau near the church, and – worth seeking out on a Friday morning – an attractive 19th-century market hall.

Tourist information
Office de Tourisme 35 Route de Nantes; ✆ 02 51 56 37 37; w paysdesaintehermine.fr, sudvendeelittoral.com; ☉ Oct–Jun 09.30–12.30 & 14.00–18.00 Fri, Jul–Aug 09.30–13.00 & 14.30–18.00 Mon–Fri, 09.30–13.00 Sat & hols

Where to eat and drink
Le Saint Georges 11 Pl de la Mairie, St-Juire-Champgillon, 4km northeast of Ste-Hermine; ✆ 02 51 27 91 87; w lesaintgeorges.wordpress. com; ☉ 08.00–15.00 Tue & Sun, 08.00–15.00 & 17.00–21.00 Wed–Sat. Smart place with a bar, café & restaurant area & a great reputation for innovative cuisine. The menu changes each month. Prices & quality are above the norm. €€€€

What to see and do
St-Juire-Champgillon (St-Juire, 4km northeast of Ste-Hermine; ✆ 02 51 27 82 04) This tongue-twisting *commune* (roughly, 'san-jweer-shong-jee-ong') is actually two separate villages, each revealing lovely houses of mellow local stone along its lanes. St-Juire has become a bit of an artistic centre, with a summer-long series of exhibitions (Un Art d'Eté) held in converted barns near the *mairie* (☉ Jul–Aug, times & dates vary; free). It also has a couple of 'secret' gardens into which you can wander: the small Jardin des Cinq Sens, behind the school, designed to please the five different senses; and a garden of fruit trees and blue flowers, behind the *mairie*.

Le Jardin du Bâtiment (Le Bâtiment, Thiré, 4km southeast of Ste-Hermine; ✆ 02 51 27 39 32; w arts-florissants.org; ☉ opening times & days vary, see website for details; €5/free adult/under 12s) These lovely formal gardens surrounding a 17th-century house, now the home of Baroque-music specialist William Christie (born in New York State but now among the Vendée's most famous residents) are occasionally open to the public. Classified as a 'Jardin Remarquable', they feature pleached hornbeams, box-edged *allées*, fine topiary and elegant vistas. The gardens are part of a foundation set up by William Christie, which also includes the world-famous baroque-music ensemble Les Arts Florissants, who perform regularly throughout the year (see the website for information). A special Festival Dans les

Jardins de William Christie is held at the gardens around the middle of August each year where you can hear the group play among the beautiful surroundings.

CHAILLÉ-LES-MARAIS The ancient capital of the 'dry' marsh, or open fenland, area of the Marais Poitevin, 14km southeast of Luçon, was once an island; the cliffs rising alongside the D25 show that you are indeed driving along the former seabed. If you travel through here in July and August, you'll get closer to the soul of the region (and probably move faster) by taking the smaller roads through the little marshland villages.

The monks from five nearby abbeys who began drainage work in the 12th century, when the estuary that covered this region began to silt up, are commemorated in the Canal des Cinq Abbés (dug around 1217). Lying just south of Chaillé, it runs roughly northeast/southwest and divides the fertile, open meadows of the 'dry' marsh (*marais desséché*) from the more picturesque, tree-lined 'wet' marshland (*marais mouillé*), known as the 'Venise Verte', or 'Green Venice', to the east (page 139). Another canal, the Ceinture des Hollandais (1645), separates the marshes from the plain lying to the north. It takes its name from the Dutch engineers brought in centuries later by Henri IV and Louis XIII to rescue the intricate system from the effects of a succession of wars.

The soil and climate here are perfect for growing melons; the town duly celebrates the fruit in early August.

Tourist information
Office de Tourisme Rue de La Coupe du Rocher; ℡ 02 51 56 37 37; w ot-isles-maraispoitevin.com; ⊕ Oct–Mar 09.30–12.30 Mon & Fri, 14.30–17.00 — Tue & Thu; Apr–Jun & Sep 09.30–12.30 & 14.00–17.00 Sun–Fri; Jul–Aug 09.30–12.30 & 13.30–18.00 Mon–Sat, 14.00–18.00 Sun & hols

 Where to stay and eat Chaillé is not exactly blessed with dining options itself, so be prepared to travel a bit, or bring a picnic.

Château de l'Abbaye (10 rooms) Moreilles, on D137, 6km northwest of Chaillé; ℡ 02 51 56 17 56; w chateau-moreilles.com. Built on the site of an abbey razed after the French Revolution, this small & now faded hotel occupies a stately mansion, with ample gardens. Half the rooms are in the old gatehouse (some gatehouse!) with jacuzzi baths & a touch more luxury. All rooms have AC, free Wi-Fi & TV with international channels. Outside, heated pool with sun loungers (⊕ Apr–Sep) & a barn, now showing its years, where you will find table tennis & table football. At extra cost, a private spa can be hired by the hour, with sauna & jacuzzi. Cosy bar, set-menu evening meals available for residents only, reservation required. Family-owned & -managed. Open year-round, with a real fire in winter. 1 room is adapted for those with restricted mobility. **€€€–€€€€€**

Côté Marais (2 *gîtes*) 38 Rue du 11 Novembre; ℡ 06 30 66 35 77; w cotemarais.fr; ⊕ Apr–Sep. Set in the grounds of a handsome, 19th-century village house, fully modernised but retaining character. Free Wi-Fi. Guests can relax in the massive gardens or dip in the pool (⊕ May–Sep). Self-catering *gîtes* costing €480–1,000/week; the small cottage accommodates up to 4 people & the large cottage will sleep 7 (one of 3 rooms is a triple). **€€–€€€**

What to see and do
Maison du Maître de Digues (7 Rue de la Coupe du Rocher; ℡ 02 51 56 77 30; w maisondumaitrededigues.fr; ⊕ Apr–Jun & Sep 10.00–12.30 & 14.00–17.30 Wed–Sat, Jul–Aug 10.00–13.00 & 14.00–18.00 daily; €5/3.50/free adult/students/under 18s) At a whitewashed farmhouse northwest of the village, you can learn about the important work of controlling the marsh waters. The *maître de digues* would supervise water levels over 5,000ha of marshland; a film shows the life of

the dyke master while another concentrates on the sluices and dykes themselves. Several rooms are furnished in period style to show the daily life of one Frédéric Collardeau, holder of this position in 1877 and part of a dynasty of dyke masters. Displays centre on birth, death, school, market day, marriage, and sociable evenings around the fireside. Outside, panels explain the functions of the various buildings, while a paddock contains some typical livestock: goats, Marans chickens, and some of the shaggy-coated donkeys called *baudets du Poitou*.

Réserve Biologique Départementale de Nalliers (Les Huttes, on the D10 near Nalliers, 6km north of Chaillé; 📞 02 51 97 69 80; w sitesnaturels.vendee.fr; ⊕ reserve accessible at all times; visitor centre: mid–end Apr 14.00–18.00 daily, May–Jun 14.00–18.00 Wed–Sun, Jul–Aug 11.00–19.00 daily, Sep–late Oct 14.00–18.00 Wed & Sat–Sun, late Oct–early Nov 14.00-18.00 daily; free) This 146ha marshland nature reserve is home to otters, kingfishers, herons and also to many rare plants typical of the watery habitat. You can tramp past brambles, ragwort and teasels (trainers or walking boots recommended), following two trails; the 1km Huttiers Trail and the 3km Naturalist Trail which has a couple of observatories. (Binoculars can be borrowed from reception.) For younger members of the family there is also a seed hunt and a smartphone-enabled otter rescue experience. From spring to autumn, the warden leads guided walks from the Maison de la Réserve (visitor centre), pointing out signs of bird and animal life and the most interesting vegetation. The centre has displays about fish and insects and a 30-minute film (in French), which takes you on a panoramic tour of the region following the story of 'Kroll', an injured seabird found on the beach.

ST-MICHEL-EN-L'HERM AND SURROUNDS
Though it rises only 17m above sea level, this former island of whitewashed houses, 15km southwest of Luçon, seems almost imposing when seen across the flat marshland. A map from the tourist office guides you on a 2.5km circular walk through the village's narrow lanes, known as *venelles*.

The village of Triaize, 7km northeast of St-Michel, is clustered around a restored 12th-century church with a spire resembling a wavy sausage-balloon. The lack of wood in this open landscape meant the inhabitants had to find other methods of cooking and heating, and Triaize has the dubious glory of having preserved the once-widespread custom of making *bouses*, dung-pats that could be burned as fuel – even the ash made a valuable fertiliser. At the annual Fête de la Bouse festival of old customs, held at the end of July/beginning of August, the stuff is put to good use for cooking eels, mussels, *mogettes* and other regional specialities – as well as for throwing, in frisbee-style competitions! En route from St-Michel to Triaize, look out on the right at the hamlet of Les Chaux; a farmhouse there is built on a bank of oyster shells – thought to have been a protection either against the sea or invading Normans.

Tourist information
Office de Tourisme 5 Pl de l'Abbaye; 📞 02 51 56 37 37; w paysnedelamer.fr; ⊕ 09.30–13.00 & 14.30–18.00 Mon–Fri, 09.30–13.00 Sat & hols

Where to eat and drink
La Rose Trémière 4 Rue de l'Église; 📞 02 51 30 25 69; w restaurant-larosetremiere.fr; ⊕ 12.15–13.15 & 19.45–21.00 Wed–Sat, 12.15–13.30 Sun. Good-value, though not inexpensive traditional restaurant serving gourmet meals with style in a tastefully restored barn, complete with wooden beams & fireplace. €€€€€

What to see and do

Abbaye Royale (Pl de l'Abbaye; 02 51 30 21 89 or tourist office, page 137; mid-Jun–mid-Sep, guided visits at 10.00, 11.00, 15.00, 16.00 & 17.00, Tue & Thu–Fri; €3.50/1/free adult/under 13s/under 7s, buy tickets from tourist office next door) Behind the boundary wall of a large house on the main square are the remains of a former royal abbey whose Benedictine monks were among those who undertook the draining of the surrounding marshes. Established in the 7th century by monks from Noirmoutier, the abbey was reconstructed several times after the ravages of the Hundred Years War, the Wars of Religion and, finally, the devastating Wars of the Vendée. Still intact are the 17th-century chapter house and the tall refectory, while skeletal ribs of vaulting are all that remain of the *chauffoir* where the monks took exercise. The interesting 45-minute guided tour of this now privately owned abbey also takes in the lapidary and refectory; it's often conducted by students, who *may* speak English. An English-language paper guide is provided. Occasional summer concerts are staged here.

Musée André Deluol (4 Rue de l'Étendard; m 06 83 31 57; mid-Jun–mid Sep 15.00–18.30 Tue–Sat; €3/free adult/under 7s) This museum houses a collection of unusual, classically inspired stone sculptures, paintings and drawings by well-known local artist André Deluol (1909–2003). His former studio (originally a barn, then a pickle factory!) is crowded with stone and marble carvings featuring Deluol's characteristically voluptuous female nudes, cavorting with fish, writhing with satyrs, or prancing exuberantly in chorus lines.

Réserve Naturelle de St-Denis-du-Payré (2 Rue du 8 Mai, St-Denis-du-Payré; 02 51 28 41 10; w reservenaturelle-saintdenisdupayre.fr; the reserve holds discovery days on Sun; outside of this it can only be visited for guided tours or themed activities & reservations are required – see website for detailed calendar; €6.50/5/free adult/under 18s/under 7s) For bird-lovers, this 207ha reserve is one of the Vendée's star locations. A rest stop for exhausted birds migrating between the wetlands of Senegal and the Nordic countries, it is well tended by the LPO and offers the opportunity to see 275 recorded bird species; mornings are the best time to visit. You should go first to St-Denis village (address as above) to get your ticket, see a short film and pick up additional information – the ticket office has a variety of books, in French, on the birds that visit or live in the region. Then, drive 2km along the D25 Triaize road and park at the site entrance, from which you follow a boardwalk for 400m across the marsh to the wooden observatory. Inside is a comfortable space with 18 high-powered telescopes, and knowledgeable volunteers to point out (often in excellent English) the most interesting birds to be seen. Year-round residents include marsh harriers, curlews, egrets and white storks. Winter visitors are widgeon, teal and greylag goose; spring sees black-tailed godwits and thousands of other waders; summer is the time for redshanks, stilts and spoonbills; and autumn is the period for migratory species like garganey and black tern. In July and August, there are occasionally special 'twilight' meetings, with guides in attendance.

ST-CYR-EN-TALMONDAIS A small village straddling the main D949, St-Cyr is situated at the southern limit of the woods and fields of the Bas-Bocage. On its east side stands a romantic-looking, 17th-century-style chateau; although private property, it now offers B&B rooms. Adjoining it is a marvellous garden, filled with luxuriant tropical plants. To the west is the village's other curiosity – a moving war memorial, with a statue of a soldier dramatically silhouetted against the sky.

Some time-warped villages with interesting little churches (see below) lie just to the south. Though only 13km from the busy resort of La Tranche, these peaceful places seem a world away from the bustle of the coast.

Tourist information

Mairie 3 Rue Tillauderie; 📞 02 51 30 82 82; w vendeegrandlittoral.fr/saint-cyr-en-talmondais

Where to stay and eat

Auberge de la Court d'Aron [map, page 122] (4 rooms) 1 Allée des Tilleuls, visible from D949, just west of St-Cyr; 📞 06 03 56 59 73; w courtdaron.com. Pretty, stone-built inn near the chateau, with simple & tidy rooms, a pool, Wi-Fi & an excellent restaurant (🕐 19.00–21.00 Mon–Sat during the summer; see website for opening times in other months; €€€€) with food verging on the gastronomic. Veranda in summer, welcome fireplace for winter. €€€€

What to see and do

Parc Floral de la Court d'Aron (On the D949, just west of St-Cyr; 📞 02 28 14 11 10; w lacourtdaron.com; 🕐 early Apr–early Sep 10.00–19.00 daily, early Sep–Oct 10.00–17.00 daily; €13/11/9 adult/disabled/5-12s, rising to €14/12/9 Jul–Aug) Having celebrated 45 years of existence in 2022, this magnificent, well-cared-for garden is lush with verdant lawns, woodland walks, spring bulbs, and jungles of bamboo and banana palms. A signposted '*itinéraire*' leads past carp-filled ponds, over quaint bridges and through shady woodland brightened with Icelandic poppies, hydrangeas and carpets of busy-lizzies. However, the garden's most outstanding feature is its large lake, covered, from June to September, in thousands of exquisite pink lotus flowers standing above the water on long green stalks. It's an unforgettable sight. With picnic areas, free mini-golf, children's playground and a mini-farm full of inquisitive goats, lazy pigs and other mammals, families could spend a good couple of hours here. There's a reasonably priced restaurant/bar in high season, but you can also bring a picnic if you prefer. A Lotus festival takes place twice a year, in July and August, and there are occasional exhibitions featuring local artists and sculptors.

Église de St-Romain (Curzon, 2.5km southeast of St-Cyr; 🕐 in daylight hours, exc during services; free) The pride of this small village church is its 11th-century crypt. Enter the church by the side door, tug open the trapdoors in the floor, press a button on the right for 5 minutes' illumination, and screw up your courage for a slightly spooky experience of strange carved faces ogling you from the tops of 1,000-year-old stone pillars down below.

Église St-Martin (La Jonchère, 3km southwest of St-Cyr) The weirdly shaped spire of this ancient church towers above another pretty village. Step inside to see an unusual interior with colourful statues, lace-trimmed altar, and a chancel decorated with simple medieval wall paintings of stylised flowers.

5

LA VENISE VERTE: 'GREEN VENICE'

An incredible 8,000km of canals spread themselves out like tentacles across the entirety of the Marais Poitevin, but it is the green and leafy eastern region of the natural park which is the most picturesque. It's an area of quaint houses, floodable prairies and endless water channels, punctuated by tiny ports with landing stages

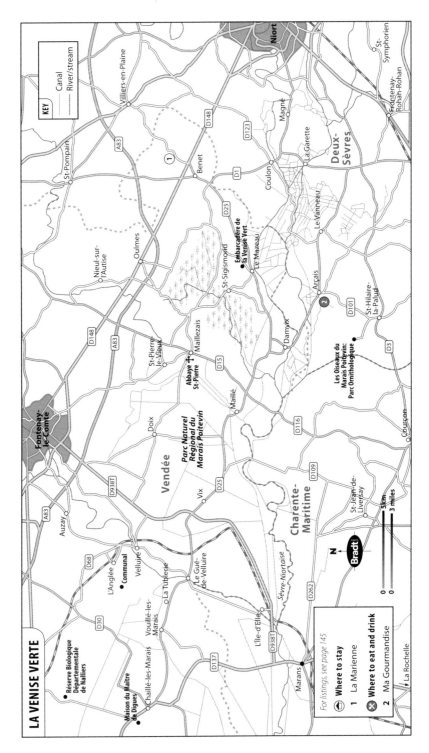

LA VENISE VERTE

For listings, see page 145

KEY
- Canal
- River/stream

Where to stay
1. La Marienne

Where to eat and drink
2. Ma Gourmandise

Niort

St-Symphorien

Fontenay-Rohan-Rohan

Villiers-en-Plaine

St-Pompain

Magné

La Garette

Deux-Sèvres

Benet

Coulon

Le Vanneau

Nieul-sur-l'Autise

Oulmes

St-Sigismond

Le Mazeau

Embarcadère de la Venise Vert

Arçais

St-Hilaire-la-Palud

St-Pierre-le-Vieux

Maillezais

Abbaye St-Pierre

Damvix

Les Oiseaux du Marais Poitevin: Parc Ornithologique

Maillé

Coulon

Doix

Maillé

Parc Naturel Régional du Marais Poitevin

Vendée

Vix

St-Jean-de-Liversay

Charente-Maritime

Auzay

L'Anglée

Communal

Velluire

La Tublerie

Le Gué-de-Velluire

Vouillé-les-Marais

Sèvre-Niortaise

N

Bradt

0 5km
0 3 miles

Réserve Biologique Départementale de Nalliers

Maison du Maître de Digues

Chaillé-les-Marais

L'Ile-d'Elle

Marans

→ La Rochelle

Fontenay-le-Comte

known as *embarcadères* that enable visitors to take to the water in boats or canoes. This 28,000ha labyrinth of tranquil, duckweed-covered waterways nicknamed 'La Venise Verte' ('Green Venice') is one of the region's most entrancing features. Almost the size of the Isle of Wight, the vast 'wet' marshland drained by 12th-century monks and 17th-century Dutch engineers stretches from Marans in the west to Niort in the east, and from Maillezais down to Arçais. It is criss-crossed with tiny *rigoles* – canals, edged with pollarded willows or rustling poplars – that run into the Sèvre Niortaise River.

Although the name 'Venice' has vaguely urban connotations, the 'Green Venice' is in fact almost entirely rural. The tree-lined waterways serve partly as drainage for little squares of green pasture and partly as avenues of transport for everything from wedding parties to cattle. Their blissful silence is broken only by the buzz of dragonflies and the giggles of incompetent crews of tourists who, unlike expert local boatmen, zigzag inelegantly from bank to bank. In most villages you can rent canoes, electric boats or workaday *plates* and *barques* (flat-bottomed metal boats) between April and October, with or without a guide. If you prefer to stay on dry land, cycle rental is on offer in larger villages, and there are signposted trails to explore on foot or by bike, maybe leading to the studios of artists and craftspeople along the way. For a dreamy aerial view, you can even be wafted by hot-air balloon over the area (page 168).

Since the Poitou Marshes straddle three départements, or counties, it can sometimes be difficult to obtain information on the area as a whole. Tourist offices stock a useful, free map called *Marais Poitevin: Carte Découverte*, which gives an overall view. Though its pinpointing of attractions can be a bit inaccurate, it shows roads and waterways and is invaluable for addresses of boat and bike hire, museums and nature reserves.

Regional specialities to sample here include eels, melons, angelica, *lumas* (snails), lamb served with *mogettes* (beans) and Fiefs Vendéens wines.

There are several *maisons du parc*, or visitor centres, with a mission to explain the ecology and traditions of the marshes: those within the area of this book are at Chaillé-les-Marais (Maison du Maître de Digues, page 136) and Nieul-sur-l'Autise (Maison de la Meunerie, page 169). Outside the area, you'll find others at Esnandes (Maison de la Mytiliculture) and Coulon (Maison du Marais Poitevin, page 146). Arranged below, roughly from west to east, are some of the most attractive villages of the Venise Verte. Chaillé-les-Marais (page 136), on the edge of the Venise Verte, would also offer a good base for exploring the area.

TOURIST INFORMATION As well as the individual tourist offices listed on the following pages, additional information can be gleaned from three websites devoted to the marshlands:

w maraispoitevin-vendee.com. For the Vendée area.

w marais-poitevin.com. For Deux-Sèvres & Charente-Maritime areas.
w parc-marais-poitevin.fr. Official park website.

LE GUÉ-DE-VELLUIRE The site of a *gué*, or ford, across the Vendée River, this waterside village has some beautiful old stone buildings in Rue de l'Église. The villagers, who these days number only around 500, are known as Guétréens.

VELLUIRE A prosperous-looking, stone-built village 21km east of Luçon, Velluire is located at a crossing point on the Vendée River. To its west is the *communal*, or common grazing land, of Le Poiré-sur-Velluire. Along the D65 southwest towards Le Gué-de-Velluire (page 141) you have the strange impression of being on a cliff overlooking the ocean – indeed, the marshland that lies 40m below was once the seabed.

Tourist information
Mairie 13 Rue Georges-Clemenceau; 02 51 52 31 04; w velluire.free.fr

 ## Where to stay and eat
Auberge de la Rivière (11 rooms) 2 Rue de la Fouarne; 02 51 52 32 15; w hotel-riviere-vendee.com. Comfortable, 2-star Logis de France hotel, with a few well-priced rooms, some with river view. Free Wi-Fi, TV. Restaurant (closed Mon, Tue & Thu lunch; €€€) is justly reputed for excellent, artistically presented food. Towards the 'special treat' end of the spectrum, but well worth the extra few euros. €€€€

What to see and do
Communal (2km west of Velluire, signposted) A traditional system of 'commons' governs this 250ha nature reserve. During winter, the pastureland is flooded. Once it dries out and the grass shoots up in spring, farmers turn out their horses, cows and geese – each marked with an identifying number – and the new season is celebrated with a colourful April festival, the Ouverture du Marais Communal. The animals are rounded up in December and restored to their owners for the winter. The *communal* is a haven for birds and the site is now classed as a Regional Reserve: storks nest from early spring; little bustard gather in autumn; and spectacular numbers of lapwing and golden plover visit between September and March. A signposted observatory 2km west of Velluire, on the road between L'Anglée and La Tublerie, is open and from here you can spot some interesting species in the waterways nearby.

VIX Vix is a large village strung out along the D25, with a riotously flowery private garden at the eastern end. In a nearby loop of the River Sèvre Niortise, 3km south of Vix, the Île Charouin nature reserve is home to otters and purple herons.

MAILLÉ Old-fashioned wells, with winding handles, lend this village a frozen-in-time atmosphere. Its Romanesque church front features some marvellous carved stone acrobats. Cycle hire is available, and there are electric *capucine* boats to rent (page 144). Sunday is market day, in July and August.

MAILLEZAIS On the edge of the Venise Verte, Maillezais (pronounced 'my-er-zay'), attracts the visitor hordes with its imposing, ancient monastic ruins that tower over the countryside to the west. Before joining them, pause first in the centre of the village to admire the Romanesque church, its main doorway decorated with carved stone birds, serpents and acrobats.

As you head towards the abbey, along Rue de l'Abbaye, look out for number 74: pieces of grey bone stick out high up in the walls – placed there, legend has it, to protect from sickness any animals kept inside.

The area's other main attraction is its collection of *embarcadères*, little 'ports' where between April and October you can hire small boats (page 144) to explore the local waterways. If you engage the services of a guide, they will do the hard work – and may decide to astonish you by stirring up the mud of the canal bed and setting fire to the gases that are released above the surface.

Tourist information

Office de Tourisme Rue du Docteur Daroux; 02 51 87 23 01; w maraispoitevin-vendee.com; Jan–Mar 14.00–17.30 Mon, 09.30–12.30 Wed–Thu & Sat, 09.30–12.30 & 14.00–17.30 Tue & Fri; Apr–Jun 14.00–18.00 Mon, 09.30–12.30 & 14.00–18.00 Tue & Thu–Sat, 09.30–12.30 Wed; Jul–Aug 09.30–12.45 & 14.15–18.30 Mon–Sat, 09.30–12.45 Sun

✖ Where to eat and drink

Auberge de l'Abbaye Impasse du Petit Versailles; 02 51 87 25 07; w restaurant-marais-poitevin.fr; 10.00–noon & 15.00–19.00 daily. Very popular restaurant, with heavy accent on regional cuisine – snails, eels, frogs' legs, *mogettes* – but crêpes are also available all day long, too. Great location, with pleasant outdoor space. €€€

L'Échauguette 39 Rue du Grand Port; 09 77 68 09 53; w echauguette-maillezais.fr; Apr–end Jun 09.00–19.00 Tue–Thu, 09.00–22.00 Fri–Mon. This rustic restaurant can be found at the foot of the Abbaye St-Pierre, down by a boat hire business on the canal. Its interior is, given the age of the place, appropriately adorned with open wood beams & well-worn stone floors. Traditional cuisine is served alongside local wines & deliciously decadent desserts. The service is equally fantastic. €€€

What to see and do

Abbaye St-Pierre (02 51 53 66 80; w nossites.vendee.fr/abbaye-de-maillezais; Mar & Oct–mid-Nov 10.00–12.30 & 14.00–18.00, Apr–May & Sep 10.00–12.30 & 14.00–18.00, Jul–Aug 10.00–19.00, all daily; €6/4/free adult/under 26s/under 12s) West of the village, where the winds sweep in off the open marshes, rise the ghostly remains of an 11th-century abbey, a striking example of Romanesque architecture. Some 200 monks lived here in the 13th century, undertaking the first draining of the area to create the productive fields that exist today. During this time, they suffered much harassment from Geoffrey la Grand'Dent ('Longtooth'), half-factual, half-fictional son of the powerful Raymondin de Lusignan and the fairy Mélusine (page 161). Some 300 years later, the writer Rabelais (page 16) spent three years within its walls. During the Wars of Religion, the abbey was seized and fortified by the Protestants – in 1589 the Calvinist writer Agrippa d'Aubigné turned it into a Protestant stronghold and remained its governor for 30 years. After this relatively stable time, the abbey sunk into a long period of decline that continued after the Revolution in 1789, when its remains were confiscated by the state and much of the stone sold.

Were there a prize for the Vendée's most high-tech visitor attraction, the abbey here would fight it out with Le Puy du Fou (page 182). The reception will lend you a smartphone (in exchange for you depositing your passport/ID card) and an app then lets you do a self-guided tour around the abbey and grounds. Insert the phone into the viewer provided and you get a 3D tour of some parts. (If you prefer 'low-tech', there's a leaflet in English describing the history of the buildings and the daily life of the monks who lived here, as well as two digital terminals which give you further insight into the architecture of the Abbaye.) From lines of foundations visible in the uneven ground, you can make out the positions of refectory, cloister and chapter house. Climb the abbey's north tower – the steps come to an abrupt halt – to view the distant marshes and, closer at hand, to look down at white stones on the ground delineating the nave and the succession of choirs that each bishop laid out. Among more intact buildings are the octagonal kitchen, the dormitory for visiting travellers and, down a flight of worn stone steps, a magnificently preserved, vaulted space called a cellarium. In the dormitory, a clever series of projections using 'talking head' actors takes you back to the age of the monastic builders. In July and August, several times daily, groups of costumed players plunge visitors into this turbulent history, popping out to describe (in French) the building of the abbey – see website for details. Between May and June, the abbey is a venue for the new Festival des Voûtes Célestes, which brings world-famous classical musicians together across three historical sites, and a Christmas market takes place in early December. Nearby are a snack bar, crêperie and a good gift shop.

Embarcadère de l'Abbaye (Le Vieux Port; ☎ 02 51 87 21 87; w marais-poitevin-tourisme.com; from €18 based on 2 people for 1hr, but prices pp reduce as group size increases) Hire a canoe, rent a rowing boat or relax while a guide does all the work, allowing you to sit back and enjoy the canals and waterways of the Venise Verte, under the shade of willows and poplars. Boats can take up to five passengers. When booking, ask for a guide who speaks English – if required.

DAMVIX This village has a delightful setting, with rows of houses overlooking a long stretch of river. Summer restaurant-cruises depart at lunchtimes from near the bridge (see below), and cycle and boat hire are also available. The Vélo Francette, a cycle route that runs from Normandy to the Atlantic, passes through the village on its way from Niort to La Rochelle (see w cycling.lavelofrancette.com).

Where to stay and eat

La Belle Époque (4 Rooms) 8 Chemin du Halage; m 06 49 89 40 68; e kowalskipawel14@gmail.com. Welcoming hosts & a smart, luxuriously fitted out interior with large bedrooms that overlook the canal make this a special & already highly rated hotel. €€€€

Le Collibert II Le Porteau, Damvix; ☎ 02 51 87 19 16; w lecollibert.fr; ☉ Apr–Sep, departure 11.45 daily. 4hr lunchtime cruises on board a glass-sided boat, with meal & wine included.

Menu prices vary. Children catered for. Booking essential. €€€€

La Récré 24 Chemin du Halage, Damvix; ☎ 02 51 87 10 11; ☉ Jul–Aug noon–14.00 & 19.00–22.00 Mon & Thu–Sun, noon–14.00 Tue. Waterside pizzeria/crêperie in a former school building. The school closed in 1970, but the scholarly theme continues. Pleasant terrace, child-friendly menu & games room. Advanced booking advised. €€€

LE MAZEAU Amid the farms and gardens of this area of the Marais Poitevin, you'll come across this small town that provides the perfect one-stop-shop for access to the 'Green Venice'. Nestled in the marshes between its better-known counterparts of Benet, Maillezais and Damvix, the place is easy to miss – but don't. If you only have one day in the area and really want to get a feel for the waterways and landscapes then Le Mazeau is ideal. The village itself is unremarkable but down by the river, which is spanned by an attractive iron bridge adorned with pink flowering shrubs, you will find everything you need. Whether it is a short, well mapped bike ride that takes you along the waterways up to the pretty village of Saint-Sigismond and back, or else a more leisurely jaunt through tree-lined canals on a traditional *yole* (punt), Le Mazeau can provide. You can hire a bicycle or boat at the Embarcadère de la Venise Verte for your morning or afternoon excursion before returning to the same place to sit beside the water and try a platter of local cuisine that includes *mogettes* and *préfou* (garlic bread), at the cheerful and laid-back Au Bord de l'Eau (see below). L'Échoppe du Marais, a wine shop that's hard to miss with its bright red façade, is on the main road at the eastern end of town and is highly regarded for its local selection of wines – it's well worth stopping at to finish off your visit.

�֎ Where to eat and drink
Au Bord de l'Eau Rue du Port; ☏ 02 51 51 20 71; w restaurantaubordeleau.com; ⏲ lunch daily & dinner Wed–Sat. Low-key, with an outside terrace that puts you right at the water's edge where you can watch the comings & goings of boat outings along the Marais. Great food & at a good price which is matched by local wines. You can eat there or they also provide the option of a picnic that you can take with you on your outing from the linked boat operator next door. €€

What to see and do
Embarcadère de la Venise Vert (☏ 02 51 52 90 73; w la-venise-verte.com; ⏲ Apr–Jun & Sep 10.00–12.30 & 14.00–18.00 daily, Jul–Aug 09.00–19.30 daily; from €15/13 adult/child) Next to the bridge at the bottom of town you can hire bicycles, paddleboards, canoes and boats for either a self-guided adventure with maps provided or a tour with a guide who can offer local insight into the towns, waterways and wildlife around the area. A recommended option is to hire electric bikes and follow the well-signposted 24km cycle route provided by the tour operator, making your way west at an easy pace through the marshes before taking the road south to the Village de la Sèvre which sits on the Sèvre Niortaise. This river forms the heart of the drainage system for the Marais Poitevin and takes the excess water all the way to the Atlantic Ocean. From there, you glide beneath weeping willows and past ivy-covered houses along the riverbank before returning to Le Mazeau. Book ahead in the summer months, particularly for boat hire, as it gets very busy.

BENET A large village on the northern edge of the Marais Poitevin, Benet is best known for the sculpted scenes from the Old and New Testaments that adorn its Romanesque church doorway.

↑ Where to stay and eat *Map, page 140*
La Marienne (4 rooms) 14 Rue de la Virée, Lesson, 3km northeast of Benet; ☏ 02 51 51 50 41; w la-marienne.com. A well-favoured B&B, with bright rooms, including family options. Free parking & Wi-Fi, b/fast inc. Spa & hammam at extra cost. €€

Ma Gourmandise 1 Pl de l'Église, Arçais, Deux-Sèvres; ☏ 05 49 73 43 84; ⏲ 11.00–15.00 & 19.00–21.00 Mon–Tue & Thu–Fri, 11.00–15.00 Wed & Sun. 14km southwest of Benet in an elegant old house; try local snails, eels, goat's cheese & angelica. Sometimes offers vegetarian options, too. €€€

THE MARAIS POITEVIN BEYOND THE VENDÉE

Those who want to venture further into the Venise Verte can cross the departmental boundaries and visit other waterside villages in Deux-Sèvres or Charente-Maritime.

Le Vanneau (Deux-Sèvres) is a popular excursion in late July, for its Marché sur l'Eau (Market on the Water) when local produce is sold from boats by costumed farmers. In **Arçais** (Deux-Sèvres), a beautiful 19th-century chateau dominates the main slipway of this charming village, where craft and antiques shops line cobbled pavements, and winding alleys lead to attractive *gîtes* and B&Bs. At **St-Hilaire-la-Palud** (Deux-Sèvres), boats can be rented on the shady canals at neighbouring Montfaucon. Birdwatchers can look for geese, ducks and wading birds at a nearby reserve, the **Les Oiseaux du Marais Poitevin: Parc Ornithologique**. **La Garette** (Deux-Sèvres) is another pretty village, with craft shops, restaurants and boat-hire places in some of the ancient houses that line its pedestrianised main street. From **Niort**, you can navigate the full 60km length of the Sèvre Niortaise to Marans on an electric houseboat designed with families in mind, which can accommodate 8 people (w aboutdumarais.com). **Coulon** (Deux-Sèvres) is officially categorised as one of the 'most beautiful villages of France'; this 'capital' of the Venise Verte contains old streets lined with craft shops, and photogenic houses reflected in the limpid waters of the Sèvre Niortaise. Along the quayside, you can rent traditional flat-bottomed boats from several companies, some of which own waterside sites where their clients can moor to enjoy their picnics. Coulon is also the location of the **Maison du Marais Poitevin** (w maison-marais-poitevin.fr), an information centre which explains the history of the marshes, how the land has been won from the sea and the natural and ethnographic points of interest in the marshlands.

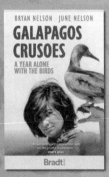
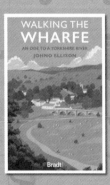
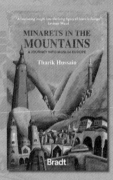

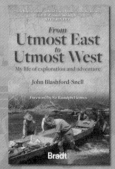

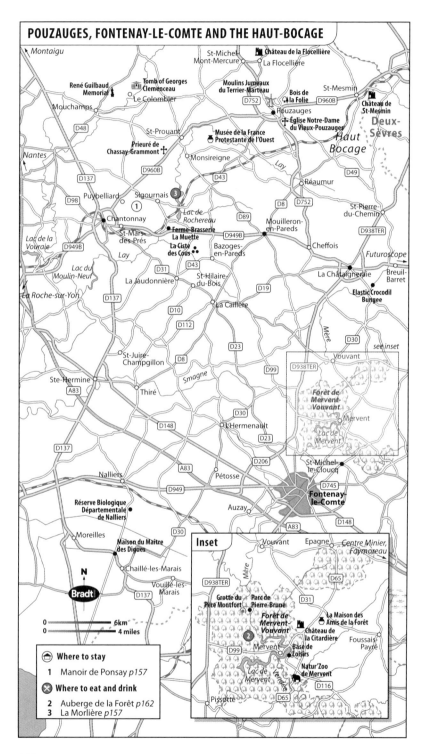

POUZAUGES, FONTENAY-LE-COMTE AND THE HAUT-BOCAGE

Montaigu

St-Michel-Mont-Mercure ☐ Château de la Flocellière
La Flocellière

René Guilbaud Memorial
Tomb of Georges Clemenceau
Le Colombier
Moulins Jumeaux du Terrier-Marteau
Bois de la Folie
St-Mesmin
D960B
Château de St-Mesmin

Mouchamps
D752
Pouzauges
Église Notre-Dame du Vieux-Pouzauges
Deux-Sèvres

D48
St-Prouant
Musée de la France Protestante de l'Ouest
Haut Bocage

Nantes
Prieuré de Chassay-Grammont
Monsireigne
Lay

D137
D960B
D43
Réaumur
D49

Puybelliard
Sigournais ③
D8
D752
St-Pierre-du-Chemin

D98
①
Lac de Rochereau
D89
Mouilleron-en-Pareds
D938TER

Chantonnay
Ferme-Brasserie La Muette
D949B
Cheffois

Lac de la Vouraie
St-Mars-des-Prés
La Ciste des Cous
Bazoges-en-Pareds
Futuroscope

D949B
Lay
D43
La Châtaigneraie
Breuil-Barret

Lac du Moulin-Neuf
D31
St-Hilaire-du-Bois
Elastic Crocodil Bungee

La Roche-sur-Yon
La Jaudonnière
D137
D19

D10
La Caillère

D112

D23
Mère
D30

St-Juire-Champgillon
D8
D99
D938TER
see inset
Vouvant

Ste-Hermine
A83
Smagne
Forêt de Mervent-Vouvant

Thiré
D30
Mervent

D148
L'Hermenault
Lac de Mervent

D137
D23

D206
St-Michel-le-Cloucq

Nalliers
A83
Pétosse
D745
Fontenay-le-Comte

D949
Auzay
A83
D148

Réserve Biologique Départementale de Nalliers

Moreilles
D30

Maison du Maître des Digues

N

Chaillé-les-Marais

Bradt
Vouillé-les-Marais
D137

0 _____ 6km
0 _____ 4 miles

Inset

Vouvant
Epagne
Centre Minier, Faymoreau

Mère
D65

D938TER
Grotte du Père Montfort
Parc de Pierre-Brune
D31

Forêt de Mervent-Vouvant
La Maison des Amis de la Forêt

Château de la Citardière
Foussais-Payré

②
Mervent
Base de Loisirs

D99
Natur'Zoo de Mervent
Lac de Mervent
Vendée
D116

Pissotte
D65

6

Pouzauges, Fontenay-le-Comte and the Haut-Bocage

This chapter explores the inland region from St-Michel-Mont-Mercure in the north to Nieul-sur-l'Autise in the southeast. Here you'll find the Vendée's largest forest, its highest village and – from pre-Revolution days when the area was known as Bas-Poitou – its former capital of Fontenay-le-Comte. The remains of feudal fortresses dominate Bazoges-en-Pareds, Vouvant, Pouzauges and Sigournais, and the water meadows near St-Mesmin. The French Revolution may have marked the decline of religion in France, but plenty of stout churches remain in this area to mourn its passing. Medieval wall paintings adorn some of these sacred buildings, while others host a series of summer concerts, 'Les Nuits Musicales en Vendée Romane'.

Away from the coast, yet not away from the water, lakes at Mervent and Sigournais provide welcome relief on hot summer days. In the east of a département fairly lightly touched by industry, it's a surprise perhaps to find the vestiges of some once-important coal mining, waiting to be discovered at Faymoreau.

ST-MICHEL-MONT-MERCURE

Its relatively dizzy altitude of 290m qualifies this picturesque spot 14km northwest of Pouzauges as the highest village in the Vendée. A microclimate up here inclines temperatures at St-Michel to be several degrees colder than in villages below.

A massive, gold-leafed copper statue of St Michael, the patron saint of high places, crowns the late 19th-century church – you can climb 199 steps inside for a 360° panorama on a clear day across five French départements. At either end of the church, outside, you'll find a *table d'orientation*, or viewing table. There are signposted country walks starting from the Moulin des Justices, a 19th-century windmill just off the D755, 3km northwest of St-Michel.

TOURIST INFORMATION
Mairie Rue de l'Église; ℡ 02 51 57 20 32; w demarchesadministratives.fr; ⏱ 09.00–noon

Thu & Sat, 09.00–noon & 14.00–17.30 Tue–Wed & Fri

WHERE TO STAY AND EAT
Château de la Flocellière (5 rooms & 5 *gîtes*) 30 Rue du Château, La Flocellière; ℡ 02 51 57 22 03; e flocelliere.chateau@gmail. com; w chateaudelaflocelliere.com. Delightful,

upmarket accommodation, in a castle continuously occupied for nearly 1,000 years & set in 15ha of grounds. You may wish you'd worn period costume when you enter the building, which

149

is adorned with antique furniture. Excellent service, charming hosts. Free Wi-Fi, billiards table. Seasonal swimming pool. B/fast inc. Dinner on request. €€€€€

Auberge du Mont-Mercure 8 Rue de l'Orbrie, behind church; 🕿 02 51 57 20 26; w aubergemontmercure.com; 🕐 lunch Tue–Sun, dinner Wed–Sun. Rather austere décor, but the good food (favouring meat over fish) includes a wallet-friendly 'workman's menu' on w/day lunchtimes, with more gastronomic options in the evenings. €€€

WHAT TO SEE AND DO

Église de St-Michel-Mont-Mercure (Pl du Sommet; 🕐 Apr–Oct 09.00–20.00 daily, Nov–Mar 09.00–17.00 daily; €1/0.50 adult/child, leave donation in the box)

The history of the church and its precious archangel is now documented with a series of wall panels inside: at times a rather sad tale, at times uplifting. St-Michel first lost a wing in 1907, then another in 1932. Particularly astonishing are the pictures of the statue being lifted back into place in 1961 after it had been dislodged by a storm four years earlier. More than 30,000 people attended a special festival organised to help raise funds for this tricky operation. The current statue has impressive stats, weighing in at 1,200kg, with a wingspan of 2.3m and a height of 9.6m. The route up the well-worn stairs to the statue is very narrow, steep and winding so take care. A notice at the foot of the stairs warns that you must strictly observe the opening times…or run the risk of being locked in!

Chapelle Notre-Dame de Lorette (La Flocellière, 2km east of St-Michel, signposted once you're in La Flocellière)

In this picturesque village stands an unusual chapel that was once part of a Carmelite convent. Its cool, white interior is a place of peace; a few wall panels (in French) give historical information about religion in the area, the church itself and other buildings of interest in the town. However, through a door to the left of the altar lies its most extraordinary feature: a room modelled in the 19th century on the Santa Casa, the 'holy house' that was the birthplace of the Virgin Mary. The whole house was said to have been transported by angels, in 1294, from Nazareth to the Italian town of Loreto, where it became a major focus of pilgrimage. Here, a reverently hushed atmosphere reigns over La Flocellière's perfect replica, with its hanging lamps and handsome statue of the Virgin – an astonishing blend of medieval-style gloom and gilded Middle Eastern-style decoration. On the left, as you enter, you can press a button to add lighting and gentle music to this atmospheric place, or another button which activates the lighting, without the music.

POUZAUGES

History seems to have dealt harshly with this attractive hilltop town. The revocation of the Edict of Nantes, in 1685, drained its strongly Protestant population; a century later, the Wars of the Vendée left only seven houses standing here, out of 300. On a (quite literally) brighter note, in 1886 Pouzauges became the first town in the Vendée to have electric street lighting and more recently it was awarded Petites Cités de Caractère (Small Towns of Character) status.

You need to be extremely adept at hill starts to drive around the precipitous streets of 'the pearl of the *bocage*', as Pouzauges is known; even the buildings seem to have difficulty clinging to the rocky slopes. It is best to park near the church and walk, following the *fil vert*, a painted green line that leads you on a roughly 90-minute trail, via shops, the chateau and major points of interest. Market days fall on Thursdays and Saturdays. For rambles further afield, the tourist office can provide maps of interesting *sentiers pédestres* (footpaths) in the countryside around the town, which includes the two routes of the Rando Bocage. The shortest is a three-day, 60km walk starting in Pouzauges called Sur les Hauteurs de Vendée.

TOURIST INFORMATION

Office de Tourisme 30 Pl de l'Église; ☎02 51 91 82 46; w tourisme-paysdepouzauges.fr; ⏰ Apr–May 14.30–17.30 Mon, 10.00–12.30 & 14.30–17.30 Tue–Fri, 09.30–12.30 Sat; Jun–Sep 09.30–12.30 & 14.30–18.00 Mon–Sat, 09.30–noon Sun & hols; Oct–Mar 10.00–12.30 & 14.30–17.00 Tue–Wed & Fri, 09.30–12.30 Thu & Sat

⭐ WHERE TO EAT AND DRINK

Le Casse-Croûte Vendéen 31 Rue de la Mare, 500m south of town centre; ☎02 51 61 72 80; ⏰ noon–14.00 daily & 19.00–21.30 Thu–Sun. Vendée specialities served in a converted barn (slightly bizarre décor, involving tractor & bicycle seats, among other oddities!), near the southern bypass. Very popular. Good-value lunch; occasional themed evenings. €€€

WHAT TO SEE AND DO

Rando Bocage (30 Pl de l'Église; ☎02 51 91 82 46; w tourisme-paysdepouzauges. fr; ⏰ Mar–Nov, organised by the Tourist Office; €170–220 pp) Designed to immerse walkers into the historical, cultural and natural heritage of Pouzages and the surrounding area, the Rando Bocage comprises two hiking options that take you across the local countryside following the GR de Pays routes. The Tourist Office (see above) takes care of everything, including accommodation, catering, visits and even transport of your luggage. The Sur les Hauteurs de Vendée circuit between Pouzauges and Saint Mesmin is a three-day, two-night option that departs from Pouzauges and covers 60km. Au Coeur des Collines Vendéennes is a slightly longer, four-day, loop trail that goes from Chavagnes-les-Redoux through Le Boupère, Pouzauges, Réaumur and back to Chavagnes-les-Redoux.

Église St-Jacques (Pl de l'Église) Pouzauges' town-centre church, dating in part from the 11th century, has some wonderful stained glass, including a window on the south side illustrating scenes from the Vendée Wars.

Château de Pouzauges (Rue du Vieux Château; ☎02 51 91 82 46; w pouzauges. com; ⏰ Jul–Sep for guided tours at 18.00 Thu, book at the tourist office; €3/free adult/under 11s) Occupying the highest point in town, alongside a modern housing estate, are the remains of an 11th-century stronghold that once belonged to the notorious Gilles de Rais (page 177) but which is now in municipal ownership. Its 12 ruined towers are gradually being revealed from their cloaks of vegetation; views from the grassy courtyard (admission free) leave no doubt as to why this was such a strategic position. Above it rises the massive, square *donjon*, or keep. You can take a guided tour of the interior – though there is little to see inside, apart from a few stone fireplaces and a list of its (many) previous owners.

Église Notre-Dame du Vieux-Pouzauges (On the D49, south of bypass; ⏰ usually during daylight hours; free) Well signposted, about 1km southeast of the town centre, is the ancient church of Notre Dame. Completed in around 1066, it's looking a little run-down these days, but it's worth a peek inside for some magnificent wall paintings on the north side of the nave. Laminated sheets provide English-language information about the frescoes and there are occasional temporary exhibitions on church architecture or related subjects. A symphony of terracotta and ochre, the frescoes are thought to date from the 13th century and were discovered in 1948 under layers of paint. Press a button nearby for a 7-minute son et lumière display with French commentary, highlighting this medieval strip-cartoon. Five scenes on the lower level depict episodes in the life of the Virgin Mary and her parents. Above are friezes of grotesque animals, and illustrations representing different months of the year. Over the west door, some more-recently uncovered paintings show Cain and Abel.

Moulins Jumeaux du Terrier-Marteau (Off the D752, 1km north of Pouzauges, signposted from town centre; w les-moulins-du-terrier-marteau.com; ⊕ Jul–Aug 09.00–12.30 & 17.00–19.00 Fri, 15.00–18.30 Sun; €3/1 adult/child) Now back in use and grinding corn for the town's shops, these two sturdy 18th-century windmills, with their canvas sails, have been restored and can be visited in high season on a guided tour. This takes you up and down rough steps, and squeezing through narrow gaps, to see the different processes. They are now under the ownership of Pouzauges-based French food giant, Fleury-Michon.

Bois de la Folie (Off the D752, 1km north of Pouzauges) Druids once worshiped the mistletoe at this mysterious, distinctively shaped hilltop clump of trees, reputed to be inhabited by the fairy Mélusine (page 161) as well as by numerous pixies and goblins. Take the Terrier-Marteau turning (see above), and you can reach the wood by a footpath that starts just beyond the windmills.

Château de St-Mesmin (La Ville, off the D960bis, 8km east of Pouzauges, from the car park, cross the railway to find it after 100m; ☏ 05 49 80 17 62; w chateau-saintmesmin.fr; ⊕ Apr–Nov, see website for detailed timetable; €8/5 adult/under 15s, multi-media guide €1 extra) This proud 14th-century fortress overlooks a tributary of the Sèvre Nantaise River at the hamlet of La Ville, just beyond St-Mesmin. Its walls and five towers seem to emerge from the very rock, while an ongoing restoration programme has revealed or refurbished its dry moat, drawbridge, chapel, spiral stairs, arrow-slit windows and rooftop sentry-way. In summer, and sometimes in the Easter holidays, there is a programme of special events, which might include food markets, medieval banquets, concerts and atmospheric evening tours. Recent years have seen actors chronicling the cruel and sometimes funny stories of soldiers involved in some of the many battles that the castle played a part in, while 2024 takes inspiration from the Paris Olympics and features medieval games.

The chateau is a marvellous place to visit at any time, but it's in July and August that it really springs to life. In these months, every day, costumed actors are present in the different tower rooms to demonstrate – remaining solemnly in character – medieval methods of cookery, herbalism, childcare, writing and so on (a different theme is explored each year). With an irresistible blend of passion, humour and enthusiasm (and a pretty good knowledge of English), they draw children in to try their hand at activities, and might even dress a small volunteer up in real armour or solve the puzzle of who poisoned Pierre de Montfaucon, the 14th-century lord of the castle. In the courtyard, children can try their hand at medieval games such as skittles, hoopla, stilts, etc. There is a short, subtitled introductory film and the multi-media guide is an audio-phone with an English-language option, or videophone option (in French) letting you do a self-guided tour. For technophobes, there is a brochure in English and fact sheets in the rooms are also in English. A family could spend a good 2 hours enjoying it all,

The Vendée is famous for its fragrant – and delicious – brioche PAGE 37
above left
(SB/VE)

Salt has played an important part in the region's economy since the Middle Ages PAGE 37
above right
(SB/VE)

Costumes and dancing enhance summer festivals in the Vendée PAGE 17
right
(PO/S)

Traditional *carrelet* fishing huts line the waterways of the Vendée coast PAGE 129
below
(SyR/D)

above
(MS/S)

The Château des Ducs de Bretagne reminds us that Nantes was once in Brittany PAGE 222

left
(AL/VE)

The ornate interior of the Château de Terre-Neuve in Fontenay-le-Comte PAGE 167

below
(PO/S)

Ruined but still imposing: the castle at Commequiers PAGE 74

The chapel of Notre-Dame-de-Bonne-Nouvelle overlooks the Port de la Meule, on the Île d'Yeu PAGE 86

above
(OM/S)

The 12th-century Église Notre-Dame in arty Vouvant PAGE 161

right
(C/D)

The atmospheric ruins of L'Abbaye de l'Île Chauvet at Bois-de-Céné PAGE 65

below
(SB/VE)

above left — The Vendée is know for its many picturesque windmills; this one stands near
(SB/VE) — Île-d'Olonne PAGE 105

above right — Get paddling – it's one of the best ways to explore the region's wetlands PAGE 44
(SB/VE)

below — Canals turn the Marais Breton into a green chequerboard PAGE 52
(SB/VE)

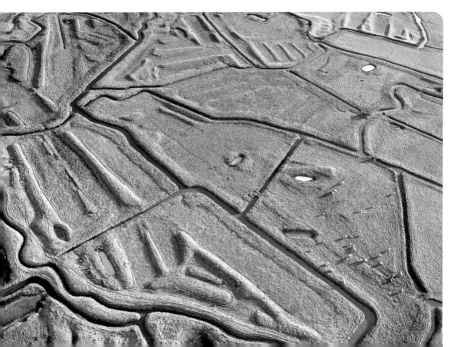

Mareuil-sur-Lay is a centre of Vendean wine-making PAGE 133

above
(SB/VE)

Take a break from the coast to visit the scenic Lac du Jaunay and surrounding forests PAGE 102

below
(JG/VE)

above left (DH/D) The middle-spotted woodpecker is one of several woodpecker species found in the Vendée PAGE 6

top right (AA/D) Black-winged stilts breed in the marshes and salt meadows PAGE 6

above right (OP/D) A migratory brent goose with its distinctive charcoal colouring PAGE 6

below (S/S) Barn owls can be spotted hunting around farms and fields at night PAGE 6

A black-tailed godwit, one of the Vendée's many waders PAGE 6
above left (RZ/D)

Huge flocks of dunlin stop in the Vendée on their way to and from Africa PAGE 6
above right (StR/D)

Red squirrels are a common sight in forests PAGE 5
right (S/S)

Look out for the *baudet du Poitou*, the distinctive, shaggy donkey! PAGE 6
below (S/D)

above
(AD/S)
Endless salt marshes lie inland from elegant La Baule PAGE 244

below left
(O/D)
The bridge near St-Nazaire links the north and south
banks of the Loire Estuary PAGE 240

below right
(MCM/S)
Take a ride on Nantes' mechanical elephant, perhaps
the city's most famous inhabitant PAGE 226

bottom right
(CL/S)
The Misconceivable, one of many outdoor artworks that line
the Loire between Nantes and the sea PAGE 252

but check with current leaflets or the website to make sure your visit coincides with the activities. There's a shop – which expands in high season – and snacks and drinks are available.

ST-PROUANT

This small village southwest of Pouzauges is best known for the charming little priory that stands in its countryside (see below). Another spiritual heritage is explored at the Château du Bois-Tiffrais, with a museum dedicated to the Protestant religion – traditionally fairly prevalent in this region – whose once-persecuted followers forswore the trappings of Catholicism in favour of the plainer Lutheran style of worship.

TOURIST INFORMATION
Mairie 1 Pl de la Mairie; ☏ 02 51 66 40 60; w saintprouant.fr, tourisme-paysdechantonnay.fr; ⏰ 09.00–12.30 Tue–Thu, 09.00–12.30 & 15.00–18.00 Mon & Fri

WHAT TO SEE AND DO
Prieuré de Chassay-Grammont (Off the D960bis, 3km southwest of St-Prouant; ☏ 02 51 66 47 18, 02 51 50 43 03; w nossites.vendee.fr/prieure-de-grammont; ⏰ Jun–Aug 10.00–12.30 & 13.30–18.00 daily, 1st half Sep same hours Fri–Sun; €4/2/free adult/under 26s/under 12s) This diminutive but extraordinarily well-preserved rural priory was founded by Richard the Lionheart in 1196. Ten hermit-like monks of the austere Grandmont order took vows of poverty, humility and chastity, existing on a near-vegan diet of fruit, vegetables and bread. (Seemingly, the more spartan the religious régime, the more good points its benefactor notched up for the afterlife.) The *prieuré* fell into disuse long before the Revolution but, having been used as farm buildings until as recently as 1983, escaped the usual wartime destruction of religious buildings.

The visit starts with a very short introductory video (available in English), but a detailed booklet distributed with your ticket provides ample information on the history and structure. An exhibition of 3D images of fabulous church treasures occupies the following room. The tall chapel, empty chapter house and restored refectory, with its vaulted, Plantagenet-style ceilings, form a harmonious group enclosing an open-air cloister. In a room marked '*celliers*' you can watch a 5-minute video of computer-generated images illustrating the priory's original appearance and its setting among dense woodland, before modern agricultural needs swept away the trees. Prestigious classical concerts are held in the chapel between spring and autumn.

Musée de la France Protestante de l'Ouest (Château du Bois-Tiffrais, Route de Réaumur, Monsireigne, 4km east of St-Prouant; ☏ 02 51 66 41 03; w bois-tiffrais.org; ⏰ Jul–Aug 14.00–18.00 Sat–Sun; €10/5 adult/under 18s) This impressive country-house museum and research centre stands in splendid isolation and explains three centuries of Protestantism in western France, during which followers were alternately persecuted or tolerated (page 154). Historic items on show in the five ground-floor rooms include huge Bibles, photographs, pulpits, documents and such objects as the metal tokens that admitted clandestine worshippers to secret services during the times of religious intolerance, a long period of persecution known as '*le Désert*' (1685–1787). One interesting picture shows a clandestine service being held outdoors during this era: high on the cliffs above the ceremony are some women with their umbrellas open, a sign to those below that all was safe. If they closed their

6

Jean Calvin (1509–64), the French Reformist, spent some time in Poitiers spreading his doctrine, giving western France a strong Huguenot (as Calvin's brand of Protestantism was described) tradition. Calvin was a disciple of Martin Luther, who was vehemently against the Catholic practice of selling indulgences, and considered the Bible, rather than the Pope, to be the final source of religious authority.

The Wars of Religion (1562–98) pitched Catholics against Protestants, causing death and the destruction of religious buildings on a grand scale. Eventually, in 1598, Henri IV issued the Edict of Nantes, allowing French Protestants freedom of worship. This was revoked by Louis XIV in 1685 – causing more than 400,000 Huguenots to flee overseas (many to Britain). The period from here to the Revolution in 1789 (when Protestants' political and civil rights were finally restored) was known as 'le Désert'. Protestant services had to be held in strict secrecy, in unfrequented corners of the countryside; worshippers themselves brought the items to be used – a portable pulpit on show at the museum (page 153) dates from this time. If identified, followers risked burning, hanging, torture, prison, or being sent off as galley slaves.

brollies, it was time to disperse, as danger approached. Other objects include *coiffes*, or headdresses; small, individual cups for Communion (used instead of a communal cup during 19th-century TB epidemics); and a copy of the 1787 Edict of Tolerance, which began the end of the prohibition on practising as a Protestant. Many Protestants still live in this area, and in St-Prouant, Fontenay, Foussais, Pouzauges, Mouilleron, Moncoutant and Mouchamps you come across small churches, known as *temples*, of the Église réformée – as the Protestant Church is known in France. Visits are by guided tour only, available at any time during opening hours, though conducted in French. An English-language leaflet may be available.

Even if you are not particularly interested in the subject, a visit here gives a rare opportunity to experience a typical country house interior that has not been over-restored. Near the car park is a 6km signposted walk called the Sentier Huguenot, which leads past megalithic stones, a Protestant cemetery, and some abandoned watermills along the River Lay.

MOUILLERON-EN-PAREDS

In Mouilleron's main square around noon, the 13 bells from the Romanesque church play 'Ave Maria' before the midday chimes. Incredibly, this unspoiled village, 16km east of Chantonnay, is the birthplace of not just one, but two of France's most famous wartime heroes: Georges Clemenceau (1841–1929), who was born above a former shop on today's Rue Clemenceau; and Jean de Lattre de Tassigny (1889–1952), who drew his first breath in a rather more prosperous-looking house on a neighbouring street.

A lesser claim-to-fame perhaps: the town holds a barrel-organ festival each May. For tourist information, see La Châtaigneraie (page 159).

WHAT TO SEE AND DO
Musée National Clemenceau-de Lattre (1 Rue Plante Choux; ✆02 51 00 31 49; w musee-clemenceau-delattre.fr; ⊕ Oct–Apr 10.00–noon & 14.00–17.00 Tue–Sun;

May–Sep 10.00–noon & 14.00–18.00 daily; €6/free adult/under 27s) Note: At the time of writing the museum was going through a redesign and the exhibits are likely to change. Cosy, 19th-century middle-class house, home of the maternal grandparents of distinguished French soldier Jean de Lattre de Tassigny and still furnished in comfortable bourgeois style. Outside is a small garden. Decorated eight times in World War I, de Lattre became a general (the youngest in the French army) at the start of World War II but was imprisoned by the Vichy government in 1943. He later escaped, joined the exiled General de Gaulle and took command of a unit in North Africa. From there he led the French First Army that landed in Provence in August 1944, liberated Alsace, crossed the Rhine and the Danube rivers, and accepted the surrender of Germany in Berlin on 8 May 1945.

The 45-minute guided tours of the house (supplemented by an English leaflet and some English-language signage) take in the kitchen, dining room and several bedrooms, all impeccably presented over three floors. They are filled with family furniture, photographs, mementoes (including some items of World War I uniform), and details of the marshal's career – including his later service as commander-in-chief of the French forces in Indo-China during the early 1950s. A short film shows highlights from his life, and his grand state funeral which was attended by fellow generals Eisenhower and Montgomery. There is also a display devoted to de Lattre's only son, Bernard, who was killed in Indo-China in 1951 and who lies buried beside his parents in the village cemetery, at the end of Rue Clemenceau. You are welcome to enjoy a picnic in the pretty garden.

A short stroll along Rue du Temple from the de Lattre birthplace, is a second museum building (19 Rue Clemenceau) devoted to twice-elected French prime minister Georges Clemenceau. In the former home of his maternal grandparents, where the politician was born on 28 September 1841, rooms have been arranged on three themes. One covers his political life and is narrated in part by Clemenceau's own newspaper articles; another looks at his passions and enthusiasms as a writer, a collector, and as a friend of artists; the third reveals the strong links that bound 'le Tigre', as he was nicknamed, to the Vendée throughout his life – including his retirement at St-Vincent-sur-Jard (page 117), and his eventual burial near Mouchamps (page 196). All information is bilingual.

Visitors wishing to follow in his footsteps will find a series of ten information panels (all with English as well as French text) at appropriate spots around the Vendée under the title 'La Vendée de Clemenceau' (w inthevendee.com/in-the-footsteps-of-georges-clemenceau).

Rochers de Mouilleron From the ancient village pump and washing-place, the Sentier des Meuniers (Millers' Path, marked with a picture of a donkey) leads up through the woods to a windy ridge crowned with three majestic windmills. Like those on the Mont des Alouettes (page 186), these and 11 others that once stood beside them played an important signalling role in the Wars of the Vendée. On the south side, a dramatically sited monument, with life-sized verdigris figures, represents Marshal de Lattre with his troops in Indo-China. To get there by car, it is signposted off the D949bis, 1.5km east of Mouilleron.

Manoir des Sciences de Réaumur (8 Rue Ferchault, Réaumur, 7km northeast of Mouilleron; ☏ 02 51 57 99 46; w manoirdessciencesdereaumur.fr; ⊕ Feb–Apr & Sep–Nov 14.00–18.00 Mon–Wed & Sun, Jun–Aug 14.00–18.00 Mon–Fri & Sun; €7/5/free adult/under 17s/under 6s) A 17th-century manor house contains a permanent exhibition on the life of René-Antoine Ferchault de Réaumur (1683–1757).

Born in La Rochelle, this versatile French scientist spent holidays here, at his family's country mansion. As well as inventing the alcohol thermometer that bears his name (on which freezing point is 0 and boiling point 80 degrees), Réaumur developed a method of making steel, invented the first coach springs to make travel more bearable, attempted to cross rabbits with chickens, and carried out studies of insect life that earned him a reputation as the father of French entomology.

Remodelled in 2016–17, the building is now a child-focused, interactive science museum suitable for children with some adult guidance. Guides are available in English. There is a display of thermometers; amazingly, the first one created by the scientist was around 1.5m in length. The exterior and grounds are delightful, planted with flowers to encourage the bees that the scientist so admired, and full of puzzles which children can enjoy solving. You can relax with a coffee or selection of artisanal teas and a side of local cookies here as well. There are interesting temporary exhibitions in the outbuildings on themes related to Réaumur's work.

BAZOGES-EN-PAREDS

You can easily spot Bazoges as you drive across the rolling green hills of the *bocage* on the D949bis; look out to the south for a tall castle keep, crowned by a jaunty little pointed watchtower. In July and August, the tower is illuminated, with the staff choosing the colour. On 14 July (Bastille Day) and around Christmas, the choice will be red, white and blue for the French flag. With its fortified stronghold, ancient church and old square edged with solid stone houses, this unspoiled village, untouched by invasive tourist-related paraphernalia retains a charmingly old-world atmosphere.

For tourist information, see La Châtaigneraie (page 159).

 WHERE TO STAY AND EAT

Auberge du Donjon 28 Rue de la Poste; ☎02 51 51 20 07; ⏲ noon–13.30 & 19.30–21.15 Wed–Sun. Good food in a prettily restored house opposite the castle, with open stone & wooden beams. Inexpensive lunchtime menu. English spoken. €€€

WHAT TO SEE AND DO

Donjon (12 Cour du Château; ☎02 51 51 23 10; ⏲ Apr–Jun & 1st half Sep 14.00–18.00 Mon & Fri–Sun, Jul–Aug 10.30–13.00 & 14.00–19.00 daily; €7/3/free adult/under 18s/under 9s, includes access to museum & garden) The village's magnificent square tower, *not* a dungeon (whatever the word may sound or look like to Anglophones), is the keep of a long-vanished castle dating back to the 14th century. A good English explanatory booklet is available to guide you around the restored interior, which contains a number of sparsely furnished rooms with armour, tapestries, oak chests and four-poster beds. The reward after climbing the uneven spiral stone stairs is a wonderful panorama of the surrounding countryside from the covered sentry-way that runs almost around the entire building. From a separate door on the ground floor, stairs lead to a first-floor room, which houses temporary exhibitions. The ticket office contains a small gift shop and cold drinks for sale.

Across the courtyard is the little Musée d'Arts et Traditions Populaires, Bazoges' museum of rural life, which has a couple of rooms set out with period furniture, and a bakehouse and barn displaying farm machinery alongside an assortment of traps for mice, moles, weasels, foxes – and even humans. Commentary (in French) starts up automatically as you enter the rooms and barn, describing local traditions as well as the typical tools, furniture, costumes and toys laid out in the two ground-floor rooms. If your language skills are not well honed, audio guides are available from reception or you can follow the French commentary from the translated scripts stuck to the walls.

Also across the courtyard is a beautifully laid-out medieval-style garden, the **Jardin médiéval**, with fruit trees and herbs growing in wattle-edged beds. Fairly recent in their design and creation, the gardens are set out in four distinct squares: one with medicinal plants, one with herbs, one with vegetables and a fourth devoted to plants associated with witchcraft. Fragrant old-fashioned roses surround a massive 16th-century *fuie*, or dovecote, once home to nearly 2,000 pigeons. Although the roof has been redone, the rest of the dovecote carpentry dates back to 1524.

La Ciste des Cous (Off the D43, 2km southwest of Bazoges) Towards La Jaudonnière, then signposted up a track to the right is a lonely site where a grove of walnut trees shelters the Vendée's oldest megalithic monument. This circular, stone-flagged enclosure – a prehistoric burial chamber – dates from 4000BC. In 1913, more than 100 skeletons were unearthed here.

CHANTONNAY

Though lacking in tourist sites of its own, this market town situated in the centre of the Vendée claims the title of 'the gateway to the *bocage*'. Some interesting 1980s panels by Dominique Landucci decorate the outside of the rather bleak, modern market hall, recalling local agriculture and scenes from the Vendée Wars. This latter theme is the basis of another Landucci design for a stained-glass window in the town's church (unmissable beneath its 68m-high spire).

To the north and east, the landscape is one of prairie lands, gentle hills and valleys, three of the latter filled with large lakes, offering welcome opportunities for boating, sunbathing, fishing or waterside walks. Interesting old villages to visit in the area include Puybelliard and Sigournais.

TOURIST INFORMATION
Office de Tourisme 65 Av du Général de Gaulle; ☏ 02 51 09 45 77; w tourisme-paysdechantonnay. fr; ⊕ 08.00–12.30 & 14.00–17.30 Mon–Fri

WHERE TO STAY
Manoir de Ponsay [map, page 148] (7 rooms) Between Puybelliard & St-Mars-des-Prés, 4km east of Chantonnay; ☏ 02 51 46 96 71; e manoirdeponsay@gmail.com; w manoirdeponsay.com. Elegant chateau/hotel, set in generous grounds, with spacious rooms decorated in period style. Free Wi-Fi, on-site parking, seasonal outdoor pool, hot-tub, billiards. Very good value. €€€

WHERE TO EAT AND DRINK
Château du Puybelliard 17 Rue des Dames; m 06 13 08 76 76; ⊕ noon–13.15 Tue & Sun, noon–13.15 & 19.00–20.45 Mon & Thu–Sat. A beautiful family run restaurant in a stunning & newly renovated 19th-century chateau serving great food in a grand setting. €€€
La Morlière [map, page 148] 7km northeast of Chantonnay, from Sigournais, take Monsireigne road for 2km; ☏ 02 51 40 41 98; ⊕ 12.15–13.45 Wed–Thu & Sun, 12.15–13.45 & 19.30–21.15 Fri–Sat. Excellent food in attractive surroundings high above the Lac de Rochereau, attracting the breeze onto its generous terrace & into a smart interior. Well worth the diversion for food & location. Children's & teenagers' menus. €€€

6

Ô'P'ti Bistrot 1 Place de la Liberte; ☎02 51 94 53 96; ⏰ 09.00–14.00 Tue–Wed & Sun, 19.00–22.00 Thu–Sat. Trendy establishment in the centre of town with outside terrace serving a seasonal menu sourced locally. €€€

WHAT TO SEE AND DO

Lakes Three artificial reservoirs surround Chantonnay. The Lac du Moulin-Neuf (also known as the Lac de l'Angle-Guignard), created by the Angle-Guignard dam on the River Lay 6km south of the town, offers fishing, signposted walks and, in summer, canoeing, pedaloes, giant inflatables for children and a café. The more recently created Lac de la Vouraie, 7km west of town, is surrounded by a 15km footpath and has picnic areas and fishing. Lac de Rochereau, 6km east of Chantonnay, has picnic places, children's play area, fishing and an excellent restaurant (page 157).

Puybelliard (2km northeast of Chantonnay) Although this sleepy village lies a mere 20m south of the busy D949bis, it produces a strong feeling of having stepped back in time. Its fortified church has useful-looking slit openings alongside the front door through which defenders could fire to protect the villagers gathered within. Opposite stands a venerable prison tower; behind that are narrow lanes and alleys – notably Rue des Dames, near the *mairie* – where buildings have arched doorways, Renaissance porches and other ancient architectural features.

Château de Sigournais (Sigournais, 4km northeast of Chantonnay; ☎02 51 40 40 71; w chateau-sigournais.fr; ⏰ early Jul–mid-Sep 14.30–18.30 Tue–Sun; €7/4/ free adult/under 15s/under 6s) High stone walls surround this imposing, beautifully restored medieval castle keep in the centre of an attractive village. Inside, one of its main features is a huge display of colourful, modern coats of arms – from 34 French provinces and 144 Vendean *communes*. Guided tours (pick up an English pamphlet at the admissions desk) take you from the guardrooms to the more refined *logis du seigneur* (lord's house). Here, a lovely modern stone staircase takes you, via the lord's stately courtroom, up to the slate-roofed sentry-way, from which soldiers had a commanding view for 20km around. Down below, in a courtyard outbuilding, a collection of before-and-after photographs show the renovation work that has been carried out. There are also animated exhibitions where actors provide a view of castle life in the 15th century, costume rental for children and medieval dances (see website for details).

Ferme-Brasserie La Muette (On the D949B, 5km east of Chantonnay; w brasserie-la-muette.fr; ⏰ 17.30–22.30 Wed–Thu, 11.30–15.30 & 17.30–00.30 Fri, 17.30–00.30 Sat, 11.30–15.30 & 17.30–22.30 Sun) Having joined the beer revolution in 2014, this farm-based brewery now offers a range of craft brews – all free from additives or preservatives and using hops grown on their own farm. You can try the beers on site at the rustic bar during the limited hours above or take away some gift packs. You will also find them in bars and cafés around the region under the distinctive 'La Musse' label.

LA CHÂTAIGNERAIE

If you approach this little hillside town from the southeast, by the D19, you see a rocky outcrop supporting a massive stone viaduct that is a popular spot for country walks…and, at the other end of the adrenalin scale, also the location of a bungee-jumping enterprise.

TOURIST INFORMATION

Office de Tourisme 1 Pl des Halles; ☎ 02 51 52 62 37; w tourisme-payschataigneraie.fr; ⏱ Jan–Mar & Oct–Dec 10.00–12.30 & 14.00–17.00 Tue–Wed & Fri, Apr & Sep 10.00–12.30 & 14.00–17.00

Mon–Fri, May–Jun 10.00–12.30 & 14.00–18.00
Mon–Fri, Jul–Aug 10.00–12.30 & 14.00–18.00
Mon–Fri, 10.00–13.00 Sun

PARC DU FUTUROSCOPE

Opened in 1987 and now stretching over 50ha in the Vienne, a département to the east of the Vendée, the Parc du Futuroscope (Av René Monory, Chasseneuil-du-Poitou, 8km north of Poitiers and 83km east of La Châtaigneraie; ☎ 05 49 49 30 80; w futuroscope.com; ⏱ around 2nd week Feb–Nov; €52/35/free adult/under 13s/under 5s; a whole range of passes available, inc family & group tickets, as well as hotel packages, see website for details) one of France's most popular attractions. More than 50 million people have passed through its gates since its creation and most go home very happy indeed.

'Theme park' is not a description that truly conjures up the array of astonishing audio-visual experiences that assault your senses. Here you'll immerse yourself in virtual reality, visiting not only 3D but 4D cinemas, encountering state-of-the-art technology, some of which is unique across the world. Plus there's a range of more traditional experiential rides and activities, some with height, age or other restrictions. With over 20 attractions, there is more than enough to entertain the curious for a full day or more and some visitors choose to stay overnight and enjoy an extra day. True, there's no Mickey Mouse to greet you here, but young children will be wide-eyed at the incredible displays created for their education and entertainment.

Even the names of the attractions are sure to generate excitement among the youngsters. There's 'Tornado Chasers', which received a 2022 Outstanding Achievement Award, and 'Destination Mars', which received an award for best new rollercoaster in 2020, as well as other suitably named attractions such as the 'Time Machine' and 'Extraordinary Journey'. The evening show, 'The Key to Dreams' is also popular, a spectacular officially described as an 'aquatic fairy tale' and performed by the world-renowned Cirque du Soleil group.

An essential part of the Futuroscope experience is the planning, as a quick visit to the website will confront you with a bewildering range of options: day tickets, hotel packages (great if you are spending two days here), passes, pre-booked meals. There are ten hotels close to the park, with full details on the website; for on-site nourishment, seven restaurants and numerous fast-food outlets can oblige at reasonable prices, though some are only in service in high season. Everything from sandwiches through steakhouse to gourmet is available, but if you prefer, feel free to bring your own picnic.

You may choose to visit out of season, but queues can still be long and eat into your time. The solution is to buy a Premium Pass, allowing you to skip most of the tedious time spent 'standing in line'. Although parts of the park are showing their age (so would we all if nearly 2 million people traipsed over us every year!), new attractions are introduced most years. If you want to make the most of your time here consider booking into one of the park's space-themed hotels or ecolodges (see website for details).

Pouzauges, Fontenay-le-Comte and the Haut-Bocage LA CHÂTAIGNERAIE

6

✕ WHERE TO EAT AND DRINK

La Pause Goût Thé Rue de Terriers, Zone de la Garenne; ☎02 51 51 50 05; w la-pause-gout-the. fr; ⊕ 09.00–19.00 Tue–Sat. A high-class tea shop, in the unlikely setting of a retail park, with homemade cakes, plus some great gift ideas. Super tea selection, but no savouries, just sweet stuff. €€€

WHAT TO SEE AND DO

Elastic Crocodil Bungee (Viaduc de Coquilleau, Route de Coulonges, near Breuil-Barret, 5km east of La Châtaigneraie; ☎05 65 60 00 45; w elasticrocodilbungee. com; ⊕ Apr–Oct 1 or 2 w/ends a month; €70 1st jump, €30 for a 2nd on the same day) Anyone brave enough to contemplate taking the 52m plunge above the valley of the River Mère should head for the disused railway viaduct on the D19. The strong latex 'rope' is so elastic that jumpers bounce back 85% of the distance covered from the platform.

Église St-Pierre (Cheffois, 4km northwest of La Châtaigneraie) Above the rooftops of Cheffois, a picturesque village near La Châtaigneraie, towers a solid, fortified Gothic church, topped with a *chemin de ronde*, or sentry-way. Its sober exterior hardly prepares you for the multitude of columns and extraordinary statues that you find inside: at first glance, you may think they are previous visitors, turned to stone! Only one, the Christ lying in his tomb, pre-dates the French Revolution, with the others being created in the late 19th century.

Église St-Hilaire (Breuil-Barret, 4km east of La Châtaigneraie) Visible from the main road, the village church in Breuil-Barret houses *Golgotha*, a magnificent painting by Jean Chevolleau (1924–96), an internationally famous Vendée-born artist known for his colourful, near-abstract works. There are also two beautiful, bright, stained-glass windows based on Chevolleau designs.

St-Pierre-du-Chemin (6km northeast of La Châtaigneraie) The village of St-Pierre-du-Chemin is known for its special greyish-pink stone, called *pierre des Plochères*. Outcrops can be seen in surrounding fields, and you can find it in the construction of several large buildings – notably some opposite the church. The village's best claim to fame, however, is that it possesses relics of 3rd-century martyr St Valentine, which have been held in the church since 1847, now displayed in an illuminated glass case near the entrance, along with other religious artefacts. For obvious reasons, in mid-February the village is the focus of a Fête des Amoureux, or Festival of Love – a popular time for local marriages.

VOUVANT

With its postern gate and cobbled streets, this attractive fortified village steeped in legend and dotted with little art galleries could almost be a film set, and richly deserves its title of one of the most beautiful villages in France. As if one accolade is not enough, it is also designated a Petite Cité de Caractère and a self-styled '*village de peintre*' (painter's village). High on a promontory in a crook of the River Mère, Vouvant is surrounded by stout defensive walls from which you can look down on the meandering waterway below, and is filled with allusions to the region's most famous inhabitant, the mythical Mélusine (see opposite). Crowds throng here in the summer to drink in the medieval atmosphere, to admire the façade of the church, to wander in and out of artists' studios or to attend some of the many special events.

TOURIST INFORMATION

Office de Tourisme Pl du Bail; ☎ 02 51 00 86 80; w vouvant-vendee.fr; ⏰ Jul–Aug 10.00–13.00 & 14.00–18.00 daily, Apr–Jun & Sep 10.00–12.30 & 14.00–18.00 Tue–Sun. Guided visits to the village may be available on Sun afternoons in summer (in French; €5). A copy of a sculpture of Mélusine lurks in one corner of the office & upstairs there is a small museum, L'Antre de Mélusine, covering medieval life in the Middle Ages & where you can even meet the fairy herself! Information on art events can be found at w vouvantvillagedepeintres.com.

WHERE TO STAY AND EAT

Les Remparts B&B (2 rooms) 12 Rue Basse des Remparts; m 06 51 75 20 12; e anitafroger85@gmail.com; w vouvant-vendee.com. Outdoor space, shared bathroom, free Wi-Fi. Bike hire available (extra charge). Central & good value, b/fast inc. €

Bar/Café Mélusine 19 Rue du Duc d'Aquitaine; ☎ 02 51 00 81 34; ⏰ Jul–Aug lunch Thu, lunch & dinner Fri–Tue. Various menus & daily dishes, plus w/end pizzas. Nothing elaborate, but a decent choice for lunch. €€€

Café Cour du Miracle 20 Rue du Duc d'Aquitaine; ☎ 02 51 00 54 93; ⏰ 10.00–18.00 Wed–Sun. A bright, British-owned café with pleasant courtyard, offering excellent salads, homemade pies, cakes & light lunches. €€

WHAT TO SEE AND DO

Village tour Pick up an English-language leaflet, with map, from the tourist office to guide you around the Vendée's only fortified town, taking in the tower, church and Romanesque bridge. Signboards correspond to the points of interest on the leaflet.

Tour Mélusine (Pl du Bail; ⏰ at the time of writing the tower was closed for restoration work, due for completion in 2024; get the key from the tourist office or Café Mélusine across the car park, see above) The ancient watchtower dominating the village and surrounding countryside was built – according to folklore – in 1242 by the fairy Mélusine. Various versions of the myth circulate, but essentially this legendary creature, who had been sentenced by a curse to become half-serpent each Saturday, has been credited with the construction of several castles in the region, each within the space of a single night. Some say her name is a corruption of 'Mère Lusignan', and that she married into the powerful local family of that name. Before agreeing to marriage, however, she made it a condition that her husband, Raymondin, should never see her on Saturday. He agreed. But one day, mad with jealousy, he spied on his wife as she was bathing naked and saw to his horror that she had a serpent's tail. Realising that her secret was out, the distraught Mélusine flew through the window on leathery wings, never to be seen again, and all her works crumbled…though enough of the stone steps remain in this case to allow you a spectacular view from the top. Virtual reality headsets are also available from the tourist office, allowing you to enjoy a 'Save the Mélusine tower' treasure hunt.

Église Notre-Dame (Pl de l'Église; ⏰ most days; free) The richly sculpted 11th-century decoration on the north front of Vouvant's Romanesque church is one of the marvels of the Vendée. Fantastical animals surround the twin doorways; above them is a series of magnificent life-sized statues dating from the 15th century. Inside the church the ornamentation is simpler, and you can have a closer look at some stone carvings reposing in the ancient crypt (mind the steps down), where there is also a film in French charting the history of the church's fortunes over the centuries. In the south aisle, a stone slab commemorates Geoffrey la Grand'Dent, or Geoffrey Longtooth, son of Mélusine and her human husband, who repented from his warmongering in time to ensure a Christian burial.

6

Cour du Miracle Behind the café of the same name lies a pretty courtyard whose name alludes to the story that one December day in 1715 a sick child begged visiting missionary, and future saint, Père Montfort (see opposite) for cherries. The priest told the boy's grandmother to go out and pick some. The old lady opened the door and, to her astonishment, saw a tree in this little yard laden with fruit.

MERVENT

Around this hillside village, there is no shortage of things to do deep in the heart of the vast Mervent-Vouvant Forest, north of Fontenay-le-Comte. In summer, the series of lakes created by dams across the Mère and Vendée rivers are ideal for watersports. The leafy D99A winds for 6km through the woods; there are also many signposted walks and rides among the 5,000ha of oak and chestnut – shady in summer and colourful in autumn – that are home to red deer and wild boar. The forest still has an active industrial side, too, its 35m-tall sessile oaks being particularly sought after for cabinet-making, carpentry, wood flooring and the production of wine barrels. And barrels are needed, as a few kilometres to the southwest is Pissotte, well known for its Fiefs Vendéens wines.

TOURIST INFORMATION

Office de Tourisme 13 Pl du Héraut; ☏ 02 51 69 44 99; w tourisme-sudvendee.com; ⊕ Jul–Aug   10.00–13.00 Tue–Thu & Sun, 10.00–13.00 & 14.00–18.00 Fri & Sat

✘ WHERE TO EAT AND DRINK

Auberge de la Forêt [map, page 148] Les Essarts (on the D99A), 3km northwest of Mervent; ☏ 02 53 72 93 11; ⊕ 11.00–18.00 Wed– Thu & Sun, 11.00–21.45 Fri & Sat. In among the leafy oaks & chestnuts, this is a place that appeals more to motorcyclists these days. The smell of smoke and stale wine hits you as you enter the dimly lit interior, where a bar and pool table finish off the biker vibe, though there is a quieter, more traditional restaurant in an adjacent room. Not a fancy place, nor is the menu huge, but no-frills, good-quality food & a friendly enough welcome. A roaring fire in winter. €€€

Chill-out 116 Route Touristique; ☏ 02 51 50 52 26; w chill-out.fr; ⊕ Mar–Oct noon–16.00 Mon, noon–15.00 & 18.00-22.00 Thu, noon–22.00 Fri–Sun. This cocktail bar & restaurant overlooks the lake from its large terrace. It also sports a private beach, hires out pedaloes & has indoor games. Good-value 'mussels & chips' sourced directly from the local fishmonger. €€€

SPORTS AND ACTIVITIES

Base de Loisirs 150 Route Touristique, D116, just below Mervent village; ☏ 02 51 00 22 13; w fontenayvendee.fr/listes/base-de-loisirs-de-mervent; ⊕ May–Jun & Sep 09.00–noon & 14.00–17.30 Mon–Fri by reservation only, 14.00–18.00 Sat–Sun & hols, Jul–Aug 10.00–18.30 daily. All sorts of activities are available to make use of the lake & surrounding forest. Choose from hiring mountain bikes, electric boats, canoes, kayaks, stand-up paddleboards or fishing boats. Instruction is available, with advanced reservation; some English is spoken. Activities priced individually.

WHAT TO SEE AND DO

Parc de Pierre-Brune (Off D99A, 2km north of Mervent; ☏ 02 51 00 20 18; w parc-pierre-brune.fr; ⊕ early Apr–mid-Sep, times vary – see website for details; €15.80/13.80/free adult/under 13s/under 3s) You know you are getting close to this pleasantly unsophisticated amusement park when you hear squeals of joy ringing through the forest. Once you get used to the razzmatazzy music, you'll find plenty to entertain the children in the way of an adventure playground, train rides, mini-golf, chair-o-planes, bumper-boats and mini-karting (extra charge for this), as well as the Vallée Enchantée, full of colourful swings, roundabouts, crazy bikes, bouncy castle and see-saws. Teenagers in touch with their inner child will enjoy the 15m-high, 50m-long slides, or the dizzying bungee-trampoline. There are a couple of restaurants onsite, including Panoramique, which provides 360° views across the Pierre-Brune valley and also has vegetarian meals available.

Grotte du Père Montfort (4km north of Mervent, signposted) Candles burn at this hillside cave in which St Louis-Marie Grignon de Montfort lived for a time in 1715, during a mission to convert the region's many Protestants to Catholicism. It's halfway down a precipitous slope in the forest, overlooking the River Mère, signposted to the east, off the main D938ter. After a – literally – rocky start, the steep path is replaced by a sturdy boardwalk with steps and handrails. Père Montfort founded several religious orders, and is buried at St-Laurent-sur-Sèvre (page 179).

Château de la Citardière (Chemin Chantoizeau, Les Ouillères, off the D99, 2km northeast of Mervent; \02 51 51 40 09; w chateaudelacitardiere.com; ⊕ open to the public only on Heritage Days) A curiously low, solid, moated Renaissance castle, its top decorated with impressive stone spouts that look like cannons, stands in the woods. The castle is used mainly as a wedding venue these days and a stunning one at that, but it occasionally opens its doors to the public on Heritage Days in September, when they offer lunch and organise guided tours of the vaulted rooms; one contains a fine *potager*, or stone cooking range, that was formerly heated by glowing embers. Concerts and other cultural events take place in summer.

La Maison des Amis de la Forêt (127 Route de la Bironnière, La Jamonière, 2km northeast of Mervent; m 06 95 05 98 36; ⊕ 10.00–noon & 14.00–17.00 Tue–Thu; contact for prices) This small ecomuseum beside a lake uses displays of mushrooms and stuffed birds, boar and deer to show the woodland's wildlife. It also demonstrates the uses made of forest materials to create wheels, clogs and other items, with the aim of capturing some of the history of the area. Guided visits and a 1-hour video on the forest are available.

Natur'Zoo de Mervent (Le Gros Roc, on the D65, 2km southeast of Mervent; \02 51 00 07 59; w naturzoomervent.com; ⊕ Jul–Aug 10.00–19.00 daily, Sep 14.00–18.00 daily, for other months see website; last admission 90mins before closure; €16/11.50/free adult/under 12s/under 3s) This ever-expanding animal park in the heart of the forest makes for a pleasant diversion. Along a 2-hour trail, amid welcome shade, you find tigers and black bears, lions, red pandas, giant tortoises, apes, antelopes and Arctic wolves. Signboards give information in English. Feeding tours are also available. There's a snack bar and gift shop, or you can bring in a picnic; just don't share it with the inhabitants.

FAYMOREAU

Metaphorically a million miles away from the hedonistic pleasure beaches of the Atlantic coast, Faymoreau sits on the eastern border of the Vendée, northeast of Fontenay-le-Comte, in an area rich with memories of 19th-century French industrialisation. Coal was mined in the region from the early 1800s, the industry reaching its peak between 1913 and 1958, when labourers brought in from

Czechoslovakia and Poland were producing up to 60,000 tonnes of the black stuff a year to fuel a local power station and a glassworks.

At the pit village of La Verrerie, 3km north of Faymoreau itself, both miners and mine masters had their homes in three parallel streets known as *corons*, the poorest houses being at the top of the valley, and the smartest – along the *coron* known as Bas de Soie, or 'silk stockings' – at the bottom. All can still be seen at La Verrerie today. A few other relics of the mining days remain, notably an evocative pit-head tower at Épagne, 8km to the northwest.

TOURIST INFORMATION

Mairie   27 Coron des Bas de Soie, La
Verrerie; 02 51 00 43 76; w cc-vsa.com;
08.30–noon Mon–Fri

WHAT TO SEE AND DO

Centre Minier   (La Cour, La Verrerie; 02 51 00 48 48; w centreminier-vendee. fr; Feb–Jun 14.00–18.30 Wed–Sun, Jul–Aug 10.00–19.00 daily, Sep–early Nov 14.00–18.30; €7.50/free adult/under 19s) This mining museum is installed in the old glassworkers' hostel. Renovated in 2018, and now bigger and more accessible than ever, it tells the history of the local industry. Visitors are transported in a rickety lift down (actually rather less far than it seems) to a re-creation of a mine in a series of seven illuminated tableaux. (Don't hang back politely at these, otherwise you'll miss the short-lived lighting effects.) An 'explosion' gives an idea of the constant danger of the volatile *grisou*, or fire-damp, dreaded by all who toiled underground. Miners would start work as young as 14 as a *galibot*, in charge of laden coal wagons. Back upstairs there are displays of mining lamps, tools and documents, a *salle des pendus* – a room where work clothes were hung to dry at the end of the day – plus a 15-minute film about working conditions in the mine. There's plenty to read (in French and English) about Faymoreau's coal industry and about the east European community who worked here; audio guides are also available. A new exhibition made out of LEGO bricks re-creates the mine as it would have been.

Chapelle des Mineurs   (Opposite Coron la Basse Terrasse) Walk down the hill from the Centre Minier to see the restored chapel, built in 1875 by the mine director of the time to keep workers more attuned to Catholicism than Communism. Dedicated to St Barbe, patron saint of miners, it has 19 modern stained-glass windows designed by French artist Carmélo Zagari (b1957) – himself the son of a miner – which evokes the hard life underground.

Foussais-Payré   (6km west of Faymoreau) The nearby village of Foussais-Payré – now basking in its status as a Petite Cité de Caractère for its historic and picturesque charm – has several Renaissance houses clustered around its ancient church. Among them, the Auberge Ste-Catherine (St Catherine's Inn), was the family home of 16th-century mathematician François Viète (page 8); across the way, a tiny open-sided building was once a market hall. However, most visitors are drawn here by the sculpted façade of Foussais' 11th-century church. Beautifully carved panels either side of the doorway show a Crucifixion scene, and the risen Christ with the disciples at Emmaus. (Sadly, over the course of the region's various wars, some of the statues have lost their heads.) Above the doorway you can make out fantastical animals, and the figure of Jesus between the symbols of the four Evangelists. A signposted village trail leads you to these, and other interesting buildings.

Ancient streets lined with Renaissance houses – once the haunts of poets, scientists, philosophers and lawyers – indicate the former importance of a town that, until the French Revolution of 1789, was the capital of Bas-Poitou (as the Vendée region was formerly known). Lying near the southeastern corner of the département at the junction of the rolling plain and the wooded hills of the *bocage*, Fontenay was much damaged by the English in the Hundred Years War. Later, having a large Protestant population, the town saw considerable turmoil during the Wars of Religion, too. But its status was overturned for good after the Vendée Wars, when Napoleon deemed Fontenay too far from the geographical centre of the département to quell any new peasant uprisings, and picked on the then small village of La Roche-sur-Yon as the Vendée's new capital. Today, as you stroll down the lengthy Rue de la République, you will be struck by the handsome three-storied buildings that set the town apart from many other Vendean settlements. The Les Halles quarter, near the river, off Rue de la République, has undergone a massive improvement programme that includes the creation of a new market hall (⊕ 08.00–12.30 Wed, 07.30–13.00 Sat) surrounded by pedestrianised streets, and a footbridge linking historic districts on both sides of the river.

The writer François Rabelais (c1494–1553), who created two legendary giants of French literature, spent several years in Fontenay as a monk, before moving to the abbey of Maillezais (page 143) in 1524. In a series of bawdy, satiric allegories

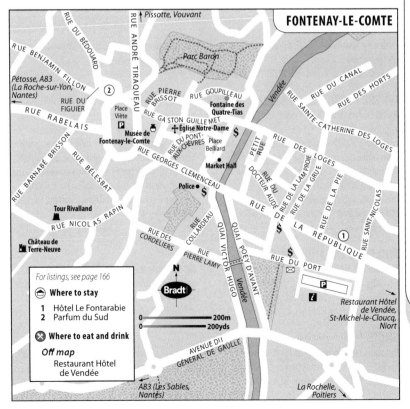

FONTENAY-LE-COMTE

Pissotte, Vouvant

Parc Baron

RUE DU BÉDOUARD

RUE BENJAMIN FILLON

RUE ANDRÉ TIRAQUEAU

RUE DU CANAL

Vendée

RUE DES HORTS

Pétosse, A83 (La Roche-sur-Yon, Nantes)

RUE DU FIGUIER

Place Viète

(2)

RUE PIERRE BRISSOT

RUE GOUPILLEAU

Fontaine des Quatre-Tias

RUE SAINTE-CATHERINE DES LOGES

RUE RABELAIS

RUE GASTON GUILLEMET

Musée de Fontenay-le-Comte

✝ Église Notre-Dame

RUE DU PONT-AUX-CHEVRES

Place Belliard

PETIT RUE

RUE DES LOGES

RUE BARNABÉ BRISSON

RUE BÉLESBAT

RUE GEORGES CLEMENCEAU

Market Hall

Police

RUE DU DOCTEUR AUDÉ

RUE DE LA LAMPROIE

RUE DE LA GRUE

RUE DE LA PIE

Tour Rivalland

RUE NICOLAS RAPIN

RUE COLLARDEAU

RUE DE LA RÉPUBLIQUE

RUE SAINT-NICOLAS

(1)

Château de Terre-Neuve

RUE DES CORDELIERS

RUE PIERRE LAMY

QUAI VICTOR HUGO

QUAI POEY D'AVANT

RUE DU PORT

Vendée

N

Bradt

0 ——— 200m
0 ——— 200yds

P

i

Restaurant Hôtel de Vendée, St-Michel-le-Cloucq, Niort

AVENUE DU GENERAL DE GAULLE

A83 (Les Sables, Nantes)

La Rochelle, Poitiers

For listings, see page 166

🛏 **Where to stay**
1 Hôtel Le Fontarabie
2 Parfum du Sud

❌ **Where to eat and drink**

Off map
Restaurant Hôtel de Vendée

with touches of local *patois* he told of Gargantua, who rode on a mare as big as six elephants, and of his son, Pantagruel, who shattered a mighty ship's chain that bound him into his cradle with one blow of his infant fist, learned all knowledge and every language, and once sheltered a whole army from the rain beneath his tongue.

The town is laid out on both sides of the Vendée River. Leafy Place Viète, at the top, is named after François Viète – a 16th-century mathematician, born in Fontenay, who is credited with the invention of modern algebra. Nearby, arcaded Place Belliard and Rue du Pont-aux-Chèvres are both lined with interesting old houses. The elegantly sculpted 16th-century spring, the Fontaine des Quatre-Tias (from which the name 'Fontenay' derives), is a little to the north of the market hall. Above it, on the site of the town's long-vanished feudal fortress, is a tree-filled park known as Parc Baron. Across the river, don't miss the ancient Rue des Loges, and several imposing old houses. It has a neglected, vaguely Bohemian feel: at No 94, you'll find the last remaining 15th-century medieval house.

A walking route is marked through the old quarters; a brochure is available from the tourist office, which also arranges regular walking tours, including some around Fontenay's Renaissance cellars. A special trail in July and August features contemporary works of art installed in the town's streets and squares.

Belgian writer Georges Simenon, who lived in the Château de Terre-Neuve (see opposite) during World War II, used Fontenay as a setting for several of his crime novels. In *Maigret a Peur*, for example, his famous fictional policeman tracks a serial killer through its old streets.

TOURIST INFORMATION
Office de Tourisme Pl de Verdun; ☏ 02 51 69 44 99; w tourisme-sudvendee.com; ⏲ 10.00–12.30 & 14.00–17.00 Tue & Thu–Fri, 10.00–12.30 Sat.

Opening times vary throughout the year, see website for updates.

 WHERE TO STAY *Map, page 165*
Hôtel Le Fontarabie (49 rooms) 57 Rue de la République; ☏ 02 51 69 17 24; w hotel-fontarabie. com. Long-established, 2-star Logis hotel set back from Fontenay's main thoroughfare. Built in the 16th century, it has some old-fashioned charm, with modern touches like free Wi-Fi & (in some rooms), AC. Private parking. **€€**
Parfum du Sud (3 rooms, 1 studio & a gîte) 4 Rue Benjamin Fillon; ☏ 02 51 69 85 75;

e parfumdusud85@gmail.com; w chambres-sudvendee.com. Up at the top end of town, a lovely *chambre d'hôte* with a fully enclosed garden, just a 5min walk from the centre. Enough English spoken to get by (just!). Free Wi-Fi throughout. The mini-studio is small, but an option for self-caterers. Cheaper weekly rates available. B/fast inc, unless self-catering. **€**

 WHERE TO EAT AND DRINK *Map, page 165*
Restaurant Hôtel de Vendée 126 Rue de la République; ☏ 02 51 69 76 11; ⏲ noon–13.15 & 19.00–20.30 Mon–Sat. Distinctly unpromising from the outside (it looks like a shabby, unloved

hotel), inside the restaurant offers arguably the best food in town. A good selection of imaginative starters, varied mains & desserts are all served efficiently in a flowery courtyard. **€€€**

SHOPPING
Emmaüs Fontenay Rue de la Meilleraie, St-Michel-le-Cloucq, 6km northeast of Fontenay; ☏ 02 51 51 01 10; w emmaus-flc.fr/accueil; ⏲ 14.00–17.30 Tue–Wed & Fri, 10.00–noon &

14.00–17.30 Sat) Large treasure trove of furniture, bric-a-brac & other household items, sold by a charitable foundation started by a French Catholic priest in 1954.

WHAT TO SEE AND DO

Musée de Fontenay-le-Comte (Rue du 137e RI, near Pl Viète & Notre-Dame church; ☎ 02 51 53 40 04; **w** fontenaylecomte.fr) Currently closed due to a large-scale modernisation project, this museum, located in a former church presbytery, gave visitors a feel for Fontenay's history before walking around its streets. Ground-floor rooms contained locally discovered antiquities and some beautiful Gallo-Roman glass, excavated from three nearby sites. Upstairs were examples of solid furniture typical of the southern Vendée and displays on the region's bird and animal life, including the sure-footed Vendean mule, a cross between the large *baudet du Poitou* donkey and a female horse. These beasts were much sought after by the French army up to World War I. There is also a cabinet with a range of *coiffes*, the traditional ladies' headgear. The second floor contained works by 19th-century painters Paul Baudry and Charles Milcendeau (page 73), wood-engraver Auguste Lepère and 20th-century Cubist-influenced Jean Chevolleau, plus a few pieces by *art-brut* exponent Gaston Chaissac (page 195). On the top floor, there was a scale model of the town itself.

Église Notre-Dame (38 Rue Gaston Guillemet) The church's slender 15th-century spire, 82.5m high, can be seen from almost everywhere in town. Steps on the north side of the nave lead down to a 1,000-year-old crypt, its vaulted ceiling supported by Byzantine-style pillars.

Château de Terre-Neuve (67 Rue Jarnigande; ☎ 02 51 69 17 75; **w** chateau-terreneuve.com; ⊕ Apr–Jun & Sep–Nov see website for details, Jul–Aug 10.00–18.00 daily, guided tours every half-hour in French, though if only English-speakers are present, it will take place in English; €7.70/3.30/free adult/under 16s/under 7s) Nicolas Rapin, 16th-century poet and magistrate, created this fairy-tale-style stately home which he trimmed with pinnacles and turrets and adorned with terracotta statues of the Muses. Today it is a private home, but 50-minute guided tours are given of some of the beautifully furnished rooms. The visit features magnificent fireplaces – one depicting the search for the 'philosopher's stone' (familiar to Harry Potter fans as the mineral that alchemists believed would turn base metals into gold). There is also some mellow wooden panelling from the Château de Chambord in the Loire Valley, plus collections of ivory, costumes and Old Master paintings. A section is devoted to the etching plates of artist Octave de Rochebrune, who was responsible for restoring the chateau in the 19th century, and there are photographs of Maigret's creator Georges Simenon, who lived here with his family between 1940 and 1942. You are shown collections of Gothic keys, flintlock pistols, 18th-century costumes and more than 100 pestles-and-mortars. A formal meal is laid out in the elegant dining room, beyond which a glazed workshop has copies of Rochebrune's works. Unusually, there is a well-stocked shop to visit at the end. You can also wander around the leafy glades that fringe the gardens. Those visiting with children can download the Piste et Trésor app; this free adventure guides youngsters to find the hidden secret of former occupant Octave de Rochebrune. The Festival de Terre-Neuve, showcasing classical French plays, takes place here in July and August.

Tour Rivalland (Rue Nicolas-Rapin; ⊕ exterior only) One of the town's lesser-known, more modern curiosities is located just outside the gates of the Château de Terre-Neuve. This strange octagonal spire, 25m tall, built by a rich freemason in 1881, is one of the earliest structures in Europe to be made of poured concrete.

Rue des Loges On the east side of the river, across the Pont aux Sardines, lies the oldest street in Fontenay. Now pedestrianised, the town's former main thoroughfare is rather run-down today, but retains some picturesque shopfronts and ancient houses of stone or half-timbering, some with plaques outside, giving their history. Covered alleys lead off, tempting you to discover hidden-away inner courtyards.

Montgolfière du Bocage (m 06 42 97 29 42; w vendeebocage.fr/pratique/activites-de-loisirs/sports-et-sensations/montgolfiere-dans-le-bocage-vendeen; ⊕ times & take-off point vary; €260 pp/hr, 4 people €240 each, children €210) When weather conditions are right, you can take a dawn or late-afternoon hot-air balloon trip from Fontenay-le-Comte over red-roofed villages or above the silvery waterways of the Marais Poitevin towards the 'Green Venice' – according to the whims of the wind.

Pétosse (8km west of Fontenay; information from Fontenay tourist office, page 166) A quiet village strung out along a main street that rejoices in the name of Rue des Chats-Ferrés ('Street of Iron-shod Cats'). Local legend says that witches, disguised as cats, clattered along in metal-soled clogs to attend their sabbaths. Whatever the truth, if you go into the church you will find near the northeast corner of the central cupola a strange little feline figure, set to pounce from the ceiling. Beneath the village is a warren of *souterrains* (underground passages), thought to have been a refuge for local inhabitants from maurauding Vikings a thousand years ago. There are occasional guided tours of them in July and August – though you need to be slim and athletic enough to wriggle through small, waist-high openings between the tunnels' 'rooms'. Dress warmly, in jeans and long sleeves to protect arms and legs; wear tough shoes, and take a torch.

Walking The tourist office can issue you with a free map and guide to 33 mainly circular, waymarked walks in and around the Fontenay region.

NIEUL-SUR-L'AUTISE

The surviving group of monastic buildings in the heart of Nieul (pronounced 'n-yerl') is the most intact in the whole region. The attractive village – another Petite Cité de Caractère – 10km southeast of Fontenay, has close links with Eleanor of Aquitaine, who is said to have been born at her father's castle that once stood here. Known as Aliénor to the French, she was Queen of France through her first marriage to Louis VII and later Queen of England after becoming the wife of Henri Plantagenêt (King Henry II).

TOURIST INFORMATION
Mairie 3 Rue Aliénor d'Aquitaine; ✆02 51 52 40 12; w rives-autise.fr; ⊕ 14.00–17.30 Mon–Tue & Thu–Fri, 09.00–12.30 Wed

✖ WHERE TO EAT AND DRINK
Crêperie du Moulin de l'Autise 15 Rue du Moulin; ✆02 51 50 47 13. Sweet & savoury pancakes, salads, omelettes & other snacks, near Nieul's watermill, served by welcoming staff. Uncomplicated fare at reasonable prices. €€

WHAT TO SEE AND DO
Abbaye Royale St-Vincent (Abbaye de Nieul-sur-l'Autise) (Rue de l'Abbaye;
** 02 51 53 66 66; **w sitesculturels.vendee.fr; ☻ Feb–Mar & Oct–Dec 10.00–12.30 &
14.00–18.00 Mon & Wed–Sun; May 10.00–12.30 & 14.00–18.00 daily; Jun–mid-Jul
10.00–19.00 daily; mid-Jul–Aug 10.00–19.00 Mon–Tue, 10.00–19.00 Wed–Sun; Sep
10.00–12.30 & 14.00–18.00 daily; €6/4/free adult/under 26s/under 12s) Founded in
1068, this Romanesque abbey was home to Augustinian monks involved in the
draining of the marshland to the south, particularly in the digging of the Canal
des Cinq Abbés (page 136) around 1217. Wonderful designs of biblical characters
and of strange animals decorate the façade of the abbey church; representations
of the Seven Deadly Sins adorn the pillars flanking the front porch. Push open
the door to view the lofty nave, with its high ceiling and its tall, rather alarmingly
inclined columns.

Access to the rest of the abbey buildings is via a pretty herb garden to the right
of the church; follow signs to *accueil* (reception), where you can pick up an English
brochure with your ticket – which also admits to the neighbouring Maison Aliénor
(see below).

On the first floor is a series of touch-screens on which you can obtain
commentaries in English on various topics. Subjects include monastic orders, the
hard life of the monks, the building of the abbeys and the hard-won draining of the
marshes. As each screen has a different bank of fascinating information, you could
be standing listening for some time. If you want to stay and take it all in, try and
visit off-season or at lunchtime, when there should be less competition for screens.

Beyond, an attic gallery presents examples of early musical instruments such
as the hurdy-gurdy, bagpipes, horn and harp; tapes start to play as you approach,
serenading you on your tour. At the end, the Canons' Dormitory contains chiselled-
stone scenes from the Bible – some arranged in a horseshoe shape that echoes the
west front of Benet church (page 145), 10km southeast of Nieul. From the dormitory,
steps lead down to the abbey's pride – the magnificently complete cloister of white
stone. Exhibits here include a slab from the grave of a 14th-century abbot and the
tomb of Aénor of Chatellrault, mother of Eleanor of Aquitaine.

In summer there are occasional plays, concerts and son et lumière performances.

Maison Aliénor (☻ daily, as abbey above; admission included with abbey ticket)
The presentations in this beautifully restored 19th-century house, on the south side
of the abbey, are a complement to the visit above. Set in various rooms, they are
narrated (in French only) by four characters: a Father Abbot, Eleanor of Aquitaine,
Prosper Mérimée (the French dramatist and historian who, in 1862, organised
the abbey's preservation), and Octave de Rochebrune (a 19th-century engraver
passionate about historical buildings; page 167). Ultra-modern techniques and
effects – such as touch-screens, a *théâtre optique* presentation which cleverly inserts
miniaturised actors into tiny stage sets, and a chance to navigate by joystick around
the cloisters from an armchair – help visitors to understand monasticism and the
area's turbulent history. You probably need an hour to take them all in.

Maison de la Meunerie (16 Rue du Moulin; **** 02 51 52 47 43, 02 51 50 48 80;
w maisondelameunerie-vendee.fr; ☻ Mar–May & Sep–Nov 14.00–18.00 Tue–Fri
& Sun, Jun–Aug 10.30–13.00 & 14.00–18.00 daily; may also open at school half-
term – see website; €5/3.50/free adult/students/under 14s) Surrounded by clucking
chickens and ancient stone outbuildings, this picturesque 18th-century watermill
has a homely feel. Refurbished in 2017, it provides a demonstration of some of

6

the flour-encrusted machinery, and a commentary, plus some information panels. There are booklets available aimed at young children and the Baludik app can be downloaded for older children, through which they can help the miller's cat solve a set of clues. You can climb the wooden stairs to see where the miller's assistant slept when on night duty. Back on the ground floor, you go through to a couple of rooms that were home to the miller and his family, charmingly furnished in traditional Vendean style. A new shop sells local products and you can watch a demonstration of the mill in action between 15.00 and 18.00 on certain days throughout the year (see website for details).

7

Clisson, Les Herbiers and the Vendée Wars

Far away from the Atlantic coast, deep in the Vendée interior, you will find the département's biggest tourist attraction and also some historical keys to unlock part of the region's identity. Who has heard of the Vendée Wars? Very few casual visitors from the Anglophonic world would register the name of those terrible conflicts, and even in France this is a subject that has been suppressed. But a visit to the main historical sites, the Refuge de Grasla, the Historial and the Logis de la Chabotterie, will kindle your understanding of this important period of French history.

On a lighter note, the superb daytime and evening amusements of Puy du Fou – often voted the world's best theme park – will leave you with memories forever. Add in the impressive displays of medieval siege weaponry at the castle of the evil Bluebeard in Tiffauges, along with other attractions among the green hills of the *bocage,* and together they make a convincing case for a few days spent touring this area. Just outside the Vendée, a tranquil mood is guaranteed along the valley of the picturesque Sèvre Nantaise River, where the Italianate buildings around Clisson never fail to surprise and captivate visitors. Other varied highlights include some unusual – even bizarre – rustic chapels and religious monuments.

CLISSON (LOIRE-ATLANTIQUE)

Your first impression on arriving at this delightful town on the banks of the Sèvre Nantaise River, only 35km southeast of Nantes and just across the northernmost border of the Vendée, is of having somehow strayed into a corner of Tuscany – an unexpected side-effect of the Vendée Wars.

The Republicans' relentless 'fire-and-sword' policy ruined the castle in 1794 and destroyed much of Clisson, leaving just two ancient bridges across the Sèvre and its tributary, the Moine. Rebuilding was started in Italian style by wealthy brothers Pierre and François Cacault, with Frédéric Lemot, a sculptor they had known in Italy. The idea caught the local imagination and from the early 19th century all kinds of Italianate buildings – including factories – grew up along the two rivers. Today, on summer nights when they are floodlit, Clisson's ruined castle, steep cobbled streets and flights of steps take on a truly magical quality. Try to avoid visiting between Sunday and Tuesday, though, as either castle or shops are closed.

Across the ancient packhorse bridge, the St-Antoine district on the north side of the river is taking on a new lease of life. In recent years, a smart hotel has opened in the restored watermill, and around the town centre are a clutch of art galleries, smart shops and one of the upmarket La Fraiseraie ice-cream parlours. Just outside town,

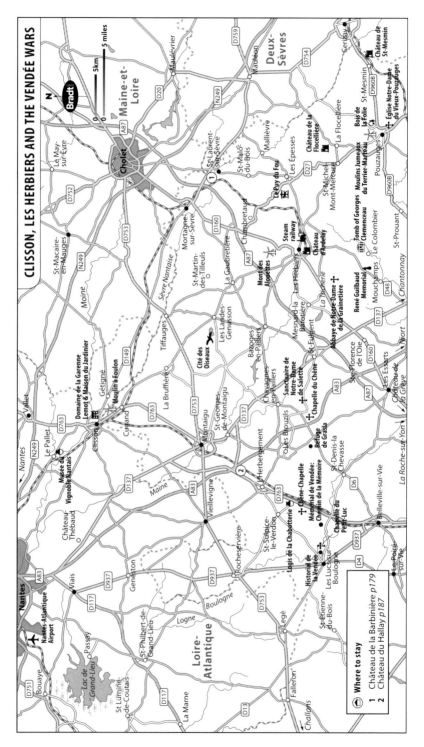

CLISSON, LES HERBIERS AND THE VENDÉE WARS

Where to stay

1 Château de la Barbinière p179
2 Château du Hallay p187

though easily walkable, is the gateway to the Garenne Lemot park (page 174). Back on the south side of the bridge, Friday mornings see Clisson's busy street market. There are restaurants to suit every taste and pocket, and shady picnic places near the Moulin Plessard watersports base, about 500m southeast. Signposted footpaths lead along the banks of the Sèvre north towards Le Pallet or south towards Tiffauges. The tourist office arranges guided tours of the town or of the surrounding vineyards (in English if requested). Its staff can also rent you an iPhone to guide you round town, or provide details of a free app to download onto your own.

Before you leave the tourist office you can obtain a map of the local vineyards from the association of 28 local producers. Armed with this, it is easy to set out by car to follow the Route Touristique du Vignoble Nantais, a signposted trail through an area famous for its Muscadet and for its Gros-Plant du Pays Nantais. (Note that you may need cash for any wine purchases, as the smaller establishments are not always equipped to take credit cards.)

Clisson enjoys a full programme of festivities throughout the year, all documented on the Tourist Board website, but oenophiles might brighten up their winters on the first Sunday in December with a visit to the Nouvel An du Muscadet, where tasting the year's new wines is the focus. Rather more left-field for this peaceful area is the Hellfest, a heavy-metal festival that rocks the place every June. Always popular (the most recent event had 240,000 attendees), tickets sell out quickly, with more than 180 bands taking part.

A mere kilometre along the riverbank, in nearby Cugand, one of the waterside Italianate buildings is the birthplace of *The Magic Roundabout*. From 1966, Serge Danot filmed *Le Manège Enchanté* – as the television series is known in France – here, writing his drily witty scripts for Margote and Zébulon (sorry: Florence and Zebedee) and the heavily English-accented Pollux (Dougal). Cugand is also the late-August venue for a well-known World Music festival.

TOURIST INFORMATION

Office de Tourisme Place du Minage; 📞 02 40 54 02 95; w levignobledenantes-tourisme. com; ⏰ Apr–Jun 10.00–12.30 & 14.00–18.00 daily, Jul–Aug 10.00–13.00 & 14.00–18.00 daily, Sep–Feb 10.00–12.30 & 14.00–17.30 Mon–Thu & Sat, 14.00–17.30 Fri. Wine tasting & shop on site. In high summer, local wine producers attend, promoting their products.

WHERE TO STAY

Hôtel & Spa Best Western Villa Saint-Antoine (43 rooms) 8 Rue St-Antoine; 📞 02 40 85 46 46; w hotel-villa-saint-antoine. com. Medium-sized hotel, formerly a mill, where some rooms have views to the chateau or over the river. Heated outdoor pool (seasonal), jacuzzi & hammam. Rooms are across 5 categories in this 4-star establishment, all with Wi-Fi, AC & TV with international channels. Family rooms are also available. Well-reputed restaurant (€€€€). **€€€**

Homgaia (4 rooms) 1 Le Bourg Cornu; 📱 06 78 94 15 27; e homgaia@gmail.com; w homgaia-chambredhotes-clisson.fr. Unusual building with garden & terrace, housing an excellent B&B built by the owners from ecological materials. Brightly coloured rooms have free Wi-Fi. Family room available. Little communal library & yurt-style wellbeing area. Very good b/fast inc. Just outside the town centre, which is easily walkable; owners also offer pick-ups from the station. Free private parking. **€€**

WHERE TO EAT AND DRINK

La Vallée 1 Rue de la Vallée; 📞 02 40 54 36 23; w restaurant-delavallee.com; ⏰ Sep–Jun lunch Tue–Sun, dinner Fri–Sat; Jul–Aug lunch & dinner Tue–Sat. Waterside restaurant with marvellous view towards town & some excellent local Muscadets. Children's menu available. **€€€**

7

Pollen 3 Pl du Minage; m 06 88 03 06 19; ⊕ noon–14.00 Tue–Fri. This small, low-key & delightful restaurant offers homemade cuisine using locally sourced & organic produce, right next to the castle. A lovely little terrace with games & books to entertain children. Also serves a range of local beers & wines. €€

L'Atelier de Laurence 3 bis Rue St-Antoine; ☏ 02 28 21 66 16; ⊕ Jul–Aug lunch & dinner Wed–Sun; Apr–May & Sep–Oct lunch Wed–Sun, dinner Sat–Sun; Nov–Mar lunch & dinner Fri–Sat, lunch Sun. A delicious crêperie; low price, high-quality place with cheerful service. Choose from savoury, sweet – or both – & don't forget the excellent homemade ice cream. €

WHAT TO SEE AND DO

Château de Clisson (Pl du Minage; ☏ 02 40 54 02 22; w chateau-clisson.fr; ⊕ Feb–Mar & Oct–Dec 14.00–17.30 Wed–Mon, Apr–Sep 10.30–13.00 & 14.00–18.00 Wed–Mon; €3/2/free adult/under 18s & students/under 14s) Successive enclosures and modifications carried out between the 12th and 16th centuries make this impregnable-looking stronghold a style-book of military architecture. Set on a rock overlooking the town, the chateau is today a dramatic ruin with defences that range from early arrow slits to the much wider openings required for the firing of cannon. There's an excellent English leaflet/map, as well as descriptive panels to guide visitors round its towers, bastions and viewpoints. Children will love climbing up into tower rooms, down into cellars, and exploring hidden passageways. A short film (English summary on a nearby board) describes how artist Frédéric Lemot, who had just built the Villa Lemot (see opposite), saw the castle falling into decay and stepped in to buy it in 1807. A longer film tells the history of local aristocrat Olivier de Clisson (1336–1407), brought up in England, who entered the Hundred Years War in 1364 in the English army. He switched his allegiance to the French side, and was eventually raised to the country's top military rank of *connétable*. There are game booklets available for children and themed exhibitions take place throughout the year (see website for details).

Les Halles (3 Rue des Rémouleurs) Wander inside the town's market hall, tucked away between the castle and the church, and look up at the intricate arrangement of 15th-century wooden beams that support its roof. The building – still in use on market days – survived the town's destruction only because of its usefulness to Republicans as a temporary barracks during the Vendée Wars. It's a bit gloomy for the few café tables that sit underneath, but comes to life on Fridays when the market invades.

Église Notre-Dame (Pl Notre Dame) Clisson's tall, Italianate church is decorated with some attractive 20th-century frescoes, inspired by Italian Renaissance artists and executed in the 1930s by local artist Georges Lusseau. The main one depicts some local personalities, including Lusseau's family; other delicate compositions adorn the walls of the baptistery.

Domaine de la Garenne Lemot and Maison du Jardinier (On the D149, 1.5km south-east of Clisson; ☏ 02 40 54 75 85; w domaine-garenne-lemot.fr; ⊕ gardens: Jan–Mar & Oct–Dec 09.00–18.00 daily, Apr–Sep 09.00–19.30 daily; free; guided visits: Feb–Apr & Oct–Dec 16.00 Sat–Sun, May–Sep 16.00 Tue–Sun; €3/2/free adult/under 18s & students/under 14s) Set in a beautiful, spacious and steeply sloping park on the north bank of the Sèvre Nantaise River is this Neoclassical villa, designed by the sculptor Frédéric Lemot (1771–1827) – whose vision is so indelibly stamped on the town – as a country retreat for himself. Statues, follies, temples and grottoes are dotted around the grounds, making it a pleasant place for a stroll, even if you don't visit the villa itself.

The **Villa Lemot** is a truly elegant mansion that opens for free temporary art exhibitions which usually run from around April to October each year. From its terrace you look across the river towards the hilltop Temple de l'Amitié, Lemot's burial place. Also on the site is the **Maison du Jardinier** (Gardener's House), a charming, Italian-style, rustic building close to one of the park entrances on the D149. Actually the first building constructed on the site, it contains an exhibition showing the influences of Italian ideas on the town's architecture. The whole site now belongs to the département and is classed as a historic monument. During the summer, it hosts a variety of cultural performances, ranging from dance and storytelling to street theatre and open-air cinema.

WINE-LOVERS' EXCURSIONS FROM CLISSON

The little town of **Vallet**, marketing itself proudly (and alliteratively) under a 'Ville en Vignes' (Town in Vines) banner, lies 10km north of Clisson and, with 60 wine producers, is the very epicentre of Muscadet production. Many of the wine-makers have grouped together to promote their products at the **Maison du Muscadet** (6 Route d'Ancenis; ☏ 02 40 36 25 95; w maisondumuscadet.fr; ⊕ Jan–Feb & Dec 10.00–noon & 14.00–17.30 Tue–Sat, Mar & Sep–Nov 10.00–noon & 14.00–18.00 Tue–Sat, Apr–May 10.00–noon & 14.00–18.30 Tue–Sat, Jun–Aug 10.00–noon & 14.00–18.30 daily) where tastings and purchases are possible. Although Muscadet is widely available abroad, Gros-Plant is harder to find, so this is a great opportunity to try some. Slightly acidic and salty, it's a good accompaniment to oysters and other shellfish. All wines here are selected in a blind tasting by experts, and if they're not good enough, they're not stocked in the shop. Before doing too much tippling, however, keep in mind the strict French drink-drive laws (page 31).

Vallet is also known for its large Sunday-morning market, and for the presence in its cemetery of some amazingly decorative graves protected behind glass and belonging to members of France's Roma community, who maintain them with reverence and devotion.

Continuing on the wine theme, the **Musée du Vignoble Nantais** (82 Rue Pierre-Abélard, Le Pallet; ☏ 02 40 80 90 13; w musee-vignoble-nantais.eu; ⊕ Feb school hols 14.00–18.00 Mon–Fri, Apr–Jun & Sep–Nov 14.00–18.00 Sun–Fri, Jul–Aug 10.00–13.00 & 14.00–18.00 daily; €5/2.50/free adult/under 18s & students/under 12s, family ticket €12) offers a superb presentation – including a tasting – of everything to do with Muscadet production, displayed in a modern, low-slung building in Le Pallet, 7km north of Clisson. An English-language audio-guide is included in the ticket price.

This village was the birthplace in 1079 of the philosopher and theologian Pierre Abélard, the subject of scandal for having fallen in love with, and secretly marrying, his young pupil Héloïse. She later entered a convent from which she wrote him a series of celebrated love letters and he – after suffering intense persecution – became first a monk and then a hermit before taking up the post of abbot at a monastery in Brittany. Héloïse died 22 years after Abélard, in 1164, and was buried beside him. The museum screens a video about Abélard and Héloïse in French; an explanatory leaflet in English summarises this love story.

Moulin à Foulon (Gaumier, 1km north of Cugand; 02 51 43 70 70; ☉ site all year; guided visits: May–Jun 15.00–19.00 Sun & public hols, Jul & 1st half Sep 15.00–19.00 Sat–Sun, Aug 15.00–19.00 Tue–Sun; free) Part of the area's industrial heritage, this small water-powered mill on the banks of the Sèvre Nantaise, 4km southeast of Clisson, was used until 1955 for fulling (bashing woollen fabric with heavy oak hammers to produce weatherproof felt). The mill and its adjacent dye-house have now been restored, with panels to illustrate the dyeing and fulling processes. From at least the Middle Ages, the waters of the Sèvre Nantaise powered more than 100 watermills near here, doing everything from grinding corn to tanning leather. Between the car park and the mill, a few panels provide information about the industry.

Le Porte-Vue et Pont Caffino (Château-Thébaud, 16km northwest of Clisson; 02 40 06 54 07; w pontcaffino.fr; ☉ 13.30–17.00 Mon & Thu, 09.30–12.30 & 14.00–17.00 Tue–Wed & Fri; access to the bridge is free, see website for activity prices) A relatively new structure, found behind the town hall in nearby Château-Thébaud, this 30m industrial-looking platform stretches out across the Maine valley giving you fantastic views of the river and vineyards. There is also a leisure centre onsite offering a range of activities – you can rent boats, canoes and kayaks or take up archery and fishing. For the more adventurous there are two zip lines (a 100m one and an 85m one) as well as a 46m Nepalese-style footbridge. You can also climb here and there are two hiking trails that lead into the vineyards.

TIFFAUGES

The ruined fortress looming over this little town belonged to the sadistic Gilles de Rais (1404–40), whose evil doings inspired the fairy tale of Bluebeard. You can spend a good half-day exploring the castle, hearing its horrible history and watching the entertaining shows. If parking looks difficult, turn off into the town centre where things are easier. This gives you the chance to stroll back down through the narrow streets and alleys, and to enjoy the views over the lovely Sèvre Nantaise River.

For tourist information, see Mortagne-sur-Sèvre (page 178).

 WHERE TO STAY

Le Petit Château (5 rooms) 6 Grande Rue; 02 51 61 08 64. Welcoming hosts & a decadent interior full of character just a stone's throw away from the castle. Choose from a range of themed rooms (not all are en suite). Terrace & outdoor swimming pool. The restaurant is also highly rated. Free Wi-Fi, b/fast included. **€€€**

✕ **WHERE TO EAT AND DRINK**

Le Presbytère Pl de l'Église; 02 51 57 63 39; w lepresbytere.fr; ☉ noon–13.30 & 19.00–20.30 daily. Cheerful place beside church, serving a traditional cuisine, with decent dessert choices. A handsome dining room in an imposing 15th-century stone building. **€€€€**

Crêperie du Vidame 23 Grande Rue; 02 51 65 76 40; ☉ noon–13.30 Mon, noon–13.30 & 19.00– 21.30 Wed–Thu, noon–13.30 & 19.00–22.00 Fri– Sun. Savoury & sweet pancakes, plus pizzas, served in a small café near village centre, all at reasonable prices. Eat in, or take-away. For sale at the time of writing, with the owners due to retire, so a question mark over whether this establishment will continue in its current form. **€€€**

WHAT TO SEE AND DO
Château de Tiffauges (Château de Barbe-Bleue) 02 51 67 60 00; w sitesculturels.vendee.fr; ☉ Apr–May & early Sep 10.00–12.30 & 14.00–18.00

Mon–Fri, 14.00–19.00 Sat–Sun; Jun 10.00–18.00 Mon–Fri 14.00–19.00 Sat–Sun; Jul–Aug 10.00–19.00 daily; €8/6/free adult/under 25s/under 6s, family tickets €24) Barbe-Bleue, or Bluebeard, was in reality the infamous Gilles de Rais, or Retz (different spelling, but both pronounced 'ray'), on whom the monster of Charles Perrault's fairy tale is loosely based. Having fought alongside Charles VII and Joan of Arc against the English in the Hundred Years War and reaching the rank of field-marshal at the age of only 25, Gilles de Rais seemed set for a glittering military career. But after the English burned Joan at the stake for witchcraft in 1431, he retired to his castle at Tiffauges and squandered his fortune with high living. He turned to alchemy and, believing gold could be made from the blood of young children, seized and murdered more than 200 from around his many properties – including the castles of Pornic and Machecoul (page 232) in the neighbouring Pays de Retz. Justice eventually caught up with him, and he was tried and hanged in Nantes in 1440.

Things kick off with a brilliant, 12-minute 3D film that takes you back to the 15th century, where you meet the main historical characters (including Gilles de Rais himself) and see an archaeological reconstruction of the castle, tracing its evolution from a monks' chapel to a keep and house. A second film, based on the latest scientific research, covers the history of the Tiffauges site to the present day. Afterwards, tours by guides in medieval garb take in the Romanesque crypt (site of many terrible deeds), the *oubliettes* (secret dungeons, in which prisoners could be 'forgotten') and, near the top of the Vidame's Tower, a whispering gallery with 37 half-moon machicolations – semicircular holes in the floor through which missiles could be dropped on invaders. (Hold on to small children here, if you don't want them to fall on later arrivals!) A shadow-puppet show in another building narrates the well-known fairy-tale version of Bluebeard, in which a young bride discovers her murdered predecessors. Outside, you can listen to stories or watch a play (in French) about Gilles de Rais, Joan of Arc and the French King Charles VII, or perhaps about weapons engineer Mestre Jehan during the Hundred Years War or the building of the castle from the tradesman's perspective. Children can try out such knightly activities as archery or jousting (on wooden horses) in a medieval-style adventure playground, and adults can haul on ropes to help with demonstrations of full-sized working replicas of 15th-century siege machinery by 'warriors' in medieval costume. English-language information is provided by a rather intense booklet that can be collected with your ticket, and signboards which detail the functions of the various pieces of impressive siege machinery.

The Wednesday night-time 'Nuits de Légende' summer events are spine-tinglingly medieval in character, revealing the chateau as it must have looked in its heyday. The courtyard is alive with the flicker of flaming torches, strains of medieval music, displays of shadow puppetry, and an eye-popping performance of juggling with fire. A lengthy play, with much declaiming between Gilles de Rais and Joan of Arc, is acted out among the ruins; it's identical to the daytime one, so you might glaze over if you have heard it before – though the lighting here does lend extra drama. Wrap up warmly for the evening; a small torch could be useful, too. You are asked to arrive half an hour before the start, as the whole audience is admitted together. There are several places to eat in the village beforehand. A Christmas craft market is also held here in December.

Cité des Oiseaux (Étangs des Boucheries, Les Landes-Génusson; ☎02 51 67 60 60; w sitesnaturels.vendee.fr; ⏲ open access to lake & hide at all times, visitor & exhibition centres: mid–end Apr 14.00–18.00 daily, May–Jun 14.00–18.00

Wed–Sun, Jul–Aug 11.00–19.00 daily, Sep–late Oct 14.00–18.00 Wed & Sat–Sun, late Oct–5 Nov 14.00–18.00 daily; free access to lake, visitor centre & exhibition centre: €4/free adult/under 12s) A lovely spot, with plenty of interest for avid birdwatchers. From the car park of this ornithological site, head to the right to skirt a lake and reach a hide overlooking the water. There are pictures of the birds to help you identify them, though the names are only in French and Latin. Totalling 56ha, the three lakes here are home to ducks, coots and moorhens, and make an important staging post for migrating birds. Warblers and golden orioles arrive in spring; grebes and cormorants take up residence in summer; and quantities of waders stop by in autumn. The best observation period is from November to March. More than 210 different species have been recorded here and you can borrow binoculars to spot some of them. Volunteers from the LPO (Bird Protection Society) will be in attendance with high-powered telescopes every Sunday from 14.30 to 17.30 between 1 September and 30 June.

Turning left from the car park, you will reach a building housing exhibitions, which change every few years. The current one (2023) focuses on migration, with videos of both birds and animals on show as you walk through a busy tunnel and five distinct displays.

MORTAGNE-SUR-SÈVRE

A quiet town on the Sèvre Nantaise River, at the eastern boundary of the Vendée and 15km northeast of Les Herbiers, Mortagne was in English hands for half of the 14th century. The town's now ivy-covered fortress, said to have been built by the brother of William the Conqueror, was mostly torn down on the orders of Cardinal Richelieu in 1626, though the remains of a circular tower called the Tour des Anglais still survive (not open to the public). Mortagne's town centre contains shady squares, steep little alleys and a few historic houses bearing information panels describing their history.

A scenic segment of railway line that once carried passengers between Cholet and Fontenay-le-Comte has been revived, and now offers popular steam-hauled train rides in summer.

TOURIST INFORMATION

Office de Tourisme 2 Av de la Gare; ℡ 02 51 65 11 32; w paysdemortagne.fr; ⊕ Apr–Jun 09.30–12.30 & 14.00–17.30 Mon–Fri, 09.30–12.30 Sat, 10.30–12.30 Sun & hols, Jul–Aug 09.30–12.30 & 14.00–18.15 Mon–Sat, 10.30–12.30 Sun & hols, Sep–Oct 09.30–12.30 & 14.30–17.30 Mon–Fri, 09.30–12.30 Sat

WHAT TO SEE AND DO

Église St-Pierre (3 Rue de la Mairie) Mortagne's tall church features sculpted Romanesque columns supporting the roof, interesting carved tombstones in the floor, and a 13th-century Gothic-style chapel containing the tombs of a prominent local family, adorned with stone effigies. An illuminated case in the main part of the church shows off the *trésor*, or church plate, as well as a grisly statue of St Sébastien transpierced with arrows.

Chemin de Fer de la Vendée (Mortagne station, Av de la Gare, 500m northeast of town centre; ℡ 02 51 63 02 01; w vendeetrain.fr; ⊕ Apr–Nov; return tickets only: €22/14/free adult/under 14s/under 3s; family ticket €65) For a ride on the Vendée's last steam train, follow signs for the tourist office, located in the old railway station near the level crossing on the Cholet road. There are two options: the 2½-hour 'Balade en Train à Vapeur' that departs at 15.30 (Jun–Sep Wed, Fri & Sun) and the 'Voitures des Grands Express' departing at noon (Apr–Nov Thu & Sat–Sun) which is a nearly 3-hour excursion with lunch. Both trips take you – at a leisurely 40km/h – along a 22km section of track between Mortagne and Les Herbiers and back, past green fields, over rivers and streams, through the Vendean hills and across dizzying viaducts. During a 30-minute halt at Les Herbiers you can watch the engine being manoeuvred to face in the opposite direction before the return journey. Advance booking is essential; arrive at Mortagne station well before departure time (ticket office opens 14.00).

ST-LAURENT-SUR-SÈVRE

Since the death here in 1716 of St Louis-Marie Grignon de Montfort, St-Laurent has become a place of pilgrimage and a spiritual centre for the religious congregations he founded. This Vendean 'holy town' lies in a curve of the Sèvre Nantaise River, on the eastern edge of the département.

Apart from the basilica (see below), notable buildings include the Maison du St-Esprit, home to an order of missionaries, and the headquarters of the Filles de la Sagesse – an order of nuns who care for the sick. The future saint also founded the Frères de St-Gabriel, a teaching order whose members work in underprivileged schools around the world. Here, on their home ground, the brothers run the Vendée's top educational establishment, the 2,500-pupil Institution St-Gabriel.

At the bottom of Rue de la Jouvenance, an iron bridge from the workshops of Gustave Eiffel straddles the Sèvre Nantaise River, in place of the old packhorse bridge that was there until the 1870s.

For tourist information, see Mortagne-sur-Sèvre (see opposite).

WHERE TO STAY

Château de la Barbinière [map, page 172] (30 rooms) La Barbinière; ☎ 02 51 92 46 00; e contact@chateau-barbiniere.com; w chateau-barbiniere.com. A recently renovated, turreted mansion on a hill that overlooks St-Laurent. Set in 13ha of grounds, the hotel offers golf, a heated swimming pool & 2 excellent restaurants. Some of the rooms inside the castle have been decorated a little more in keeping with their surroundings than those in the outbuildings, which are more modern but a good option. Family & reduced mobility rooms available. Free Wi-Fi, TV, b/fast. €€€

WHAT TO SEE AND DO

Basilique (2 Pl Grignion de Montfort; ☎ 02 51 67 81 34; w basiliquemontfort. com; ⊕ 08.00–19.00 daily; free) Among a forest of marble columns inside the huge 19th-century basilica is the ornate tomb of St Louis-Marie Grignon de Montfort, alongside that of Marie-Louise Trichet, the nun who co-founded with him the Filles de la Sagesse. Born in 1673 in Brittany, the newly ordained Montfort became a chaplain at a hospital in Poitiers in 1700 and three years later founded with the young Trichet a nursing order of nuns. He made a pilgrimage to Rome, where he asked Pope Clement XI to send him abroad as a missionary. The pontiff refused, and instructed him instead to evangelise his own region. The zealous Grignon de Montfort returned to France, keen to rekindle religious ardour in a world he considered to be full of vice and materialism, but met with hostility from the bishops of Normandy, Brittany and Saintonge. Made more welcome in this area, he based himself at St-Laurent, taking his missionary fervour to the countryside, visiting the poor and the sick and training others to spread the word, and, in 1715, spent time living as a hermit at Mervent (page 163). He was canonised in 1927. The saint's writings were a favourite source of inspiration to Pope John Paul II, who came to the basilica in 1996 to pay homage to his hero.

MALLIÈVRE

With an area of just 17ha, and fewer than 300 inhabitants, the attractive, granite-built village of Mallièvre, 15km northeast of Les Herbiers, is the Vendée's smallest *commune*. The steep, narrow streets are bordered by large houses once inhabited by rich weaving masters, who installed their workers in cellars beneath their homes (the dark and damp made ideal weaving conditions). Later, water power was harnessed on a large scale, and home-workers lost out to the mills and factories that grew up alongside the Sèvre Nantaise River.

A walking trail called the Circuit des Fontaines leads you past points of interest marked with blue plaques; its flower-spangled route is interspersed with seven bollards on which you can press a button to hear a French commentary about the village and its industrial past. (A map across the road from the Cave du Tisserand (see below) shows you the route.) Mallièvre's big festival is the Festival de Poupet, held annually in July with occasionally some heavyweight acts providing open-air music and comedy (w festival-poupet.com). Previous editions have featured Joan Baez and Jean-Michel Jarre.

TOURIST INFORMATION
Mairie 13 Pl des Tisserands; ☏ 02 51 65 30 69; w mallievre.fr; ⊕ 13.30–16.30 Mon, 09.00–noon Tue–Wed & Fri

WHERE TO STAY
Terragora Lodges (20 lodges & cabins) La Poizelière, 1.5km west of Mallièvre; m 06 24 70 75 99; e contact@terragora-lodges.com; w terragora-lodges.com; ⊕ Apr–Sep. Somewhat bizarre wooden cabins & clay 'lodges'; ecologically friendly but with overtones more of Africa, rather than rural Vendée. Ready-made picnics available, grocery store onsite & a wine bar. Not suitable for those with limited mobility. Cheaper units have shared bathroom. Free Wi-Fi in eating area only. English spoken. A walking trail passes the site. €€€–€€€€

✕ WHERE TO EAT AND DRINK
Auberge de Poupet Poupet, St-Malô-du-Bois, 2km northwest of Mallièvre; ☏ 02 51 92 33 25; w auberge-restaurant-poupet.com; ⊕ Apr–Sep noon–21.30 Tue–Sun, Oct–Mar 11.00–15.30 Mon–Fri, 18.00–02.00 Fri–Sat, 11.00–01.00 Sun. Pretty riverside setting for drinks & meals, midweek lunch menu is a particular bargain. Booking is strongly advised in summer. Unusually late w/end opening. Canoes can be hired nearby. €€€

La Trèfle 1 Rue du Haut de la Ville; ☏ 02 51 92 60 10; ⊕ 07.30–10.00 Mon–Fri, 08.00–22.00 Sat–Sun. Lovely little café, bar & shop just off the town square & run by a charming mother-daughter pair. There is a good contingent of locals throughout the week giving the place a nice community vibe. Small, freshly prepared meals ranging from crêpes to plates of fresh oysters. A small terrace outside gives you views of the town & surrounding countryside. €€

WHAT TO SEE AND DO
La Cave du Tisserand (Rue du Haut-de la-Ville; ⊕ mid-Apr–mid-Sep 10.30–19.00 Tue–Sat; free) Opposite the small market square, you can step into the single, earth-floored room of a tiny weaver's cottage equipped with a loom, plus

its attendant threads, bobbins and shuttles. Press the button on the beam above to start up a 7-minute commentary (in French) about the life of a weaver a century ago, who needed strength and dexterity to produce enough fabric – cotton, wool, serge or satin – to support his family. The commentary tells you how he worked six days per week, with Sundays dedicated to Mass, followed by digging the allotment.

LES ÉPESSES

This small village in the Haut-Bocage, 10km northeast of Les Herbiers, is known for its close geographical proximity to the département's most celebrated place of entertainment. The ruined granite-and-brick Renaissance castle of Le Puy du Fou, burned down by Republicans in 1794, has become synonymous with the dazzling Cinéscénie sound-and-light show staged in the chateau's grounds on two nights a week during the summer months. On an adjoining part of the same site – though totally separate – is a truly stunning daytime attraction, Le Grand Parc, that is open every day in summer. Though there is plenty to entertain the whole family here by day or night, it's probably too exhausting to try and cram visits to both into a single day. There is themed modern hotel accommodation on site for those who wish to spread the treats over a couple of days.

TOURIST INFORMATION

Mairie 2 Pl Monseigneur Bonneau; ☎ 02 51 57 31 30; w les-epesses.com; ⏲ 09.00–noon & 14.00– 18.00 Mon–Wed, 14.00–18.00 Thu, 09.00–noon & 14.00–17.00 Fri, 09.30–noon Sat

WHERE TO STAY AND EAT More than most places in the Vendée, this is an area that requires serious advanced planning – and not just in high season – to ensure that you have a bed for the night. Even if you're not intending to visit Puy du Fou yourself, you can be sure that thousands of others are, which puts some pressure on accommodation availability and prices for many miles around. If you are lucky enough to be attending the Cinéscénie (page 183), or spending two days in Le Grand Parc, you should give consideration to staying in one of the Parc's own hotels. As well as sheer convenience, this also means you can avoid the peak-time traffic jams when arriving or leaving.

Château du Boisniard (27 rooms) Le Boisniard, Chambretaud, 5.5km northwest of Les Épesses, near J28 of A87 motorway; ☎ 02 51 67 50 01; w chateau-boisniard.com. A beautiful, turreted 5-star hotel, with luxurious, individually decorated rooms, some with four-poster beds. Accommodation options include 10 large wooden houses that have been built in the woods & sleep up to 6 people, which would work well for a family. Free Wi-Fi, free parking, pool, tennis, indoor spa (extra cost), just 10mins from Puy du Fou (& one of the few partner hotels that can guarantee your seats at each performance of the Cinéscénie show). Set in attractive grounds with a fantastic 1-Michelin-star restaurant, La Table du Boisniard (€€€€€), as the icing on this very luxury cake. €€€€
Le Puy du Fou On-site accommodation, 2km north of Les Épesses; ☎ 08 20 09 10 10;

w puydufou.com. Choose between staying the night in a mock 18th-century lodge, a convincing (though brand-new) citadel, a fake Gallo-Roman villa or under canvas in a stripy-tented Renaissance campsite. Sounds cheesy? Not at all! Hotel staff are often in period costume & room standards are high. Accommodations can hold 4 or even 5 people, b/fast is included as is entry to the Grand Parc. Rates are quoted per person & also include entry to the Cinéscénie on evenings when it is on – though these rates are of course much higher. Take some time on the website exploring the many options before making your choice. €€€–€€€€
La Gapette 25 Rte de Saint Mars la Reorthe, Les Épesses; m 07 86 18 83 69; w lagapette.net ; ⏲ 17.00–midnight Wed & Sun, 17.00–02.00 Thu & Fri. An industrial-looking building in Les Épesses that hides a vibrant music bar. Local meats

& cheeses available at the bar with food trucks serving a variety of fast-food-style cuisines on rotation depending on the night. Great if you are looking for something a little different. €€

WHAT TO SEE AND DO

Le Puy du Fou (2km northwest of Les Épesses; ℡08 20 09 10 10; w puydufou. com; ⊕ Apr–end Sep 09.30–19.00 daily, closes 22.30 when Les Noces de Feu is taking place & 21.00 when the Cinéscénie is on – see website for detailed calendar; 1-day pass: €55/39/free adult/under 14s/under 3s, or €44/31/free if booked online in advance; 2-day pass: €94/66/free, or €75/53/free; for other prices, including combined with on-site accommodation, consult website) Astonishing special effects, dancing horses, castles that rotate, Viking longships that emerge from underwater, audiences that revolve, jousting knights, fantastic panoramic cinemas, spectacular dance sequences, fire and smoke, automated minstrels…surely there can be no better way to have a history lesson than to visit the Puy du Fou? A whole day is not enough to take in the ever-increasing amount of entertainment on offer at this immaculately conceived, wonderfully crafted and impeccably organised multi-award-winning 'historical theme park' which celebrated its 45th anniversary in 2022. Every year, the park develops, constantly innovating to maintain its place as one of the world's very best.

Le Grand Parc Advance booking for Le Grand Parc on its own is not necessary (though it is cheaper), but you could use the website to plan your trip with military precision to ensure that you really get the best out of it. Alternatively, arrive as early as possible, and pause in one of the 27 cafés/bars/restaurants to organise your day around the schedule of performances – a glossy programme (with useful site map) is produced daily. You can hire a small translator box and headphones for two people, which provides English versions for most of the exciting Grand Parc set-pieces (with their slightly disappointingly soupy romantic themes), as well as that of the evening Cinéscénie. Everyone to their own taste, but surely the most spectacular events are the breathtaking falconry display ('Le Bal des Oiseaux Fantômes'); the story of Joan of Arc and the Hundred Years War ('Le Secret de la Lance'); the emotionally charged dramatisation of the Vendée Wars ('Le Dernier Panache'); the colosseum and its chariots and gladiators ('Le Signe du Triomphe'); and the attack by Vikings ('Le Drakkar'). One of the newest shows at the time of writing was 'Le Mime et L'Étoile', a jump away from the whirling blades and muskets of the Vendée Wars to the year 1914 and the golden age of cinema. With massive scenery, hundreds of actors and the usual special effects, it has gone down extremely well with the Puy du Fou audience. 'Les Noces de Feu' is a night show that is included in the price of the standard ticket. Voted 'Best Show of the Year 2020', it follows the wedding of two musicians with music prepared by the famous virtuoso sisters, Camille and Julie Bertollet. For all of the various performances, it's essential to be at the gates at least 30 minutes before the advertised start.

Between these spectaculars, rest assured that there will never be a dull moment. You will visit immaculate gardens; a reconstructed 18th-century Vendean village (including a spookily gloomy tunnel with re-creations of scenes from the Vendée Wars); a 'medieval' township full of costumed entertainers and wandering pigs and poultry; a fort and thatched village typical of the year 1000; a World War I trench and dug out; fountains that 'dance' to Baroque music; and the secret world of the Templars, guided by a medieval knight. A large indoor theatre houses the 'Mousequetaire de Richelieu' show, its weak plotline compensated by much

17th-century swashbuckling, fantastic equestrian displays on water, swordfights and a stomping dance finale that rightly belongs in Andalucia.

Don't forget sunhats, suncream, water and other protective clothing; though many of the paths meander through leafy woodland, some of the main shows are in the open, with little shelter. Some of the restaurants on site offer period entertainment with their meals (reserve on arrival at the park). Elsewhere, drinks and snacks are on sale at nearly 20 restaurants/fast-food joints; you are not allowed to bring picnics into the grounds, though you may leave to eat your own sandwiches, and be readmitted later. If you hate queuing, you can buy a Pass Émotion, which gives you quicker access to some (though not all) of the major performances and gets you a privileged seat in the stands for an extra €49 (€28 if booked online in advance) per person, per day. For those with limited mobility, there is a 'Little Train' service, wheelchair hire and discounted entrance tickets (for more information, call ☏ 02 21 67 55 00).

If the budget allows, you could book into the reasonably priced on-site hotels (there are six of them) and take two days to enjoy the attractions: by doing this, you will avoid the traffic jams (well, to some extent!) and this is especially true if you are attending the Cinéscénie (see below) and don't want to leave the car park late at night at the same time as everyone else.

Cinéscénie: Jacques Maupillier, paysan vendéen (⊕ Only around 30 performances take place annually, so early booking around Jan is essential; €27/19 adult/under 13s; €11 extra gets you into Silver seating in the central section of the grandstand, €22 will give you Gold seating, which are the best seats on offer; combined 1-day tickets with the Grand Parc are €73/60 adult/child, 2-day tickets are €102/81; for tips on booking, see below) Some 360,000 spectators a year come to see this incredible open-air, night-time show, first performed in 1977. A gobsmacking total of more than 2,500 actors and 130 horsemen, all volunteers, act out the Vendée's history through the life of 'Jacques Maupillier', an archetypal

ADVICE ON BOOKING AND ATTENDING THE CINÉSCÉNIE

As two-thirds of the seats tend to be sold by January, you do need to apply early by phone or online. Note, however, that the show continues whatever the weather and that absolutely no refunds are made. Once the sun sets, the night breeze can whistle across the lake even on the balmiest evening, so dress warmly and take rugs or sleeping bags to cover legs. Rain capes, or even large plastic bin-liners, are a wise standby if it looks like rain. Arrive at the box office at least an hour before the start to find your places in the grandstand.

If you are desperate for tickets at the last minute, it's still worth turning up on the night, and presenting yourself at the box office at the starting time of the show (*not* an hour beforehand). By then, the ticket holders are seated and staff can often squeeze a few extra people in; group organisers standing alongside the box office also offer tickets that some of their party have been unable to use.

Stewards organise the parking efficiently, but there can be delays after the show when everyone is trying to leave. If you pack a flask of coffee, you can sit and drink it by your car while the other vehicles are queuing for the exit; once you have finished it, you should have a clear run out onto deserted country roads.

7

Vendean, to the accompaniment of lasers, drones, fountains, fireworks and the most sophisticated of sound and lighting techniques.

The commentary, using the voices of famous actors, is entirely in French. You can hire a small translator box and headphones (with a second set of headphones), which interprets some of the commentary. But in truth, the overall visual effect is so breathtaking that total understanding of the story hardly matters. Galloping horses thunder out of the castle to fall over at your feet, ballet dancers pirouette seemingly upon the very surface of the lake, and sudden bursts of light reveal hundreds of actors who have composed themselves into living tableaux in the darkness. The picturesque castle and its lake provide the backdrop to this thrilling spectacle, the ultimate in son et lumière performances.

Montgolfière du Bocage (m 06 42 97 29 42; w en-montgolfiere.com; ⊕ morning & eve flights, exact times & location by appointment; €260 pp/hr, 4 people €240 pp, children €210) Dawn or dusk hot-air balloon trips in the Puy du Fou area, taking off from near there or Le Poupet, or alternatively start from Fontenay-le-Comte for a flight over the Marais Poitevin. All flights depend on weather conditions being favourable; you'll be carried for an hour high over the countryside, and then returned to your departure point by vehicle.

LA GAUBRETIÈRE

Known as the 'Pantheon of the Vendée', the cemetery of this village 9km northwest of Les Herbiers is the last resting place of many who fought in the 18th-century Vendean uprising. During the long series of battles and reprisals, La Gaubretière lost 1,200 of its 1,700 population. Its rather austere Château de Landebaudière (not open to the public) has links with two Vendean leaders: the Duc d'Elbée (page 12), who was married here in 1788; and the Marquis de Bonchamps (page 12), who rested here after being wounded in battle. Another general – Charles-Henri Sapinaud – survived the troubles and died here in 1829 after having served as La Gaubretière's first mayor; he is commemorated on a memorial next to the church.

TOURIST INFORMATION
Mairie Pl Sapinaud; ☎ 02 51 67 10 21; w lagaubretiere.fr; ⊕ 09.00–noon & 15.00–17.30 Mon, Wed & Fri, 09.00–12.30 Tue, Thu & Sat

✗ **WHERE TO EAT AND DRINK** L'Esquisse (3 Pl Sapinaud; ☎ 02 51 91 06 97; €€€) is a central place for lunch, but as this is not a town with too many choices for eating, you might plan to eat elsewhere before or after your visit. (Les Herbiers, a 15-minute drive away, has a good choice of restaurants; see opposite.)

SHOPPING
L'Entrepôt 38 Rue Commandant Sauvageot, D9; ☎ 02 51 66 36 65; w lentrepot-lagaubretiere. fr; ⊕ 10.00–19.00 Mon–Sat. Visitors flock to this gaudily painted fashion footwear outlet, with racks of shoes for men, women & children in zany colours & designs, as featured in *Vogue*, *Elle* & other magazines. Your chance to buy some yellow cowboy boots, perhaps?

WHAT TO SEE AND DO
Église St-Pierre et St-Paul (Pl du Marché) Inside the town's church is an altarpiece dedicated to St Bartholomew, whose expression of terror in front of the

executioner who is flaying him alive has earned him the nickname, in local *patois,* of 'St Épourail' ('scary saint'). Mothers used to bring young children here to cure them of fearfulness – though you would imagine the sight of this gruesome statue might have produced a totally opposite effect.

Cimetière/Panthéon de la Vendée
(Rue du 11 Novembre, off the D9 Tiffauges road) Local victims of the Vendée Wars are buried at this cemetery either in family tombs or in a mass grave beneath a large granite obelisk, flanked by memorials to the fallen of the two World Wars. Pedestrians can reach the cemetery shortly after the church; for drivers, it is signposted from the roundabout by the factory shop L'Entrepôt.

Chapelle des Martyrs
(St-Martin-des-Tilleuls, 4km northeast of La Gaubretière, east of village centre) The victims of a Republican massacre in 1793 are commemorated by a little granite chapel. Built in 1925, it contains two stained-glass windows depicting episodes from those tragic times and – most poignantly – framed extracts from 18th-century registers giving the names and ages of the 53 who died.

LES HERBIERS

A busy manufacturing town overlooking the Grand Maine River, at the northwest end of the Vendean hills and 25km southwest of Cholet, Les Herbiers can offer some good shops in the centre, and bigger retail areas on the northwest and southwest bypasses. A much-expanded factory-shop area opened in 2010. In town, market days are Wednesday and Saturday; on your retail spree, look out for Albert Chocolatier chocolates and Mélusine beer.

Among many local industries are the Jeanneau boat-building company (now part of the Bénéteau group), and several nationally known clothing manufacturers. Les Herbiers' old station is the southern terminus for the steam train that runs in summer from Mortagne-sur-Sèvre (page 178). The nearby lake of La Tricherie offers a small sandy beach for family entertainment, with boat hire, fishing, mini-golf and a crêperie.

TOURIST INFORMATION
Office de Tourisme 12 Rue des Arts; \02 44 40 20 20; w ot-lesherbiers.fr; ⊕ Jan–Mar & Oct–Dec 14.00–18.00 Mon, 09.30–noon & 14.00–18.00 Tue–Wed & Fri, 09.30–noon Sat; Apr–Jun & Sep 14.00–18.00 Mon, 09.30–noon & 14.00–18.00 Tue–Sat; Jul–Aug 09.30–12.30 & 14.00–19.00 Mon–Sat, 09.30–13.00 Sun

WHERE TO EAT AND DRINK Les Herbiers lays claim to a dozen or so restaurants, mainly located around the town centre.

L'Envers du Décor 23 Rue de la Bienfaisance; \09 86 19 30 21; w envers-du-decor.fr; ⊕ 12.15–13.30 Tue–Wed, 12.15–13.30 & 19.30–21.00 Thu–Sat. Definitely a place for a splurge, with fine dining in a chic environment. €€€€
Aroma 7 Rue du Brandon; \02 51 91 05 48; ⊕ noon–13.30 & 19.15–21.00 Tue–Sat. In a very contemporary, bright setting, fine dining from a mouthwatering choice of menus. €€€

Les Jardins du Lavoir 10 Rue Nationale; \02 51 67 03 28; ⊕ noon–14.15 & 19.00–22.30 Tue–Sat. Just a few hundred metres east of the town centre, with outdoor space where you can enjoy pizzas, meat dishes, salads, fish of the day & pasta. Children's menu. €€

WHAT TO SEE AND DO

Mont des Alouettes (On the D160, 3km north of Les Herbiers; ☏ 02 51 66 80 32; ⊕ free access to site all year, but the mills themselves are not open to visitors) At a lofty 231m of altitude, by Vendean standards Mont des Alouettes ('Lark Hill') classifies as a veritable mountain, with great views over the surrounding flatlands. In pre-motorway days this windy ridge was considered a gateway to the Vendée. The three windmills that remain out of the eight originals here were important semaphores for the Vendean forces during the 18th-century uprising. Hidden in the leafy *bocage* below, the Vendée's royalist guerrillas could be informed of their Republican enemy's movements through the position in which the mills' sails were parked: signals included X for 'all clear' and + for 'alert'. This use led many to be destroyed by the Republicans. A chapel completed in 1823 by the Duchesse de Berry (page 13), on the other side of the busy D160, commemorates the wars.

Château d'Ardelay (Rue du Donjon, Ardelay, 2km south of Les Herbiers; ⊕ year-round, unrestricted access to exterior; free during exhibitions) Rather impressively towering above the surrounding houses of Ardelay, just south of Les Herbiers centre, this small, square castle, with its distinctive, red-tiled pointed roof can usually only be seen from the outside. You can tramp into the courtyard across a narrow wooden drawbridge spanning the moat. During the temporary art exhibitions held here, you can also visit the restored 15th-century rooms inside, empty but for some magnificent granite fireplaces.

Vieille Église St-Christophe (Mesnard-la-Barotière, off the D11, 8km west of Les Herbiers; ☏ 02 51 66 02 74; ⊕ 09.00–18.00 daily; free) This pretty 11th-century church near Les Herbiers contains some interesting medieval wall paintings. A 10-minute sound-and-light show starts automatically as you enter, listing other places in the Vendée with wall decorations, and describing the techniques used. This preparation adds to your appreciation of the frescoes as you walk around the interior (watch your step on the sloping ramps). The most gruesome depict an unfortunate martyr being barbecued, and the beheading of John the Baptist. Tamer subjects include the Annunciation, the Nativity and the Last Supper, and a scene thought to show the paintings' wealthy 13th-century sponsors. Columns in the chancel are decorated with primitive stone carvings of leaves and animals. There's a brief description in English on the left-hand wall, and more detailed commentary via headsets on the table (select language first, then the subject).

Abbaye de Notre-Dame de la Grainetière (Signposted off the D160, 8km southwest of Les Herbiers; ☏ 02 51 67 21 19; w abbayedelagrainetiere.fr; ⊕ 10.30–11.50 & 14.00–17.30 Mon–Sat, 14.00–17.30 Sun; guided tours: €5/2/free adult/under 19s/under 10s) In a peaceful, rural location, this fortified abbey was founded in 1130 by Benedictine monks and was sturdy enough to withstand an English siege in 1372. (Students of French literature may also like to know that Abbé Prévost wrote several chapters of his sentimental novel *Manon Lescaut* here, around 1731.) The abbey's fortunes declined, and after being severely damaged by Protestants during the Wars of Religion it was further ruined in the aftermath of the Revolution and the Vendée Wars, and then sold off for use as a farm and a quarry.

Today partially restored, it is a delightful spot. You could spend half an hour visiting its grassy grounds at your own pace, soaking up the tranquillity. One side of its stone-flagged cloister, supported on graceful twin columns, remains intact; opposite it is a magnificent vaulted *salle capitulaire* (chapter house). Since 1978, the abbey has been home once again to a small group of Benedictine monks. They run a small shop at the refectory where you can purchase religious medallions, cards or miniatures.

MONTAIGU

Once part of the 'Marches of Brittany', a free-trade zone between the former Dukedom of Brittany and the Kingdom of France, this attractive town overlooks the confluence of the Maine and Asson rivers and is still partially surrounded by medieval stone ramparts. Apart from the square Pavillon des Nourrices in one corner, little remains of the 12th- to 15th-century castle. Fortified and moated by Louis XI, it was dismantled in 1586 to prevent it falling into Protestant hands. Today, gardens have been planted in the drained moat and around the walls. On Saturdays, the Place de l'Hôtel de Ville (town hall square) is given over to the town market.

TOURIST INFORMATION

Office de Tourisme 67 Rue Georges-Clemenceau; \02 51 06 39 17; w officedetourisme.terresdemontaigu.fr; ⏲ Sep–Jun 10.00–13.00 & 14.30–18.30 Tue–Fri, 10.00–13.00 & 14.30–18.00 Sat, Jul–Aug 10.00–13.00 & 14.30–18.00 Mon–Fri, 10.00–13.00 & 14.30–18.00 Sat, 10.00–13.00 Sun

WHERE TO STAY

Château du Hallay [map, page 172] (5 rooms) Lieu-dit Le Hallay, Boufféré ; m 07 67 21 11 66; e contact@chateauduhallay.com; w chateauduhallay.com. A tastefully renovated castle set in 11ha of woods & meadows offering B&B accommodation. The owners, Céline & Olivier, have created an idyllic place for visitors to relax complete with stunning rooms, orangery & even a Byzantine chapel. There are 5 rooms available & each has been decorated in a style that is in keeping with the feel of the castle. Free Wi-Fi, fitness room & dinner available by reservation. **€€€**

WHERE TO EAT AND DRINK

Le Petit Saint Georges 5 Rue Durivum, St-Georges-de-Montaigu; \02 51 42 03 17; ⏲ noon–13.30 & 19.00–21.00 Tue–Sat. An elegant, highly rated place on the main road. Half-a-dozen choices of starter, mains & excellent desserts, with menus translated into English. Welcoming staff. **€€€**

WHAT TO SEE AND DO

Maison de la Rivière (Pl du Gué des Joncs, St-Georges-de-Montaigu; \02 51 46 44 67; w maisonriviere.terresdemontaigu.fr; ⏲ May–Jun & Sep 14.00–18.00 Wed & Sat, 14.00–19.00 Sun & hols; Jul–Aug 11.00–19.00 daily; access to mill free, guided walks €8/6/free adult/under 14s/under 3s) In a village dominated on high by its rather intimidating church, the real visitor attraction lies down below. In an immaculately restored former watermill, at the bottom of a steep path, is a visitor centre devoted to freshwater fish, plants and insects. The visit gets off to a rather slow start, while you stand and listen to a lengthy recorded commentary about life at the mill, but things liven up once you go up the spiral stairs and can press buttons to call up clips of film about birds and river life. A final section presents a nature 'experience' with visuals projected onto the walls at a scale that makes you feel insignificant compared with the insects shown. Occasionally, the mill also houses temporary exhibitions. Outside, in a beautiful setting, with water lilies and lush vegetation all around, you can experience the world of nature for real, by exploring the Grande Maine River on foot (there is a waymarked path) or

7

by boat. You can spice the latter option up by choosing a package with brunch or an evening cruise accompanied by an aperitif (see website for timings and prices).

CHAVAGNES-EN-PAILLERS

A profusion of bell towers and churches indicates that this small town 12km southeast of Montaigu is one of the Vendée's 'holy places'. In 1801, a local priest, Father Baudouin, founded its imposing seminary and two convents. Spiritual fervour extended to the surrounding countryside, too, where you come across some unusual religious structures. For fun, the town hosts a Fête de la Brioche in May, held simultaneously with a 100km foot race. You'd be ready for some brioche after 7 hours of gruelling running.

TOURIST INFORMATION
Office de Tourisme 2 Rue Jules Verne, St-Fulgent, 9km south of Chavagnes; ↆ02 51 43 81 61; w ccfulgent-essarts.fr; ◷ 08.30–12.30 & 13.30–17.30 Mon–Fri (closes 16.30 Fri)

✗ **WHERE TO EAT AND DRINK** Despite a population of around 3,000, there are limited choices for eating here. Try the centrally located **Bar Restaurant Le Gavroche** (71 Pl de l'Église; ↆ02 51 42 23 60; €€€) for a cheap lunch, refreshment or weekend pizza.

WHAT TO SEE AND DO
Sanctuaire de Notre-Dame de Salette (Off the D17, between La Rabatelière & St-Fulgent, 3km south of Chavagnes; ◷ access to site at all times; free) Some 20 towers and turrets of stone and brick teeter at the top of an impossibly steep slope about 5km south of Chavagnes. Built in 1889 by the Abbé Hilairet, a priest who served for 35 years in the neighbouring parish of La Rabatelière, they are interspersed with colourfully painted figures representing visions that appeared to two children at Salette, in eastern France, 43 years earlier. A simple chapel built like a castle keep stands at the highest point, and the whole site is beyond bizarre, certainly unlike anywhere else in the Vendée. There is a picnic area at the bottom, beside a pretty, tree-lined stream. Notices remind you to respect this holy place so, however tempting the idea, children should not make unseemly noise or climb on the monuments. Nearby is a restored windmill, open on Sunday mornings.

Chapelle du Chêne (Signposted off the D6 at La Haie, 2km south of Chavagnes, just before the junction with the D17) Another extraordinary, yet entirely different, religious structure is this little stone chapel grafted onto an ancient oak tree. Constructed in 1874 by the zealous Abbé Hilairet (see above), it has a large bell dangling outside. Push open the door to see an altar in the hollow of the tree, flanked by offerings from the faithful. Its wooden surrounds are worn smooth by countless hands and knees. The tree itself is long since dead, having been destroyed by lightning in 1972. A notice begs any visiting pilgrims to refrain from lighting candles, to prevent any further fires.

LES BROUZILS

On the edge of one of the Vendée's rare inland forested areas, this small village 12km south of Montaigu is one of the centres of cultivation for the *mogette*, the white haricot bean that has for so long been the staple food of the Vendeans. At the annual October 'beanfeast', 200kg of them are simmered in cauldrons over wood fires, and then spread on toast to create *grillée de mogettes*.

If you want to experience the sensation of life in the time of the Vendée Wars, don't miss the atmospheric reconstruction in Grasla Forest of an 18th-century woodland refuge (see below) where soldiers and farmers hid from marauding Republican troops.

TOURIST INFORMATION

Mairie Pl Pierre-Monnereau; ☏ 02 51 42 91 04; w les-brouzils.com; ⏰ 08.30–12.30 Mon–Wed, 08.30–12.30 & 14.00–18.00 Thu, 08.30–12.30 & 14.00–17.00 Fri, 08.30–12.30 Sat (except Jul–Aug)

WHAT TO SEE AND DO

Refuge de Grasla (At Les Brouzils, off the D7, 2km south of town; ☏ in season: 02 51 42 96 20, out of season: 02 51 43 85 90; w refugedegrasla.fr; ⏰ May–early Jul 14.00–18.30 Sun & hols, early Jul–late Aug 11.00–18.30 daily, late Aug–mid-Sep 14.00–18.30 Sun; €8/5/free adult/under 15s/under 6s) During 1794 – the bloodiest year of the Vendée Wars – almost 2,500 men, women and children would seek safety each night from the *colonnes infernales* (page 13) deep in the forest in which the Vendean leader Charette often concealed his troops. Today, signposts guide you from the D7, 2km southeast of the village, to an area where the atmosphere of those times has been brilliantly recaptured. As the lookout's horn toots from the treetops, you experience the surprise felt by the Republican General Terrand when he stumbled upon an empty encampment after venturing into this area that was then still roamed by wolves as well as by hostile Vendeans, on 10 July 1794.

A short film (in French) explains the beginnings of the Vendée Wars, and how local villages were among the first to take up arms to defend their way of life and their religion. Paintings and maps illustrate the progress of the war and the terrible reprisals that followed.

Before you set out to explore the woods, pick up the English-language booklet that explains what you are about to see. Rough shelters of branches and bracken include such 18th-century necessities as chapel, smithy, saw-yard and workshops – complete with appropriate sound effects and occasional motionless figures. At cleverly disguised information points, your arrival will trigger accompanying commentaries, or you can press buttons to hear them (all in French, though your booklet will assist in places). Visitors can play a few period games, such as skittles, or have a go at treasure hunts and puzzle games. You could easily spend an hour or more in this lovely spot – especially on a hot day when the tall trees provide welcome shade. There is a lake, where you might see wading herons and other birdlife, a children's play area, café and a small shop. By the car park is another small lake with picnic tables. Combined with a visit to the Chabotterie (page 191) and the Historial (page 193), it makes an ideal way of getting to grips with the Vendée Wars.

On summer Fridays, and occasional Sunday evenings, a new theatrical promenade performance called Le Vent de Grasla, provides interesting living-history sessions (see website for times and prices). Produced by the Association du Refuge de Grasla, these shows see actors and numerous volunteers dressed as 18th-century 'refugees' re-enact scenes from the period, leading spectators around the encampment to bring to life the memories and stories of the ordinary people who were part of the first rebellion in March 1793. In high season, there are also occasional guided tours (in French, a small extra charge applies), but off-season, a midweek visit devoid of other visitors can add to the ambience, leaving the eerie impression that the 18th-century refugees might have abandoned the site only the night before. If you want to extend your visit to this forest, there are a couple of waymarked walks detailed on an information board in the car park.

Musée des Ustensiles de Cuisine Anciens (Pl Georges Clemenceau, St-Denis-la-Chevasse; \07 57 45 75 69; w musee-ustensiles-cuisine-anciens.fr; ⊕ May–Jun & Sep–Oct 15.00–18.30 Sun & hols, Jul–Aug 15.00–18.30 Thu– Sun; €4/2/free adult/ under 16s/under 5s) France's only museum devoted to kitchen utensils presents, on two floors, a plethora of over 1,500 domestic items used between 1850 and 1960 for chopping, baking, churning, grating, slicing, roasting and a host of other processes. You can see pans in copper, pewter, aluminium, enamel and cast-iron, and study the evolution of everything from cooking stoves to potato peelers, coffee roasters to yoghurt-makers – plus some lethal-looking pressure cookers.

ROCHESERVIÈRE

This attractive village in the valley of the Boulogne, 15km west of Montaigu, is easily missed, since the D937 sweeps past it over an enormous viaduct. Today, the spruced-up square around the *mairie* gives due prominence to a few 16th- and 17th-century houses and a small market hall. The Gallo-Roman bridge across the river was the site of fierce fighting between Republicans and royalist Vendeans in 1793 (and of a further battle in June 1815). The stained-glass windows on the east side of the church illustrate another bloody episode, a massacre on 27 February 1794. The end of the long-drawn-out Vendée Wars came in 1796 with the capture of General Charette in woods near the country house of La Chabotterie (see opposite) – now an understandably important point on the Vendée's historical map.

For tourist information, see Montaigu (page 187).

✕ WHERE TO EAT AND DRINK

La Chabotterie Logis de la Chabotterie (see opposite); \02 55 90 02 85; w lachabotterie.com; ⊕ 12.15–13.30 & 19.30–20.30 Mon & Thu–Sun. Previously owned by the renowned French chef Thierry Drapeau, who held 2 Michelin stars for the venue before his departure. Now husband-&-wife team Benjamin & Audrey Patissier have taken over. Benjamin, who won the prestigious Meilleur Ouvrier de France in 2015 for his culinary skill, has already earned the restaurant a Michelin star, along with a few other awards. The duo have created a welcoming environment with exceptional food. The Discovery menu provides 3 courses at the more accessible price of €52. The Prestige menu, a 6-course extravaganza, is €115. €€€€

Crêperie les Lutins 2 Pl du Nord; \02 51 06 59 77; ⊕ noon–13.30 & 19.00–21.00 Thu–Sat, noon–13.30 & 19.00–20.30 Sun. Pleasant place with bright décor, offering standard, delicious crêpes/galettes, all made with organic flour. On the D7, south side of the river. €€

WHAT TO SEE AND DO

Site St-Sauveur (Pl St-Sauveur; \02 51 48 23 56; w sitesaintsauveur.fr; ⊕ 16.00–18.00 Mon, 10.30–12.30 & 15.00–19.00 Wed, 16.00–19.00 Fri, 10.00–noon Sat; access to site is free, guided tours available to groups of 10 or more from €3 pp) This museum of religious art is located in the village's old chapel. The chapel itself was destroyed during the Wars of Religion, rebuilt, then damaged during the French Revolution and finally underwent a full restoration in 2010. It now houses amazing religious-themed embroideries, including *La Broderie de St-Jean*, representing 25 years of painstaking work by Nicole Renard who stitched every word of St John – his gospel, epistles and the Book of Revelation – running to over 140m in length. An English-language leaflet is available and there are two films in French, one projected on a screen in front of the chapel's altar. Additional exhibitions are held each year, one of the latest being photographs on the theme of animals and plants.

Logis de la Chabotterie (St-Sulpice-le-Verdon, on the D18, 11km southeast of Rocheservière; ☎ 02 51 42 81 00; **w** sitesculturels.vendee.fr; ⊕ Apr–May & Sep 10.00–12.30 & 14.00–18.00 daily, Jun–Aug 10.00–19.00 daily, Oct–Dec & Feb–Mar 10.00–12.30 & 14.00–18.00 Wed–Mon; €7/5/free adult/under 26s/under 12s) This excellent site uses hi-tech equipment to give you the best introduction to the Vendée Wars and the heroes that it spawned, especially the revered Vendean leader Charette. In an exquisitely refurbished manor house, your tour is 'guided' by your hand-held remote control, which you point at various screens to activate commentaries about the wars' key battles, and some of the major figures, through headphones. (Commentary is in English, but you might need a bit of assistance to set up the remote.) Once you exit the major display area, the tour then takes you through the various rooms of the manor house, the commentary cleverly changing automatically as you exit one room and enter the next. The rooms themselves are full of period furniture from the 16th to 18th centuries. The kitchen contains the very table on which Charette was laid to have his wounds dressed after his capture on 23 March 1796 by General Travot's exultant Republican troops; in another room you can watch a 12-minute video about the arrest and execution of the charismatic leader. English-speakers can boost their visit with a descriptive booklet. Do go to the top, to see the 16th-century wooden rafters and hear the creaky floorboards. Finally, there is a display of models of other Vendean *logis*, or manor houses. (La Chabotterie is the only one open to the public.)

The immaculately planted garden features flowers and vegetables in geometric borders and an arbour of deliciously perfumed old-fashioned roses. You can walk and picnic in the wider grounds, and follow the Chemin de Charette trail to a granite cross at the spot where the Vendean leader was taken. Events with an appropriately period flavour are organised on summer afternoons, and a prestigious annual festival of Baroque music is held in summer. There is also a gift shop and an adjoining upmarket Michelin-starred restaurant (see opposite).

Chêne-Chapelle (3km southeast of St-Sulpice & 1km southeast of La Chabotterie; signposted from roundabout at La Grande Chevasse) Sandwiched between the roadside and the front garden of a house is this tiny chapel grafted onto a hollow oak tree. One story says that as the tree neared 500 years in age it was struck by lightning, with the resulting fire creating a hollow at its centre. Two monks interpreted the lightning strike as an act of God and decided to craft the chapel out of the embers at the end of the 17th century. In later years, further additions have been made to counter the problems caused by the age of the tree such as poles to shore up the weight of some of the branches, which, alongside the wooden staircase and balustrades, give it an increasingly fairground ride look. The tree is supposed to be between 800 and 1,200 years old, but although its 16m circumference still impresses, sadly it is now dead, its previous vivacity curtailed by workmen who cut through its roots when building the adjacent road.

LES LUCS-SUR-BOULOGNE

On 23 February 1794, the Republican *colonnes infernales* (page 13) wiped out 564 women, children and old people by setting fire to a hilltop chapel in which they had sought sanctuary. The village of Les Lucs-sur-Boulogne, 23km north of La Roche-sur-Yon, has become a shrine to not only the local victims but to all who fell in the post-Revolution civil war. The church, the rebuilt chapel, the modern memorial building, and even a traffic island on the D937 all tell the story in different ways, and the Vendée's impressive historical museum sheds further light.

TOURIST INFORMATION

Mairie 164 Av des Pierres Noires; ☏ 02 51 31 21 29; w leslucssurboulogne.fr, tourisme-vie-et-boulogne.fr; ⏰ 08.30–13.00 Mon–Thu, 08.30–13.00 & 14.00–17.00 Fri

✖ WHERE TO EAT AND DRINK

L'Auberge du Lac 250 Rue du Général Charette, off D18, 500m northeast of Les Lucs-sur-Boulogne; ☏ 02 51 46 59 59; w aubergedulac85.com; ⏰ noon–13.30 Mon–Tue & Sun, noon–13.30 & 19.00–20.45 Thu–Sat. Lovely lakeside setting, professionally managed & with delicately composed dishes. €€€

WHAT TO SEE AND DO

Église St-Pierre (Pl Mercier de Grammont; ⏰ usually open; free) The church on the crossroads at the centre of Les Lucs is really the place to begin visiting the evocative sites about the Vendée Wars. Its 20th-century stained-glass windows tell the tale of the tragic events that took place in the chapel on the hill above Les Lucs (see opposite), as related by the *curé* Barbedette, a local priest who noted the names and ages of all the village's dead. To hear an in-depth French commentary on the Vendée Wars and an explanation of each window, look beside the organ pipes and press the coloured button. Not advisable during Mass, however.

Mémorial de Vendée: Chemin de la Mémoire (On the D18, 1km northeast of Les Lucs; ☏ 02 28 85 77 77; ⏰ 10.00–18.00 daily; free access & admission) On the banks of the Boulogne River, at the foot of the hill crowned by the Petit-Luc chapel (see opposite), this low, slab-sided building is a hall of memory, paying homage to all who died during the 18th-century counter-revolution. Some consider the actions taken against the Vendée population as a concerted attempt at genocide.

The building on the right of the gateway to the site houses a small cinema, playing a film of the memorial's opening ceremony (performed by Russian dissident writer Alexander Solzhenitsyn in 1993 – the bicentenary of the start of the Vendée Wars), and a second film whose subject matter is the massacres which took place here. The commentary is in French so best to read up about the wars on page 9 – or first visit the Logis de la Chabotterie site (page 191) to give you some background on the events commemorated.

The path down to the moated memorial building is lined with panels in both English and French giving context to the massacres that took place. Inside, a few exquisitely chosen items are spot-lit, but it's best to stop thinking of this as a museum, and begin to let the hypnotic music take over – the overall effect becomes extremely moving. Roughly crayoned abstract sketches projected on screens suggest murder, fire and pillage. Real examples of the menacing weapons that the peasants improvised from their farming tools, re-angling the blades of scythes, sickles and hedgers to create lethal bayonets, look as chilling now as they did two centuries ago.

After you emerge at the other end, blinking in the sunlight and somewhat subdued, you are faced with a steep wooded slope where you can take the path to the right to climb up to reach the chapel of Petit-Luc.

Chapelle du Petit-Luc (Rue des Martyrs; on foot: see opposite; by car: drive back into Les Lucs, then out again on the D39 towards St-Denis-la-Chevasse, & turn left where indicated, after about 500m) At the top of the hill above the Mémorial de Vendée stands a chapel, raised on the site of the 1794 massacre. A stepped path leads up to it from the memorial; on the way up, there are signs with philosophical quotes (in French) pondering what might be learned from massacres such as this. It is also possible to drive round to the chapel. Constructed using the stones of the original church, the building contains marble panels bearing the names and ages of each of the 563 who died there, as noted by the *curé* Barbedette. (You can illuminate them by pressing a button inside, to the right of the door; be patient, as the light can be slow to fade up.) The 564th victim – the Abbé Voyneau, the village priest – is commemorated by a simple stone column a bit further on. Walk along the lane from the chapel to the D39, go straight across and past the old presbytery; the memorial marking the place where the cleric was put to death stands in a tree-shaded spot near a little stream.

Historial de la Vendée (Allée Paul Bazin, 1km northeast of Les Lucs, next to the Mémorial de Vendée – see opposite; ☎02 28 85 77 77; **w** sitesculturels.vendee. fr; ⊕ Jan–Jun & Sep–Dec 10.00–18.00 Tue–Sun, Jul–Aug 10.00–19.00 daily; €8/6/ free adult/under 26s/under 18s) The Vendée's major historical museum, in a grass-roofed building beside the Boulogne River, shows the region from prehistoric times to the present. Resolutely modern, and sharp-edged in its architecture, it has a rather daunting flight of steps leading down to the entrance, but a lift is also available.

You could take half a day or more to visit its many rooms, especially if you speak French; only limited English summaries are provided on the major exhibits, and for the many short film shows and sound commentaries, just a few have English commentary via headphones. It's essential, therefore, to collect the English-language booklet, available with your ticket.

Historical periods are colour-coded, which helps to visit the seven rooms in the right order. After looking at the wonderful relics of prehistoric times, when dinosaurs roamed the area, don't miss the 'helicopter ride' in the purple-coded 'L'Antiquité' section. Look in here for the '*Prenez de la hauteur*' sign, with its coloured lights, and when these turn green, push through plastic flaps into a small room with a helicopter cabin. If there is space (probably best to go at lunchtime), you can sit in the pilot's seat to watch aerial views that reveal evidence of Gaulish and Roman archaeological sites, before taking you around the rest of the region – a useful, as well as fun, experience.

In the succeeding rooms, the Vendée's history continues, through medieval and Renaissance times, followed by an extremely comprehensive section on the Vendée Wars, continuing into the aftermath and showing heroic artworks on the subject that were produced 100 years later. The 19th-century room shows agricultural development, and typical rural architecture of barns and *bourrines*, as well as industrialisation and religious revival of the time. The final part covers the period since the end of World War II, coming up to date with the latest industries. There is usually also a well-researched temporary exhibition on some aspect of the Vendée's history or culture.

Tablets are available that provide some interest for children and teenagers – puzzles include solving the Robuchon case or joining the Resistance to help Jack, an allied aviator, get back to England. An area on the left of the main hallway is devoted to younger visitors, where children can pop their heads into boxes to see themselves in mirrors, play at being an archaeologist, or do some pretend cooking.

Everything is in French, with no translations, but the small-scale features are good fun just the same. You can buy snacks at the bar behind reception, or leave to enjoy a restaurant meal elsewhere or even a riverside picnic, and then return to continue your visit later (ticket re-admits throughout the day).

LES ESSARTS

This industrial and market town 20km southwest of Les Herbiers possesses an ancient church crypt and a romantically ruined feudal castle. A more modern claim to fame is that Les Essarts lies near France's fifth-largest motorway intersection – a complex rural 'spaghetti junction' linking two *autoroutes*: the Nantes–Niort–Bordeaux A83, and the A87 Angers–Cholet–La Roche-sur-Yon.

At nearby Ste-Florence-de-l'Oie, an unusual 'museum' introduces visitors to the eccentric 20th-century artist Gaston Chaissac (see opposite). Though his wacky paintings are not on display here, you can learn a lot about Chaissac's character, and see a couple of rough works – on the lavatory walls of Ste-Florence's former village school.

TOURIST INFORMATION
Mairie 51 Rue Georges-Clemenceau; ☏ 02 51 62 83 26; w essartsenbocage.fr

WHAT TO SEE AND DO
Château des Essarts (On the D160, north side of town; ☏ 02 51 62 10 43; w chateau-des-essarts.com; ⊕ see website for opening hours and prices) Henri of Navarre (later King Henri IV) is said to have stayed at this now-ruined castle in 1588. It can be visited from the outside and occasional events are held in summer, including plays such as *Tales of Lady Cornedibule* (contact number above, or see website). The surviving parts that fringe the large, grassy courtyard are the ancient doorways; a bakehouse; the square, 11th-century Tour Sarrasine; and the remaining wall of the *logis*, or main house, now exposed to the elements, featuring a curious 'barley-sugar'-style column and a handsome Renaissance fireplace dangling at second-floor level. Plenty of adventures have been added to entertain children, from escapades with Roman legionnaires to searching for treasure with 16th-century Vendéean brigands. An earth-covered tumulus near the entrance is thought to be a Gallic burial mound.

Église St-Pierre (Pl de l'Église; ⊕ 09.00–19.00 daily) Beneath the floor of this twin-spired 19th-century church at the hub of the town's one-way system is a Romanesque crypt, survivor of an ancient priory that once stood on the site. Entering via the south door, turn right and go down a little stone stairway. (Press buttons to light steps and crypt; a torch would also be useful.) Among the sculpted pillars and vestiges of wall paintings, a French voice narrates the crypt's history.

Château de la Grève (La Grève, 2km west of St-Martin-des-Noyers & 8km south of Les Essarts; ☏ 02 51 07 86 36; w chateaudelagreve.wordpress.com; ⊕ currently closed for renovations) In a hamlet southeast of Les Essarts stands a domestic-scale castle, built in the 12th century and fortified during the Hundred Years War. For the past 200 years the chateau – which has changed hands only three times in eight centuries – has been used as farm buildings. It is currently closed to the public due to safety concerns and is awaiting funds for renovation to make it visitable again. However, while it is gradually being restored by volunteers, visitors can still view the moat, turrets and mullioned windows, and at some point will regain access to view the granite fireplaces, as well as the vaulted cellars – once used as a prison – and the hinges of a 14th-century door that are made of sword blades. Occasional events are held in summer and at Christmas, which will hopefully recommence once the castle is open again.

Espace Gaston Chaissac/La Boîte à Sucre Bleue (1 Rue de la Scierie, Ste-Florence-de-l'Oie, 7km northeast of Les Essarts; 02 51 66 10 84; w gastonchaissac-sainteflorence.fr; ☉ Sep–Jun 14.00–17.00 Tue–Fri, Jul–Aug 10.00–noon & 14.00–18.00 Tue–Fri, 15.00–18.00 Sun by reservation; €4.50/3.50/2/free adult/student/under 19s/under 3s) Taking its name from the traditional blue cardboard boxes containing sugar lumps in France, this converted school building next to the *mairie* of neighbouring Ste-Florence is a curious homage to Art Brut painter Gaston Chaissac (1910–64). Chaissac used all sorts of bizarre media for his vividly coloured works – from the aforementioned sugar boxes to old wooden doors and lengths of striped mattress ticking. During the 13 years that his wife was the teacher at this village school, he even daubed some of his childlike paintings on the walls of the playground toilets – now preserved as a listed monument! An amusing indoor trail takes you through a wardrobe, hung with the artist's clothes; past walls of mirrors that hint at the way Chaissac fragmented his subjects, bits of old bicycles, and swathes of correspondence with fellow artists. You even hear snatches of whispered gossip from behind closed shutters, revealing the locals' mistrust of the unconventional Chaissac as he pedalled obsessively past their houses. A detailed booklet in English is available.

None of his paintings is on show here, but you can see a large collection of them at the Musée de l'Abbaye Ste-Croix at Les Sables-d'Olonne (page 110). You can also explore the new 17km Sur les Pas de Chaissac bicycle route, which takes you through some of the places that inspired the artist. A route map is available at reception.

MOUCHAMPS

Perched on a hilltop, Mouchamps and its lanes are better explored on foot than by car. The precipitous streets twist and drop towards the River Lay, revealing misty views of the hills beyond, and sometimes become so narrow that a vehicle could become stuck fast. Petite Cité de Caractère status has been conferred upon the town, recognising its heritage.

The name of Georges Clemenceau resonates everywhere here – the French politician is buried at his family's country house nearby (page 196). Market day is Friday; the newsagent-cum-giftshop on Rue du Commandant Guilbaud, just north of the main square, carries a good selection of books on the Vendée, with a few titles in English.

TOURIST INFORMATION
Mairie 11 Rue du Commandant Guilbaud; 02 51 66 21 01; w mouchamps.com; ☉ 14.00–16.30 Mon, 09.00–12.30 & 14.00–16.30 Tue–Thu & Sat, 14.00–16.15 Fri

WHERE TO EAT AND DRINK
Le Canotier 5 Pl Clemenceau; 02 51 66 28 49; w restaurantlecanotier.fr; ☉ noon–14.00 Mon–Fri, noon–14.00 & 19.00–21.00 Sat. Attractive, well-established place on main square, with tables inside & out. Standard brasserie menu, grill menus in winter & gastronomic choices served if your whole table is up for it. Children catered for, too. €€€

Crêperie du Soleil 6 Pl Clemenceau; ☏ 02 51 63 99 29; ⊕ noon–14.00 & 19.00–22.00 Wed–Sun. Straightforward, blue-shuttered place with some outside tables, serving a good range of tasty crêpes, galettes, pizza & pasta. €€

WHAT TO SEE AND DO

Église St-Pierre (Pl de l'Église) Inside this stocky Romanesque church is a memorial to 43 local people who died during the post-Revolutionary wars, meticulously categorised according to whether they were guillotined, massacred, shot or died in prison.

René Guilbaud memorial (Av des Marronniers, off the D48 Les Herbiers road) A sleekly elegant monument, by sculptors Jan and Joël Martel (page 16), commemorates aviator René Guilbaud (1890–1928). Born in Mouchamps, Guilbaud disappeared with Norwegian explorer Roald Amundsen over the North Pole while on a mission to rescue the stranded crew of an Italian airship.

Tomb of Georges Clemenceau (Signposted off the D13, 5km northeast of Mouchamps; ⊕ free access at all times) From the Rochetrejoux road, a few faded signs lead to the grave of the eminent politician Georges Clemenceau (1841–1929), next to that of his father in grounds close to the family's turreted 16th-century manor house (not open to the public). Born in the Vendée, at Mouilleron-en-Pareds (page 154), Clemenceau became an MP in the 1870s and soon earned a reputation as a ferocious left-wing politician – he was nicknamed 'le Tigre' ('the Tiger'). After losing his seat in 1893 he turned journalist, before returning to politics in 1902. Prime Minister from 1906 to 1909, and called on again in 1917, he successfully negotiated the Treaty of Versailles after the end of World War I, for which he received the affectionate nickname of 'Père la Victoire' ('Father of Victory'). He returned to the Vendée to spend his retirement years in his seaside home at St Vincent-sur-Jard (page 117).

From the road next to the site, go through a little wooden gate and follow a short path to the spot where the distinguished statesman lies – under a cedar overlooking the Petit-Lay River, his grave as simple as that of his father beside him. A monument above was made by the sculptor François Sicard, a friend of Clemenceau.

Sentier à la Découverte de Mouchamps This 2-hour walk will take you around the town's attractions, spread over a 6km circuit. Bilingual signboards correspond with the text on the leaflet available from the tourist office or the *mairie*.

Part Three

NORTH AND SOUTH OF THE VENDÉE

8

La Rochelle and the Île de Ré

Less than a half-hour's drive south of the Vendée sits the capital of Charente-Maritime département, the lively seaport of La Rochelle. A modestly proportioned town of 80,000 inhabitants, this is a fascinating place with history oozing from its arcades, harbour and quaint streets, before you even get to its collection of diverse museums.

To the west of town, the Île de Ré stretches out into the Atlantic, sprinkled with pretty villages all within cycling distance of each other. With enough annual hours of sunshine to rival the Mediterranean, and gorgeous beaches to lie or play on, this is a perfect escape destination with a gentle ambience of its own.

LA ROCHELLE

'*Belle et rebelle*' ('Beautiful and rebellious') is the Rochelais motto, apt for a city that is both elegant and steeped in a history of resistance. Fully deserving of its reputation as one of France's best-known and most attractive ports, this historic city is within easy reach for anyone staying in the south Vendée. Indeed, its airport and railway station make La Rochelle highly accessible from Britain as a short-break destination in its own right, and it's also a renowned stopover for sailors. Its pleasure-craft marina is the largest in France, with capacity for 3,500 vessels and La Rochelle is also now firmly on the cruise-ship circuit. Thankfully spared from heavy bombing in World War II, the famous Vieux-Port and its immediate surroundings are the home of its most attractive sights. Here you'll also find streamlined yachts floating beside the three 14th-century towers guarding the harbour entrance. Proud and forward-thinking, La Rochelle was the first town in France to introduce pedestrianised streets (in 1970), and to offer a 'city bike' scheme, four years later.

At various points in history La Rochelle has found itself under English control, from the time of Eleanor of Aquitaine until the Hundred Years War. A great salt-and wine-trading port, the city was fiercely Protestant in the 16th century and was thus bloodily involved in the Wars of Religion. It successfully resisted a long siege by the Duke of Anjou in 1573, but a subsequent 13-month-long siege in 1627–28, led by Cardinal Richelieu (who was determined to unify France by stamping out Protestantism), left only 5,000 survivors from a population of 28,000. At the end of the 17th century, an exodus of Huguenots took place. Ruined for a time, La Rochelle again became prosperous on the back of West Indian sugar and slave trading.

The principal shopping streets are the Rue des Merciers, full of half-timbered buildings, and Rue du Palais, which has a branch of the Galeries Lafayette department store. Particularly pleasing are the arcaded galleries which hide the shopfronts for those who want to see unspoiled façades, but allow the retail fun to

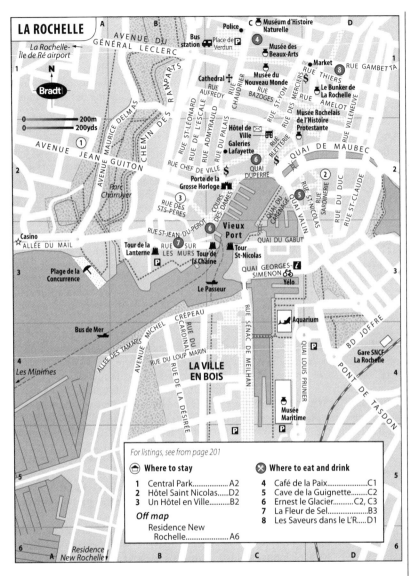

LA ROCHELLE

La Rochelle-
Île de Ré airport

Bradt

0   200m
0   200yds

Off map
Residence New
    Rochelle

Muséum d'Histoire
Naturelle
Police
Bus station
Place de Verdun
Musée des Beaux-Arts
Market
RUE GAMBETTA
RUE THIERS
Cathedral
Musée du Nouveau Monde
Le Bunker de La Rochelle
RUE AUFREDY
RUE CHAUDRIER
RUE BAZOGES
RUE ST-YON
RUE DES MERCIERS
RUE AMELOT
RUE VILLENEUVE
Musée Rochelais de l'Histoire Protestante
Hôtel de Ville
Galeries Lafayette
RUE BLETTERIE
QUAI DE MAUBEC
Porte de la Grosse Horloge
QUAI DUPERRÉ
RUE SARDINERIE
RUE ST-CLAUDE
RUE DU DUC
RUE ST-NICOLAS
QUAI VALIN
RUE ST-LÉONARD
RUE DE L'ESCALE
RUE ADMYRAULD
RUE DU PALAIS
RUE CHEF DE VILLE
RUE DES STS-PÈRES
COURS DES DAMES
QUAI DU CARÉNAGE
Vieux Port
RUE ST-JEAN-DU-PÉROT
RUE SUR LES MURS
Tour de la Lanterne
Tour de la Chaîne
Tour St-Nicolas
QUAI DU GABUT
QUAI GEORGES-SIMENON
Yélo
Casino
ALLÉE DU MAIL
Plage de la Concurrence
Le Passeur
Aquarium
Bus de Mer
ALLÉE DES TAMARIS
AVENUE MICHEL CRÉPEAU
RUE DU CARDINAL
RUE DU LOUP MARIN
RUE DE LA DÉSIRÉE
LA VILLE EN BOIS
RUE SÉNAC DE MEILHAN
QUAI LOUIS PRUNIER
Musée Maritime
BD JOFFRE
Gare SNCF La Rochelle
PONT DE TASDON
Les Minimes
AVENUE DU GÉNÉRAL LECLERC
AVENUE MAURICE DELMAS
CHEMIN DES REMPARTS
AVENUE JEAN GUITON
Parc Charruyer
Residence New Rochelle

For listings, see from page 201

Where to stay

1 Central Park.................A2
2 Hôtel Saint Nicolas......D2
3 Un Hôtel en Ville...........B2

Where to eat and drink

4 Café de la Paix.....................C1
5 Cave de la Guignette.........C2
6 Ernest le Glacier...........C2, C3
7 La Fleur de Sel....................B3
8 Les Saveurs dans le L'R.....D1

continue in bad weather. The market on Wednesday and even more so on Saturday is a must, with the surrounding streets closed to traffic. In the roads around the fairy-tale-style *hôtel de ville* (town hall), look out for the 16th-century Maison Henri II, the mirrored gilt splendour of the Café de la Paix on Place de Verdun, and the Porte de la Grosse Horloge – the gateway between port and city. La Rochelle also offers a small, town-centre beach: tiny Plage de la Concurrence, just west of the Tour de la Lanterne.

The town's layout is quite compact, so it's best to leave the car and explore on foot. Do wear comfortable shoes, though, as the cobblestones are hard on the legs – and slippery if it rains. There's a large underground car park on Place de Verdun, and some pay-and-display places around the Tour de la Lanterne, the casino, and near the aquarium. Watery areas intervene a good deal, but there are footbridges or little ferries for pedestrians, and a system of inexpensive yellow bicycles for hire.

With more than 400 restaurants, La Rochelle does not come up short on the culinary front and a healthy student population ensures its nightlife remains lively. A well-established international film festival takes place annually in early July, followed closely by the Francofolies festival – a hectic celebration of French music at various venues around the town.

From La Rochelle, it is easy to visit the Île de Ré (page 205), a sun-kissed island beloved by vacationing French celebrities, which can be reached by road across a toll bridge. Devotees of the *Fort Boyard* TV series can take a 2-hour boat trip from La Rochelle that circles the famous 19th-century island fortress. (Boats leave from near Tour de la Chaîne, though landing at the fort is not permitted.) Built to protect the military installations of Rochefort, Fort Boyard was actually rendered obsolete by advances in technology even before its full complement of guns was installed.

GETTING THERE AND AWAY   Several direct **flights** operate to **La Rochelle-Île de Ré** [199 A1] (off the N237, 4km northwest of city centre; ☏08 92 23 01 03; w larochelle. aeroport.fr) from the United Kingdom, Ireland and elsewhere.

From the town's big, bold and beautiful train station, **Gare SNCF La Rochelle** [199 D4] (w sncf.fr), you can catch **trains** south to Bordeaux, north to Nantes and northeast – in only 3 hours – to Paris.

GETTING AROUND   Being flat, pleasing on the eye and with points of interest around every corner, La Rochelle is best enjoyed by **walking**. There is a modern, efficient **bus** service (w holidays-la-rochelle.co.uk/offres-inclues-la-rochelle-ocean-pass/yelo-bus) with tickets purchasable on board (€1.30, single). The tourist office also has full details. The transport hub is Place de Verdun [199 C1], where you can catch the airport bus (line Illico 1b Mon–Sat, line D5 Sun) as well as the bus to the Île de Ré. Also accessing the island throughout the year is the Yélo bus (line 3 or 3E, or Jul–Aug line 50 or 51), with the latter equipped to carry pre-booked bicycles. It only reaches Sablanceaux at the island's eastern end, however, and the Yélo city bikes (see opposite) are not allowed on the island.

The city bus line known as Illico and marked as such on the vehicles, will take you to Les Minimes marina area – handy if you're staying in that part of town and don't fancy a 20-minute walk from the city centre.

You can also connect to Les Minimes via the *Bus de Mer* **boat**, departing by the Tour de la Chaîne [199 C3] (⊙Apr–May & Sep 10.00–19.00, Jun 09.00–19.00, Jul–Aug 08.30–23.30; €3; 20mins) and hop across the harbour to the La Ville en Bois area on the electric *passeur* (⊙Jan–Mar 07.30–20.00, Apr–May 07.30–22.00, Jun–Sep 07.30–midnight, Oct–Dec 07.30–20.00; €1; 3mins) from the same place.

CITY PASS

If you're staying here for a whole day or a long weekend, and intending to cram in as much as possible, consider buying yourself a City Pass. Available for 48 hours, 72 hours or 7 days (€44/57/75 respectively), this then allows you free access to the museums, aquarium, and the three towers, as well as transport and discounts on shopping. It also lets you jump the queues! You can pick them up at the tourist office or online at w larochelleoceanpass.com.

If you fancy **cycling**, city bikes can be found between May and September at the Yélo cabin [199 C3] (w yelo.agglo-larochelle.fr; €1.50 for first 30mins & €2 for every half hour after that) just in front of the tourist office where wheelchairs can also be hired. Cycle helmets and maps of all the cycle routes are provided.

TOURIST INFORMATION

Office de Tourisme [199 C3] 2 Quai Georges-Simenon; 05 46 41 14 68; w larochelle-tourisme.com; ⊕ Nov–Mar 09.00–13.00 & 14.00–17.00 Tue–Sat; Apr–Oct 10.00–13.00 & 14.00–18.00 Mon–Sat, 09.00–13.00 Sun; Jul–Aug 09.30–18.30 daily. Excellent multi-lingual office. Pick up the 100-page *City Guide*, which has 2 walking tours visiting the major sites. With notice, they can also organise a real, live English-speaking guide to take you around.

WHERE TO STAY

Central Park [199 A2] (41 rooms) 4 Av Jean Guiton; 05 46 66 06 06; e contact@ hotelcentralpark.fr; w hotelcentralpark.fr. Just 5mins' walk from the centre, this is ultra-modern, with chic rooms offered in 6 different categories from the more basic Classic Room to the Terrace Suite that has its own private jacuzzi. Pleasant English-speaking staff. The spa is charged extra, consisting of jacuzzis, a sauna & massages. Fitness room, free Wi-Fi, TV with international channels. €€€€–€€€€€

Hôtel Saint Nicolas [199 D2] (86 rooms) 13 Rue Sardinerie; 05 46 41 71 55; e info@hotel-saint-nicolas.com; w hotel-saint-nicolas.com. Part of a 3-hotel chain, this is a 3-star central option, well managed & with a good standard of room housed in a renovated mansion. Free Wi-Fi, buffet b/fast (extra charge), close to good restaurant area. Private parking, bicycle rental & gym. English spoken, wheelchair accessible. €€€€

Un Hôtel en Ville [199 B2] (11 rooms) 20 Pl du Maréchal Foch; 05 46 41 15 75; e contact@ unhotelenville.com; w unhotelenville.fr. He may have been in the business for over 30 years, but English-speaking Laurent's enthusiasm is undimmed. A warm welcome is ensured in this small, owner-managed delight. Rooms vary in size, but the standards are high. Laurent is proud of his (expensive) coffee machine & fresh juice-maker. Take advantage, too, of the cosy roof terrace. AC, free Wi-Fi. €€€

Residence New Rochelle [199 A6] (100 studio rooms) 17 Av du Lazaret, Les Minimes; 05 46 50 11 11; e contact@residence-newrochelle. com; w residence-newrochelle.com. Part student accommodation, part residence, this functional block in Les Minimes is a cheaper option than the town centre. Institutional in feel & soundproofed apartments are bland, but with hob, private bath, parking (extra cost for long stays), TV, free Wi-Fi & unheated, seasonal pool. Restaurants are nearby &, though it's 25mins' walk from the centre, there is a good bus line outside & a boat service, too. €€

WHERE TO EAT AND DRINK La Rochelle is full of quays, and those quaysides are full of restaurants. When the quays run out, the restaurants continue on streets such as Rue St-Jean-du-Pérot and Rue St-Nicolas. As well as fine dining, bistro and fusion, you can find international cuisines such as Japanese and Indian.

Café de la Paix [199 C1] 54 Rue Chaudrier, on Pl de Verdun; 05 46 41 39 79; ⊕ noon–14.30 & 19.00–21.00 Mon–Sat. Ignore the negative reviews online, this is still the 'bucket list' café in town, if only for a drink: brasserie food is average, but served amid dazzling head-to-toe Art Nouveau décor, without a hint of snootiness. Tempting cakes &, with a bow to modernity, free Wi-Fi. €€€

La Fleur de Sel [199 B3] 45 Rue St-Jean-du-Pérot; 05 46 41 17 06; ⊕ noon–14.00 & 19.00– 22.00 daily. Immaculately turned-out dining room on 2 floors is the setting for artistically presented food. Popular, booking advisable in what is one of the town's best dining streets. €€€

Les Saveurs dans le L'R [199 D1] 18 Rue Gambetta; 05 46 34 44 78; ⊕ noon–14.00 & 19.30–21.00 Tue–Sat. Carefully crafted cuisine, beautiful presentation, restrained & tasteful setting, hard-working staff…add it all up & you have an unbeatable combination. Slightly more expensive in the evening, but worth it at any time. €€

Cave de la Guignette [199 C2] 8 Rue St-Nicolas; ⏰ 11.00–13.00 & 17.00–21.00 Mon–Sat. Totally unreconstructed, not a penny has been spent on décor…perhaps even since it opened decades ago! A wine bar of sorts, but the speciality is the aromatic, wine-based drink that carries the bar's name, quaffed in bottles by groups of animated students at scruffy tables beneath ancient wooden rafters. The Guignette drink also comes in various colours, by the glass. Wine is available, if the house special drink doesn't appeal. Something of an institution, with food served here as well. €

Ernest le Glacier [199 C2 & C3] Rue des Dames/ Rue St-Jean-du-Pérot corner, & two other larger venues at 13–15 & 16–18 Rue du Port; ⏰ 13.00– 19.00 daily. Generally accepted as serving the town's best ice creams, award winning & with more than 70 flavours. €

WHAT TO SEE AND DO

Tours de La Rochelle (Vieux-Port; w tours-la-rochelle.fr; ⏰ Apr–Jun & Sep 10.00–13.00 & 14.15–18.30 daily, Jul–Aug 10.00–18.30 daily, Oct–Mar 10.00– 13.00 & 14.15–17.30 daily, closed 1st Mon of the month Sep–Jun; guided tours at 10.30 in French only; admission to all 3 towers: €9.50/free adult/under 18s & EU citizens under 25) No visitor can fail to be impressed by the three historic towers that dominate the Vieux-Port area, the most visible remains of the city's ancient fortifications. Each has identical opening hours and admission charges – but very different displays within.

Starting from the west, the **Tour de la Lanterne** [199 B3] – topped with a Gothic spire and looking a touch Gaudi-esque – is a former prison. On its ground floor, a list of ships whose crews were held here includes many English vessels taken during the American Revolutionary War of 1778–83. In the rooms above, walls are 'decorated' with fascinating graffiti etched by captive sailors, who inscribed in the soft stone images of the ships in which they had served. The tower is also known as the Tour des 4 Sergents, after four officers of La Rochelle guillotined in 1822 for plotting to overthrow the restored Bourbon monarchy.

TAKING TO THE OCEAN

No surprise, surely, that a variety of opportunities for boat trips await in La Rochelle's harbour. Nearly all vessels depart from the Cours des Dames quay [199 C2] in the Vieux Port and options include trips to the nearby islands (Île de Ré, Île d'Oléron and Île d'Aix) and a chance to see Fort Boyard, the mid-ocean fort built in Napoleonic times and the 'star' of the gameshow of the same name. Other trips take you past the German submarine base, built in World War II. Some trips have commentary or audio-guides; check that English versions are available. A few of the companies are listed below, but the Tourist Office (page 201) has details of others.

Croisières Inter-îles ☎ 05 46 50 55 54; w inter-iles.com; ⏰ Feb & Apr–Nov. From €28/18/5 adult/under 18s/under 5s. Whole- & half-day trips to the islands or to Fort Boyard.

La Rochelle Croisières ☎ 05 46 50 18 99; w larochelle-croisieres.com; ⏰ Jun–Sep. Excursions from 45mins to 2hrs, from €22/14/5 adult/child/ under 4s. Tours of the ports, to Fort Boyard & the submarine base.

Navipromer m 06 08 31 04 62; w navipromer.com; ⏰ Apr–Nov. From €21/13/4 adult/under 18s/under 4s. Various options, including Aix, Oléron & Fort Boyard. Written English translation of commentary available.

The circular **Tour de la Chaîne** [199 C3], on the busy Cours des Dames, has a permanent exhibition 'La Rochelle-Québec', tracing the emigration of local people between 1604 and 1763. These folk took their possessions and their different dialects with them to 'la Nouvelle France' (Quebec, Montreal and New Orleans). Audio guides in English may be rented at reception, describing the hard lives of both immigrants and missionaries on arrival in 'New France'. The chain of the tower's name, used to keep away hostile ships, can be seen outside.

For the square **Tour St-Nicolas** [199 C3], across the harbour entrance, you need to walk around to the other side of the Vieux-Port. Displays in here (with a detailed, returnable English-language booklet available to accompany you or else an audio guide in English rentable for €3) recount the history of the tower since it was built around 1345, and include engravings showing the massive barrier built by Richelieu across the estuary during the 1627–28 siege, to prevent English supply ships bringing aid to the city's Protestant defenders. You can climb the 180 stone steps to the tower's *chemin de ronde*, or sentry-way, for a wonderful view – though the large openings make it a bit perilous for young children. There's a good bookshop, with several English publications on the Hundred Years War. Outside, an archaeological dig is underway.

Markets [199 D1] (Pl du Marché; ⊕ every morning, best on Wed & Sat) The city's market balloons in size twice a week. The market hall is surrounded by cafés and restaurants, awash with excited chatter. Between mid-June and mid-September, you'll also find a daily crafts market near the Tour de la Chaîne and a Saturday flea market on the Rue St-Nicolas.

Musée du Nouveau Monde [199 C1] (10 Rue Fleuriau; ☎ 05 46 41 46 50; w museedunouveaumonde.larochelle.fr; ⊕ mid-Sep–mid-Jun 10.00–12.30 & 13.30–17.30 Mon, Wed–Fri, Sun & hols, 13.30–17.30 Sat; mid-Jun–mid-Sep 10.00–18.00 Mon, Wed–Fri, Sun & hols, 14.00–18.00 Sat; €8/free adult/under 18s, students & disabled) Housed in a grand 18th-century mansion, this museum contains paintings, drawings, sculptures and maps telling of French settlements in the New World – America, Canada and, in particular, the West Indies – over the last 400 years, through emigration, plantation owning and the slave trade. Stones from the St Lawrence River, used as ballast by ships bringing furs from Canada, can be seen here (and also, as cobblestones, on nearby Rue de l'Escale). Begin your journey at the foot of a remarkable marble reproduction of Christopher Columbus, the man who launched the discovery of America by European powers. It is a copy of a much larger version originally created by Aristodemo Costoli for the city of Genoa in 1845, and has been installed at the bottom of the museum's grand staircase. The first floor explains the city's involvement in 18th-century 'triangular commerce': shipping goods to Africa to trade for slaves; transporting these enslaved people across the Atlantic to work on the plantations; and bringing home to France the cotton and sugarcane produced there. Displays also evoke France's links with Canada, which go back to 1534 when King François I despatched Jacques Cartier to seek riches there, while the top floors often house temporary art exhibitions. Make sure you ask for an English-language audio-guide at reception, though many of the rooms have laminated leaflets which explain what you are seeing.

Muséum d'Histoire Naturelle [199 C1] (28 Rue Albert-1er; ☎ 05 46 41 18 25; w museum.larochelle.fr; ⊕ mid-Jun–mid-Sep 10.00–18.00 Tue–Fri, Sun & hols, 14.00–18.00 Sat; mid-Sep–mid-Jun 10.00–12.30 & 13.30–17.30 Tue–Fri & Sun,

13.30–17.30 Sat; €8/free adult/under 18s, students & disabled) Concentrating on ecosystems, seashells, world cultures and rites and beliefs, the range of this museum is wide. Exhibits include everything from local sea fauna and pressed flowers to pickled snails, stuffed bears and a magnificent giraffe – the first live one seen in France – presented to King Charles X in 1825. There are 10,000 objects across 32 rooms and five levels; the upper floors have beautiful ethnographic weapons, masks and clothes, prehistoric tools and Indonesian shadow-puppets. A jazz festival is held in the museum's botanical gardens every August.

Musée des Beaux-Arts [199 C1] (28 Rue Gargoulleau; ☎ 05 46 41 64 65; w museedesbeauxarts.larochelle.fr; ⊕ closed for renovation until 2026) Closed to the public since 2018 due to substantial renovation works that have kept it hidden behind a wall of scaffolding, this museum should look almost new when it reopens in 2026. Laid out on three floors of a distinguished-looking stone town house that was formerly a bishops' palace, the collection here holds mainly European paintings from the 15th to 20th centuries. These include works by Camille Corot and Gustave Doré, plus scenes of North Africa by 19th-century La Rochelle artist Eugène Fromentin. More modern views of the city are supplied by such 20th-century painters as Albert Marquet and Paul Signac.

Le Bunker de La Rochelle [199 D1] (8 Rue des Dames; ☎ 05 46 42 52 89; w bunkerlarochelle.com; ⊕ Apr–Sep 10.00–19.00 daily, Oct–Mar 10.00–18.00 daily; €9/6.50/free adult/under 13s/under 5s) Le Bunker tells the story of how in 1941 the occupying Germans requisitioned the hotel that stood above this very bunker and set about building a fortified shelter for officers of the 3rd Submarine Fleet. Vivid 'real-life' scenes, contemporary newsreel and hundreds of artefacts depict La Rochelle's role as a submarine base in World War II. Incredibly, after the conflict, the bunker lay forgotten for more than 40 years before being rediscovered, saved and eventually put to its current excellent use in 2013. Even more surprising, the site was created with the help of German U-Boat officers who had been stationed here in wartime.

English-speakers can get an audio-guide or a booklet with their ticket to help them learn about the 350 Allied bombing raids, the resistance to the Germans, daily life under occupation and the eventual liberation of La Rochelle. The location of the submarine base away from town meant that the town's elegant buildings themselves remained relatively unscathed. A visit here is recommended; there's even a treasure hunt for the youngsters. An excellent booklet (€5) can be bought here, if you want a succinct but comprehensive record of La Rochelle during this period. You can also purchase a virtual visit that gives you 24-hour access to a guided virtual tour of the museum, which you can do from the comfort of your own home/hotel/B&B.

Musée Rochelais de l'Histoire Protestante [199 C2] (2 Rue St Michel; w protestantisme-museelarochelle.fr; ⊕ Jun–Sep 14.30–18.00 Mon–Sat; €5/2.50/ free adult/under 26s/under 18s) Accessed through the Protestant temple, this museum tells the tale of Protestantism in La Rochelle. Today, around 500 Protestant families still live in the town. Fascinating artefacts include the 'dismantle-able pulpit', which was ferried to and from clandestine services held in the woods and elsewhere when Protestantism was outlawed in the 17th century. Each piece was carried by a different attendee, to avoid discovery. There is also a collection of Bibles, some dating back nearly 400 years. The austerity of the temple itself – still used on Sundays – is of course in stark contrast to the usual ornate Catholic décor.

If you're lucky, there may be an English-speaker to assist you; otherwise there is only one sparse leaflet.

Hôtel de Ville [199 C2] (Pl de l'Hôtel de Ville) The city's town hall, which has been in use since 1298, has been recently renovated following a catastrophic fire in June 2013. An elegant building, it is the oldest-serving French *hôtel de ville* still functioning. If you look at the cobbles in the square, you can make out the Huguenot Cross, whose four points radiate out from the centrally placed statue of 17th-century mayor Jean Guiton. Signage outside gives details of the restoration work, albeit in French.

Aquarium [199 C3] (Quai Louis Prunier; ☎05 46 34 00 00; w aquarium-larochelle. com; ⊕ Jul–Aug 10.00–20.00 daily, for other months see website; €17.50/12.50/ free adult/under 18s/under 3s; audio-guide €3 extra) A couple of minutes' walk from the tourist office, La Rochelle's aquarium opens every day of the year and provides an incredible experience. Though the admission charge may seem high, you can look forward to some superb displays and a good 2 hours' entertainment viewing thousands of sea creatures, from fragile seahorses to large sharks. Visitors descend in a clunky lift, building the atmosphere, and then enter through a glass tunnel entirely surrounded by tiny, translucent jellyfish swimming gracefully in all directions. Throughout the tour, the lighting and other effects are magical, transforming shoals of sardines into shimmering silver hordes, and knightfish into strange glowing forms. Various films are available, though these are in French; items are labelled in both English and French. At the end, you cross a wobbly bridge amid a humid rainforest. It is understandably popular (especially on a wet day), so try and go midweek, off-season or around noon, when the crowds may be slightly smaller. (You can bypass the sometimes long queues by buying tickets online, or from tourist offices, here or in neighbouring towns.)

Musée Maritime [199 C4] (Pl Bernard-Moitessier; ☎ 05 46 28 03 00; w museemaritime.larochelle.fr; ⊕ mid-Jun–mid-Sep 10.00–18.00 Tue–Fri & Sun, 14.00–18.00 Sat; mid-Sep–mid-Jun 10.00–12.30 & 13.30–17.30 Tue–Fri & Sun, 13.30–17.30 Sat; €8/free adult/under 18s & students under 26 yrs) A display of huge metal buoys advertises this large, refreshingly old-fashioned museum of maritime history in La Rochelle's former fish-auction building, just south of the aquarium. There is some maritime history of the town and its leisure, fishing and commercial ports; displays of fishing techniques, using models of trawlers, dredgers, drifters, lobster- and line-fishing boats; and navigation and sonar aids, plus reconstructed workshops showing the now-defunct boatbuilding and coaling businesses of the adjacent La Ville en Bois district. Outside is a variety of ships to visit – a tug and a fishing boat among others – though you need to be pretty agile to cope with the steep stairs and uneven decks. There are also temporary exhibitions, which at the time of writing included the legendary around-the-world ketch built by Bernard Moitessier. English information is available for the outdoor exhibits, but not the indoor ones.

ÎLE DE RÉ

Once four separate islands, Île de Ré is now just one – and a rather delightful one, too. Joined to the mainland by an impressive bridge that connects just northwest of La Rochelle, the island can hardly be called 'undiscovered' by visitors, whether

Although beach-orientated, the Île de Ré is an upmarket destination and certainly not full of kiss-me-quick hats or tacky plastic souvenirs. If you want to take home more than memories and photos, you can certainly find unique items in most villages. If it's **art** you're after, pick up the tourist office's *Art à la Carte* booklet, listing over 30 island-based artists with studios and shops. For those who like a drink, do visit the wine co-operative (page 213), where, alongside the **wines** themselves, you can buy **Pineau** or island **cognac**. **Artisanal beers** to sample include the dozens of tasty brews of Bières de Ré at their shop on the D201 at Ste-Marie-de-Ré (🕿 05 46 43 82 63; w bieresdere. fr). As well as their own brewed beers, the shop of the Brasserie des Flibustiers (7 Pl du Bois de l'Ardilliers, La Flotte; m 06 08 91 91 88) sells flavoured **salt**, island-made **biscuits** and much more. At the various village markets, look for the Paradis en Ré brand, which can be found on **T-shirts** and small souvenirs such as **fridge magnets** and **jewellery**. For something quirky, the island's unusual mascot of a donkey wearing pyjamas decorates many souvenirs. To find a collection of characterful shops in one place, head for the Village Artisanal in Loix (page 211).

they come from the rest of France or further afield. Undiscovered, no, but – to the outsider eye at least – largely unspoiled. True, the infrastructure is firmly in place here to greet the crowds that arrive year after year in the summer holidays. Campsites, hotels, holiday villages and *chambres d'hôte* are all here to host you, while there are plenty of delicious markets and good-quality restaurants to feed you. More than half of the properties here are second homes, shuttered up for most of the year while their owners reside in Paris or elsewhere in mainland France. The result? House prices resemble telephone numbers! The good news for visitors is that this influx of outsiders has raised the level of cuisine on offer here a notch up from what you might expect. Island prices are high though, so expect to pay more for your morning coffee.

If you decide to bring your car and then insist on using it to any degree, you will find yourself in the minority, for two wheels are better than four on Ré. Ample cycle paths lace this flat island and they are well used, even in off-season and on the odd days when it rains. Bikes can be hired in every village of note, with electric ones for those who need assistance.

The ten quaint island villages are impeccably kept, from low-level La Flotte to the more imposing but elegant three-storey 'bourgeois' edifices of St-Martin-de-Ré, the island capital. Some of the 30 beautiful beaches become visible from the bridge before you even arrive on the island, but the best ones decorate the southern shores a little further west. As well as the tourist offices listed, there are further offices – some seasonal – at Rivedoux-Plage, Ste-Marie-de-Ré, La Couarde-sur-Mer, Loix, St-Clément-des-Baleines, and Les Portes-en-Ré. The island's overall tourist office maintains a well put-together website (w experience.iledere.com), which makes it very easy to find activities, events and places to visit on Île de Ré – it also allows you to purchase tickets that come with a 'best price guarantee'.

GETTING THERE AND AWAY

By road For day trippers there should be a strong temptation to leave the car 'on the continent' (mainland) and take the **bus** from Place de Verdun or from the train station in La Rochelle. A €4.10 day (line 3/3E) ticket allows you to hop on

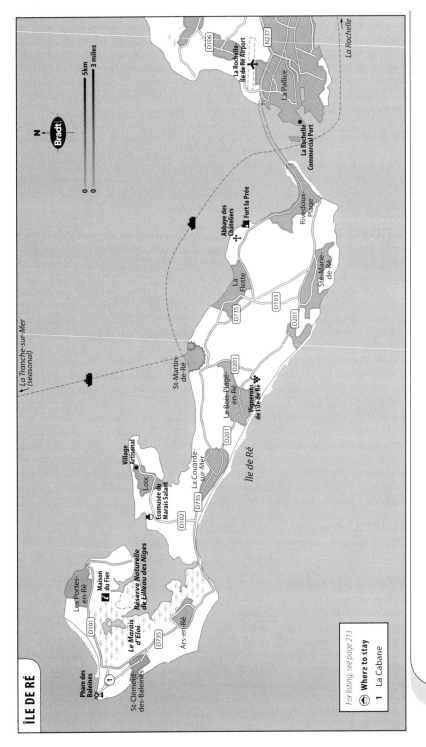

ÎLE DE RÉ

Phare des Baleines

Les Portes-en-Ré

St-Clément-des-Baleines

Ars-en-Ré

Maison du Fier

Réserve Naturelle de Lilleau des Niges

Le Marais d'Éloi

D101

D735

Loix

Village Artisanal

Écomusée du Marais Salant

La Couarde-sur-Mer

D102

D735

D201

Le Bois-Plage-en-Ré

Vignerons de l'île de Ré

St-Martin-de-Ré

D201

La Flotte

D735

D103

Ste-Marie-de-Ré

D201

Abbaye des Châteliers

Fort la Prée

Rivedoux-Plage

La Rochelle Commercial Port

La Rochelle Île de Ré Airport

La Pallice

N237

D106

La Rochelle

La Tranche-sur-Mer (seasonal)

La Rochelle

Île de Ré

N

Bradt

0   5km

0   3 miles

For listing, see page 213

🏠 **Where to stay**

1 La Cabane

and off around the island and you can forget the worry of finding and paying for parking, the cost of the **bridge toll** (a whopping €16 in high season, €8 in other months, return) and the sometimes tricky task of navigating your way through narrow streets while trying to enter or escape from seemingly labyrinthine villages. Between mid-April and September, a free **electric bus**, the *Navette du Pont*, crosses the bridge every day, with free car parking provided on either side of it. Frequency varies according to the time of day.

By boat You can ignore the bridge, of course, and arrive by boat. From La Rochelle's Old Harbour, Croisières Inter-Îles (w inter-iles.com) takes passengers to St-Martin-de-Ré between April and September. Return fares cost €25/17/5 adult/under 18s/under 5s. There is an additional cost if you are taking your bike (€6.70 return). In July and August, you can also connect to the island from La Tranche-sur-Mer, in the South Vendée.

GETTING AROUND Once on the island, there is an **electric village shuttle service** (w holidays-iledere.co.uk/practical-information/transports/bus-schedules-and-village-shuttles) that connects the villages from April to September, and which anyone can access for free.

Otherwise, assuming that you have left the car behind and thus avoided the traffic jams in high season, taking a bike around the island is easy. Most hirers offer electric bikes as well, though these are more expensive. From the tourist offices you can equip yourself with a map of cycle paths, also available at w iledere.com.

Cycland ☏ 05 46 09 08 66; e st-martin@cycland. fr; w cycland.fr; ⏰ Apr–end Oct daily; €13/9 per day adult/child. With offices in 9 island villages.

Cyclo Surf ☏ 05 46 30 19 51; e contact@cyclo-surf.com; w cyclo-surf.com; €12/9 per day adult/child. With 8 offices across the island.

LA FLOTTE The favourite village of many islanders, La Flotte delights visitors with its U-shaped harbour, surrounded on three sides by restaurants and cafés. Further joy awaits you in the market, which takes place year-round, seven mornings a week, and there is a little museum focusing on local history. A particular claim to fame for the town is that an ancestor of America's first president, George Washington, was born here. Nicolas Martiau is duly remembered by a plaque at the base of a statue beside the tourist office that portrays his illustrious descendant.

Tourist information
Office de Tourisme Quai de Sénac; ☏ 05 46 09 00 55; w holidays-iledere.co.uk; ⏰ Apr–Nov

09.30–13.00 & 14.00–17.00 Mon–Sat, Dec–Mar 09.30–13.00 & 14.00–17.00 Tue–Sat

 Where to stay and eat
Le Mole (2 rooms, 1 studio, 7 apts) 2 Cours Félix Faure; ☏ 05 46 09 60 43; e lemole17@hotmail. com; w le-mole.com. A mix of rooms, apts & studios, with an adjoining *brocante* (bric-a-brac) shop & a restaurant inside, this is a seafront choice with renovated accommodation in an old building almost next to the tourist office. Some rooms have a sea view, some apts can accommodate 6, with sofa beds & further beds on a mezzanine level. Free Wi-Fi, TV. **€€€**

L'Ecailler 3 Quai de Sénac; ☏ 05 46 09 56 40; ⏰ 12.15–14.00 & 19.30–22.00 Wed–Sun. Definitely to be classified as 'fine dining,' the excellent fish & seafood here, artfully created & presented, comes at a price. But if this is your holiday treat, you're unlikely to be disappointed. Turbot & sole are recommended; high-quality wines are available to accompany the cuisine. **€€€€€**

Chai Nous Comme Chai Vous 1 Rue de la Garde; ☏ 05 46 09 49 85; ⏰ Apr–Oct 19.00–20.30

daily. In a quiet alley close to the port, this small restaurant is run by the husband & wife team of Laurent & Florence Favier, who provide a warm welcome, great service & excellent food. Cuisine is French in style with produce & menus linked to the seasons, leaning towards fish which is sourced straight from the port. The sand-baked sea bass served whole is impressive & there is a well-curated wine cellar to match. €€€

L'Endroit du Goinfre 1 Rue Jean Henri Lainé; 📞 05 46 09 50 01; ⏰ noon–14.00 & 19.00–21.00 Mon–Sat, noon–14.30 Sun. Specialising in meat & specifically pork, although the stuffed cow head on the door might suggest otherwise, they pay close attention to where the meat comes from & how the animals have been looked after prior to reaching the table. A big hit with locals who are drawn by the well-priced food & friendly atmosphere. €€

What to see and do

Market (Accessed off Rue du Marché; ⏰ 09.00–13.00 daily) In a little square just back from the seafront, the island's most characterful market takes place every day. There are a few of the ubiquitous stalls selling clothing, but island products are very much to the fore here – wines, jams and other specialities – all sold in a pleasant ambience. Shoppers will also find interesting boutiques in the neighbouring streets.

Musée du Platin (4 Cours Félix Faure; 📞 05 46 09 61 39; w museeduplatin. fr; ⏰ Apr–Jun & Sep–Oct 10.00–12.30 & 14.30–18.00 Mon–Fri, Jul–Aug 10.30–12.30 & 14.30–18.30 Mon–Fri; €5/3.50/free adult/under 19s/under 6s) On the waterfront, this small museum is set over four floors. The focus is on local costumes and traditions, daily island life, the island's relationship with the 'continent' (mainland) and the nearby Abbaye des Châteliers (see below). They run guided tours of the village of La Flotte and the Abbaye des Châteliers throughout the year, and there is the opportunity to go out collecting crustaceans on the foreshore (boots and buckets recommended) – see website for dates.

Fort la Prée (Route de Rivedoux, RD 735, east of La Flotte; m 06 87 21 90 29; w fort-la-pree.com; ⏰ days & times vary, see website for details; €6/4.50/2.50/ free adult/under 25s/under 14s/under 4s, family tickets available; guided visits in French at 10.30 & 16.00, reservation required) As the island's oldest fortification, this star-shaped fort built in the 17th century has played its part in the island's troubled history. It faced off against the Protestants in the religious wars and was occupied by the Germans in World War II. It was given the 'Vauban treatment' at the end of the 17th century, undergoing strengthening at the direction of France's famous military engineer. Today, the addition of escape room games, concerts, treasure hunts and seasonal events provides further interest for visitors.

Abbaye des Châteliers (Route la Prée, La Flotte) Standing alone in a field just east of La Flotte, this ruin is accessible at all times, except when a wedding is taking place here (quite frequently on summer weekends!). Built in the 12th century by Cistercian monks, the abbey has endured a lifetime of being destroyed, pillaged and set on fire. It was finally abandoned in the 17th century, after repeated Protestant attacks.

ST-MARTIN-DE-RÉ The island capital, historic port and administrative centre, St-Martin is a delightful place to potter, though on weekends and in high season you won't be alone. The port's structure is a bit unusual, with an 'island' in the middle of the harbour itself. Vauban, the renowned 17th-century military engineer, was responsible for the sturdy fortifications that can be seen all around, the town having experienced many sackings over the centuries – including by those pesky

English, of course. Nowadays it's happy visitors who do the besieging and there are plenty of them. Enjoy the excellent shopping in Rue Sully and Rue Jean-Jaurès – the latter of which hosts the town's market – and take time to climb the clocktower and meander down the beautiful, cobbled side streets, full of flowers. St-Martin's prison has been important at various times in French history, serving as a detention centre after the Revolution for more than 1,000 priests who were then deported to French Guiana and other far-flung places. It's still in use today.

Tourist information

Office de Tourisme 2 Av Victor Bouthillier; ℡ 05 46 09 00 55; w holidays-iledere.co.uk; ⏰ May–Jul & Sep–Oct 09.30–13.00 & 14.00–18.30 Mon–Sun, for other months see website

Where to stay

La Maison Douce (14 rooms) 25 Rue Merindot; ℡ 05 46 09 20 20; e contact@lamaisondouce.com; w lamaisondouce.com; ⏰ early Apr–Nov. In a quiet & beautiful part of town, a quiet & beautiful hotel. Elegant rooms – 4 different standards, but all tasteful – around a flowery courtyard, plenty of communal lounges in which to relax, play chess or read a book. With English-speaking staff, this is a great place to take time out & relax. Also has family rooms. Private parking on reservation (extra charge). €€€–€€€€€

Le Galion (29 rooms) Allée de la Guyane; ℡ 05 46 09 03 19; e contact@hotel-legalion.com; w hotel-legalion.com. Just off the harbour front, upper-floor rooms have sea views. A popular place in a great location, so reserve well in advance. Free Wi-Fi. Private, on-site parking is possible, at extra cost. Small restaurant open to guests in the evening by reservation (⏰ Tue–Sat; €€€€). €€€

Le Poulailler de l'Île de Ré (3 rooms) 5 Rue Etienne d'Hastrel; m 07 70 59 03 47; e lepoulaillerdeliledere@gmail.com. In this weather-beaten, characterful old manor house, just 3 rooms are offered to guests, 2 of which are in the garden. Not particularly spacious & 'bedroom headroom' is a precious commodity here in some rooms, so not suitable for the non-agile. The garden is ample (it doubles as a free car park) & the bare stone walls & stained-glass windows lend it plenty of personality. B/fast (extra charge) is excellent & served in the garden, if the weather is kind. Communal TV lounge, free Wi-Fi in the main building. Just 5mins' walk from the port. 2-night min stay. €€

✕ Where to eat and drink

Ben Hur Char à Huitres Av Victor Bouthillier (in winter, it moves onto the quay in the port); ⏰ May–Sep noon–14.30 & 19.00–22.30 daily, hours may be shorter in winter. A very simple place, with a summer base in the park & a winter one in the port area. Coloured plastic tables may not promise much, but don't be fooled – the food is fresh, tasty & reasonably priced. The chef stands like an orchestra conductor, perched up in a former fishing boat, grilling up sardines & doling out oysters. Service is cheerful. €€€

Le Bistrot du Marin 10 Quai Nicolas Baudin; ℡ 05 46 68 74 66; ⏰ 08.00–02.00 Mon–Wed & Fri–Sun. Rather than join the throngs on the main quay, cross the bridge onto the 'island within the island' & watch the crowds across the water. Blackboard menus tell you what's on offer; tables fill quickly so don't delay. Fish is to the fore, though excellent steaks also make up a fair part of the menu. €€€

La Martinière 17 Quai de la Poithevinière; ⏰ 11.00–21.30 daily, closes 23.00 Jul–Aug. Even in quiet times, the sheer length of the counter at this ever-so-popular ice-cream parlour will tell you that they are expecting plenty of customers, & with an incredible range of flavours, it's clear that they'll be turning up soon. €

What to see and do

Musée Ernest-Cognacq (13 Av Victor Bouthillier; ℡ 05 46 09 21 22; w musee-ernest-cognacq.fr; ⏰ see website for hours; €4.50/free adult/under 19s) This is a bright and modern museum charting the island's history, full of colourful signboards, old-time film footage and artefacts. For English-speakers, a booklet is available to accompany your trip. There is much made of the island's historic role as a detention/transfer centre for prisoners, though the English translation lacks a bit of detail on this subject. The building itself was originally constructed in the 15th century as the Hôtel de Clerjotte, but also served as an arsenal before being acquired by the township to become the current museum. A good representation of island history is provided here and exhibitions change regularly throughout the year.

Église St-Martin (Pl Eudes d'Aquitaine; ⊕ Feb–mid-Nov & Christmas hols daily) A great view is to be had from the top of the Église St-Martin and there's a bit of fun in getting there – a certain agility is an advantage. Over 100 steps are required and so narrow are the stone, then wooden, stairs that a traffic-light system is in place to prevent those descending and those ascending getting to an impasse. It's comical, to say the least, as is the fact that the ticket office is about one-third of the way up! A great favourite at sunset and the tower stays open late to oblige. If you are next to the bells (halfway up) when they chime, you'll need to cover your ears. Once you've navigated the ascent, you get your treasured view over the town.

Fortifications Take a stroll along the sea wall and you are already on the powerful defences built by Vauban. A quick look at the town map will show you just how the layout of these solid walls has been preserved.

LOIX Somewhat isolated on the northern coast, Loix did not join up physically to the other three islands that now make up Ré until the 19th century. Today, one solitary road makes that connection, a reminder of the fragility of the landscape across the salt-marshes.

What to see and do
Village Artisanal (Chemin du Corps de Garde, signposted in town; ⊕ May–Sep, hours vary, some shops open all year) At this grouping of artisans, you'll find a magnificent bookshop, the *Atelier Quillet*, which sells and preserves old books and documents and has a huge comic-strip collection; a shop selling local honey; Loix & Savons, with scented handcrafted soaps; the Fromagerie Chèvrerie Lefort, producing homemade goat's cheese; some quirky souvenir shops; and the Vacances à la Mer design shop (w designlocal.fr), where everything (bags, jewellery, gifts) is made either on the island or in nearby La Rochelle.

La Banane Bleue (13 Rue du Couvent; m 06 81 88 40 47; ⊕ Easter–Nov daily, other times by arrangement, phone in advance) The delightful and delightfully named Sidné le Fou ('Sidney the Madman', and proud of it) sits in his studio creating artwork that perhaps justifies his nickname. Also represented at this small art gallery is the contemporary artist Miss Mirza. Choose from a machine gun made from coke cans and chair legs, or some very colourful paintings and collages.

Ecomusée du Marais (On the main road from La Couarde to Loix; ☎05 46 29 06 77; w marais-salant.com; ⊕ mid-Mar–end Apr & early Oct–early Nov 14.15–17.00 Tue–Sat, end Apr–early Jul 14.30–18.00 Tue–Sun, early Jul–early Sep 10.00–12.30 & 14.00–19.00 daily, early Sep–early Oct 14.30–18.00 Tue–Sat, early Oct–early Nov 14.15–17.00 Tue–Sat; €6/5/2.70/free adult/under 19s/under 12s/under 8s) This museum was set up in 1997 as a way of promoting the culture of the Marais and conserving the practices of the salt marshes. While waiting for your guided tour to begin, you can spend time in the small exhibition hall, watching a video or reading the information panels (all in French, though a laminated handout in English will give you some limited information). A scale model shows the level of activity that might have taken place here around the late 19th century. Interesting fact: only 10% of salt use can be attributed to cooking, the rest being industrial. The tour then continues outside in the saltpans.

ARS-EN-RÉ Amid the flatlands of the island, the spire of Ars-en-Ré's church is unmissable. Painted black and white, it stands like a rocket waiting to be launched into outer space. The village is classed as one of France's 'most beautiful' but for some can't quite match La Flotte or St-Martin for sheer prettiness. However, it is still important for the distribution of the locally produced salt and a lure for expensive yachts, which tie up here in high summer.

Tourist information
Office de Tourisme 25 Pl Carnot; 📞 05 46 09 00 55; ⏲ Dec–Mar 10.00–13.00 & 14.00–17.30 Tue; Apr–Jun & Sep–Oct 09.30–13.00 & 14.00–18.00 Mon–Sat, 09.30–13.00 Sun & hols; Jul–Aug 09.30–18.30 Mon–Sat, 09.30–13.00 & 14.00–17.00 Sun & hols

✖ Where to eat and drink
Aux Frères de la Côte 99 Route de la Grange; 📞 07 69 97 28 09; ⏲ 07.00–02.00 daily. Here's the backstory: Ars-en-Ré wanted to clean up its town centre, so they moved out the 'Bohemians'. Those same Bohemians solved their exile by starting their own bar & here it is. Food is average, service gets mixed reviews: some love it, some hate it. The location, at the edge of Plage de la Grange, is wonderful & despite a recent year-long hiatus, with no immediate competition it looks sure to continue. €€€

Le Café du Commerce 6 Quai de la Prée; 📞 05 46 29 41 57; w cafcom-ars.com; ⏲ Jul–Aug noon– 15.00 & 19.00–22.00 daily, other months vary – contact for details. Not the best food on the island, but the décor alone makes it worth poking your head inside this popular port-side establishment to see the strange knick-knacks that adorn the surfaces, including a bewildering range of ships in bottles & random sports equipment. There are also 2 mirrors from El Paso, Texas & a huge sequoia wood statue on the bar (origin Oregon), while the back of the bar itself is a former ice-cream bar from a drugstore in Boston. Food is equally eclectic: Tex-Mex, salads, burgers & fish dishes. Pleasant terrace. €€€

LE BOIS-PLAGE-EN-RÉ Its many beaches and numerous adjacent campsites ensure that Le Bois attracts its fair share of visitors. For wine buffs, the co-operative is well worth a visit.

Tourist information
Office de Tourisme 87 Rue des Barjottes; 📞 05 46 00 99 55; ⏲ Nov–Mar 09.00–13.00 & 14.00–17.00 Tue–Sat, Apr–Oct 09.30–13.00 & 14.00–17.00 Mon–Sat

✖ Where to eat and drink
L'Aile de Ré 2 Raise Flottaise; 📞 05 46 09 29 87; ⏲ noon–14.00 & 19.30–20.30 Wed–Sun. On the D201, halfway from Le Bois to St-Martin, this place enjoys a good reputation for creative meals crafted from fresh ingredients. €€€

La Martinière 16 Rue du Colombier; 📞 05 46 09 01 20; ⏲ 10.30–19.30 daily, closes 22.30 Jul–Aug. Previously the location of Kustoms Diner, this place has been taken on by the same family chain of stores that are prolific across the island, & can be relied on to serve delicious iced treats wherever they are & at whatever time of year. €

What to see and do
Vignerons de l'Île de Ré (Route de Ste Marie; ☎ 05 46 09 23 09;
w vigneronsiledere.com; ⊕ Apr–Jun 09.00–12.30 & 14.00–18.30 Mon–Sat; Jul–
Aug 09.00–12.30 & 14.00–19.00 Mon–Sat, 10.00–13.00 Sun; Sep 09.00–12.30 &
14.00–18.30 Mon–Sat; Oct–Mar 10.00–12.30 & 14.00–18.00 Mon–Fri) All the
island grapes intended for wine production end up here, in the one and only
co-operative. As well as reds, whites and rosés, you can try and buy the island's
fortified Pineau des Charentes and even cognac. There are free guided tours in
French, followed by tastings; these take place at 10.00 and 15.30 Monday–Friday
in July and August, and 15.30 on Tuesdays and Thursdays in April, June and
September. A separate schedule of wine tastings can be found on the website.

THE FAR WEST Heading west out of St-Martin, the landscape is all about wine,
salt and oysters. If you're in the mood to taste the latter, there are plenty of
producers waiting for you along the route. Taking the D735 as far west as you
can, you end up in the car parks that service the island's most visited spot, the
Phare des Baleines (Lighthouse of Whales). You're not likely to see any whales on
your visit, but the beauty of this place has ensured that a full range of facilities is
here, including campsites, restaurants and souvenir shops selling island products.

Where to eat and drink There are a number of restaurants on the approach road
to the lighthouse, of which **La Cabane** [map, page 207] (m 06 37 44 51 66; ⊕ Apr–
Nov; €€) is probably the pick. It is also good for tea or an ice cream.

What to see and do
Le Phare des Baleines (155 Route du Phare; ☎ 05 46 29 18 23;
w pharedesbaleines.com; ⊕ Apr–Jun & Sep 10.00–19.00 daily, Jul–Aug 09.30–
20.00 daily, Oct–Mar 10.00–17.30 daily; admission to all 3 sites: €12.95/7.65/free
adult/under 13s/under 7s, cheaper tickets for individual sites) Ever-popular with
visitors, this 57m-high lighthouse occupies the western tip of the Île de Ré. There
are three sites to explore here: the Phare des Baleines itself, plus the 'Old Tower'
that preceded it and a museum on both structures' history. You can visit just one
or two of these for less money; as none of the museum's exhibits currently has
any information translated into English, pure Anglophones might do well to just
climb the 'new' lighthouse (€4.35/2.85/free), built in 1854 and still in use, and
forget visiting the other two. The view from the top is wonderful, but if you can
combine it with sunset, all the better.

The Old Tower was constructed as a lighthouse in 1669 at a height of 29m,
originally powered by whale oil, then coal. In the building at its foot is the museum,
where you will find exhibitions with old photos of the island's various ports and
history as to how crossings were made to the island over the centuries. (Before
the bridge was built in 1988, a tunnel, a monorail and a submersible road were all
proposed at one time or another.) Even if you decide to visit _none_ of the three sites,
it's still worth walking up to the sea wall to look out over the ocean.

LES PORTES-EN-RÉ The northernmost village and on the road to nowhere, Les
Portes is nevertheless close to the pleasant beaches of La Loge and La Patache.

What to see and do
Réserve Naturelle Lilleau des Niges/Maison du Fier (☎ 05 46 29 40 74;
w maisondufier.fr; ⊕ Exhibition Centre: Apr–Jun 10.00–12.30 & 14.30–18.30

Mon–Fri, 14.30–18.00 Sat–Sun; Jul–Aug 10.00–13.00 & 14.30–18.30 daily except Sat morning, Sep–early Oct 10.00–13.30 & 14.30–18.00 daily except Sat morning; €4/3/free adult/student or limited mobility/under 5s, €10 family ticket; there is free access to the reserve outside these opening times) The park's information centre, the Maison du Fier, is a converted salt hangar, where you are welcome to hire binoculars to cast your eye out over the marshes in search of an avian gem or two. Information panels outside in French will assist you and provide details about the birds' migratory patterns. Back inside, an English-language audio-guide tells you the essentials of the exhibition, which naturally focuses on the flora and fauna in this distinctive bay and marshland terrain. Families can go on a learning quest to explore the island's biodiversity with various discovery games, and there is also a 2km walking circuit around the marshes.

Nantes, Pays de Retz and the Loire Estuary

Up the estuary of the majestic Loire River lies the energetic city of Nantes, by far the biggest conurbation in this area and a former industrial giant now rich in points of interest for visitors. Once the capital of neighbouring Brittany, these days it has to content itself with being boss of the Loire-Atlantique département. Its quirky, creative dynamism reveals surprises at every turn.

Just a few kilometres south of town, the rural charms of the Pays de Retz (pronounced 'ray') – the unsung area sandwiched between the Vendée and the River Loire – should not be overlooked. Its highlight is perhaps the nature reserve around the enigmatic lake, the Lac de Grand-Lieu, a haven for birdlife and whose waters contract and expand with the seasons. In winter, it is indisputably France's largest lake.

Continuing west towards the ocean, family-friendly resorts are strung out along the Atlantic coast between the border with the Vendée and the Loire Estuary: Les Moutiers, La Bernerie, Pornic and St-Brevin, each with its own attractions. Northwards, a giant estuary bridge arches between the two banks of the Loire, taking you across to the important port town of St-Nazaire. Here you'll find a few scars of necessary industry, perhaps the looming bulk of a giant cruise ship under construction and a fleet of ships waiting offshore to load and unload. More interestingly, you'll stumble across fascinating reminders of the significant part played by this coast and St-Nazaire in World War II: the town's former German U-Boat base, which now hosts a French submarine and an enjoyable and imaginatively created simulation of life aboard an ocean liner.

West of industrial St-Nazaire, leisure takes over once more, with the popular resort towns of Pornichet and La Baule providing more beaches and all the wonderful trappings necessary for a seaside holiday. The influences of neighbouring Brittany become increasingly stronger here, too.

Returning along the south bank of the estuary towards Nantes, it's clear that the city's innovative spirit has escaped and flowed down the river towards the ocean, with nearly 30 installations on the Parcours Estuaire art trail between the city and the sea.

NANTES

'If you think that culture is expensive, then just consider the cost of ignorance'
(A favourite Nantes saying)

Shipbuilding, biscuit manufacturing, sugar refining and food canning were the traditional livelihoods of this pleasant river port of just under 300,000 inhabitants,

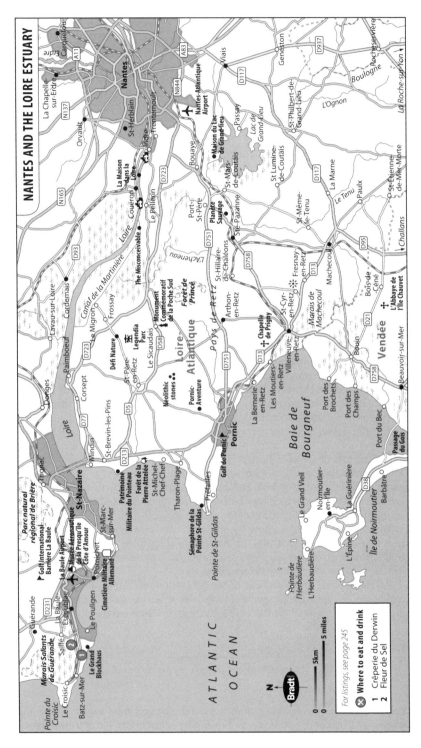

For listings, see page 245
⊗ Where to eat and drink
1 Crêperie du Derwin
2 Fleur de Sel

Bradt

0   5km
0   5 miles

making it France's sixth-largest city. Include the larger metropolitan area and the population doubles. And it's a population that's steadily increasing: a former European Green Capital and straddling the Loire, Nantes is regularly voted by readers of influential French magazines as the town in which they would most like to live and certainly has enough to justify a couple of days' stay. For visitors, this is perhaps a city still lacking a bit of international high profile, but it's certainly not through want of trying. Renovated museums, constantly changing art installations and a well-presented history added to a decent gastronomy and a swish transport network ensure that the city is always ready to welcome you. And with a huge increase in visitors from abroad, it's clear that Nantes' efforts are being rewarded. As are its tourists: after all, this is a city that's bound to impress.

It was from the proceeds of the sugar and slave trades that the city grew rich in the 17th and 18th centuries. During the Wars of the Vendée, Nantes was the site of a ferocious battle during which the Vendean leader Cathelineau was mortally wounded. Later it became the headquarters for the notorious Republican General Carrier who delightfully instituted wholesale drownings of prisoners in the Loire. Though you would not guess it from the profusion of old buildings, some dating back to the Middle Ages, the town was subjected to heavy Allied bombing in September 1943.

Along the river to the west, you will easily spot *la grue jaune*, one of the two decommissioned giant Titan cranes that still keep alive a trace of the city's shipbuilding past. Located opposite the *Maillé-Brézé* warship, now a visitor attraction in its own right, this brightly painted yellow crane reminds us that thousands used to work here, commuting on the old transporter bridge, a model of which you can see in the Chantiers Navals museum. Harnessing the city's traditional metalworking heritage, an inventive company has installed workshops to produce Les Machines de l'Île (page 226) – crazily inspired creations that are a cross between the dreams of Jules Verne and of William Heath Robinson. Ever ridden on a mechanical elephant? Or a giant spider? Now is your chance! As well as this 'surrealistic bestiary', other inhabitants of the creative quarter of the Île de Nantes include a maritime-themed carousel and a host of other thought-provoking artworks, including *Les Anneaux de Buren*, a series of 18 enlightened rings that frame the river landscape.

Visiting Nantes between Wednesday and Saturday will ensure that nearly all the shops, sites and museums will be open, though even on other days the glut of freely accessible outdoor points of interest will still make any trip here more than worthwhile. Rue Kervégan is the central street of the 'Île Feydeau' ('Feydeau island') district, formerly surrounded by the Loire, but now landlocked in a tide of swirling traffic. The island's narrow and cobbled streets have had something of a makeover, giving deserved prominence to the homes of wealthy 18th-century shipowners. Their houses feature ornate balconies and decorative carved stone faces, called *mascarons*, over doors and windows.

Nantes' historical quarters have two distinct characters, divided by the Cours des 50 Otages – a central north–south boulevard. To the east is the old town, a series of narrow pedestrianised streets around the chateau and the Ste-Croix church, containing 15th- and 16th-century houses and many small shops, plus a branch of the Galeries Lafayette department store [218 D1] (on Rue de la Marne). To the west lies the busy Place du Commerce, a bustling interchange for tram and bus passengers. Off it, Rue de la Fosse has some chic shops en route to smart Place Royale [218 C2]. Also off Place du Commerce is the Passage Pommeraye [218 C2], a unique 19th-century arcade on three different levels linked by decorated steps that

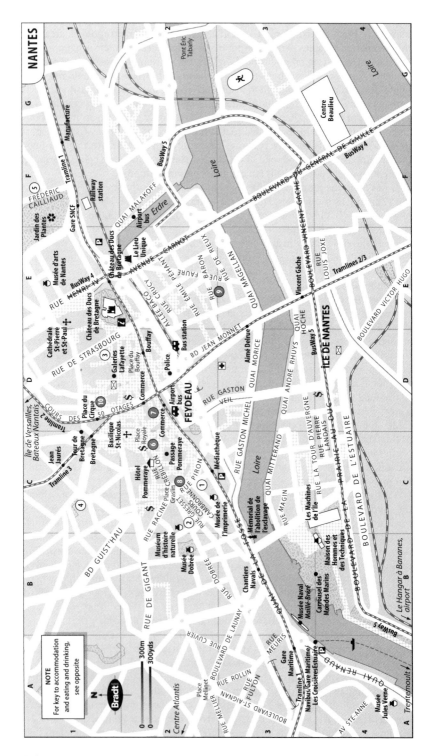

NANTES

NOTE
For key to accommodation
and eating and drinking,
see opposite

Bradt

0   300m
0   300yds

rise steeply to finish at Rue Crébillon – the city's smartest shopping street. (Whether you choose to shop there or not, walking the Passage Pommeraye is a must.) Up here, turn left for Place Graslin [218 C2], with its shiny-stoned opera house and glorious turn-of-the-century brasserie, La Cigale, which demands of you at least a coffee stop. Just south of Place Graslin lies an elegant, traffic-free avenue of 18th-century houses called Cours Cambronne. In the historic centre, look out for street signs in both French and Breton, reminding you again that Nantes was once the capital of Brittany.

For fun, there's the annual Voyage à Nantes (page 220) and the Folle Journée, a themed classical-music festival which stretches across five days in early February. Jazz fans flock to town at the beginning of September for Les Rendezvous de l'Erdre.

GETTING THERE AND AWAY Nantes is well served for transport. The city has an international **airport** a mere 8km southwest of the centre, with several flights from the UK and Ireland (page 22).

As well as having fast **trains** which link it to Paris (Montparnasse) in just over 2 hours, Nantes railway station [218 F1] also has a regular TGV service from Lille-Europe, making an easy link with Eurostar trains to and from London. You can also take trains to other places covered in this book, such as Clisson, St-Gilles-Croix-de-Vie, Les Sables-d'Olonne, Pornic, St-Nazaire and La Baule. Note that currently there are *two* exits at Nantes station, north and south (*sortie nord* and *sortie sud*) – worth knowing if you are planning to meet someone. In 2020, an ambitious new renovation to increase the station's passenger capacity was completed, with an eco-friendly approach that is reflected in the architecture – the resulting mezzanine level that replaced the underground tunnel between north and south terminals is adorned with trunk-like columns that resemble trees, with canopies of concrete branches that cover the ceiling. If you prefer to travel by **bus**, most of the towns mentioned in this chapter as far west as St-Nazaire are connected to Nantes through the Lila bus network (w lila.paysdelaloire.fr), though services can be infrequent.

GETTING AROUND Driving around the confusing one-way system can be tricky, so abandon the car as soon as possible and visit on foot, or by tram and bus. There is a large underground car park beneath the Tour de Bretagne – a skyscraper visible from almost anywhere in town – a multi-storey one near the railway station plus a dozen or so others marked on the Tourist Board map. Be warned: these can cost up to €20 per 24 hours. Alternatively, try the pay-and-display parking on the streets north of the station. If staying out of town or day tripping in here from the Vendée, consider travelling in by train or coach (confusingly, this last is called a *car*). Alighting from a train here, choose the north exit (*sortie nord*) to emerge opposite the tram stop and the Jardin des Plantes (page 223), ready to start exploring. A coach will drop you at the station's south exit (*sortie sud*), so you need to walk through the station's underpass to reach the trams. The south exit also takes you to

Nantes, Pays de Retz and the Loire Estuary   NANTES

9

WALKING THE LINE

The most comprehensive (and tiring!) way to see all of Nantes' sites and attractions, both historical and modern, is to walk the thin green line painted on the city's roads and pavements. This leads you around town on the Voyage à Nantes, a walking tour of around 14km, complete with various bilingual information panels along the way. You can walk the line at any time of year, but in July and August, when the city bills itself as the 'loopiest in Europe', the route is enhanced with temporary additions from artists and gardeners who have been invited to install their works as part of the Voyage à Nantes festival. The opening of the festival takes place at the beginning of July on La Nuit du Van, when there are concerts, special events and barbecues to announce the city's celebration of itself. The fun then continues until nearly the end of August. Although ostensibly temporary, the new installations may become permanent if the Nantais decide that they particularly like one of them. To walk the whole of the green line route would take you around 5 hours, but that would give you no time to enjoy the sites en route. Far better to split it over two or more days, or do a bit of planning and identify those sites where you actually want to spend some time. For more information on the route and the annual programme of the Voyage à Nantes festival, visit w levoyageanantes.fr.

one of the shuttle-bus stops for Nantes-Atlantique airport (service every 20 or 30 mins; €10). An alternative, slightly longer route is via tram line 3 from Commerce to Neustrie and change for an airport shuttle bus.

Taking advantage of the many pedestrianised streets in the centre, **walking** is an attractive way of seeing the best of the town. North of the Loire, Nantes rises quickly away from the river, but apart from that and a few other undulations it is reasonably flat. The city's efficient **tram** system has three lines intersecting near Place du Commerce and running east–west or north–south; a fourth line – called the 'BusWay' – runs north–south from near the cathedral down to the covered shopping centre of Beaulieu and beyond, and BusWay Line 5 goes from the railway station to Le Hangar à Bananes. If you choose to buy a **Nantes Pass**, your bus and tram transport is included for 24/48/72 hours or 7 days. Travel is free for all on weekends in the city; otherwise, a single ticket (€1.80) is valid for an hour anywhere on the network from when you first punched it, even when you change tram, bus etc. A *carnet* of ten tickets is slightly cheaper, advantageous for long-stayers. Good-value day tickets (€6.40 at the time of writing) make sense, as do day tickets designed for four people travelling together (€12). Tickets are valid on both bus and tram, and can be bought from machines at tram stops before boarding, or on board buses, but not on board trams. Ticket machines accept Carte Bleue credit cards. The ticket has to be punched, or *composté*, to validate it on entering the tram. (For an all-day ticket, you do this just on the first trip.) Tickets are also valid on the **Navibus** (waterbus services), but note that the airport bus is not included. A good first stop for visitors is the tourist office, where you can pick up a Nantes Pass, free town plan, ask for information and browse through brochures.

TOURIST INFORMATION

Office de Tourisme [218 E2] 9 Rue des Etats; ☎ 02 72 64 04 79; w levoyageanantes.fr; ⏱ Sep–Jun 10.00–18.00 Mon–Sat, 10.00–17.00 Sun & hols, Jul–Aug 09.00–19.00 daily. Guided tours of the city are available in English, usually once a day in Jul–Aug only. Various routes are available. Alternatively, you can hire an audio-guide (leaving a passport as deposit), or hop on board the Little Train, which offers English-language commentary.

WHERE TO STAY Good-quality apartments are an alternative option to the hotels listed below, though beware that many demand a stay of two nights or more, and some are located out of the centre. A few upmarket apartments can be found under the Destinations Surprenantes banner (w surprenantes.com), with many more listed on the Nantes tourist office website.

Okko Hotels Nantes Château [218 D1] (80 rooms) 15 bis Rue de Strasbourg; ☎02 52 20 00 70; e nantes0041@okkohotels.com; w okkohotels. com. Super, modern, designer hotel where everything – except the parking – is included. Business-orientated, with a swish communal lounge, gym & sauna. Centrally located, eco-friendly & welcoming, if a little pricey. Free Wi-Fi throughout. Limited parking is available, at extra cost, only bookable on morning of arrival. €€€€

Radisson Blu [218 C1] (142 rooms) 6 Pl Aristide-Briand; ☎02 72 00 10 00; e info.nantes@ radissonblu.com; w radissonhotels.com. A 4-star hotel in the beautiful former Palais de Justice (law courts), opened in 2011. Modern, but with many original features retained. A gourmet restaurant (€€€€) occupies the old courtroom itself. Rooms feature free Wi-Fi, AC. €€€€

Sozo Hôtel [218 F1] (24 rooms) 16 Rue Frédéric Cailliaud; ☎02 51 82 40 00; e reception@ sozohotel.fr; w sozohotel.fr. Located behind the Jardin des Plantes, this small hotel has been built inside a hollowed-out church. All rooms retain a vestige of the building's religious past, 2 with stained-glass windows. Free Wi-Fi, TV with international channels. Furniture is all ultra-modern & chic, despite the old building. €€€€

Hôtel le Cambronne [218 C2] (19 rooms) 11 Rue Fourcroy; ☎02 40 44 68 00; e contact@ hotel-cambronne.com; w hotel-cambronne. com. A good, cheaper option in a decent location. Reasonably priced b/fast, public parking nearby, free Wi-Fi. Not all rooms are accessible by lift. Good value. €€

Hotel Voltaire Opéra [218 C2] (37 rooms) 10 Rue Gresset; ☎02 40 73 31 04; e resas@hvonantes. com; w hotelvoltaireoperanantes.com. A friendly place, a 2-star option in an elegant 19th-century building. TV, free Wi-Fi. Nothing fancy, but a good central choice. Note the more-than-unusual 'universal sheep counter' on the outside wall, a legacy from the Voyage à Nantes festival. €€

WHERE TO EAT AND DRINK

La Cigale [218 C2] 4 Pl Graslin; ☎02 51 84 94 94; w lacigale.com; ⊕ 07.30–00.30 daily. Opened in 1895, La Cigale has since been the beacon of elegance & opulence for les Nantais & their visitors alike. (Though to tell the whole story, it had to be rescued from dilapidation in 1982.) Some say it rests on its past glories, but although the food & service can be bettered elsewhere, the interior is stunning & for that alone it remains a 'go-to' destination when you're in town. Unusually, it's open for b/fast, though the stinger is that it is expensive. €€€€

L'Entrecôte [218 D2] 2 Rue du Couëdic; ☎02 40 48 62 83; ⊕ noon–14.00 & 19.00–22.15 daily. This is a bit of a 1-dish wonder, definitely to be avoided unless you like steak & fries – but if you do like them, you'll love this Nantaise institution & its 'secret sauce'. The good news for the sweet of tooth is that there is a choice of desserts – more than 20 of them! No reservations, so get there early or join the queue – it's popular. €€€€

Lulu Rouget [218 D1] 1 Rue du Cheval Blanc; ☎02 40 47 47 98; ⊕ noon–13.30 & 19.30–21.00 Tue–Sat. A well-recommended, now Michelin-starred place, towards the upper end of the price range. Creative dishes by a renowned chef with a menu that is kept a closely guarded secret – so you'll have to eat here to find out. €€€€

La Récré [218 E3] 5 Rue Baron; ☎02 40 89 50 51; ⊕ noon–14.00 & 18.00–23.00 Tue–Sat. Taking the phrase 'old school' to a new level, this is a novelty place housed in a former school which delights young & old alike. Old-style games entertain you, friendly service & good food centred around burgers & skewers. A fun experience but a little out the way. Booking advised. €€€

During your visit to the city, check the restaurant menus for *beurre-blanc nantais*, a rich buttery sauce offset by a slightly citrus tang, often served with fish, and *canard nantais*, which is duck. For the sweet of tooth, check the shops for *berlingots nantais*, pyramid-shaped boiled sweets, as well as the famous LU-brand biscuits which are also local specialities.

Le Hangar à Bananes [218 B4] 21 Quai des Antilles; w levoyageanantes.fr/lieux/hab-galerie. Best visited in the evening. Once the place where bananas & pineapples were left to ripen, this old warehouse has been converted into an exciting space where people gather in the evenings to drink, eat & relax. In addition, the HAB Galerie hosts around 3 or 4 art exhibitions each year. Take the Chronobus number 5, or be prepared for a walk to reach it, at the west end of the Île de Nantes. Once

there you'll find cafés, restaurants & even a disco. €€–€€€

Crêperie Heb Ken [218 C2] 5 Rue de Guérande; ☎02 40 48 75 03; ⏰ 11.45–22.45 Mon–Fri, 11.45–23.00 Sat. Recently renovated, this is a decent & well-priced crêperie with an endless range of filling pancake combinations. Side salads are cheap; overall this is good value given its central location. Lunchtimes are busy, service is brisk. Also serves homemade pastries such as the traditional rum-flavoured Nantais cake. €€

SHOPPING The ornate Passage Pommeraye [218 C2] (page 224), all columns and carvings, is unmissable whether you shop or not, and you could easily spend a happy day's retailing around the city centre. More mundane shopping malls are available on the fringes of town. South of the station, on a large island that lies between the two branches of the River Loire, is a huge modern *centre commercial*, or shopping mall, the Centre Beaulieu [218 G4], which has a hypermarket and many French high-street clothes shops. There's another – the Centre Atlantis – at St-Herblain [218 A2], off the ring road to the northwest of Nantes (J32 or J33). For markets, the main Nantes food fair operates from Tuesday to Sunday on the Rue Talensac, north of the Tour de Bretagne. There's a giant *brocante* (flea market) in the Place Viarme, also north of the centre, held over three days in early October.

SPORTS AND ACTIVITIES

Bike n' Tour m 06 52 62 94 64; e contact@bikentour.com; w bikentour.com; €44 for 2hr tour – min of 4 persons required. Nantes' many pedestrianised streets provide good reasons to take a guided bike tour around the city. Even

better when the bikes are electric & the young guide is English-speaking, full of fun & armed with amusing anecdotes. Advanced booking required. Longer vineyard tours & bespoke itineraries also available.

WHAT TO SEE AND DO

Château des Ducs de Bretagne [218 E1] (4 Pl Marc-Elder; ☎08 11 46 46 44; w chateaunantes.fr; ⏰ courtyard & ramparts: 08.30–19.00 daily, closes 20.00 Jul–Aug; moat garden: 08.00–19.00 daily, closes 20.00 Jul–Aug; castle interior, museum & exhibitions : Sep–Jun 10.00–18.00 Tue–Sun, Jul–Aug 10.00–19.00 daily; courtyard, ramparts & moat garden: free; museum & temporary exhibitions: €9/5/ free adult/under 26s/under18s, audio-guide in English €2) This majestic 15th-century castle lying between the Île Feydeau and the railway station was formerly the residence of the dukes of Brittany and then the kings of France. Its name is a reminder that at one time, Brittany was outside the Kingdom of France, ruled by its own dukes. Entering the courtyard, you seem to have left the medieval-style fortress behind you on the outside and discovered a true chateau on the inside, with its Italian Renaissance windows bestowing elegance. From this beautifully renovated courtyard, you enter the pretty, white-painted building containing an excellent museum on the history of Nantes. (Anglophones are aided by a leaflet, bilingual 'pull-out' cards, touch-screens and an optional but recommended audio-guide.) It covers more than 800 years, so allow at least a couple of hours to follow the chronological displays. A multi-lingual touch-screen explains the Edict of Nantes, that gave Protestants the right to worship. The visit is in the form of a constant progress up from floor to floor, via trade with the West Indies, slavery and buccaneering, followed by a descent through more rooms towards ever more recent history such as shipbuilding, biscuits (LU, born from the marriage between members of the Lefèvre and Utile families), and Amieux sardines. Look out for the room displaying old maps of the city, which will help you understand how the Loire and its tributaries used to intrude into the city centre much more than they do today. Both world wars are included too: the city's role in manufacturing food for the war effort, and the fact that 150,000 British soldiers passed through the ports of Nantes and St-Nazaire during World War I; and the story from World War II of the 50 French hostages shot on 22 October 1941 in reprisal for the assassination of a German officer. Nantes' main north–south boulevard, 50 Otages is named in their honour. Temporary thematic exhibitions are put on throughout the year, with a focus on Nantes the city and the connection between Nantes and the rest of the world – at the time of writing, this included a detailed Genghis Khan exhibition, supported by an app providing a free English and French audio guide that could be downloaded on to a smartphone. Guided tours are also available (€12/7.50/free adult/under 26s/under 7s).

Cathédrale St-Pierre et St-Paul [218 E1] (Pl St-Pierre; w cathedrale-nantes. fr ; ⊕ closed for renovation until 2025) Following a devastating fire in 2020, the the city's flamboyant Gothic cathedral was closed to visitors at the time of writing and expected to reopen in 2025. Within its lofty, white tuffeau-stone interior is the spectacularly decorated tomb of Duke François II of Brittany and his wife, commissioned in 1502 by their daughter Anne, Duchess of Brittany and Queen of France. Construction began in the 15th century but was completed only in the 19th century. Unlike many French places of worship, this huge holy building strikes you with its sheer luminosity, with light flooding through the many high-level, clear-glass windows.

Musée d'Arts de Nantes [218 E1] (10 Rue Georges-Clemenceau; ☎02 51 17 45 00; w museedartsdenantes.nantesmetropole.fr; ⊕ Sep–Jun 11.00–19.00 Wed–Mon, Jul–Aug 10.00–19.00 daily, closes 21.00 Thu; €9/4/free adult/under 26s & students/ under 18s) Midway between the cathedral and the Jardin des Plantes, Nantes' arts museum is a light and bright space in which to reflect and admire the extensive works forming both permanent and temporary exhibitions. Artists whose works form part of the permanent collections include Wassily Kandinsky, Peter Paul Rubens, Claude Monet, Anish Kapoor and Georges de la Tour.

Jardin des Plantes [218 F1] (1 Pl Charles Leroux; ☎02 40 41 65 09; w nature. metropole.nantes.fr; ⊕ 08.30–17.30 daily; free) Birdsong drowns the hum of traffic once you step inside the city's delightful botanical gardens, modelled by their founder upon those of Kew and since 1860 one of the most cherished of the city's 100 green spaces. Opposite the north exit of the railway station, or alternatively

accessed from Rue Georges-Clemenceau, the garden makes a marvellous open-air 'waiting room' if you have time to kill between trains. There are wonderful spring magnolias, camellias and rhododendrons, plus green lawns and summer colour. The city's creative spirit cannot be kept at bay by green spaces and you'll find a few artworks here, too, such as a giant wooden bench that straddles the path. Inevitably, the more adventurous and athletic visitors climb up for a photo-shoot (not strictly allowed). There's also good entertainment for children, with a roundabout, climbing frame and sandy play area.

Le Lieu Unique [218 E2] (2 Quai Ferdinand-Favre, off Av Carnot; ☏02 40 12 14 34; w lelieuunique.com; ⊕ timings vary depending on what you want to see – visit the website for details) One of the most conspicuous buildings in Nantes stands just south of the railway line, near the station's *sortie sud*, or south exit. Extravagantly decorated and magnificently restored, this 1905 domed tower – once the glory of the city's LU biscuit factory – is now an avant-garde arts centre, with a lively programme of events, a relaxing café, bookshop and other facilities. The biscuits themselves are still made, though no longer in the city itself.

Place du Bouffay [218 D2] This unexceptional-looking square was the site of the guillotine during the Vendée Wars (page 9). In those days, the Loire flowed right in front of the square – shackled prisoners were also thrown into the waters to drown.

Île de Versailles [218 D1] (Quai Henri Barbusse; ☏02 40 41 90 00; ⊕ mid-Jan–mid-March & mid-Oct–mid-Nov 08.30–18.30, mid-Nov–mid-Jan 08.30–17.30, mid-Mar–mid-May 08.30–20.30, mid-May–early Sep 08.30–21.30, early Sep–mid Oct 08.30–20.00, all daily; free) Once marshland, this island was artificially created in 1831 and became a centre for metalworkers, boat repairmen and mechanics. Now it is revitalised as a tranquil, pretty Japanese-style garden on the River Erdre, north of the city centre, easily accessible by tram. Camellias, azaleas, rhododendrons and cherry trees flower in spring; all year you will find bamboos, reeds, cloud-pruned pines and, in the small Maison de l'Erdre, a few aquariums containing eels and freshwater fish.

Basilique St-Nicolas [218 C2] (Rue Affre; ⊕ 08.00–17.00 daily) This church was designed in 1837 as one of France's first examples of Gothic religious architecture. Known for its stained-glass windows, and eight gilded angels on one of its spires, it can be packed at Sunday evening services.

Passage Pommeraye [218 C2] Built in 1834, this three-level arcade allowed the bourgeoisie to safely transit between the lower and upper parts of the town, without getting mugged, rained on or worse. (As a maritime town, Nantes certainly had its rough elements.) It was one of the first places to be illuminated, using gas lamps. Renovated only once, in 2010, and with an additional arcade built off it in modern, but sympathetic style, this is an essential photo-stop. The sturdy steps were part of the renovation, but were built using 200-year-old chestnut. The passage is endowed with 'historic monument' status. Notice that the top floor of this amazing structure consists of private residences.

Musée de l'Imprimerie [218 C2] (24 Quai de la Fosse; ☏02 40 73 26 55; w musee-imprimerie.com; ⊕ Sep–Jun 10.00–noon & 14.00–17.30 Mon–Sat, Jul–Aug 10.00–

noon & 14.00–17.30 Mon–Fri; €8/5/free adult/students & scholars/under 6s) The pungent smell of printing ink pervades this museum on the history of printing, which shows the materials used for illumination, woodcuts and other techniques. A returnable English-language handout is available for visitors, but as it does not bear direct reference to the exhibits, this is perhaps a museum best suited to those who already know what they're looking at!

Muséum d'Histoire Naturelle
[218 C2] (12 Rue Voltaire; 🕿 02 40 41 55 00; w museum.nantesmetropole.fr; ⊕ 10.00–18.00 Wed–Mon, closes 1st half of Nov; €5/2 adult/under 26s & students) Enjoyable natural history museum, full of stuffed animals – from weasel to polar bear, plus quantities of birds – and skeletons of a whale, rhinoceros, horse and deer. The museum has a large collection of minerals, displayed in pleasantly old-fashioned style; the walls of its staircase are lined with slices from 1,000 different trees. An astonishing 1,600,000 specimens feature in the collections here. Some but not all information panels are translated into English.

Musée Dobrée
[218 B2] (18 Rue Voltaire; 🕿 02 40 71 05 79; w collections.musee-dobree.fr; ⊕ 08.00–18.30 daily) Thomas Dobrée (1810–95), son of a rich Protestant shipowner, built this granite palace to house his fine collections of furniture, prints, enamels, porcelain, sculpture and curiosities from medieval times, via the Renaissance to the late 19th century. Collecting such items became his lifetime's 'work' and included weaponry, enamels, coins, ivories, alabaster, paintings – and even a reliquary containing the heart of Anne, 15th-century Duchess of Brittany who became twice Queen of France (by marrying first Charles VIII and, later, Louis XII). Housed across the courtyard (though this may change after the current renovation works), a modern archaeological museum holds all manner of fossils and Neolithic treasures dug up in the Vendée and Loire-Atlantique, continuing through Gallo-Roman pieces up to the 10th century. If it all sounds a bit dry for the youngsters, there are puzzles, jigsaws and games to help hold their interest. There's also a treasure hunt available via the free Baludik app, providing a more interactive visit. An English-language leaflet and translated wall-panels are available.

Memorial de l'Abolition de l'Esclavage
[218 B3] (Quai de la Fosse; ⊕ mid-May–mid-Sep 09.00–20.00 daily, mid-Sep–mid-May 09.00–18.00 daily; free) On the banks of the Loire you'll find this reminder of a dark period in Nantes' history. The so-called 'triangular trade' took guns from the city's arms manufacturers to Africa, where the weapons were traded for enslaved people; the enslaved people were taken to the West Indies, where they were traded for sugar and spices; these foodstuffs were then brought back to Nantes, where the whole cycle started again. The memorial is in two parts, above and below ground. Above, reflective panels embedded in the pavement give the names of all the slave-trading boats that left the town, while below there is a tunnel with a chronology of the slave trade and quotes from those who brought about its abolition.

Musée Naval Maillé-Brézé
[218 B3] (Quai de la Fosse; 🕿 09 79 18 33 51; w maillebreze.com; ⊕ by guided visit only, see website for timings; various tours from €12/10/8/free adult/students & under 18s/under 12s/under 4s) This 3,900-tonne French destroyer is permanently moored along Quai de la Fosse, directly across the water from the giant yellow crane. The guided tour (in French only; English-language leaflet available) takes you up and down ladders and

companionways of the 1955-built vessel that was once home to 300 sailors. You see everything from engines to missiles, barber's shop to the sick bay. It seems strange to stand on the bridge of the ship and look out at the city centre, rather than the empty ocean, and at the trams running past.

Les Machines de l'Île [218 C3] (Parc des Chantiers, Bd Léon Bureau; ☎02 51 17 49 89; w lesmachines-nantes.fr; ⊕ check website for detailed opening hours as it varies within each month & is sometimes closed for maintenance; elephant ride or Galerie des Machines *atelier*: €9.50/7.50/free adult/under 18s, students & disabled/under 4s; carousel with ride: €9/7.10/3 adult/under 18s & students/under 4s, without ride: €6.50/5.50/free; discounts can apply if visiting more than 1 attraction – see website) The weirdest and most wonderful concepts are brought to life in this massive arts project that has been a key to regenerating the site of the city's former shipyards on the Île de Nantes. Most spectacular is the now-famous 12m-high **mechanical elephant** – a wrinkled, *much* larger-than-life-sized mechanical pachyderm (created for the centenary of Jules Verne's death) whose silhouette dominates the site's open hangars. It can take 50 passengers for a stately 45-minute ride around the Île, flapping its leathery ears, fluttering its eyelids and mischievously spraying onlookers with a fine mist from its jointed wooden trunk.

If you'd rather observe the elephant from the ground as it saunters across the concrete, it's entirely free to do so. An additional/alternative attraction is to buy a ticket to visit the **Galerie des Machines'** *atelier* (workshop) to see smaller, even wackier creations, which change from year to year – in which a few passengers can sit and pull levers to operate wagging tails and snapping mouths, or make the creatures tilt or spin (English-speaking staff are usually at hand). Not to be missed is the massive spider that rises to the roof of the workshop, climbing along its thread and, carrying its human cargo, hissing and spitting in a mechanical cacophony. Future years will bring new 'animals', currently under development. *Atelier* visitors can also look down from a gantry to observe work on the next projects, and watch a film (with English subtitles) about the whole grandiose project, which involves 155 people from 30 different trades.

If you want to know what happens to some of the lesser-sized mechanical animals that are created in the Galeries des Machines workshop, the three-storey **Carousel des Mondes Marins**, 25m high, provides the answer. Here you'll discover horses, fish and insects as well as giant seashells and fishing boats in residence on this maritime-themed roundabout. From the top, you get a great alternative view of the elephant, if he's on walkabout, as he drops off his passengers outside the entrance. You can choose between simply exploring the three floors of the carousel, or taking a ride on the character of your choice.

A schedule of live events following the seasons take place here each year, from 'Indian Summer' to 'Noël aux Nefs', complete with Christmas trees, roasted chestnuts and festive illuminations. Future plans include the creation of a 'Heron Tree', an incredible multi-year project to be based in a nearby quarry and subtitled the 'City in the Sky'. A metal structure with walkways and entwined with foliage, it will be topped with two giant herons carrying 20 passengers in a 45m-high carousel. It started in 2018 and is due for completion in 2027. In the meantime, a prototype is on show in the Galerie des Machines' *atelier*, which includes a large 1:5 scale model of the trunk, branches, struts and roots, along with a giant hummingbird swigging nectar from a flower and other fascinating creations including sloths and a giant chameleon.

Maison des Hommes et des Techniques [218 B4] (2bis, Bd Léon Bureau; ℡02 40 08 20 22; w maison-hommes-techniques.fr; ⊕ 10.00–13.00 & 14.00–18.00 Mon–Fri, w/end opening times vary – consult the website for details; free, though contributions welcome) Next to the Machines de l'Île, above, stands the large building that was once the administration offices of one of Nantes' three shipbuilding companies. Part of it has become a small but endearing museum dedicated to this important industry, which wound up in 1987. Inside, there are descriptions of the decades when hundreds of skills and trades flourished in this seafaring city, until silting-up of the Loire caused such business to be moved downriver to St-Nazaire. It's unusually hands-on, with clocking-on cards to punch, and buttons to press to hear the sound of riveting or to make a propeller revolve. Photos allow you to see what the island looked like before the decline of shipbuilding. The museum is set up on a shoestring, but very effective – and even moving at times – with model boats, life-sized silhouettes of men at work, a model of the transporter bridge (now replaced by a fixed bridge) that could carry 300 men at once from the town quay to the island for work, recordings of former workers lamenting the missed camaraderie of the workplace, and a film in English showing you how to launch a ship. There is also a folder with an excellent English translation lying on the windowsill (or ask for it at the desk). Changing temporary exhibitions are put on throughout the year.

Musée Jules Verne [218 A4] (3 Rue de l'Hermitage; ℡02 40 69 72 52; w julesverne. nantesmetropole.fr; ⊕ Sep–Jun 14.00–18.00 Mon & Wed–Sun, Jul–Aug 10.00–19.00 daily; €4/1.50/free adult/under 26s & to all visitors 1hr before closing/under 18s) Although born in Nantes (at 4 Cours Olivier de Clisson, near the main tourist office), the great visionary writer Jules Verne (1828–1905) never actually lived in this lovely, late 19th-century house on a clifftop site overlooking the river. You start in a plush little seating area alongside some of his furniture and domestic items, watching a film about Verne's wife of 50 years, Honorine, and her reflections about her husband. You learn that Verne was a prodigious eater, who thought nothing of downing a leg of lamb while waiting for tardy guests to arrive; that his son Michel got seriously into debt; and that Verne was so busy with his publisher and his work that he paid little attention to either his wife or his son.

Exhibited here are poems and drawings by Verne, so some familiarity with his work would be helpful. You can see a model of the *Nautilus,* from his epic *20,000 Leagues Under the Sea*, a reminder that he anticipated the submarine, as well as foreseeing space exploration. An adventurer, Verne wrote that he could not see any ship sail – whether warship or fishing boat – without feeling his whole being going aboard.

Also on display you'll find toys from Japan, China, Russia and Germany, inspired by Verne's literary inventions. Try and peep into *all* the rooms on *all* the floors, as there are lots of little surprises. Two floors down, you can press buttons on a map to light up the places where his books were set. Serious students of Verne's large output will appreciate the many editions of *20,000 Leagues Under the Sea* and other titles on display over three floors of the house, but the collection has a distinctly 'glass-case' feel that may not appeal to children or non-enthusiasts. In a small room near the entrance is some of Verne's own furniture; his much-fingered globe can be seen on another level. New artefacts are always being acquired, the most recent of which is a set of letters from a young Verne to his family, providing a fascinating insight into the author's daily life growing up in the midst of the 1848 Revolution. On the lowest floor a half-hour film on Verne's life and works is screened, and children can try and work out the rules of a board game based on *Around the World*

9

in 80 Days. Good museum notes are available in English, on request. Down the hill a little way, a couple of life-sized statues recall Captain Nemo brandishing a sextant and a young boy gazing wistfully at him.

Bateaux Nantais [218 D1] (Quai de la Motte Rouge, Pl Waldeck-Rousseau; ☎02 40 14 51 14; w bateaux-nantais.fr; prices from €15.50/8.50 adult/child, lunch/ dinner cruises from €65/24) The Erdre River is somewhat hidden away to the north of Nantes. It's a beautiful waterway, lined with green fields and bordered by several grand country chateaus dating from Renaissance times. A boat can take you on enjoyable cruises, with commentary, along this peaceful river, aboard rather grotesque, glass-sided vessels. Though somewhat ugly from the outside, they're comfortable enough within. Prices for the 3-hour lunch or dinner cruises include a meal. Allow plenty of time for parking; the company suggests using the underground car park near the cathedral.

Les Croisières Estuaire [218 A4] (Gare Maritime, Quai Ernest-Renaud; ☎02 40 69 40 40; w marineetloire.fr; ⊕ see website for dates; from €27.50/16.50/3 adult/ under 18s/under 3s one-way) Take a boat all the way down the river to St-Nazaire, spending 2½ hours on the water, enjoying the scenery and spotting the artworks and villages along the way. Various trips are available – make sure you book a return, either by boat, train or bus.

Trentemoult (7km southwest of Nantes) An attractive waterside village on the south bank of the Loire, almost in the shadow of the Cheviré bridge, this was once the home of eel fishers. Today it has a marina, riverside bars and restaurants, and some quirkily decorated houses in the back streets. Go there by car, or by Navibus (6min crossing, every 20mins from the Gare Maritime, near the Maillé-Brézé ship – see map, page 218).

THE PAYS DE RETZ

Far removed in terms of character from bustling, dynamic Nantes, the Pays de Retz provides both a peaceful haven with its inland lake, just a short drive from the city, as well as the more lively ambience of accessible seaside resorts along its Atlantic coast, just a little further away.

LAC DE GRAND-LIEU Just south of Nantes, and thus a popular escape for city-dwellers, Lac de Grand-Lieu is invisible from the main roads and has always exuded an air of mystery. Claimed to be the oldest inland lake in France, it is in winter also the largest, when it swells from its summer area of 3,500ha to as much as double that. With its floating forests, peat bogs and many rare plants, this wildlife haven is a breeding site for white spoonbills as well as grey herons and many other species. It is fed by three rivers: the Acheneau, the Ognon and the Tenu. This last flows north towards the Loire in winter, when the marsh is overloaded; and south in the summer, bringing water from the Loire to replenish falling levels inland. As such, it is the only French river that flows in two directions. The lake's last private owner – the perfumer Jacques Guerlain – gifted it to the nation in 1980, to be a nature reserve.

Here, in a clockwise direction from Bouaye, you can find the few points around the perimeter that give views of the elusive water, or information about the lake and its varied wildlife.

Bouaye At the northwest corner of the lake, this small town (its name pronounced 'boo-eye-ee') is now the venue for a comprehensive information centre. A visit here can also include the opportunity to explore Jacques Guerlain's shooting lodge on the banks of the River Acheneau, a good birdwatching site.

What to see and do

Maison du Lac de Grand-lieu (Rue du Lac, D264; ☏ 02 28 2519 07; w maisondulacdegrandlieu.org; ⊕ closed Mon, see website for detailed opening times; self-guided visit: €5/4/free adult/under 18s & students under 26/under 6s, guided visit: €8/5/free adult/under 18s & students under 26/under 6s, audio-guides in English: €2) A great deal of thought and presumably money has been expended in creating this superb centre, which covers the history, geography, flora and fauna of the lake. It is also well equipped for foreign visitors, providing high-quality audio-guides in English to accompany you. The visit breaks down into three parts, starting at the exhibition centre, which has more detailed information than most people will need. Secondly, there is a 1km trail, with further information points along the way, which brings you to the final stop, the former hunting pavilion of Jacques Guerlain, the famous reclusive creator of perfumes. This third part of the visit can only be done accompanied by a guide, as it falls inside the protected area of the lake. The pavilion has been renovated and contains clever sound and light scenography, but the highlight has to be to stand on the terrace and see which birds are frequenting the marshes at the time of your visit. Stretching out in front of you is a channel created by one of Guerlain's employees to allow his master to access the lake and shoot ducks. Best visiting seasons for migratory birds (and therefore birdwatchers) are spring and autumn. Visitors seeking guided visits should enquire in advance; options include dawn excursions to the lake and autumn tours to witness the bird migrations (see website for details).

Planète Sauvage (La Chevalerie, Port-St-Père, 8km southwest of Bouaye; ☏02 40 04 82 82; w planetesauvage.com; ⊕ Mar–Nov, see website for detailed opening hours, last admission 2hrs before closing; €28.50/22/free adult/under 13s/under 3s) Lions, tigers, giraffes and zebras are among the 2,000 animal residents of this excellent drive-through safari park, which could easily provide a whole day's entertainment. The safari trail winds for 10km – a 2-hour journey – so, on a hot day, it's wise to take something with you to drink. If you prefer to let someone else do the driving, and to go off the beaten track, it is possible to have a guided tour in a tall, 40-seater 4x4 vehicle (supplementary charges apply). Later, on foot, you can look at reptiles in a reconstructed African village, watch an aquatic show (possibly dolphins or sea lions with the option for younger children to take part in a dolphin training session where they can meet the team of caretakers and discuss what it's like to be a dolphin trainer), and embark on an amazing aerial ramble along jungle-style bridges watching macaque monkeys cavort below you. (As you need both hands to hold onto the sides of the swaying, undulating walkway, this last part is unsuitable for pushchairs, for those carrying small children, and for people with mobility problems.) If this really floats your boat, you can also buy the 'bivouac' packages, with dinner, overnight stay among the animals and two days in the park. The whole place is busiest, of course, in July and August, so go early, if you have to visit in that period. Hot days are best avoided – it can become unbearable to be crammed into a roasting car, crawling slowly around the safari park.

Passay A pretty lakeside fishing village, Passay sits out on a limb, 9km north of St-Philbert. Passay gives perhaps the best access to the elusive lake, whose vastness can be truly appreciated only by passengers coming in to land at nearby Nantes-Atlantique airport. Village fishers net tench and other freshwater fish, and catch eels in long, black-netting traps, keeping them alive afterwards in the sinister-looking tarred boxes resembling miniature wartime landing craft. Carp and catfish are also present. Nowadays, there are only seven fishers left who are licensed to fish the lake, down in numbers from 120 in 1920. Visitors are allowed to join them on a couple of days a year in August, during the summer fishing festival (Fête des Pêcheurs), taking a trip into the interior by *plate* (a flat-bottomed boat) to see the catch being hauled in.

Tourist information

Office de Tourisme 2 Place de l'Hôtel de Ville, La Chevrolière; ☎02 40 13 30 00; w mairie- lachevroliere.com; ⊕ 08.30–noon & 14.00–17.00 Mon–Wed & Fri, 08.30–noon Thu & Sat

What to see and do

Maison Touristique de Passay (All contact details & opening hours as per tourist information, see above; €4/2/free adult/under 15s & students/under 6s) A lighthouse-like observation post looms 12m above the village, marking the position of this museum of local life among the low, white-painted cottages. Inside, you can find out about the birdlife of the lake – 263 different species have been recorded – including spoonbills, egrets, herons, cormorants and a recent intruder, the sacred ibis. Outside, beyond a small garden planted with reeds and grasses, is a further visitor centre with aquariums featuring the types of fish that inhabit the lake, such as eels, pike and carp. You can sit and listen to the voices of fishers talking about fishing techniques with the different types of net that you see on display: the *tramail*, or vertical net; the *louve*, or hooped net; the long *senne* net that is pulled in by two or more fishers; and the long, black-mesh eel traps. Trek up the stairs of the observation post to peer through the fixed binoculars. The tourist office is housed in the same building and has details of some waymarked walks in the area.

Observatoire Ornithologique (La Chevrolière; m 06 79 65 63 67; w observatoire-ornithologique-grandlieu.fr; ⊕ guided tours May–Oct 14.30, 16.00 & 17.30 Sat–Sun; €3/1/free adult/under 19s/under 7s, tickets on sale at the Maison Touristique de Passay, see above, or on site) The wildfowlers of Passay have set up an observatory on a promontory in the marshes, and conduct regular guided walks. Commentary is in French. Waterproof footwear is essential.

St-Philbert-de-Grand-Lieu Near the southern limit of the great wetland known as the Lac de Grand-Lieu, stands one of the oldest churches in France. In this attractive village 23km south of Nantes, you can rent boats, or fish in the calm waters of the Boulogne river. Opposite the campsite to the north of the river is a cheery playground equipped with bouncy castles, mini-golf and other delights. Market day here falls on a Sunday.

To take full advantage of your visit, try the local specialities of eels and freshwater fish, washed down with Muscadet Côtes de Grand-Lieu, Grolleau or Gros-Plant wine.

Tourist information

Office de Tourisme 2 Pl de l'Abbatiale; ☎02 40 78 73 88; w stphilbert.fr; ⊕Apr–Oct 10.00–12.30 & 14.00–18.30 Tue–Sun, Oct–Mar 14.00–17.30 Wed & Fri–Sun. With a boutique selling crafts, the office also serves as the ticket office for the Abbey.

Where to eat and drink

Crêperie le Tourmentin 40 Rue de l'Hôtel de Ville; m 07 70 79 5286; ⏰ 19.00–21.00 Tue & Fri, 18.00–19.00 Wed–Thu, noon–14.00 & 19.00–21.00 Sat–Sun. An excellent, stylish crêperie with a good choice of tasty crêpes & galettes. Very welcoming, friendly owners. Online orders also possible €€€

Des Voyageurs 6 Pl de l'Église; 📞02 40 78 89 29; ⏰ 07.00–19.30 Mon–Fri, 08.00–13.30 Sun. Good value, pleasant surroundings & a welcoming serving staff ensure this place stays popular. Food is tasty, though not over-fancy. €€€

What to see and do

Abbatiale St-Philbert (Pl de l'Abbatiale, entrance via tourist office; 📞02 40 78 73 88; w abbatialedeas.fr; ⏰ as tourist office, see opposite; €5/3/free adult/under 19s/under 6s) More than 20,000 visitors flock each year to this ancient abbey church, built in AD815 by monks from St Philbert's Abbey on Noirmoutier (page 61) to preserve the relics of their founder (known also as Philibert) from repeated Norman invasions. Though continuing raids by the Norsemen on Deas (as this settlement was then called) meant that the saint's remains had to be carried eastward again in 846 for safety as far as Tournus in Burgundy (where they are venerated to this day), you can still see Philbert's empty marble sarcophagus in the crypt. The chunky columns of the church's interior are built from alternating bands of white stone and warm brick, creating a surprising chequerboard effect. Concerts, theatrical performances and exhibitions are held in the church during the summer; a medicinal garden has been laid out behind it with signs that provide information on the many plants that are present. There are plenty of explanations in French at the site, but a rather meagre leaflet for English-speakers.

Base de Loisirs (Av de Nantes; ⏰ 2nd week Jul–end Aug 14.00–19.00 daily) As the lake itself is strictly off-limits for swimmers, water-lovers can try this artificial alternative, where bathing *is* permitted during the summer months. Complete with beach, barbecue facilities and various children's activities (beach soccer, volleyball, etc).

Observatoire du Clocher (St-Lumine-de-Coutais, 8km northwest of St-Philbert; €2/1 adult/child) Strictly for the fittest, the church tower of St-Lumine-de-Coutais affords a view of the lake and its surrounding area. The climb of 158 steps involves some near-vertical ladders, and you should avoid passing the bell chamber on the quarter hours! Charmingly, the four bells, dating as far back as 1856, are called – in descending size order – Henriette, Marie, Marguerite and Rosalie. Stone steps give way first to wooden ones, followed by two sets of almost unbelievably steep metal ladders. From the top, the lake is surprisingly distant, the wind often strong. The key can be obtained from the *mairie*…or the *boulangerie*. Or, sometimes from the Cheval Mallet café, opposite the church.

MACHECOUL Dominated by the twin spires of its 19th-century church, the attractive market town of Machecoul nestles on the edge of the Marais Breton, near the border of the Vendée and Loire-Atlantique. At the start of the Vendée Wars, Machecoul saw one of the first risings against the Republicans, on 11 March 1793, when 3,000 Vendeans massacred those whose sympathies lay with the new régime (page 12). Today, the town is thankfully quiet – especially on Mondays – but livens up a level for the enjoyable Wednesday market. Local specialities to try and buy from there include *machecoulais* cheese and other dairy products from Fromagerie

Beillevaire, and *mâche* (corn salad). The town is also renowned for *muguet* (lily-of-the-valley), a traditional French gift which is presented on 1 May.

The jagged silhouette of a ruined castle that once belonged to the sadistic Gilles de Rais, or Bluebeard (page 177), can be glimpsed among the trees bordering the old Rue de Nantes. The locals use its sinister connections to the past as the subject of medieval dinners in May and for an excellent week of son et lumière shows acted out against the chateau ruins in late July.

Rue du Marché, leading from the picturesque market hall, is lined with interesting shops; the tourist office can advise on local footpaths and cycle trails, riding and fishing, canoeing at nearby St-Même-le-Tenu, and on wine producers to visit in the surrounding Pays de Retz.

Try and make a trip around the marshes to the west by car, bike, canoe or on foot (routes are available on the tourist office website and range from 2.8km to 11km); it's particularly beautiful towards sunset, when herons flap languidly across the landscape and keen-eyed hawks hover above smaller, unsuspecting wildlife on the ground.

Tourist information
Office de Tourisme 14 Pl des Halles; `\`02 40 31 42 87; w sudretzatlantique-tourisme.fr; ⊕ Oct–Mar 09.00–12.30 & 14.00–17.00 Tue, Wed & Fri, 09.00–12.30 Sat; Apr–May 09.00–12.30 & 14.00–17.30 Tue–Fri, 09.00–12.30 Sat; Jun–Sep 09.00–12.30 & 14.00–17.30 Tue–Sat; Jul–Aug 09.00–12.30 & 14.00–17.30 Mon–Sat, 09.00–12.30 Sun & hols

✖ Where to eat and drink
Machecoul offers its visitors half a dozen dining choices in its town centre, mainly around the Rue du Marché and its side streets.

Chez Fred 1 Rue de Brie Serrant; `\` 09 55 44 33 20; ⊕ 07.30–10.00 & noon–14.00 Mon–Fri. Set up by the owners of the now closed Coelho Resto of the same address, this is a charming little establishment that serves simple French b/fasts & lunches at a very affordable price. €€

What to see and do
Château de Machecoul (Av du Château; `\`02 40 78 50 42; w chateaudemachecoul. over-blog.com; ⊕ by guided visit Jul–mid-Sep 16.00 Wed only (meet in front of gate); €10/free adult/under 15s) In summer it is possible to tour the town's castle ruins, preceded by a talk and slide show giving details of its history. Constructed in the 13th century to protect the frontiers of Brittany, it became the property of the notorious Gilles de Rais during the Hundred Years War, before being destroyed on the orders of King Louis XI. It was rebuilt in 1490, fortified in the 16th century, then served time as a prison during the Vendée Wars before being reduced to its present rather piteous state in 1793.

St-Étienne-de-Mer-Morte (10km southeast of Machecoul) In this picturesque village ('St Steven of the Dead Sea'), bypass the church and look at a much-older, free-standing bell tower with a pointed spire, the last remnant of its 12th-century predecessor. This is the remains of an ancient church into which stormed Gilles de Rais on Whit Sunday 1440, at the head of a band of men. In the middle of High Mass, he seized Jean le Ferron, one of the congregation, and dragged him to his castle at nearby Machecoul. (A bronze plaque commemorates this event.) For this act of sacrilege, Gilles de Rais was later arrested and taken to Nantes, where he at last confessed to his many horrible crimes before he was hanged on 26 October 1440. His body was then burned at the stake.

VILLENEUVE-EN-RETZ This large village – shown on older maps as Bourgneuf-en-Retz – lies 33km southeast of the St-Nazaire bridge and just inland from the Bay of Bourgneuf. Its muddy seabed is an excellent habitat for shellfish – particularly oysters which are raised here in large numbers. Of course, shellfish attract birds and if you make your way 2km west towards the shore, beyond the quaint little Port du Collet you can watch thousands of egrets and other waders moving inshore poking in the mud for choice morsels as the tide rises. For some poking around of your own, market days fall here on Tuesdays and Saturdays.

Tourist information

Mairie Pl de la Mairie; ☏ 02 40 21 40 07; w pornic.com; ⏰ Jan–Apr & Oct–Dec 09.30–12.30 & 13.30–17.30 Tue–Wed & Fri, 09.30–12.30 Thu, 09.00–13.00 Sat; Apr–May & Sep 09.30–12.30 & 14.30–18.00 Tue–Sat; Jul–Aug 09.30–13.00 & 15.00–18.30 Mon–Sat, 10.00–13.00 Sun

Where to eat and drink

La Bourrine 5 Chemin de la Culée; ☏ 02 40 21 40 69; w restaurant-labourrine.com; ⏰ Jul–Aug noon–14.00 & 19.00–21.00 daily, other months closed Mon & Sun eves. Seafood & marshland specialities in a 17th-century building. €€€

What to see and do

Musée du Pays de Retz (6 Rue des Moines; ☏ 02 40 21 40 83; w museedupaysderetz.fr; ⏰ Jul–Aug 15.00–19.00 daily, Apr–Jun & Sep–Oct 14.30–18.30 Tue–Sun; €7/4/3/free adult/students & disabled & under 18s/under 13s/under 6s) Housed in an 18th-century convent building opposite the church, this fascinating museum shows the history of the entire area from the River Loire to the border with the Vendée. Displays include fossils and folk traditions, salt production and shopping, plus Neolithic stones, local costumes (including headdresses) and some typical room-settings. A good video is shown, in French, on the region, and excellent English notes on the collection are available on request.

Table d'orientation (St-Cyr-en-Retz, 4km southeast of Villeneuve) Even from its paltry 34m height, the ridge above St-Cyr-en-Retz offers a beautiful panorama of the Machecoul marshes. An attractive ceramic orientation table identifies the various landscape features. Turn north off the D13, and follow '*point de vue*' signs.

LES MOUTIERS-EN-RETZ Some intriguing ecclesiastical features may be found in the leafy centre of this appealing old village, 4km northwest of Villeneuve. Les Moutiers' curious *lanterne des morts* was built around the same time as the Vikings departed the nearby village of Prigny, in AD938. The church dates from the 11th century.

On the beach at low tide, locals root among the rockpools or push giant shrimping nets through the shallows. Others retreat to quaint, spider-legged *pêcheries*, the wooden huts on stilts that are strung along the coast from Villeneuve to St-Nazaire. Rather in the same way as the UK's pigeon lofts or allotment sheds, these isolated structures provide an escape for people – a place offering licence to sit and dream, away from the obligations of home. As the tide rises, the occupants let the large square nets down into the water, hoping to winch them back up loaded with mullet, plaice and other small fish to take home for supper.

Some 3km northwest of Les Moutiers, the little family resort of La Bernerie-en-Retz has a sandy beach with the added attraction of a captive sea-water pool, so that children can bathe whatever the state of the tide.

Tourist information

Office de Tourisme 14 Pl de l'Église Madame; 📞02 40 82 74 00; w pornic.com; 🕑 Jan–Apr & Oct–Dec 09.30–12.30 & 13.30–17.30 Tue–Wed & Fri, 09.30–12.30 Thu, 09.00–13.00 Sat; Apr–May & Sep 09.30–12.30 & 14.30–18.00 Tue–Sat; Jul–Aug 09.30–13.00 & 15.00–18.30 Mon–Sat, 10.00–13.00 Sun (when closed, try the mairie next door)

✘ Where to eat and drink
You'll find most of Les Moutiers' restaurants in the main square by the church.

La Fraiseraie 2 Rue Jean-du-Plessis, La Bernerie-en-Retz, 3km north of Les Moutiers; 📞02 40 64 64 82. Delicious strawberry sorbet, jams & liqueurs made from locally grown fruit, plus excellent ice creams in myriad flavours. Look out for branches in other towns. €

What to see and do

Église St-Pierre (Pl. de l'Église) In the cool interior of Les Moutiers church, a handsome model sailing ship hangs below a wooden ceiling shaped like the upturned hull of a boat. Insert a €1 coin in the box by the pulpit to illuminate the huge 17th-century altarpiece.

In the shady square outside the church stands a strange 7m stone column dating from the 11th century, a rare structure known as a ***lanterne des morts*** (lantern of the dead). Although there are around 100 of these left in France, this is the only one still in use. Whenever a death occurs in the parish, a lamp (electric today, of course) is lit inside; the light glows through the slit windows day and night until the burial has taken place. Its purpose? To guide the dead into the afterworld.

Chapelle de Prigny (Route de l'Abbaye; 🕑 guided tours: Jul–Aug 14.00–18.00 Wed; free) Guided tours are given of this tiny 11th-century chapel, just east of the D13. Built in primitive Romanesque style, it has some surprisingly colourful Baroque altarpieces, and a pretty slate-roofed bell tower added by the Knights Templar as a lookout point around the 13th century. Classical concerts take place here in the summer on Wednesday evenings.

PORNIC Starting with its very name, there is a real Breton flavour to this chic seaside resort full of narrow lanes and steep steps, once a favourite of Gustave Flaubert, George Sand and other 19th-century literary luminaries. Some 18km south of the St-Nazaire bridge, Pornic has a rocky coastline dominated by a fairy-tale castle with pointed slate roof, whose prettiness belies the fact that it once belonged to Gilles de Rais (page 177). Pornic's regular market unfolds year-round on Thursday and Sunday mornings in the Place des Halles. For foodies doing some shopping, look out for Curé Nantais cheese and locally brewed Brigantine beer; for a souvenir or gift, try some Pornic pottery, produced in the town for more than 70 years.

On Tuesday and Friday evenings in July and August, Les Estivales festival of street theatre makes the town centre echo to the sounds of music and laughter – programme details are available from the tourist office.

The clifftop Sentier des Douaniers (Customs Path), on either side of town, provides fantastic views over the sea. The sandiest beach is the Plage de la Noëveillard, just beyond the marina. Further west, some exquisite villas look over the sea in the smart Ste-Marie district.

West of Pornic, 12km away, the village of Préfailles has much charm. France's yachting icon, the late Éric Tabarly spent his childhood holidays here, in a villa on the street that now bears his name; it has quaint shops, an iron-rich spring, and an interesting visitor centre in the former semaphore building, from which messages could be passed between ship and shore in the days before wireless telegraphy.

Tourist information
Office de Tourisme Pl de la Gare; 02 40 82 04 40; w pornic.com; Jan–Apr & Sep–Dec 09.30–12.30 & 13.30–17.30 Mon–Wed & Fri–Sat, 09.30–12.30 Thu; Apr–early Jul 09.30–12.30 & 14.00–18.00 Mon–Sat, 10.30–13.00 & 15.00–17.30 Sun & hols; Jul–Aug 09.30–19.00 Mon–Sat, 10.00–13.00 & 14.00–18.30 Sun & hols

Where to stay
Une Escale à Pornic (5 rooms) 2 bis Rue des Alisiers; 02 40 21 91 31; e escaleapornic@ orange.fr; w escale-a-pornic.com. Pornic's hotels are acceptable but unexceptional. However, just outside town, this B&B has a pool, warm welcome & b/fast inc. €€€

Where to eat and drink
Pornic is not short of restaurants, though in August booking is advisable. Most of the choices cluster around the waterside, in particular along the Quai Leray, which occupies the north bank of the estuary.

L'Alplaya 56 Av de la Convention, Tharon-Plage, 8km northwest of Pornic; 02 40 64 90 06; noon–14.00 Tue–Thu & Sun, noon–14.00 & 19.00–21.00 Fri–Sat. This smart place near the beach has taken over from the hugely popular Le Belem that had run in the same location for 33 years previously. The new owners have maintained the high standards & offer fresh, homemade local cuisine with a touch of the Savoyard. €€€€

Le Retz 12 Rue de la Marine; 02 40 82 19 78; w leretz.com; noon–13.30 & 19.00–21.30 Tue–Wed & Fri–Sat, noon–13.30 Sun & Thu. Nearly always full – so book in advance; everything from a reasonable dish of the day to a monstrously extravagant seafood platter for 2, which must be pre-ordered. Central location. €€€
La Fraiseraie Pl du Petit-Nice; 02 40 82 49 51. Delicious ice creams, plus jams, syrups & liqueurs from a popular kiosk near the castle. €

Sports and activities
Golf de Pornic Av Scalby-Newby, Ste-Marie-de-la-Mer, 2km northwest of Pornic; 02 40 82 06 69; w bluegreen.com. Established for more than 100 years, an attractive 18-hole course, over 6,000m off medal tees. Lessons, driving range & clubhouse restaurant. Price for 18 holes: €75, though sometimes discounted & packages/passes available.

What to see and do
Faïencerie de Pornic (Rue de la Faïencerie, west of Pornic town centre; 02 51 74 19 10; w faiencerie-pornic.fr; mid-Jul–end Aug 10.00–12.30 & 14.00–18.30 Mon–Sat, Jan 10.00–12.30 & 14.00–17.00 Tue–Sat, other months 10.00–12.30 & 14.00–18.00 Mon–Sat) Inside this excellent factory shop you can pick up half-price bargains in some of France's favourite pottery designs. Best known around here are the popular 'Petit-Breton' bowls, with names inscribed, launched in the late 1940s. To date, they have sold more than 18 million units! Look for the ingeniously designed circular plates with painted numbers around the edge to help you fairly divide slices of pizza or gâteau among different amounts of people. There's a small 'museum' of designs from all over France. The factory produces 400,000 pieces of pottery a year and offers 45-minute guided tours on Thursday afternoons (14.30 with an additional tour at 15.00 in the summer, numbers limited & booking advisable; €5/3/free adult/under16s/under 7s).

Cimetière Anglais (Pl Joseph-Girard) Pornic's Commonwealth (not English) war cemetery – immaculately maintained by the gardeners of the Commonwealth War Graves Commission – holds 399 graves, mostly from those who lost their lives in June 1944, in the sinking of the *Lancastria* (page 238). It is on the north side of the river, on higher ground, north of the railway station.

Dolmens Well signposted among the villas to the west of Pornic is the Dolmen (Tumulus) des Mousseaux, an impressive stone funeral chamber thought to date from 3500BC. On the southeast side of town stands the Dolmen de la Joselière, where walkers can also enjoy a fantastic view over the Bay of Bourgneuf.

Pornic-Aventure (Chemin des Trois-Croix, Le Val St-Martin, east of Pornic; m 06 16 05 55 36; w pornic-aventure.com; ⊕ Jul–Aug 10.00–20.00 daily, days & times vary in other months, consult website for details; €25/23/20/15/free adult/under 16s/under 12s/under 8s/under 4s) The buzzing and whining of 1,500m zip-wires is all around in this fantastic family tree-top adventure park, spread across 9ha of land with nine different courses. Kids and adults zoom with great aplomb across lakes, and negotiate wobbly ladders, climbing nets and even an aerial bike and a high-wire skateboard between trees. It's all highly disciplined, yet huge fun.

Exposition Cerfs-Volants (Grand Bazar, 31 Grande Rue, Préfailles, 10km northwest of Pornic; ☏ 02 40 21 61 22; ⊕ 08.00–noon & 13.30–17.30 Mon–Wed & Thu, 08.00–noon & 13.30–16.30 Fri, 08.00–noon Sat; free). Dangling from the ceiling of a century-old general store in the tranquil resort of Préfailles is a collection of around 30 historic kites (*cerfs-volants*), discovered in an old trunk in the attic by this quirky shop's proprietor in 1990. They include hundred-year-old examples that carried advertisements, cameras, and wireless and meteorological equipment. One, dating from 1912, is called the 'Roi des Airs' (King of the Air), perhaps unsurprising as it can reach 2,800m in height! Occasionally, the kites go 'on tour', but otherwise are around all year for viewing. Look among the fish hooks, pottery, stationery and household items on sale beneath them, for modern kites to buy and fly on the headlands nearby.

Sémaphore de la Pointe St-Gildas (Pointe St-Gildas, 12km northwest of Pornic; ☏ 02 40 21 01 21; w pornicagglo.fr/lieu/semaphore; ⊕ Apr–Jun & Sep 10.00–13.00 & 14.30–18.00 Wed–Mon, Jul–Aug 10.00–13.00 & 14.30–19.00 daily, Oct 14.30–17.30 Wed–Sun; €4.50/3.50/free adult/under 18s/under 7s) This quaint little building, dating from 1938, stands on the coast surrounded by large, colourful buoys and wind-twisted bushes. On its three floors, you can learn the intricacies of the coastal semaphore system, a six-armed mast set on the roof of the building used as a method of ship-to-shore signalling before the days of GPS and radar. The system was perfected by the French, who developed a series of coded sentences relating to the position of the arms, so quite detailed messages could be passed quickly.

The treacherous approaches to the Loire made many wrecks, including the English warship HMS *Maidstone*, sunk in 1747. You can see more than 250 of their locations on a chart, and a few relics from some of the vessels. Other maritime disasters off the coast here included the sinking of the French warship *Juste* in 1759, the *St-Philibert* pleasure steamer in 1931 with the loss of almost 450 lives, and the troop-laden Allied merchant ship *Lancastria* in 1940 (page 238). Arm yourself with the English-language leaflet from the ticket office as, considering that many wrecks were British, there are not too many explanations in English.

There is a film and a lot more information on the operation of lighthouses too, and a rare chance for a close-up look at the glass lens developed in 1823 by Augustin Fresnel. Better than mirrors, this technique refracted light and made lighthouses 4.5 million times more powerful than hitherto; the system was in use until the mid 20th century. Fresnel also invented a way of rotating the light smoothly, floating the equipment on a bed of mercury. Up on the first floor you can play with a model semaphore; on the top floor there is a panoramic view over the sea from a windswept walkway.

Don't miss the large concrete German lookout posts on the coast path here, redundant but still gazing blindly out to sea. A series of panels explains their history.

ST-PÈRE-EN-RETZ It all seems pretty quiet today, but back in Roman times this little town was hugely important, with almost all the roads across the rural Pays de Retz seeming to converge here. It was once formed of two parishes: St-Père and Ste-Opportune. Although the latter was merged after the Revolution, its name still often pops up in the names of local associations. Vestiges of even earlier times can be discovered – there are a surprising number of Neolithic stones scattered in the surrounding countryside. Markets on Sunday morning and every other Tuesday imbue the sleepy village with a bit of activity.

Tourist information
Mairie Pl de la Mairie; ☏ 02 40 21 70 29; w saintpereenretz.fr; ⏱ 09.00–noon & 14.00–17.00 Mon–Fri

What to see and do
Maison du Lavoir (Rue de Pornic; ☏ 02 40 21 83 45, 02 40 21 74 46; w en.saint-brevin.com/the-wash-house-museum.html; ⏱ Jul–Sep 14.30–18.30 daily, outside of these months visits can be made by reservation; €6/free adult/under 13s, for this & the Conservatoire des Vieux Métiers) Alongside a pretty, restored *lavoir*, or washing place, still in use until the 1960s, set among gardens on the River Grésilon, is a museum about the life of washerwomen and laundresses. On a wall beside the *lavoir*, some notices document the 1871 meetings of the Parish Council as they identified the need for this facility, set up a committee and then finally approved its construction for 1,500 francs. Rather oddly, a big notice announces the hours during which the site is *closed,* rather than open.

Conservatoire des Vieux Métiers (Chemin Ste-Opportune; ⏱ contact details & opening times as Maison du Lavoir) You cannot imagine how many types of business were carried out in and around the village. In this large barn, off the main street, you can see some of the fruits of their labour: carts, barrels, clogs, bricks and harnesses as well as souvenirs of World Wars I and II.

Monument Commémoratif de la Poche Sud (On the south side of La Sicaudais, 8km southeast of St-Père) An imposing grey monument marks the southern limit of the 25km-radius Poche de St-Nazaire, the area to which 30,000 Germans withdrew in the summer of 1944 with orders to fight to the death to hold it. While the rest of France was progressively liberated by the Allies, these German-held 'pockets' (as well as St-Nazaire, there were others at Dunkerque, Lorient and La Rochelle) were left until the end of the war. Some 130,000 civilians were stuck in the area, too. This memorial is dedicated

9

to residents and Resistance members of the Pays de Retz who lost their lives during World War II.

Neolithic stones (To the west of the D5, 4km southeast of St-Père) There is a wealth of ancient stones scattered through the Pays de Retz, with quite a concentration between St-Père and Chauvé. Armed with a good map, set out to track down the menhirs du Chevanou, de la Pierre Lematz and des Platennes.

Forêt de Princé (On the D266/D66, 16km southeast of St-Père-en-Retz) This pretty, forested area hides some strange memories and traditions. At least three stone crosses can be discovered at different locations; one – the Croix des Vendéens – commemorates some 2,000 people massacred in these woods between 1793 and 1796, during the Vendée Wars (page 9). Legend has it that anyone who walks seven times around the Pierre-Levée menhir on a moonless night, at the eastern edge of the forest, will glimpse Hell. During the 15th century, Hell would almost certainly have been glimpsed by the many children from the surrounding area who died at the hands of the evil Gilles de Rais (page 177) at one of his castles just north of Chéméré.

ST-BREVIN-LES-PINS With mini-golf and casino, cycle hire and quad biking, street entertainment and forest walks, kitesurfing, sand yachting, and tennis, there is something for all ages and tastes at St-Brevin besides the obvious attractions of its 8km of sand. No wonder that the resort is the most popular holiday centre on this part of the coast. Just 2km south of the St-Nazaire bridge, St-Brevin is divided into two districts: a northern part full of shady pine trees, and the more open, southwest-facing beach area known as St-Brevin-l'Océan.

If you are wondering about the purpose of the bizarre-looking structures on stilts, with square fishing nets dangling from long poles, these are fishing cabins whose owners visit to lower the nets as the tide rises, in the hope of winching up something tasty for supper.

The fast road sweeping down from the St-Nazaire bridge towards the Vendée links many seaside resorts. Fluttering flags along its length officially proclaim it to holidaymakers as the Route Bleue, or 'Blue Route'. South of St-Brevin-l'Océan, a wonderful smell of baking tells you that you are level with St-Michel-Chef-Chef, the home of the St-Michel biscuit factory, whose products you will find laid out on the shelves of every supermarket. South of St-Michel lies Tharon-Plage, with another 8km stretch of sand and some fine examples of seaside architecture.

Just off Mindin, at the mouth of the River Loire, occurred one of the greatest maritime disasters in history. At least 3,000 Allied troops and civilians (some estimates put the number as high as 6,000) were drowned on 17 June 1940 when the *Lancastria*, a merchant ship evacuating them to Britain following the fall of France, was sunk by enemy bombing in just 24 minutes. (For comparison, the number that perished on the *Titanic* was 1,517.) Commonwealth War Graves Commission headstones in many cemeteries along the coast mark the places where the *Lancastria* victims were washed ashore during the ensuing months and, later, buried.

On a lighter note, the town hosts an international firework festival (Festival Pyrotechnique) each August, with teams judged by a jury. Markets take place on Thursdays and Sundays, in the Place Baslé, and on Saturdays on the Avenue Roosevelt.

Tourist information

Office de Tourisme 10 Rue de l'Église; ☎ 02 40 27 24 32; w saint-brevin.com; ⊕ Jul–Aug 09.30–13.00 & 14.00–19.00 Mon–Sat, 10.00–13.00 Sun & hols; Apr–Jun & Sep–Oct 09.30–12.30 & 14.00–18.00 Mon–Fri; Nov–Mar 09.00–12.30 & 14.00–17.30 Mon–Sat

Where to eat and drink
Avenue de Mindin, the road that runs parallel to the seafront, but two blocks inland, is home to a smattering of a dozen or so restaurants. Coastal options in town are a bit more limited.

La Cuisine d'Apolline / La Cabane des Pins Bd Padioleau (seafront); m 06 71 00 71 26; ⊕ 10.00–23.00 daily. A fun beachside restaurant & bar with tables overlooking the sea. Eat in or else take your burgers, waffles or ice cream back to your spot on the sands. €€

Shopping

Les Délices de St-Michel 8 Rue du Chevecier, St-Michel-Chef-Chef, 8km south of St-Brevin; ☎ 02 51 74 75 44; w stmichel.fr; ⊕ 09.30–12.30 & 14.00–19.00 Mon–Sat, 09.30–12.30 Sun. Follow your nose to the boutique of the St-Michel biscuit factory, whose products (galettes, *madeleines*, etc) & their distinctive chicken motif will be familiar to those who have browsed the biscuit aisle of any French supermarket.

What to see and do

Musée de la Marine (Fort de Mindin, Pl Bougainville, Mindin, 2.5km north of St-Brevin; ☎ 02 40 27 24 32; w museemarinemindin.fr; ⊕ May 14.30–19.00 Fri–Sun, Jun 14.45–19.00 Tue–Sun, Jul 14.15–19.15 Mon–Fri & Sun, Sep 14.15–19.00 Tue–Sun; €7/5/free adult/under 17s/under 13s) Inside a 19th-century fort almost under the south approach road to the St-Nazaire bridge is an interesting museum of the sea. Within its solid stone walls, there are just a few huge model ships which form the permanent exhibition, but an additional maritime-themed exhibition is put on which differs from year to year. It might be centred around steamships, or the history of sailing or the slave trade that enriched the city of Nantes in the 18th century, or perhaps even boating novelties. Outside the museum, gardens have been planted to commemorate French explorer Louis Antoine de Bougainville, who sailed from here on 15 November 1766 on a three-year circumnavigation.

Once you've visited the museum, walk down to the beach directly in front of it to admire the **Serpent d'Océan**, a giant metal sculpture of a skeletal serpent nestling just offshore. All 130m of this monster's length is visible at low tide. It's the work of Huang Yong Ping and is one of the many art installations which decorate the Loire Estuary between Nantes and the ocean.

Patrimoine Militaire du Pointeau (Av du Maréchal Foch, Le Pointeau, 2km southwest of St-Brevin) The headland overlooking the approaches to the River Loire was a strategic point for the occupying Germans during World War II. A group of blockhouses on the dunes still bears witness to those times; the coastal footpath has ten panels explaining the different types and uses.

Forêt de la Pierre Attelée (5km southwest of St-Brevin-les-Pins) An unspoiled area of pine and holm-oak forest just inland from the Plage de la Roussellerie, at the southern end of the resort, that takes its name from a large menhir located on the south side. A farmer is said to have harnessed (*attelé*) his oxen to the stone and tried – but failed – to pull it out. The oxen mysteriously died within 12 months, and their owner a year later (so, don't even think about it). Paths are laid out to prevent walkers from trampling the fragile dunes, and no bikes or horses are permitted.

NORTHWARDS ACROSS THE ESTUARY

With 3km of bridge to cross to the north side of Loire Estuary, you'll have plenty of time for an aerial view – of the goods yards and cargo ships to the east and the city of St-Nazaire and its shipbuilding yards to the west – as you leave the Pays de Retz behind you.

ST-NAZAIRE As you cross the Loire heading north, from the Pays de Retz over the Pont de St-Nazaire bridge, the rooftops below change from rounded Roman tiles, with their Mediterranean feel, to the more business-like slate of Brittany. As an important U-Boat port during World War II, St-Nazaire suffered so much Allied bombing that 85% of its buildings were flattened. Surely we can forgive the town, then, for lacking any quaint, old-world charm? The heavily fortified German submarine base here was the target of an audacious Anglo-Canadian commando raid, codenamed Operation Chariot, on 28 March 1942. The destroyer HMS *Campbeltown*, crammed with explosives, was rammed into the gates of the huge lock and blown up, disabling the lock for the remainder of the war. Among the awards made to participants were five Victoria Crosses; those who lost their lives are buried in the CWGC cemetery at La Baule-Escoublac (page 246).

After the D-Day landings in Normandy, in June 1944, many German troops in Brittany continued to hold out in St-Nazaire as well as other large ports. The Allies chose to leave these 'pockets' while they continued their advance on other fronts, and so St-Nazaire was not liberated until 11 May 1945, three days after VE Day.

Today entirely rebuilt, St-Nazaire has a bright, modern face…but what to do with the ugly concrete remains of the German submarine pens? Turn them into a venue for first-class tourist attractions, naturally – and that is exactly what the town has done. As a result, you can clamber onto a real submarine, then trade up to take a voyage on a simulated ocean liner.

The main shopping centre is focused on the semi-pedestrianised Avenue de la République and on nearby Rue de la Paix. The Place du Commerce is the venue for the town's principal market, on Tuesday, Friday and Sunday.

The shipbuilding company that built such great ocean liners as the *Normandie* (in 1935), the *France* (1962), the *Queen Mary 2* (2003), and now the massive *Symphony of the Seas* (2018) still dominates the northern shore of the estuary. Now nationalised, though perhaps still prey to a foreign takeover, it reportedly has enough work to keep thousands employed for a few more years.

To the west, the town claims to have at least 20 beaches, starting from just south of the Escal'Atlantic centre (page 242) and stretching westwards to include that of St-Marc-sur-Mer, the setting for the Jacques Tati film *Monsieur Hulot's Holiday*.

St-Nazaire has also featured in literature, as the backdrop to Tintin's adventure *The Seven Crystal Balls*. The town's Tintin fans have installed comic-strip panels at certain points to remind you where the fictional boy detective and his faithful dog Snowy are reputed to have passed.

The port's visitor centre also offers bus and walking tours of the shipyards (*chantiers navals*) where the vast liners are built, and even visits to l'Aérospatiale where parts of the Airbus plane are assembled. (These tours – which can be in English during July and August – need to be booked well in advance, and you have to show a passport for the Airbus visit.) In summer there are also night-time boat trips around the docks, past the majestic cranes and artistically illuminated quays.

A decent walk along the coast path would take you to the nearby village of St Marc-sur-Mer, from where the U3 bus line will return you to the city centre. For drivers, take care with the town's bus lanes, which appear both on your left and right: slightly disconcerting at times.

Tourist information

Office de Tourisme Bd de la Légion d'Honneur; ☏02 40 22 40 65; w saint-nazaire-tourisme. com; ⏲ Jul–Aug 09.30–18.30, Jun & Sep

09.30–12.30 & 13.30–18.00 daily, for other months see website

Where to stay

Chambres d'Hôte St-Nazaire La Milonga (5 rooms) 52 Rue Jules Verne, Trignac; ☏02 40 42 65 37; e lamilongabb@gmail.com. This *chambre d'hôte* is a bit out of town, but still a good choice. Family & trpl rooms available. Bike-friendly, free parking, free Wi-Fi, shared kitchen & garden. B/fast inc; very good value. €€

B&B Hotel St-Nazaire (83 rooms) 5 Rue de Troènes; ☏08 92 23 37 73; w hotel-bb.com. Just west of town, 10mins from the train station & on a bus route, with free Wi-Fi & abundant parking. A modern, very budget-friendly place, spick & span, devoid of any character, but nice & easy if you are just looking for a bed. The excellent-value buffet b/fast includes local & organic products. €

Where to eat and drink

Le France Plage de Monsieur Hulot, St-Marc-sur-Mer, 11km southwest of St-Nazaire; ☏02 40 91 96 13; ⏲ noon–14.00 Mon–Thu, noon–14.00 & 19.00–22.00 Fri, noon–15.00 & 19.00–22.00 Sat, noon–15.00 Sun. Popular with locals, a beach bar & restaurant with wooden terrace right down on the sands. Tuck in to seafood, fish & grills. Situated directly beneath the statue of Monsieur Hulot. €€€

Restaurant le 16 16 Bd de Verdun; ☏02 40 15 41 89; w restaurant-le-16.fr; ⏲ lunch (from

noon) & evenings (from 19.15) Tue–Sat. Opposite the ocean, with choice of menus. A few outside tables, & a decorative & tasty cuisine. €€€
Restaurant Panem 10 Av Général de Gaulle; ☏02 40 22 59 58; ⏲ noon–14.00 & 19.00–22.00 Tue–Thu, noon–14.00 & 19.00–22.30 Fri–Sat, noon–14.00 Sun. A well-established & welcoming place, with English-speaking host. Pleasant terrace for sunny days, high-quality food. €€€

What to see and do

***Visite du Sous-marin* Espadon** (Av de la Forme-Écluse; ☏02 28 54 06 40; w saint-nazaire-tourisme.uk; ⏲ see website for calendar of opening hours, closed last 3 weeks Jan & much of Nov–Dec; €12/10/6/free adult/students & scholars/under 18s/under 4s, combined tickets are cheaper, page 242) As you enter the concrete-roofed, German-built submarine dock that lies across the water from the Escal'Atlantic base, you cannot refrain from giving a shudder when you first glimpse the sinister silhouette of the 1950s-built French submarine *Espadon* ('swordfish'). And if you get claustrophobic after 45 minutes on board, try imagining the feelings of those confined to the vessel for 45 *days* at a stretch. Thankfully never involved in any military skirmishes, this sub nevertheless covered a distance equivalent to 17 times around the world, before being 'retired'. Picking up an audio-guide, in English, at the admission desk, you step on board for a self-guided tour. (Virtual tours are also available for those with disabilities that prevent them from going onboard.) Up and down narrow companionways and steep ladders, you listen to descriptions of life aboard, when there were bunks for only two-thirds of the crew (the other third was on duty), and just two lavatories for the 65 men. Your visit on board ends in the missile chamber. Afterwards you can climb to a viewing platform (*'terrasse panoramique'*) on the top of the dock to look down on the Forme-Écluse Joubert, the large lock that was attacked by Allied commandos in 1942, and in more modern vein, admire the artwork of Felice Varini. To do this, you have to line up the red fragments painted on various buildings to see the whole of his picture, called the *Suite de Triangles*.

Escal'Atlantic: L'Aventure des Paquebots (Bd de la Légion d'Honneur; ℡02 28 54 06 40; w saint-nazaire-tourisme.uk; ⊕ see website for calendar of opening hours, closed last 3 weeks Jan & much of Nov–Dec; €15/13/7.50/free adult/student & scholar/under 18s/under 4s, combined tickets are cheaper, see above) *Paquebot* is the French for ocean liner and, as soon as you have climbed the gangway and entered the chic, wood-panelled foyer within Escal'Atlantic, you forget you are inside a massive, reinforced-concrete structure and feel you really have stepped aboard a luxurious 1930s floating palace. At times you emerge during your tour of corridors and cabins, saloons and engine room – all newly created inside the monolithic World War II building – to find yourself on 'deck', with the (fake) wind in your hair, (real) salt water lapping below and icebergs with polar bears passing by. You finish your tour with a wordless film that traces the decline of the transatlantic crossing market: by 1958, airline passengers were outnumbering those travelling by ship, and by 1974 the French crossings to the USA had ceased. After the film, the finale sees you returned to ground level in a surprising way. It takes a good hour and a half to see it all. English-language information panels accompany your visit, there are games to play – taking decisions as the imaginary captain of a liner – a café 'on board' and a gift shop.

Écomusée: Mémoire d'Estuaire (Av de St-Hubert; ℡02 28 54 06 40; w saint-nazaire-tourisme.uk; ⊕ see website for calendar of opening hours, closed last 3 weeks Jan & much of Nov–Dec; €4/3.60/2/free adult/students & scholars/under 14s/under 4s, combined tickets are cheaper, see above) After the submarine visit and the liner experience, the town's museum (near the submarine dock) is inevitably a bit of an anticlimax. There is information on St-Nazaire's important shipbuilding heritage, including some splendid model ships. (An unexpected British connection is that in 1860 the town's original shipyards were designed and built by Scott & Co of Greenock, Clydeside.) You learn, too, how skills were adapted in more modern times to embrace the aerospace industry as travellers' preferences changed. If you're interested in recent history, you can marvel at the photos of the city's post-war reconstruction. As in bomb-scarred British cities, many inhabitants lived for up to 30 years in 'temporary' prefabricated houses. An English-language leaflet is available and a few information panels are translated to English.

If you want to see how these massive boats are made nowadays, then you can visit Chantiers de l' Atlantique (1.6km north of the museum), the shipyard famous for the construction of legends such as *France, Queen Mary 2* and *Harmony of the Seas* (2hr guided tours in French can be booked at w saint-nazaire-tourisme.uk; English audio guides also available).

EOL Centre Éolien (2 Av de la Forme-Écluse; ✆ 02 28 54 06 40; w saint-nazaire-tourisme.uk; ⊕ see website for calendar of opening hours; €6/5/3/free adult/students & scholars/under 18s/under 4s, combined tickets are cheaper, see opposite) Touted as France's first ever tourist site dedicated to offshore wind power, this visitor centre celebrates the 80 wind turbines that have been installed off Guérande Beach, with the ability to meet the energy needs of 20% of the Loire-Atlantique. Visitors are taken on a journey from the first windmills to the 21st-century wind turbines. There are interactive exhibitions for the whole family to get involved with, such as static bikes that you can ride while learning how power is generated, quizzes on how much electricity is required to run different household items, and turbines that you can get to work with your own wind power.

Boat trips (Av de Saint-Hubert, near the Écomusée; w saint-nazaire-tourisme.uk/attractions-and-tours/discovery-cruises; ⊕ cruise times and prices vary, see website for details and bookings) There are five cruises to choose from, which last between 1.5 hours and 3 hours and run during the summer. The daytime cruises take you out to the wind turbines, across to Noirmoutier or down the Loire River. There is even a musical cruise where you can be serenaded by a band and learn about the history of St-Nazaire from a guide. The night-time cruise takes you out to the lighthouses. Commentary is in French.

La Plage de Monsieur Hulot (St-Marc-sur-Mer, 8km southwest of St-Nazaire) Devotees of Jacques Tati's classic 1953 film *Les Vacances de Monsieur Hulot* can have fun at St-Marc-sur-Mer trying to spot the locations used in the movie. Be prepared for a bit of walking: the village is incredibly busy on summer weekends, and parking can be a problem. The beachside Hôtel de la Plage has been given a lick of paint and is still in action, and a bronze statue of the gawky Monsieur Hulot now stands forever gazing down onto the sands, which have been renamed in his honour. Strangely, the French seem baffled by the British reverence for Tati's engaging fictional character – for really side-splitting entertainment, they much prefer Mr Bean!

Parc Naturel Régional de Brière (15km north of St-Nazaire; w parc-naturel-briere.com) North of St-Nazaire lies a marshy, secretive landscape of peat bog, wildfowl and thatched cottages. The prettiest spots in this 40,000ha national park are the village of Kerhinet on the west side of the reserve, and the Île de Fédrun on the east, both of which have cottage-museums open in summer, informing on different aspects of life in the marshes. Almost invisible from the road, Kerhinet is full of beautifully restored houses, some of which are now craft shops (after crossing the St-Nazaire bridge, take the direction of Guérande, and then turn off to St-André-des-Eaux; 5km after St-André, on the D47, look for a sign to Kerhinet, on the left). On the opposite side of the park, the Île de Fédrun is a small island lined with pretty, stone cottages, approached by a raised causeway across the marsh from St-Joachim (from the St-Nazaire bridge, take the Nantes direction, and turn off north at Montoir-de-Bretagne on to the D50). You can enjoy birdwatching for geese, ducks and kingfishers, or excursions in a traditional *chaland* (flat-bottomed boat) or by horse-drawn wagon. (Canoes, kayaks and other watercraft are not permitted here.) Boats can be hired through **Anthony Mahé** (La Chaussée Neuve, St-André-des-Eaux; ☏ 02 40 91 59 36; w decouvrir-la-briere.fr; ⊕ all year, but advanced booking is advisable; €18–35 according to number of passengers). Guided tours with French commentary are also possible.

LA BAULE AND THE PRESQU'ÎLE La Baule-Escoublac, to give it the correct name, owes its development from sandy semi-desert to elegant international resort to the arrival of the railway in 1879. Hotels and villas followed and a casino arrived after World War I. With the infrastructure in place, together with the natural advantage of its superb 9km crescent of beach – from Le Pouliguen in the west, with its pretty harbour, to child-friendly Pornichet in the east – it was no surprise that this resort west of St-Nazaire became one of the most glamorous destinations in France before the outbreak of World War II. For five years of the war itself, the town and surrounds were heavily occupied by the Germans and it was one of the last areas of France to see their departure. Today, modern apartment blocks and signs of mass tourism have somewhat marred La Baule's immediate seafront, and the resort has moved a fraction downmarket, but just a couple of blocks inland the elegant villas of days gone by still nestle among the pine woods. A mosaic of architectural styles reflects the diverse origins of their original owners: Parisians, Basques and those from further afield. And the resort's popularity is undimmed, with the 16,000 Baulois (as the inhabitants are known) joined by up to 135,000 visitors in peak season.

Avenue de Gaulle, linking the beach to the railway station, and Avenue Louis Lajarrige, are the principal shopping streets; live jazz is performed in the former each evening in July and August. Some of the town's other roads (there are no 'streets' here; only avenues) ramble in slightly eccentric directions, following the lines of paths in the grounds of the resort's original grand houses. Horseriding, sailing and golf are the chic pastimes on offer, along with sessions of pampering in the town's two thalassotherapy centres (sea-water treatment spas). La Baule's market is open from Tuesday to Sunday in the Place du Marché (where else?).

Pornichet, slightly more down to earth than its more famous neighbour, runs almost seamlessly into La Baule, which then borders on to Le Pouliguen, before the coast continues further west onto the *presqu'île* (peninsula) with Batz-sur-Mer and Le Croisic. The further west you go, the more Breton character the places exude, and when you see 'Bzh 44' painted on a wall or signpost, it's a reminder that at least a few people with spray-cans believe that Loire-Atlantique (département 44) should still be part of Brittany ('Breizh' in the Breton language) rather than of the less romantic Pays de la Loire region.

Tourist information

Office de Tourisme 8 Pl de la Victoire; ☏ 02 40 24 34 44; w en.labaule-guerande.com; ⊕ Apr–Jun & Sep 10.00–12.30 & 14.00–18.00 Mon–Sat, 10.00–13.00 & 15.00–17.00 Sun & hols; Jul–Aug 09.30–19.00 Mon–Sat, 10.00–13.00 & 14.00–19.00 Sun & hols; Oct–Mar 10.00–12.30 & 14.00–18.00 Tue–Wed & Fri–Sat. Audio-guides available for self-guided tours around town. Free Wi-Fi is available, here & at several places around town.

⌂ Where to stay

Villa Bettina (35 rooms) 5 Av Bettine; ☏ 02 40 60 23 93; w bettina-labaule.com. A few hundred metres from the beach, in a quiet area away from high-summer madness, an impressive-looking, brightly painted villa with its own restaurant, free Wi-Fi, table tennis & bike hire. Some rooms are in a separate building. Fully renovated in 2015, the

interior is bright & modern. Free on-street parking usually available outside. Good-value buffet b/fast, friendly owners. Restaurant & bar. **€€€€**

✖ Where to eat and drink

Le 14 Avenue 14 Av Pavie, La Baule; 📞02 40 60 09 21; **w** 14avenue-labaule.com; ⏱ 12.30–13.30 & 19.30–21.30 Wed–Thu, 12.30–13.30 & 19.30–22.00 Fri–Sat, 12.30–13.30 Sun. Wholeheartedly recommended for its delicious fish & seafood. No cheap meals here, but not many mediocre ones either from its shortish à la carte or more extensive blackboard choices. Booking advisable. **€€€€€**

Le Lénigo 11 Quai du Lénigo, Le Croisic, 8km west of La Baule; 📞02 40 23 00 31; ⏱ noon–14.15 & 19.00–21.00 Wed–Sun. Next door to good-value La Criée (see below), here you'll find more sophistication & inevitably more euros added to the price. A special-occasion place, strongly recommended by locals with money to spend. **€€€€€**

Café Jules 15 Quai Jules-Sandeau, Le Pouliguen, 5km southwest of La Baule; 📞02 40 42 31 79; ⏱ 10.00–23.00 daily. Trendy brasserie overlooking the harbour, at the west end of the bay. Mussels, oysters, fish & a few meat options, plus good-value, weekday lunch menus. A great quayside choice for coffee & people-watching, too. Limited children's menu. **€€€€**

La Criée 10 Quai du Lénigo, Le Croisic, 8km west of La Baule; 📞02 40 62 91 72; ⏱ closed Mon eve, Tue & Nov–Feb. La Criée ('The Shout') is the name

given to the wholesale fish market, referring to the noisy setting of prices that happens each morning. This is a great quayside restaurant, serving huge portions of seafood to throngs of contented customers. You can get cheaper elsewhere, but maybe not better value. **€€€**

Crêperie du Derwin [map, page 216] Le Derwin, off the D45 east of Batz-sur-Mer; 📞02 40 23 90 06; ⏱ noon–14.00 & 19.00–22.00 Wed–Mon during school hols, closed Nov–Mar. Seafront, though being slightly set back from the road it attracts mainly those 'in the know'. Serves mainly crêpes & seafood. No reservations. **€€**

Fleur de Sel [map, page 216] 42 Rue de la Chapelle, Kervalet, near Batz-sur-Mer, 7km west of La Baule; 📞02 40 23 90 73; **w** creperiefleurdesel. fr; ⏱ daily most of the year, closed Fri–Sun in winter, see website for full opening hours. Much-loved crêperie, a quaint little granite house in pretty salt-makers' village; delicious Breton-style snacks, crêpes, galettes & local cider. Low prices, too. No reservations, so turn up early. **€€**

Le Bidule 122 Av de Mazy, Pornichet; 📞02 40 61 03 54. In this lively Pornichet bar, all social classes & age groups gather for an aperitif or 2. Red or white Muscat is what's on offer: everyone who's anyone is there to drink it & have fun. Bring your own crisps! **€**

Shopping

Confiserie Manuel 2 Av du Général de Gaulle, La Baule; 📞02 40 60 20 66; ⏱ 09.30–13.00 & 14.30–23.00 daily. A legendary sweetshop, guaranteed to widen the eyes of young visitors.

This family business, handed down through the generations, is a true institution, famous for its lollipop-style niniches confectionery made to the same recipe since 1946.

Sports and activities

Golf International Barrière La Baule Route de St-Denac, St-André-des-Eaux, 7km northeast of La Baule; 📞02 40 60 46 18; **e** golfinterlabaule@ groupebarriere.com; **w** hotelsbarriere.com. There are 4 other courses in the area, but this one is the top of the range, with its 3 courses providing 45

holes in total. There is a restaurant, & lessons are available. €54–74 for 18 holes.

Golf de la Vigne Rue des Sports, Mesquer; 📞02 40 42 64 37; **w** golfmesquer.fr. Beginners might prefer to head to Mesquer, 15km north of La Baule, for the cheaper, more relaxed 9-hole course. €15.

What to see and do

Océarium du Croisic (Av de St-Goustan, Le Croisic, 8km west of La Baule; 📞02 40 23 02 44; **w** ocearium-croisic.fr; ⏱ see website for details; closed 3 weeks in Jan; €15.50/12.50/free adult/under 13s/under 3s) Allow 2 hours to visit this excellent modern aquarium that attracts 250,000 visitors each year and stands near the wild point beyond the picturesque fishing port of Le Croisic. There is a real will to make visitors understand more about the fish and shellfish they see on their plates. From 3cm-long lobsters and spotted skate the size of a €2 coin, you move on to scallops and turbots, and then to ghostly stingrays and Australian sharks cruising in deep tanks. Zones are divided into tropical, Atlantic, Pacific and Arctic; there are penguin feeding times to enjoy, and starfish in touch-tanks for some hands-on experiences. Finally, you walk through an amazing glass tunnel that gives the feeling of moving across the sea bed among eels, skate and glittering sea bass.

Musée des Marais Salants (Pl Adèle Pichon, Batz-sur-Mer; ✆ 02 40 23 82 79; w museedesmaraissalants.fr; ⏲ Jun & Sep 10.00–12.30 & 14.00–18.00 Tue–Sun, Jul–Aug 10.00–19.00 daily, Oct–May 10.00–12.30 & 14.00–17.00 Tue–Sun; €5/4/3/ free adult/seniors/under 27s & disabled/under 13s) Northwest of La Baule stretch endless sparkling salt marshes, producing the crystals sold as *sel de Guérande*. This museum takes you through the history of salt here, combining artefacts with modern technology to help you understand its importance to the region.

Le Grand Blockhaus (Allée Dervin, on the D45 coast road, between Batz-sur-Mer & Le Pouliguen; ✆ 02 40 23 88 29; w grand-blockhaus.com; ⏲ Feb–mid-Nov 10.00–19.00 daily; €9/6.50/free adult/under 13s/under 5s) Everyday items from toothbrushes to phrasebooks, lent by American, British, French and German war veterans, form part of the collection amassed in this fascinating place, west of La Baule. Inside an impregnable-looking World War II German artillery and observation post, transformed into a museum by two brothers between 1994 and 1997 and now set out over three levels, you can see dormitories as well as radio, weaponry and machine rooms; be prepared to climb a vertical ladder if you want a sentry's-eye view of the sea. An informative film is shown in the basement at 15 minute intervals. An English-language leaflet is also provided, and there are good explanations of the 1942 St-Nazaire Raid, plus details of the Poche de St-Nazaire, one of the German forces' last outposts in Europe, which was not liberated until 11 May 1945 – a year after the Normandy landings and three days after VE Day. The bizarre trompe-l'oeil windows on the west side were part of the wartime camouflage, designed to convince Allied reconnaissance planes that the blockhouse was merely a harmless seaside villa.

World War II cemeteries Allied and German war dead are buried in two immaculately tended graveyards. The white headstones provided by the Commonwealth War Graves Commission can be seen in the La Baule War Cemetery (marked on some maps as *Cimetière Anglais* – incorrectly, as there are Scots, Welsh, Irish, New Zealanders and others buried here), in a residential area of Escoublac, near the southeast corner of the town's airport. For the most part, these are victims either of the *Lancastria* sinking of June 1940 (page 238), or of the St-Nazaire Raid of March 1942 (page 240). There is a register of the graves and a visitor book to sign.

The 4,800 German troops who died in the Vendée, Loire-Atlantique and Maine-et-Loire are remembered in an even more sombre setting. At the Cimetière Militaire Allemand, on the north side of the D92, just to the east of Pornichet, and 5km southeast of La Baule, their names are marked on flat slabs set into the grass among weeping cedars.

Musée Aéronautique de la Presqu'île Côte d'Amour (Aérodrome de La Baule-Escoublac, 4km east of La Baule; ✆ 02 51 75 10 43; w mapica.org; ⏲ Jul–Aug

14.00–17.00 daily, Sep–Dec 14.00–17.00 Mon & Wed–Fri; free, though donations welcome) This collection of old aircraft, including rare biplanes, has been restored to flying condition – or is in the process of being so – by dedicated volunteers. Enthusiasts give guided tours of the static machines, and organise a couple of flying days a year (in spring and summer).

Tropicarium Bonsaï: Parcours Tropical (Route de Brédérac, near Pornichet railway station, 2km southeast of La Baule; m 07 50 06 79 08; w tropicarium-bonsai-la-baule.fr; ⏲ 09.00–noon & 14.00–18.00 Mon–Tue & Thu; €6/4/free adult/under 13s/under 4s) This bonsai specialist centre opens its greenhouse doors to the public each summer. Around 2,000 types of plant flourish in the 30°C temperatures, along with tarantulas, scorpions, turtles and giant (noisy) frogs. Outside, a garden of exotic plants increases in size each year.

Peninsula walk Le Pouliguen village is the start of the *presqu'île*, or peninsula, and locals enjoy taking to the coastal path to take in the sea air. It's easy to follow, waymarked, and if you're walking clockwise then the sea is always on your left. Even better, if you get tired, there are buses to return your weary legs back to base.

GUÉRANDE Sturdy stone ramparts still completely encircle this beautifully preserved medieval town, in the centre of the large *presqu'île* (peninsula), 20km west of St-Nazaire. Park outside the town walls before exploring the maze of picturesque streets full of restaurants, crêperies and shops, and the tall collegiate church with Romanesque decorations carved on its granite pillars. A colourful market fills the town centre on Wednesdays and Saturdays, and you can patrol the ramparts between April and October to survey whatever's happening down below.

Guérande's fortune was founded on the salt-producing industry at Saillé, just to the south. This business declined in the 19th century after Frenchman Nicolas Appert discovered that canning was a more convenient way of preserving food. However, salt-making is enjoying a revival, and today many *paludiers* are producing the famous *sel de Guérande* for the world's foodies. There are interesting establishments at Saillé (page 248) and at Batz (see opposite) that explain the salt industry and the way of life that grew up around it. Guérande tourist office has details of visits to working saltpans in the area. In May, the town holds a medieval festival, with street entertainment to the fore. Costumed locals enjoy dance, music, banquets and more.

Tourist information
Office de Tourisme Pl du Marché au Bois; ☎ 02 40 24 34 44; w labaule-guerande.com; ⏲ Jul–Aug 09.30–19.00 Mon–Sat, 10.00–13.00 & 14.00–19.00 Sun & hols, Sep 10.00–12.30 & 14.00–18.00 Mon–Sat, 10.00–13.00 & 15.00–17.00 Sun & hols, Nov–Apr 10.00–12.30 & 14.00–18.00 Tue–Wed & Fri–Sat. Guided visits of the town are occasionally organised.

Where to stay
La Guérandière (8 rooms) 5 Rue Vannetaise; ☎ 02 40 62 17 15; w guerandiere.com. In a gorgeous 19th-century house just inside the solid town walls, beautifully, classically furnished & with a warm welcome. Free parking & they'll lend you bikes to explore the marshlands nearby. Free Wi-Fi, coffee/tea-making facilities. €€€

Where to eat and drink
L'Agapé Bistrot Gourmand 11 Faubourg St Michel; ☎ 02 40 11 78 78; w lagapebistrot.com; ⏲ noon–13.15 Tue–Thu, noon–13.15 & 19.30–20.15 Fri–Sat. High-quality food, but not high

prices, given the calibre, freshness & decorative presentation. Pleasant ambience. €€€

Les Remp'arts 14 Bd du Nord; ☎ 02 40 24 90 69; ⏰ noon–14.00 & 19.00–21.00 Wed–Sat, noon–14.00 Sun. A long-established restaurant, serving good fish & traditional dishes, just outside the walls. €€€

Crêperie Roc Maria Rue du Vieux Marché aux Grains; ☎ 02 40 24 90 51; w hotel-creperie-rocmaria.com; ⏰ Apr–Aug lunch & dinner daily, other months vary, check website for details. Popular crêperie on small street in town centre – formerly a women's prison! Crêpes, galettes, plus salads & fish soup. €€

What to see and do

Musée du Pays de Guérande (Porte St-Michel; ☎ 02 28 55 05 05; w portesaintmichel.fr; ⏰ opening times vary each month – see website for details) The museum of local history is housed on three floors in one of the town's massive 15th-century gatehouses, so there are plenty of stone steps to climb. Rooms inside contain furniture of the area, including the enclosed beds known as *lits clos*, that gave some privacy to parents sharing rooms with their family, and the typical red-painted pieces traditional to salt-workers. There are 2,500 objects tracing the history of life in the Guérand, among them weapons, furniture, church plate, archaeological discoveries including paintings, *coiffes* (lace headdresses), decorative porcelain from nearby Le Croisic, and *globes de mariées* – glass domes, inside which a new bride would preserve her wedding headdress. Temporary exhibitions are held each year. You'll also find maps of the area's many dolmens and menhirs. The top floor presents a wonderful collection of clothing, alongside salt-making equipment, and the especially quaint costume worn by Guérande and Saillé salt-makers. The ramparts outside offer fantastic views over the countryside. A good English-language leaflet is available.

Maison des Paludiers (18 Rue des Prés Garnier, Saillé, 3km south of Guérande; ☎ 09 53 07 74 06; w maisondespaludiers.fr; ⏰ eco-museum: Apr & Sep 10.00–12.30 & 14.30–17.30 daily, May–Aug 10.00–12.30 & 14.00–18.00 daily, Oct 14.30–17.30 Mon–Sat; saltpan visit & film: €10.50/6/free adult/under 16s/under 6s, eco-museum only: €8/5/free adult/under 16s/under 6s) The back-breaking work of a *paludier* (salt-maker) is explained in this modern building next to the village church in Saillé – a place surrounded in summer by hundreds of glittering saltpans. Allow an hour for this visit, which includes an excellent audio-visual show (English version on request), describing the body's need for salt, and how humans excrete it through tear ducts, sweat glands and kidneys, and likening the salt-maker's life to that of the farmer in its seasonality, unpredictability and reliance on good weather. A large model demonstrates how sea water brought into the circuit of ever-shallower *oeillets* (a series of basins) is slowly evaporated by wind and sun to saturation point, when it begins to deposit the fine crystals that are raked off and gathered for sale.

In fine weather, you can join a 90-minute guided tour to see a salt-maker at work. There is also a self-guided treasure hunt (€10 per group, max 4 people), available in either a child or adult version; set in 1902, it tasks you with tracking down a mysterious salt thief.

FROM THE OCEAN BACK TO NANTES: THE LOIRE'S SOUTH BANK

A leisurely drive back to Nantes gives you the chance to contemplate the river's industry as it once was, a time when marine traffic ploughed its way inland to reach Nantes during the city's heyday as a port of greater significance. You can admire some crazy artworks along the way, dive inland to expend some energy in the treetops at Défi Nature, enjoy a boat trip or take advantage of the free ferries that connect south bank to north.

PAIMBOEUF On the south shore of the Loire, 11km east of the St-Nazaire bridge, this once-thriving port is characterised by its old quays and alleys. In days long gone, these thronged with whalers and cod fishers, witnesses to the town's glory days as the main port for Nantes. During the 18th century, shipowners who had made their fortunes from the sugar and slave trades built handsome houses on Quai Éole, west of the *mairie*; fancy wrought-iron balconies testify to the wealth that was once here. Today, the remaining commercial fishing activity takes place in winter, with a few boats trailing fine-meshed nets for the tiny, critically endangered *civelles* (elvers, or baby eels, also known as *pibales*), as thin as spaghetti, that can fetch prices as high as €5,000 a kilo if smuggled beyond the EU and out to the wealthy gourmets of Asia. Paimboeuf has seen its jobs and its status migrate across to the north shore: shipbuilding to St-Nazaire and industry – in the form of oil-refining – to Donges across the water.

Its squat, 19th-century lighthouse has seen countless ships sail off to exotic climes. Near the *mairie* stand several cannons from the 18th-century French warship *Juste*.

In the late 1830s, the 11-year-old Jules Verne was retrieved from Paimboeuf by his father. Driven by an insatiable thirst for exotic travel, the boy had managed to reach the port from his home in Nantes, with the intention of stowing away on a sailing ship bound for the South Seas.

At about that time, too, Impressionist artist Jean-Baptiste Corot is known to have stayed with a wealthy friend and pupil just along the river at Corsept, southwest of Paimboeuf. During his stay, he painted some of the walls of his host's house with whimsical bunches of flowers. (Unfortunately, the building is not open to the public.)

Tourist information
Office de Tourisme Quai Sadi-Carnot; 📞02 40 27 53 82; w paimboeuf.fr; ⏰ Nov–Mar 09.00–13.00 Tue–Sat, Apr–Jun & Sep–Oct 09.30–12.30 & 14.00–18.00 Tue–Sat, Jul–Aug 10.00–12.30 & 14.30–18.30 daily. Occasionally organises guided tours of the town, in French, in Jul–Aug.

Where to eat and drink Paimboeuf has few choices for those wanting to linger, so bring supplies for a waterfront picnic, choose the crêperie below, or dine before or after your visit.

Restaurant Crêperie de l'Estuaire Chemin de l'Estuaire; 📞02 44 06 20 42; w restaurant-lestuaire. com; ⏰ noon–15.00 Tue–Thu, noon–15.00 & 19.00–22.00 Fri–Sun. A wide range of cheap, tasty galettes the main attraction, though you'll also find fish & mussels on offer in this unpretentious place. Children's menu available. A few hundred metres west of the town centre, this place hosts occasional 'theme evenings' which might be a concert, a debate or a literary reading. €€

What to see and do
Église St-Louis (Rue de l'Église; ⏰ free access during the day) Modelled on Santa Sofia in Istanbul, the town's extraordinary neo-Byzantine church was designed by two Nantes architects, Alexis and Ludovic Douillard. They had submitted the plans to a competition to build a basilica church at Montmartre in Paris in the 1870s. Though the Douillards' design came only fourth in the contest, they were persuaded by Paimboeuf's priest of the time to scale down their vision and to realise it closer

to home. Inside it is equally unusual, containing 19th-century frescoes and an unexpectedly Baroque altar (from a disused abbey in the area) made of 14 different types of marble.

Le Jardin Étoilé (Quai Edmond-Libert, 500m southeast of centre; ⊕ 09.00–21.00 daily; free) This extraordinary 'starry garden' is the work of Japanese artist Kinya Maruyama, who conceived it for the biennial arts project 'Estuaire'. Running through the summers of 2007, 2009 and 2011, Estuaire saw many delightfully crazy art installations spring up along both sides of the Loire Estuary, between Nantes and St-Nazaire, some of which have become permanent. Maruyama modelled his creation on the Great Bear constellation, using found materials, local reeds, slate, sand, earth and fishing nets. The result is an amusing 'playground' for all ages, with viewpoints, stairways, colourful vegetables and flowers, and a host of fluttering flags and carp-shaped kites. An informative site-related gamebook with puzzles and crosswords can be downloaded or picked up from the tourist office (page 249).

Walking tour of Paimboeuf Arm yourself with a leaflet and map from the tourist office and set off on a stroll around town. There are several courses available, including a nature walk that takes you along the banks of the estuary, highlighting the various wildlife that makes the mud flats and water its home, and '100pression collective', an initiative designed by 13ARTS association and Paimboeuf municipality that takes you on a tour of the town's history. This includes *La Méduse* (see above), a ship once visited by Napoleon and which later sank; the Kuhlmann factory, which hints at the town's industrial past and which produced fertiliser for 80 years; and a number of frescoes produced by members of the arts association.

Dominique Leroy's House (21 Quai Boulay Paty; ⊕ access at all times to view exterior) It's worth checking out this small house, just opposite the little river-lighthouse, with its façade decorated with a bizarre collection of objects. The artist has promised to constantly change it (at the time of writing it was strewn with thousands of circuit boards), but it is unlikely to be anything other than atypical!

FROSSAY As you drive across the green countryside in the heart of the Pays de Retz, it is impossible to miss this village: Frossay's vast 20th-century church dominates the landscape for miles around. It's worth stopping for a look inside the cavernous building to see the brilliant modern stained glass. Set within a tracery of concrete, the windows are a curious marriage of the flamboyant-Gothic style familiar from more traditional churches, and the techniques and materials of the 1930s.

North of Frossay lies the hamlet of Le Migron. At one time it was an island and a prosperous little trading port. Nearby is the north end of the now-abandoned Canal de la Martinière (page 252), or Canal de la Basse-Loire, and the gateway to the Île Massereau, which serves today as a bird reserve popular with storks, ducks and herons in the springtime.

Tourist information

Mairie 4 Rue du Capitaine Robert Martin; ☎ 02 40 39 72 72; w frossay.fr; ⏱ 09.00–13.00 Tue–Sat

Where to eat and drink
Most visitors to Frossay are heading for one of the two parks listed below, both of which offer food. Legendia Parc has both a fast-food outlet and a more traditional restaurant.

L'Ogre Bleu 5 La Poitevinière; ☎ 02 40 39 94 23; w ogrebleu.fr; ⏱ noon–14.00 Tue–Thu & Sun, noon–14.00 & 19.00–21.30 Fri–Sat. Good, straightforward food in a pleasant setting close to the entrance of the Legendia park. €€€

What to see and do

Défi Nature (Parc du Château de la Rousselière, 2km southwest of Frossay; ☎ 02 40 39 79 59; w definature.com; ⏱ Jul–Aug 10.00–19.00 daily, for other months see website; prices depend on activities chosen, various combinations possible) Allow at least 3 hours to try out the treetop trails through the mighty oaks in the grounds of a 19th-century stately home, signposted off the D78. The staff dish out harnesses and give instruction on the safe use of the wires, platforms and walkways set up among the trees. There are inflatables for bouncy small children, games and puzzles, laser games and a paintball setup. Groups of ten can also book to do the whole thing by night, on Thursdays in July and August.

Legendia Parc (Sentier des Daims, La Poitevinière, off the D78 5km southwest of Frossay; ☎ 02 40 39 75 06; w legendiaparc.com; ⏱ Jul–Aug 10.00–22.30 daily, for other months see website; Jul–Aug €27/20/free adult/under 13s/under 3s, slightly cheaper outside peak months & if booked online) A little further along the D78 from Défi Nature, and well signposted from everywhere, is this curious park, somewhere between a zoo, a farm and a theme park on the idea of 'legends'. It takes a few hours to walk the trail and watch the shows – six new ones have been added that provide 'Puy du Fou' type spectacles (on a much smaller scale) with a slightly mad, fairy-tale version of French history (not available in low season, see website). You can also stroke donkeys and fallow deer, see camels and alpacas, and marvel at brown bears and Siberian lynx. In total, there are more than 400 animals. There is an option to spend a night in the park's lodges among the wolves, with dinner and breakfast provided.

LE PELLERIN Something of a seaside atmosphere pervades this little riverfront town on the south bank of the Loire, west of Nantes but definitely a good distance from the ocean. Its name comes from the *pèlerins*, or pilgrims from countries further north who arrived here in large numbers by cargo boat during the Middle Ages to start their long walk to Santiago de Compostela, in northwest Spain (page 8).

Fans of French cinema might like to know that Jean-Loup Hubert's charming 1987 film *Le Grand Chemin* was shot in the hamlet of the same name, 2km west of Le Pellerin. The plot concerns a nine-year-old boy from Paris, sent to stay with relatives in the countryside, and the freedom and friendship he discovers.

Tourist information

Mairie Rue du Docteur Gilbert Sourdille; ◥02 40
04 56 00; **w** ville-lepellerin.fr; ⊕ 09.00–noon &
14.00–17.30 Mon-Fri

What to see and do

Canal de la Martinière (La Martinière, off the D58, 3km west of Le Pellerin)
Near the water tower at the northwest end of Le Pellerin is an interesting industrial
relic: a 15km canal that was opened in 1892 to allow sailing ships to reach Nantes
by bypassing the sandy shallows of the Loire. The canal's usefulness was short-lived,
however. It closed to navigation in 1914, following the arrival of steam-driven
dredgers that could easily keep the river itself open. Today this artificial waterway
is a vital element in controlling the water system for the marshes, and a paradise
for walkers, birdwatchers and fishers. Nearby is an attractive waterside park, and
the 19th-century locks and hydraulic works at Buzay, 2km west of La Martinière
village, are showpieces of industrial archaeology.

Parcours Estuaire artworks Of all the artworks making up the Parcours
Estuaire trail between Nantes and the sea, *The Misconceivable* (La Martinière,
follow signs for canal, as above; ⊕ open access at all times) – a warped boat, draped
over a lock – is surely one of the strangest. A little further along the river, 1km east
of Cöueron, lies another weird installation: *La Maison dans la Loire* (Quai Jean-
Pierre Fougerat; ⊕ open access at all times). The work of Jean-Luc Courcoult, it
depicts a full-sized house apparently tilting into the river!

Across the river from Le Pellerin A free car-ferry service – signposted as 'Le
Bac' – runs every 20 minutes between 06.00 and 20.00 across the fast-flowing river
to Couëron on the north shore, a 5-minute trip that saves a long drive around via
the bridges of Nantes or St-Nazaire. (A similar free ferry service runs between
Indre, 7km to the east, and the outskirts of St-Herblain, every 15 minutes.) There is
no doubting the dangerously fast currents in the river, when you look at the boats'
crabwise route across it.
    The American bird artist John James Audubon (1785–1851), born in what is now
Haiti, spent his childhood at his stepmother's home near Couëron, and developed
his interest in ornithology by roaming the marshes along this side of the Loire.
Further northwest, Cordemais has a conspicuous oil- and coal-fired power station;
for Estuaire 2009, a jokey structure called the Villa Cheminée was built near it,
echoing the tall red-and-white chimneys – with a holiday *gîte* installed on top (you
can rent it via **w** reservation.nantes-tourisme.com). Northwest again, and at the
end of the village of Lavau-sur-Loire, a charming crêperie – La Maison du Port –
shares a quaint old building overlooking the marshes with a secondhand bookshop;
from here, you can follow a long boardwalk into the reed-beds to a tall wooden
observatory that gives views across the river back towards Paimboeuf.

✗ Where to eat and drink

Le Bistrot du Paradis Paradis, Couëron; ◥09 52
27 03 69; ⊕ 10.00–18.00 Mon–Tue & Thu–Sat.
You'll need to take the ferry across the water from
Le Pellerin to dine at this simple place. Sit outside,
watch the ripple of the river & listen to the grind &
bump of the shuttling ferry. Food is straightforward,
choice fairly limited, service is swift. €€

Appendix 1

LANGUAGE

ESSENTIALS

English	French
Good morning/afternoon	*Bonjour*
Good evening	*Bonsoir*
Hello	*Salut*
Goodbye	*Au revoir*
My name is…	*Je m'appelle…*
What is your name?	*Comment vous appelez-vous?*
I am from…	*Je viens d'/de...*
England	*Angleterre*
Scotland	*Écosse*
Wales	*Pays de Galles*
Ireland	*Irlande*
the United States	*États-Unis*
Canada	*Canada*
Australia	*Australie*
New Zealand	*Nouvelle Zélande*
How are you?	*Ça va?*
Very well, thank you	*Très bien, merci*
Pleased to meet you (m/f)	*Enchanté/enchantée*
Thank you	*Merci*
Please	*S'il vous plaît*
Sorry!	*Pardon, or désolé/désolée*
You're welcome (don't mention it)	*De rien*
Cheers	*Santé*
Yes	*Oui*
No	*Non*
I don't understand	*Je ne comprends pas*
Could you speak slower?	*Pouvez-vous parler plus lentement, s'il vous plaît?*

QUESTIONS

How?	*Comment?*
What?	*Quoi?*
Where?	*Où?*
What is it?	*C'est quoi, ça?*
Which?	*Lequel/Laquelle?*
When?	*Quand?*
Why?	*Pourquoi?*
Who?	*Qui?*
How much?	*Combien?*

NUMBERS

1	*un*
2	*deux*
3	*trois*
4	*quatre*
5	*cinq*
6	*six*

7	sept
8	huit
9	neuf
10	dix
11	onze
12	douze
13	treize
14	quatorze
15	quinze
16	seize
17	dix-sept
18	dix-huit
19	dix-neuf
20	vingt
21	vingt et un
30	trente
40	quarante
50	cinquante
60	soixante
70	soixante-dix
80	quatre-vingts
90	quatre-vingt-dix
100	cent
1,000	mille

TIME

What time is it?	Quelle heure est-il?
It's (8) o'clock in the morning/afternoon/at night	Il est (huit) heures du matin/de l'après-midi/du soir
today	aujourd'hui
tonight	ce soir
tomorrow	demain
yesterday	hier
morning	le matin
afternoon	l'après-midi
evening	le soir
night	la nuit

Days

Monday	lundi
Tuesday	mardi
Wednesday	mercredi
Thursday	jeudi
Friday	vendredi
Saturday	samedi
Sunday	dimanche

Months

January	janvier
February	février
March	mars
April	avril
May	mai
June	juin
July	juillet
August	août
September	septembre
October	octobre
November	novembre
December	décembre

GETTING AROUND
Public transport

| A (single/return) ticket to…please | Un (aller simple/aller-retour) à…s'il vous plaît |
| I want to go to… | Je voudrais aller à… |

How much is it?	Ça fait combien?
What time is the train/bus to…?	A quelle heure part le train/le bus vers…?
ticket	le billet
ticket office	le guichet
timetable	les horaires
from	de
to	à
port	le port
bus	le bus
bus station	la gare routière
coach	le car
plane	l'avion
train	le train
train station	la gare
boat	le bateau
ferry	le ferry-boat (sea-going), le bac (river)
car	la voiture
taxi	le taxi
motorbike	la moto
bicycle	le vélo
here	ici
there	là
bon voyage!	bon voyage!

Private transport

How can I get to…?	Je prends quel chemin pour aller à…?
Where is the service station?	Où est la station-service?
Full, please	Le plein, s'il vous plaît
Ten euros of unleaded, please	Dix euros de sans plomb, s'il vous plaît
diesel	le gazole
I have broken down	Je suis tombé en panne

Road signs

give way	cédez le passage
danger	danger
diversion	déviation
entry/entrance	entrée
one-way	sens unique
toll	péage
no entry	défense d'entrer
exit	sortie

Directions

Where is the…?	Où est le/la…?
go straight ahead	Allez tout droit
turn left…	Tournez à gauche…
turn right…	Tournez à droite…
at the traffic lights	aux feux
at the roundabout	au rond-point
north	nord
south	sud
east	est
west	ouest
behind	derrière
in front of	devant
near	près de
opposite	en face de

Street signs

entrance	entrée
exit	sortie
open	ouvert
closed	fermé
toilets	toilettes/WC
information	information

ACCOMMODATION

Where is a cheap/good hotel?	*Où se trouve un hôtel à bon prix/bon hôtel?*
Do you have any rooms available?	*Avez-vous des chambres disponibles?*
How much is it per night?	*Ça coûte combien la nuit?*
I'd like…	*Je voudrais…*
a single room	*une chambre individuelle*
a double room	*une chambre double*
a room with two beds	*une chambre avec deux lits*
a room with a bathroom	*une chambre avec une salle de bain*
a dormitory bed	*un lit en dortoir*
Is there free Wi-Fi?	*Il y a du Wi-Fi gratuit?*
What is the Wi-Fi password?	*Quel est le mot de passe pour le Wi-Fi?*
Is breakfast included?	*Est-ce que le petit déjeuner est compris?*
How much is breakfast?	*Ça coûte combien, le petit déjeuner?*

FOOD

What time does the restaurant open?	*A quelle heure ouvre le restaurant?*
Do you have a table for…people?	*Vous avez une table pour…personnes?*
Do you have a children's menu?	*Vous avez un menu enfant?*
I am a vegetarian	*Je suis végétarien(ne)*
Please may I have the bill	*L'addition, s'il vous plaît*

Basics

bread	*le pain*
butter	*le beurre*
cheese	*le fromage*
oil	*l'huile*
pepper	*le poivre noir*
salt	*le sel*
sugar	*le sucre*

Fruit

apples	*les pommes*
bananas	*les bananes*
cherries	*les cerises*
grapes	*les raisins*
lemon	*le citron*
melon	*le melon*
nectarine	*la nectarine*
orange	*l'orange*
peach	*la pêche*
pear	*la poire*

Vegetables

carrots	*les carottes*
garlic	*l'ail*
onions	*les oignons*
pepper	*le poivron*
potatoes	*les pommes de terre*

Fish

anchovies	*les anchois*
cod	*la morue, le cabillaud*
cuttlefish	*la seiche*
hake	*le merlu, le colin*
monkfish	*la lotte*
sea bream	*la dorade*
squid	*le calamar*
oysters	*les huîtres*

Meat

beef	*le bœuf*
chicken	*le poulet*
lamb	*l'agneau*
pork	*le porc*

Drinks

beer	*la bière*
coffee	*le café*
fruit juice	*le jus de fruits*
milk	*le lait*
tea	*le thé*
water	*l'eau*
red wine	*le vin rouge*
white wine	*le vin blanc*

SHOPPING

I'd like to buy…	*Je voudrais acheter…*
How much is it?	*C'est combien?*
I don't like it	*Je ne l'aime pas*
I'm just looking	*Je jette juste un coup d'œil*
It's too expensive	*C'est trop cher*
I'll take it	*Je vais l'acheter*
Please may I have…	*S'il vous plaît, puis-je avoir…*
How much do I owe you?	*Combien je vous dois?*
Do you accept…?	*Acceptez-vous…?*
bank cards	*des cartes bancaires*
more	*plus*
less	*moins*
smaller	*plus petit*
bigger	*plus grand*
That's enough	*Ça suffit*

COMMUNICATIONS

I'm looking for…	*Je cherche…*
a bank	*une banque*
an internet café	*un cybercafé*
a post office	*un bureau de poste*
a tourist office	*un office de tourisme*

HEALTH

I have…	*J'ai…*
diarrhoea	*la diarrhée*
nausea	*la nausée*
I need…	*J'ai besoin de/d'…*
a doctor	*un médecin*
a prescription	*une ordonnance*
painkillers	*antidouleurs*
a pharmacy	*une pharmacie*
antibiotics	*antibiotiques*
antiseptic	*antiseptique*
tampons	*tampons*
condoms	*préservatifs*
contraceptive	*contraceptif*
sun block	*écran total*
I am…	*Je suis…*
asthmatic	*asthmatique*
epileptic	*épileptique*
diabetic	*diabétique*
pregnant	*enceinte*
I'm allergic to…	*Je suis allergique…*
penicillin	*à la pénicilline*
nuts	*aux noix*
bees	*aux abeilles*

TRAVEL WITH CHILDREN

Is there a…?	*Y-a-t'il…?*
baby changing room?	*un espace bébé?*
a children's menu?	*un menu enfant?*
Do you have…?	*Avez-vous…?*
infant milk formula	*du lait maternisé*

a nappy	une couche
a potty	un pot de bébé
a babysitter	un baby-sitter
a highchair	une chaise haute
Are children allowed?	Est-ce que les enfants sont permis?

OTHER

my	mon/ma/mes
our	notre/nos
your	votre/vos
and	et
some	du/de la/des
but	mais
this/that	ceci/cela
this one/that one	celui-ci/celui-là, celle-ci/celle-là

Adjectives

It is…	C'est…
cheap/expensive	bon marché/cher
beautiful/ugly	beau/laid
old/new	vieux/nouveau
good/bad	bon/mauvais
early/late	tôt/tard
hot/cold	chaud/froid
difficult/easy	difficile/facile
boring/interesting	ennuyeux/intéressant

Appendix 2

FURTHER INFORMATION

BOOKS
In English

Harper, Rob *Fighting the French Revolution: The Great Vendee Rising of 1793*, Pen and Sword Military, 2019. An excellent book with lots of detail, especially on the counter-revolutionary aspects of the war.

Hayward, Tim *Genocide – The Civil War in the Vendée Militaire 1793–99.* e taghuk@yahoo.co.uk. Self-published, 2000. Useful background and outline to the conflicts.

Schama, Simon *Citizens* Penguin, 2004. Highly readable history of the French Revolution, with a substantial section on the Wars of the Vendée.

Secher, Reynald *A French Genocide, The Vendée* University of Notre Dame Press, 1986. The claim of genocide by Secher gained this book some notoriety when it was first published, and it was denounced by many as anti-revolutionary and anti-republican. However, strong academic and institutional support has helped it maintain its credibility. Translated and published into English in 2003.

Trollope, Anthony *La Vendée* Dodo Press, 2008. Historical novel, based closely on the memoirs of Madame de la Rochejaquelein, which first appeared in 1850. It paints a vivid picture of the early part of the war and of its principal characters.

In French

Martin, Jean-Clément *Blancs et Bleus dans la Vendée déchirée* Découvertes Gallimard, 2008. Pocket-sized, information-packed book, alive with evocative paintings and drawings.

Ragon, Michel *L'Accent de ma mère* Albin Michel, 2006. Autobiography of a present-day writer and critic whose memories of his Vendean childhood are interwoven with accounts of the wars 150 years earlier.

Ragon, Michel *Les Mouchoirs rouges de Cholet* Albin Michel, 1983. Historical novel about the Vendée Wars.

FILMS
In French

C'Était une fois dans l'Ouest (*Once Upon a Time in the West*) (2015) It may sound like a cowboy film, but it's actually a French-made documentary about the Vendée Wars.

Le Général du Roi (2014) Based loosely on a Daphne du Maurier novel, a romance with the Vendée Wars as a backdrop.

Vaincre ou Mourir (2022) Released to fairly average reviews, this is the first production from Puy du Fou Films and focuses on the Vendée War. It does give you a flavour of the brutality of the 'Infernal Columns', the type of guerrilla fighting conducted by the counter-revolutionaries, and an introduction to some of the key figures of the war.

Index

Page numbers in **bold** indicate major entries; those in *italic* indicate maps.

INDEX OF ADVERTISERS